# Intertidal History in Island Southeast Asia

Jennifer L. Gaynor

# Intertidal History in Island Southeast Asia

## Submerged Genealogy and the Legacy of Coastal Capture

SOUTHEAST ASIA PROGRAM PUBLICATIONS
an imprint of
Cornell University Press
Ithaca and London

SEAP Publications Editorial Board
    Mahinder Kingra (*ex officio*)
    Thak Chaloemtiarana
    Chiara Formichi
    Tamara Loos
    Kaja McGowan

First published 2016 by Cornell University Press
First printing, Cornell Paperbacks, 2016

Printed in the United States of America

ISBN 978-0-99104-805-2 (cloth: alk. paper)
ISBN 978-0-99104-780-2 (pbk. : alk. paper)

Cornell University Press strives to use environmentally responsible suppliers and
materials to the fullest extent possible in the publishing of its books. Such materials
include vegetable-based, low-VOC inks and acid-free papers that are recycled, totally
chlorine-free, or partly composed of nonwood fibers. For further information, visit
our website at www.cornellpress.cornell.edu.


Cover design by Kat Dalton

# TABLE OF CONTENTS

Acknowledgments     vii

List of Abbreviations     xi

Note on Transcription and Spelling     xiii

**Chapter 1**     1
Introduction: Geographies of Knowledge and Archipelagic Belonging

**Chapter 2**     33
The Northern Littoral Route and Makassar's Hinterseas

**Chapter 3**     65
"That Nasty Pirates' Nest": Tiworo and Two Wars over the Spice Trade

**Chapter 4**     107
Sama Ties To Boné and Narrative Incorporation

**Chapter 5**     167
Stakes and Silences: Lawi's Capture during the Darul Islam Rebellion

**Chapter 6**     201
Conclusion: Maritime History in an Archipelagic World

Bibliography     207

Index     223

# ACKNOWLEDGMENTS

This book grew out of research supported by the generosity of numerous institutions. An International Pre-dissertation Fellowship Program award from the Social Science Research Council supported early intensive language study of Dutch, Sama, and Bugis. Research in archives and at field sites in Indonesia, kindly permitted by the Indonesian Institute of Sciences (LIPI), and archival research in the Netherlands and Great Britain, was jointly funded by the Social Science Research Council's International Dissertation Field Research Fellowship and a Fulbright-Hays Doctoral Dissertation Research Abroad Fellowship (P022A80050). Time dedicated to writing was generously provided by Cornell University's Society for the Humanities, and the Humanities Institute and Office of the Vice Provost for Research of the University at Buffalo (UB), State University of New York. Further assistance was provided by UB: its Gender Institute made possible additional field research in the summer of 2011; its Baldy Center for Law and Social Policy supported archival research during the summer of 2012; and its College of Arts and Sciences provided support through the Julian Park Publication Fund.

For providing access to their collections, I gratefully acknowledge the KITLV (Royal Netherlands Institute of Southeast Asian and Caribbean Studies), the National Archives of the Netherlands, the British Library, the Royal Asiatic Society, the Indonesian National Archives (ANRI) Jakarta and South Sulawesi Branches, and the Indonesian National Library. The staff at the National Archives of the Netherlands, who run a very tight ship indeed, graciously let me examine fragile seventeenth-century manuscripts that could not be brought out into the public viewing area.

A workshop sponsored by the Baldy Center for Law and Social Policy, a wonderfully interdisciplinary institution at UB's Law School, generated stimulating conversation and productive feedback on the book manuscript, thanks to the interest and generosity of Kerry Ward, Barbara Watson Andaya, and Eric Tagliacozzo, who went out of their way to offer extensive comments. I am also grateful for the participation and commentary of UB colleagues in this workshop: Jim Bono, Tom Burkman, Susan Cahn, David Engel, Roger Des Forges, Charles O. Frake, Walt Hakala, Hal Langfur, Adam Malka, Ndubueze Mbah, and Mateo Taussig-Rubbo.

One does not delve into seventeenth-century Dutch sources lightly, and the same may be said for Bugis-language manuscripts. This gratifying and enriching experience could not have been undertaken without the help of others. Thanks to Mathilda Knoop for archival assistance; Henrike Florusbosch for a native speaker's ear; Ton Broos for weighing in on a particular passage; Martijna Briggs for helping to decipher and discuss many details of early modern Dutch; and Annabel Teh Gallop for guidance with royal seals, *kitmir*, and more in the British Library. For help with Spanish and other Iberian linguistic matters, for thinking in complex, evidence-based historical ways about language change, and for the sheer pleasure of intellectual engagement in flagrant disregard of disciplinary boundaries, I am grateful to Bruce Mannheim. Thanks also to John Wolff, who advocated for retaining the flavor of colloquial speech in translation, and for help with phonetics, sound shifts, and linguistic borrowing between Malay and European languages; as well as to Robert Blust for weighing in on loanwords in Malay and other Austronesian languages.

Henk Schulte Nordholt generously commented on the manuscript at different stages of its development. Philip Taylor offered helpful remarks at an early stage, as did Campbell Macknight, whose graciousness in having young scholars over for tea and cake to discuss their work is matched only by the depth and rigor of his interdisciplinary insights. Thanks also to Sirtjo Koolhof for sharing knowledge about Sulawesi, all things Bugis, and for great breaks from research in Makassar; Steve Druce for correspondence related to the earliest European sources on Sulawesi; Kathy Wellen for her interest in looking beyond the peninsula, her collegiality, and friendship; Wil Burghoorn for corresponding about family; Thomas Suárez for communicating about early maps; and Valerio Valeri, who long ago urged me to return to Tomé Pires. For their lively engagement through maritime conferences, talks, and emails, thanks to Kären Wigen, Michael Pearson, Marcus Rediker, Roy Ritchie, John Gillis, and Pierre-Yves Manguin. Charles O. Frake's work has been an inspiration and I treasure our get-togethers. The scholarly examples set by Janet Hoskins and by Ann Stoler have made a deep and lasting impression, for which I will always be grateful. Inestimable credit must also be given Ken George, who, in an offhand way, once remarked in an email, "But above all, write the book that makes *you* happy." For vastly improving the book's readability, and more, my thanks to Sarah E. M. Grossman and Fred Conner.

In Indonesia, Abdurrauf Tarimana (*almarhum*) and Mukhlis Paeni graciously sponsored periods of research. Muhamad Salim (*almarhum*) patiently sat with me day in and day out for months explaining Bugis grammar, discoursing on differences between dialects, and ironing out my errors. Kamaruddin Thamzibar did something similar with the Sama language. Kamaruddin was the person who first introduced me to his Sama kin, effectively placing me in the care of trusted relatives—an experience that expanded like a snowball rolling down a hillside. His warm family always welcomed me, making me feel at home, and a better, truer friend in the world could not be found. Yohana Talabessy (*almarhumah*), who also took me in, on occasion lovingly scolded me for not staying with her even when there were laws against putting up foreigners. Collectively, her entire family was like a rock, especially Jeni Gamganora, who took her mother's maiden name, and who takes after her mother in so many ways, a woman of shining intelligence, warmth, and integrity amidst a sea, as her mother used to say, of all kinds. Among the others, too many to list, thanks go to Marhalim (*almarhum*), who inspired people's respect and not fear; Tikungrahman for assistance during field research; the brave and gracious Hajjah Sitti Alwia and her daughter Erna; Haji Mansyur and Hajjah Sarwana in Tanjung Pinang; and on Pulau Balu, Nurhawana, who, along with Nuhba (Si Ce), first eased my socialization into Sama life, and always thereafter greeted me like a long-lost sister. Special thanks to Gebing, friend and steady captain, who looked after my safety at sea and on land; and Hatia, who could have been a captain, and who has, I am sure, always been game for much more than what life has thrown her way.

To the memory of my father, Dr. Arthur Gaynor, who literally healed hearts, and my mother, Dr. Evelyn Gaynor, scientist, artist, nurturer, who celebrated life. Also in memory of my maternal grandparents: Louis Chartoff, who, with his cornet, escaped impressment with the Russian Army (was it the red or the white?—we never knew), and stowed away across the Black Sea to play a freer tune in a Turkish circus; and Rose Chartoff née Klein, who, as a young girl playing in a tree, saw the Cossaks coming and warned her village, saving it. Their stories, within wider histories, bear the legacy of survival, memory, hope, and connection.

Deep gratitude to Dave Register, fearsomely grounded, for keeping my spirit afloat.

This book is for Max, may your compass always be true.

# ABBREVIATIONS

ANRI  Arsip Nasional Republik Indonesia, National Archives of the Republik of Indonesia

BKI  *Bijdragen tot de Taal-, Land- en Volkenkunde*, Journal of the Humanities and Social Sciences of Southeast Asia, issued by the KITLV

BR  Emma Blair and James Alexander Robertson, eds., *The Philippine Islands, 1493–1803* (Cleveland: A. H. Clark Company, 1903–09), 55 volumes

DI-TII  Darul Islam—Tentara Islam Indonesia, lit., "Abode" or "House" of Islam—Indonesian Islamic Army

KITLV  Koninklijk Instituut voor Taal-, Land- en Volkenkunde, The Royal Netherlands Institute of Southeast Asian and Caribbean Studies

MS  Matthes Stichting, the colonial-era Matthes Foundation

NA  Nationaal Archief, National Archives of the Netherlands

PMC  Armando Cortesão and Avelino Teixeira da Mota, *Portugaliae Monumenta Cartographica* (Lisbon: Coimbra University Press, 1960)

TAG  *Tijdschrift van het Koninklijk Nederlandsch Aardrijkskundig Genootschap*, Journal of the Royal Netherlands Geographic Society

TBG  *Tijdschrift voor Indische Taal-, Land- en Volkenkunde*, Journal for Indies Linguistics, Geography and Ethnology, issued by the (Royal) Batavian Society of Arts and Sciences

TNI  Tentara Nasional Indonesia, Indonesian National Army

UBL  Universitaire Bibliotheken Leiden, (Leiden University Libraries), University of Leiden

VBG  *Verhandelingen van het (Koninklijk) Bataviaasch Genootschap van Kunsten en Wetenschappen*, Proceedings of the [Royal] Batavian Society of Arts and Sciences

VKI  *Verhandelingen van het Koninklijk Instituut*, Proceedings of the KITLV

VOC  Vereenigde Oost-Indische Compagnie, (United) Dutch East India Company

# A NOTE ON
# TRANSCRIPTION AND SPELLING

Place names in this book use Indonesian spellings. However, colonial names, such as "Celebes" for what is now "Sulawesi," are often used to refer to places in the pre-independence period. The letter "q" represent a glottal stop, which often appears at the end of Bugis words, such as *lontaraq* (manuscript). The Sama dialect in Southeast Sulawesi differentiates a glottal stop like that in Bugis, from a softer non-plosive gottal stop, represented here with an apostrophe: *tikolo'na* (her hair). Occasional prevocalization and preglottalization of consonants in Sama has been represented with superscripts, such as *di$^n$da* (woman), and *$^{qm}$boq* (grandparent), except when the latter is a title of respect for elders: *Mboq*.

Transliteration of Bugis texts commonly presents challenges, as from an alphabetic viewpoint, the orthography seems graphically incomplete, sometimes "missing" the final consonants in syllables. However, I have always felt that the writing system in some ways is particularly suited to the way the language geminates consonants. For instance, "*aru*" standing alone may be read "*arung,*" the word for "lord," even though the "ng" is not represented. When combined with the place name "ᰛᰘᰍ" ("Palakka"), for "Lord of Palakka," the combination is not pronounced "Arungpalakka," but instead, the "ng" transforms to become either "*Aruqpalakka*" or "*Aruppalaka.*" Although it may seem cumbersome from an alphabetic language ideology, the syllabic writing system used for the Bugis and Makassar languages suits them pretty well. Muhammad Salim gave assistance and advice in transliterating and translating texts.

In the transliteration and transcription of oral and written texts below, I preserve the distinction between "é" and the unstressed vowel "e," often called a "schwa." I mark the stress in many personal and place names where Indonesian documents have historically done so (hence, "BoEpinang" here is "Boépinang," "BajoE" is "Bajoé"), and to prevent misapprehensions ("Boné" rather than "Bone"). Except where they appear in transliteration or transcription, I do not mark the stressed "é" in names and terms where it commonly is not represented (hence, "Karaeng Bayo" and "*kelong*").

# CHAPTER ONE

# INTRODUCTION:
# GEOGRAPHIES OF KNOWLEDGE AND
# ARCHIPELAGIC BELONGING

*Intertidal History* begins and ends in the 1950s. Yet what it shows about littoral society and the maritime world of the 1950s takes on particular salience in light of new information the book presents concerning the role of Southeast Asian maritime people during the seventeenth-century spice wars. At that time, important polities such as Makassar made alliances with Southeast Asia's so-called sea people, who played a pivotal role in efforts to oppose European domination of the spice trade. Often considered stateless pirates and nomads, sea people were in fact part of a vibrant socially complex world in which polities of maritime-oriented Southeast Asians maintained alliances with regional states, and at times sea people held prominent rank in them. Their knowledge, skills, and networks benefitted their allies, who were tied to them through webs of kinship and shared interests that crossed both waters and ethnicity. Drawing on underutilized Southeast Asian and European sources, *Intertidal History* illustrates a new view of the region's maritime past, one that contributes to the revision of a world history narrative in which the spice wars are portrayed as a conflict between competing European mercantile empires. Yet the book does more than help reframe that Eurocentric narrative. It shows how social and political connections along and between the region's coasts changed over time, by revealing maritime-oriented people's participation in the dynamics of trade, war, and kinship. Demonstrating that littoral society was not just based in cities, this work alters our understanding of the littoral and its place in the region's past, helping to conceptually integrate the archipelago within wider frameworks of Asian maritime history along with the Indian Ocean and the South China Sea.

Chapter two looks at the northern east-west route across the archipelago, and at Makassar's hinterseas, delving into the historical background of seventeenth century maritime networks. While subsequent chapters consider the significance of enduring dynamics in the archipelagic world, in this book I primarily approach maritime history via the strands of the networks that people made. The point is not just to see the networks' connected elements, but also to understand what those connections were made of and how they worked. Intersecting maritime networks formed nodes, and tugging gently at them shows how networks fit together in archipelagic space, which was not two-dimensional. At once ecologically and historically made, it was also a social and political space. What can be discovered about this archipelagic past depends on the use of some mixed methodology, and, as with all history, on the point of view of the sources used and how the historian handles them. The key here is not to go to sea from the land, for if one does that one will always return to it. Instead one must launch, as people did, from the littoral itself.

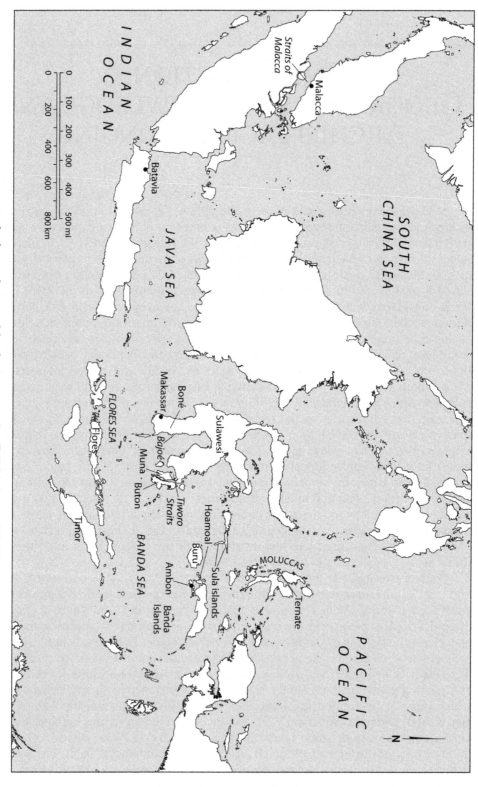

Indonesian archipelago; map by Bill Nelson, 2015

## CAPTURE, CONNECTION, AND FOLLOWINGS

When Lawi was taken in 1954 from her coastal village in the Straits of Tiworo, Indonesia was barely a nation. Although Lawi, too, was quite young, she had her eye on a man named Umar. She had been promised to him, and while no formal gift exchange—no deal-sealing—had yet taken place between their families, her relatives had already begun to gather the quantities of rice that would be needed for a wedding. Then the rebels came for her.[1] Lawi was Sama, an ethnic group often referred to as "sea people," usually called "Bajo" by others. She was "captured" (taken against her will) in order to be married to a regiment commander in the Darul Islam rebellion, which was then spreading throughout most of south and southeast Sulawesi.

Darul Islam, or "DI-TII," the common acronym that includes its armed wing, the Indonesian Islamic Army (Tentara Islam Indonesia), was just one of many groups that struggled over the new nation's future during the early post-independence period. The Bugis dominated the Sulawesi branch of DI-TII, which had two other main branches and smaller offshoots elsewhere in the country. Jufri Tambora, the regiment commander to whom Lawi was wed, was ethnically Bugis. Lawi's capture and marriage to Jufri came as an unwelcome development in the predominantly Sama Tiworo Straits. After she was taken, two rebel men dared to visit her village once again, apparently to persuade relatives to join her at their base in the hills. They compounded the offense of her capture by attempting to extort money from her father, who had been away at the time she was taken, on a trading trip to Lombok with his youngest son, Buraéra. When the two rebels returned, recognition of them by Lawi's relatives led to retaliation against them.

While Lawi's kin were angered and distressed about her capture, it also put them in the difficult position of having to suppress knowledge of her whereabouts. When her captors permitted her a visit to her natal village, people even felt compelled to turn her away because they could not afford to have it appear, in the eyes of the TNI (Tentara Nasional Indonesia, Indonesian National Army), that they were siding with the rebels. Convincing the TNI of their allegiance to the nation was a matter of collective survival for Lawi's neighbors and relatives, and among wider networks of Sama kin. The ramifications of her capture, therefore, played out both at the level of intergroup relations and in the wider struggle of post-colonial politics. At the same time, intergroup relations and their part in the broader maelstrom of the early post-colonial period unfolded between littorals. That is, they took place between land and sea, directly involving the maritime-oriented Sama people of Tiworo and the surrounding region.

Lawi's spouse, Jufri, knew a great deal about how maritime trade worked. During the Second World War, before he became a Regiment Commander, he had been an informant for the occupying Japanese, filling them in on who was spying for the Dutch, the previous colonial overlords. The trust he gained as an informant earned him a position as harbormaster (*syahbandar*) for Binsen Ongkōkai, the

---

[1] Author's interview with Habiba, June 27, 2011, Raha, Southeast Sulawesi. Lawi was also called "Haji Lawi," using the local, nongender specific title for one who has done the *haj* (rather than "*hajjah*"). Habiba is Lawi's sister-in-law. She mentioned the rice gathering and that the gift exchange had not yet taken place. Lawi mentioned the prospective groom, Umar, in Sama, also called Ummareng (the /e/ is an unstressed schwa), Haji Subaeda's son. Lawi said in 2011 that the rebels had shot him. Author's interviews with Haji Lawi, May 4, 2000, and June 22, 2011, Wawo, North Kolaka.

Japanese Tramp Shipping Transport Company, in the town of Kolaka, on the Gulf of Boné's east coast. He managed the paperwork for "tramp" freighters, cargo boats that had no fixed schedule. The paperwork included permits to sail, as well as bills of lading. Common in the world of shipping even today, bills of lading serve both as a receipt for goods delivered to carriers and as a description of the goods, as well as evidence of title to them. They show that a shipper is not carrying contraband. Jufri's position as the enforcer of rules about shipping papers taught him many things. He not only learned who carried what cargo under which terms, but also came to understand that notions of legitimate trade were flexible under wartime interpretations of legality. One thing Jufri's experience drove home was the importance of having the right papers, which seemed to confer legitimacy not only to shippers, but also to the governing body that recognized their documents. Later, during the Darul Islam years, this lesson came into play when his sister, Sitti Hami, ran a smuggling ring for DI-TII, issuing papers under its authority, even as smugglers also carried counterfeit passes in case they were stopped by the other side in the conflict. Jufri, in his administrative role over mariners at Kolaka's harbor during the Japanese occupation, kept an eye out for paperwork that came up short. If and when it did, the potential for lucrative gain, or for brokering knowledge about smuggling opportunities, would have been obvious to him. In effect, the job as harbormaster under the Japanese gave him a deep understanding of how smuggling worked in practice. All he lacked were the nautical skills, the distant clandestine connections, and the *savoir faire* to pull it off. For these he would need real mariners with experience.[2]

He obtained the allegiance of his most trusted smuggler during the Darul Islam rebellion through his marital connection with the Sama. While most of Lawi's relatives kept quiet about her link with the rebels, her brother, Buraéra, who had been captured by the rebels on a separate occasion, eventually managed to take advantage of his new kin connection as the regiment commander's brother-in-law. In a bid to extricate himself from a combat position under Jufri's nephew, Buraéra offered his services as a smuggler for the rebellion. A Sama man with a special set of nautical skills, he drew on the experience and knowledge he had gained as a young mariner on trading ventures across the archipelago with his father. Jufri derived benefits from Buraéra's skills, knowledge, and networks. Buraéra, in turn, eventually became the regiment commander's trusted adjutant.[3]

While discussing the clandestine maritime trade of the 1950s with me, Jufri, then in his dotage, raised the topic of his personal relation to Sama people, namely, his marriage to Lawi. He said he had married a Sama woman from the *raja* class, in other words, a woman from a high status lineage, and he noted that it had caused some fear. That he drew a link between clandestine trade or smuggling on the one hand, and his marriage to Lawi on the other, indicated that in his mind the two were related. His comment about fear in the same breath made me think that the manner

---

[2] Author's interviews with Jufri, March 5 and 6, 2000, Lambai, North Kolaka. He said it was the "Binsen Ongkōkai," which would be "Tramp Steamer Transportation Company." (*Binsen* would be 便船 = "available steamer," i.e., "tramp steamer," freighters without set schedules.) Wartime Japanese firms operating in southern Borneo included the Kasen (river) Ongkōkai (transport company). See: Ooi Keat Gin, *The Japanese Occupation of Borneo, 1941–1945* (London and New York: Routledge 2011), 77.

[3] Author's interviews with Haji Buraéra March 5 and 6, 2000, Rantéangin and Wawo, North Kolaka; and Sitti Hami, March 6, 2000, Wawo, North Kolaka.

in which their kinship connection was brought about also mattered. Fear of him and for Lawi, he implied, helped motivate the compliance of her Sama kin, even though there had been some retaliation. It was via kinship and fear that Jufri endeavored to create, and to some degree succeeded in creating, a path to gain followers with specialized nautical skills, from whose networks he could benefit. Without this kin connection, Jufri may have wound up commandeering their boats anyway, as he did on occasion, simply for a show of strength. However, had it not been for Jufri's union with Lawi, it is unlikely that her brother Buraéra would have become a smuggler for the rebellion. Their marriage provided Buraéra a way to improve his circumstances, and concern for his sister's well-being kept him from absconding. Jufri cemented Buraéra's loyalty with the position of adjutant, and, to hear Buraéra tell it, with fear as well.[4]

These events during the 1950s provide rich material for exploring the politics that took shape around the need for seafaring skills, nautical manpower, and specialized social knowledge in the maritime world. When set alongside this book's examination of the seventeenth-century archipelago, the 1950s material suggests the durability of a politics in which forging social connections with maritime people conferred nautical advantages. In this archipelagic environment, cultivating such connections opened up, or reinforced, access to the intangible yet invaluable assets of maritime people's skills and networks. Since maritime people usually inhabited the littoral, often in places distant from land-based powers and in ecological zones that made it hard for others to reach them, they were able to maintain a measure of maneuverability independent of established polities on land. If powers based primarily on land wished to benefit from maritime skills and networks, it behooved them to form compelling links with maritime people.

For Lawi and Buraéra, whose stories I return to in chapter five, capture, kinship, fear, and conferral of rank were political tools that made and maintained their connections with Bugis leaders during the Darul Islam rebellion. Yet these methods of gaining nautical advantage were not a new part of intergroup dynamics in the archipelagic world. During the seventeenth century, as this work shows, the bestowal of rank, both by the Gowa court at Makassar, and subsequently by the Bugis realm of Boné, also cemented the loyalty of maritime-oriented people who possessed both nautical and martial skills. Rank was conferred on people viewed as having, or having the potential, to garner followings. Likewise, during the seventeenth century, capture had an impact on followings that was not simply about the acquisition of dependent labor. For instance, the capture of women led to new, subordinate kin connections, yet it also sundered existing ties of foes, thereby weakening the longstanding friendships and relations they maintained with maritime allies and their networks.

Tiworo's ties with Makassar endured just this sort of blow. Closely allied with Makassar, the most powerful port polity in the central and eastern archipelago, Tiworo's people suffered the capture of three hundred women and children, which sealed its military defeat in 1655. Although this large scale capture did not prevent Tiworo's rejuvenation over the next decade, the redistribution of Tiworo's women and children to Makassar's enemies not only wrested them from where they lived, but also removed them from Makassar's political orbit and made them, however

---

[4] Jufri interview, March 6, 2000; and Haji Buraéra interviews.

reluctantly, into "followers" of its foes. Such capture and redistribution of victims among foes was a tool of politics and a means of domination.

Whether used to forge or to rupture connections, the capture of women, in particular, was never simply neutral. Its salience is evident in how Sama capture narratives got taken up and adapted to new contexts, in literary-historical texts from southern Sulawesi (Celebes) that euphemized capture and effectively erased it. To understand the cultural history of this process requires a look at how particular kinds of writing, especially those focused on particular lineages, such as genealogical narratives, related to the social contexts of their production and transmission. Decisions about how to represent elite kin connections, and why it mattered to show, or to obfuscate, the ways they came about, were inseparable both from genre expectations, and, more broadly, from the relation of writing to societal structures. Chapters four and five, respectively, address these qualitative dimensions of capture, representation, and intergroup connection through the analysis of locally produced manuscripts and the examination of events at the local scale. Yet, maritime people's networks and links with others have also made their impact felt on a global stage.

*Intertidal History* shows that networks of maritime people played a vital role, until now virtually invisible, in opposing European efforts to control the seventeenth-century spice trade. By giving concrete shape to the much talked about, but less well understood, place of the sea and those who lived by its tides in the past, my research alters what once seemed a familiar story in world history. Scholarship on the region had already shown that it was only possible to sustain a neat narrative about mercantile competition and conflict among European powers by disregarding their need to ally themselves with Southeast Asians in order to achieve their ends. *Intertidal History* shows how Southeast Asian powers, which had their own aims and agendas, themselves relied on alliances and partnerships with regional maritime people. It thereby opens a window on the dynamics of politics, trade, littoral society, and military cooperation in the maritime world of island Southeast Asia.

In revealing how maritime-oriented people contributed to wider historical dynamics, the book furthermore enters ongoing conversations about maritime history. *Intertidal History* takes maritime history's focus on the sea and turns it toward the dynamics of densely archipelagic regions, with their interlinked seas, clusters and chains of islands, bustling ports, and havens off the beaten track. While the word "intertidal" refers to the littoral, its use in these pages also signals what connects sites along a shore, as well as points between disparate coasts. *Intertidal History* intervenes in maritime history debates in three ways. First, with respect to littoral societies, it offers a view in which their locus did not radiate from urban centers, but instead encompassed complex webs that also contained vital nonurban hubs of maritime activity. Second, the book helps to bring the archipelagic region within wider frameworks of Asian maritime history, by shifting the focus from a largely ocean-crossings approach that basically became tri-coastal: East Africa, the South Asian coast, and a bit of Southeast Asia, and also by peering south and east beyond the porous edge of the South China Sea, to a realm not just of goods but of accomplished mariners, as well. Finally, with its emphasis on the relation between archipelagic geography and the social forms of politics, my findings offer analytical approaches to oceanic history analogous to those that "Zomia" has opened for mainland Southeast Asia.[5]

While the region's maritime people have often been depicted as "stateless," comparison of the intertidal concept with Zomia is not meant to suggest that my book argues that maritime people were defined by techniques and geographies merely of avoiding the state.[6] Nor does it go the opposite direction, overextending its reach by beefing up claims about "states" constituted by maritime people's networks where, indeed, more modest and diffuse political configurations existed. Instead, much as Zomia represents an upland space of interaction not delineated by state-formation, the "intertidal" focuses attention on spaces of littoral and maritime interaction.

*Intertidal History* argues that while maritime-oriented people used distance and connection strategically, the value of both their nautical skills and their networks made land-based polities seek them out as partners, clients, and dependents. Their connections with others in this archipelagic geography show that maritime people operated interstitially between states, sometimes on their behalf, and at times as part of the inner circle at their highest echelons. What connected maritime people with others, as well as how these connections were broken and new ties established, constituted tools of politics through which people exercised power in archipelagic interactions.

A focus on the networks and connections of maritime-oriented Southeast Asians represents but one way to come at the long unfolding historiographic shift away from European expansionist approaches in the writing of maritime history. This shift, which accompanied the rise in transnational perspectives and world history, initially led, in maritime history, to studies of separate ocean basins. The attention to ocean basins seemed to leave the archipelago in an awkward place, as though, unlike them, it had no obvious political or natural boundaries with which scholars could work.[7] Elucidating how the archipelago and those in its littorals were part of interlinked maritime worlds not only integrates its history with that of other parts of Asia and the globe, but also provides a small corrective to the predominant focus on outsiders and sojourners in Southeast Asia's maritime history. *Intertidal History*'s approach to the region navigates its past through a focus on the maritime networks of Southeast Asians. This breaks with the the false dichotomy of inward- and outward-looking analysis, showing how archipelagic dynamics interfaced with the cross-currents of history at different scales.

The focus on archipelagic networks also helps to expose how kinship politics supported the political and military roles played by maritime-oriented people, particularly the Sama, the most numerous and widespread of Southeast Asia's so-called sea people. Marriage politics among elite lineages have long-standing precedents across the region and even interregionally. That they served a diplomatic function is nothing new. However, such practices were also important to mobilizing

---

[5] See: Willem van Schendel, "Geographies of Knowing, Geographies of Ignorance: Jumping Scale in Southeast Asia," *Environment and Planning D: Society and Space* 20 (2002): 647–68; and James Scott, *The Art of Not Being Governed: An Anarchist History of Upland Southeast Asia* (New Haven: Yale University Press, 2009).

[6] On such depiction as "stateless," see, for example, Anthony Reid, *Charting the Shape of Early Modern Southeast Asia* (Singapore: ISEAS, 2000), 4.

[7] Jennifer L. Gaynor, "Ages of sail, ocean basins, and Southeast Asia," *Journal of World History* 24, 2 (2013): 309-333.

maritime power in archipelagic history. Networks of kin related by marriage supported interethnic alliances, such as those the Sama had with Gowa in Makassar and later with the Bugis realm of Boné. Such intergroup kin connections undergirded the ties land-based elites had with maritime leaders capable of mobilizing nautically skilled followings.

Capture was also part of kinship politics, whether it led to new alliances, ruptured old ones, or forestalled future ties. Unions resulting from capture and those resulting from negotiated marriages registered their significance in relation to each other, as part of practices that produced and reproduced social hierarchy in these interlinked stratified societies. The sense that capture made, in other words, relied in part on how it differed from other ways to make kinship and alliances. Marriage, which united not just two individuals, but rather different kin groups brought public recognition—through negotiation, gift exchange, and celebration—to claims about status and the parity of different lineages. Capture, in sharp contrast, breached the respect and expectations manifest in such marital procedures.

Shared practices of cultural production, particularly oral and written knowledge about the past, conferred a status-corroborating authority that intertwined with the kinship and status system pervading much of south and southeast Sulawesi, as well as its offshore regions. Surviving written materials from Sulawesi convey social distinctions, points of view, spheres of meaning, and, indeed, facts, many of which visiting European observers found insignificant or simply missed. Hence, these Southeast Asian sources, both published and in manuscript, help to explain and illustrate the social and political character of intertidal connections.

Perhaps one of the greatest surprises the Southeast Asian sources yield is that the Sama were not, as is generally thought, peripheral to regional states. Makassar's court diaries and chronicles demonstrate that during the seventeenth century, prominent Sama men and women were included in the writings of Makassar's royal inner circle. Sama people held office as harbormaster or chief-of-port (*sabannaraq*, cf. Malay *syahbandar*), a high-ranking position in Makassar's political structure, and Sama people also led naval endeavors. Rare Bugis-language manuscripts similarly describe multiple and complex links through politics and kinship among regional Sama people and the rulers of the Bugis realm of Boné.

The two known examples of these Bugis-language manuscripts about the Sama past adapt, in their opening sections, a widespread story from Sama oral traditions. Compared with the documentary register of the rest of their contents, this initial section employs a narrative structure and it has a legend-like feel that makes it reminiscent of Homeric references in the start of some works on Greek history. In its varied oral versions, the story typically tells of a high status Sama woman, the daughter of a Sama leader, who gets relocated among ethnic others as the result of capture. However, in the Bugis manuscripts' adaptations of this Sama story, the narrative portrays her relocation as an accident. There is no mistaking that this is a literary device, since a well-known event from Bugis myth sets her accidental relocation in motion. The narrative also sets the tone for what follows in the rest of the texts, much of which is not in a particularly narrative form, providing an interpretive context that lays down certain points as presumptions for the audience's understanding of information in subsequent sections.

Who, exactly, this female Sama figure in the narratives purportedly represents remains hazy in one of these manuscripts, and is hard to pin down historically, due to the use of pseudonyms and the lack of clearly datable events. Yet, the other version ascribes her a specific place in a genealogy and makes the claim that she was a forebear of the famous Bugis leader Arung Palakka. During the late 1660s, Arung Palakka helped the VOC (Vereenigde Geoctroyeerde Oost-Indische Compagnie, United Dutch East India Company) defeat Makassar, and on his way to doing so, incorporated people from the maritime hub of Tiworo into the leadership under him. It is certainly possible, perhaps even likely, that the ascription of such a relationship between the story's female Sama protagonist and Arung Palakka is apocryphal. Yet, whether or not the kin connection is true, the story's use of a narrative device to depict as accidental what appears as capture in numerous similar Sama tales, cries out for analytical attention. What made this genre-crossing, interethnic adaptation possible historically, and what explains the need to euphemize "capture"?

Attention to these questions deepens our comprehension of capture in the region. This is important because the role of capture has pertinence for our understanding of slavery, dependency, and followings in Southeast Asian history. Most attention to capture in this period has focused on captives' sale and use as dependent labor, primarily in urban centers like Batavia (present-day Jakarta). Considerably less is known about other forms of dependency, outside of cities and colonial cultures. Capture was not only a means to acquire dependent labor. It was also used to increase followings. Particularly when it involved elite women, capture provided a way either to make or to break intergroup connections, and, as such, formed a part of political conduct.

*Intertidal History* treats the capture of elite women as a phenomenon from that midtemporal scale, concerning persistence and change in social institutions, that Fernand Braudel described between the history of events and the effects of geography on the *longue durée*. While the latter exerts obvious influence on the concept of "intertidal history," the middle temporal scale breathes life into the study of capture. Hard to investigate, the capture of high status women, like smuggling, erases traces of itself in the historical record. *Intertidal History* turns to a recent, more accessible example as an opportunity to think comparatively and over the long term about the capture of elite women in Tiworo's past.

This brings into a single analytical field a number of seventeenth-century captures from Tiworo, and the capture of a single Sama woman from Tiworo in the 1950s. It sets the causes of silences about the latter alongside the reasons for capture's effacement from the Sama narrative in Bugis-language manuscripts. It takes this story in Bugis-language manuscript inherited through a Sama lineage and its exhortation to remember descent from a maternal Sama line, and juxtaposes it with how the childless Bugis sister-in-law of the Sama woman captured in the Darul Islam rebellion took and raised her daughter, enlisting others in the project of hiding her true maternal Sama parentage.

Historically, the capture of elite women was not unique to the Sama. However, as a practice that could make or break connections, capture acquired particular salience in the archipelagic world due to the importance of followings in this context. We know from the archaeological record that capture has an extremely long history in the region, since raiding was endemic to island Southeast Asia, predating both European and Chinese travel to and involvement in the region.[8] Raiding could

---

[8] Laura Lee Junker, *Raiding, Trading and Feasting: The Political Economy of Philippine Chiefdoms* (Honolulu: University of Hawai'i Press, 1999).

increase followings directly through capture, as well as potentially, through reproductive labor or by drawing in people through networks of new kin ties.

Historians of Southeast Asia generally concur on the importance of followings in regional dynamics, and have explained this at the theoretical level with reference to the relative abundance of land. The idea is that the relative abundance of land made labor relatively scarce, hence highly valued. This proposition has been used to explain the demand for manpower and the prevalence of debt bondage and other forms of voluntary and involuntary servile dependency in the region's early modern urban centers. As Anthony Reid has emphasized for the region's cities, manpower, not fixed capital, was the principal asset to be protected, and the fundamental aim of warfare in the region was to increase the availability of workers.[9]

However, in the intensely maritime-oriented zones of the region, among its littoral society, land was a relatively unimportant factor in the significance of followings. Consider that since at least the seventeenth century, maritime-oriented people in the region built houses on stilts in the intertidal zone, rather than on land, and sometimes lived on boats. Moreover, as outlined in the following chapter, like many other regional ethnic names that derive from references to the environments in which people lived, the ethnic name "Bajo," applied to regional sea people, can be traced to the "shallows." The populace in this littoral environment does not become tied to land as it would with settled agriculture. Thus, relations of debt and dependency were not primarily grounded in land ownership and rents, or their inheritance. Instead, the conduct of politics and economy in this context entailed expending considerable energy on the ability to muster people.

The need to muster followings was not unique to coastal states of the region. However, the relative insignificance of land throws into stark relief how the creation and disruption of connections made it possible to forge or fracture followings. As Kenneth Hall explains, the key to a center's authority over manpower was the ability to form personal alliances with locally based elites. Rulers fragmented potential enemies by reaching agreements with leaders of local population centers, turning them from potential opponents into subordinate allies. In return for their patronage of the state's monarch they enjoyed enhanced status in the eyes of their own followers. Allied populations received protection of the state's armies, as well as the symbolic benefits of a state's ritual cults, and they shared in successful states' prosperity.[10]

Within maritime-oriented spheres, primarily land-based polities like Makassar needed followings with nautical skills and networks to gain commercial, political, and military advantage. They secured these followings through various means, such as by gaining people's loyalty and obligation through the conferral of rank, forming kinship ties, amassing dependents, and fostering markets. While capture provided a route to gather subordinates and create dependent kin, at times it also severed the ties of foes and their allies, fragmenting them. Whatever means were used to achieve followings, connections with maritime people were desirable for the skills and knowledge they provided, along with the people-mobilizing potential of their maritime networks.

---

[9] Anthony Reid, "The Structure of Cities in Southeast Asia, Fifteenth to Seventeenth Centuries," *Journal of Southeast Asian Studies* 11, 2 (1980): 243.

[10] Kenneth R. Hall, *A History of Early Southeast Asia: Maritime Trade and Societal Development, 100–1500* (Lanham: Rowman and Littlefield, 2011), 14.

## TIWORO

This is the first study to look at Tiworo's place in history. However, this is not simply a work about Tiworo. Drawing on rarely accessed archives of the VOC, this book shows how maritime people were involved in events of the latter half of the seventeenth century. It taps cartographic materials and the writings of various European observers—Dutch, English, Portuguese, and Spanish—to sketch aspects of the archipelagic world's historical background during the sixteenth and early seventeenth centuries. Southeast Asian sources offer further evidence of maritime people's connections to one another and to others, especially in and around Sulawesi (Celebes), in subsequent eras. These Southeast Asian sources, both published and in manuscript, also help to illustrate the social and political significance of these links. A closer look at the dynamics of the 1950s, touched on at the beginning of this chapter, draws both on interviews with those present at events, as well as on scant but relevant archival materials from the post-independence period, when the Dutch were already gone.

Located in what is now Southeast Sulawesi, the Straits of Tiworo comprise the northern margins of Muna Island, the waters between this large island and the peninsular "mainland," as well as the peninsula's opposite coast. Covering about 876 square miles (2,270 square kilometers), its shores embrace reefs, shoals, small islands, mangrove stands, and sources of fresh water. Regarded by the Dutch as a subordinate ally of Makassar, Tiworo served as a nonurban maritime hub vital to Makassar's endeavors in the seventeenth-century spice trade. The role its maritime-oriented people played led the VOC to target Tiworo twice in what are conventionally taken to be different wars: The Great Ambon War of the mid-1650s and the Makassar War of the latter 1660s.

Defeated in the first conflict, over the following decade Tiworo bounced back and its people resumed their nautical pursuits and assistance to Makassar. Both of these wars ultimately had to do with control of the spice trade. However, control of spices was not the sole motivating factor, for Makassar's Sultan Hasanuddin invoked Tiworo's first defeat in 1655 as a reason for its campaign of re-expansion in the eastern archipelago during the period between the wars. This campaign to reassert Makassar's power in the waters and islands east of Celebes revived Tiworo's role as a naval staging area and as a haven for fleets sailing under Makassar.

After Tiworo's second defeat in 1667, sixty of its men were incorporated with high-ranking positions in an elite Guard of Prime Commanders under Makassar's Bugis foe, Arung Palakka of Boné, the VOC's principal ally in the Makassar War. This outcome contrasts sharply with the aftermath of Tiworo's first defeat a dozen years earlier, when, in addition to some two hundred men killed, three hundred of its women and children were captured and granted to the VOC's allies as spoils of war. Although markedly different outcomes, both this "transfer" of the dependents of the vanquished and the incorporation of former foes at the forefront of Boné's armed fighting force, represent approaches to remaking the connections between maritime people and other ethnic groups—an important feature of the archipelago's social and political history.

Nevertheless, Tiworo went from infamy to obscurity. "That renowned realm Tiworo, which since the old days has been a nasty pirate's nest," held its notorious reputation well into the first quarter of the eighteenth century. At least, such was the view of its nautical character in François Valentijn's *Oud en Nieuw Oost Indiën*

(Old and New East Indies).[11] This scornful depiction can be traced to Admiral Cornelis Speelman's extensive notes, or *Notities*, compiled in 1669 after his forces defeated Makassar with the help of Bugis allies. Speelman singled out the straits as *"dat leelijcke roofnest Tiboore"*—that nasty pirate's nest Tiworo.[12]

Given the strength of Speelman's characterization and its prominent placement on the opening page of Speelman's narrative, one wonders about the lack of subsequent commentary, aside from Valentijn's remark, about this "nasty pirate's nest." Although the aphorism that history is written by the victors holds some truth, other factors help account for why Tiworo slipped through the historiographic cracks. For one thing, the sources use variant spellings, as well as entirely different place names to refer to Tiworo. For another, its inclusion under different subregions in emergent administrative practice resulted in references to it scattered across the topological structure of subsequent archival organization. Both of these factors complicate the task of historical research.

Larger methodological issues also play a role, such as a predominant focus on states in the writing of Southeast Asian history. Yet, was Tiworo a state? States in Southeast Asian history have garnered much attention for how they often do not fit with analysts' expectations. This applies especially, but not only, to the island and peninsular world in the pre-seventeenth-century period, whose states were less influenced by Indian models than were the agrarian states of the mainland.[13] States tended to be weakly integrated and often not bound territorially. For instance, early "amorphous coastal polities" had restricted centers and extended peripheries.[14] Java's coastal enclaves would reach a threshold beyond which they separated from the main body of a state to become the foci of different smaller sorts of "states." Even in agrarian Java, with its greater human density than the rest of the archipelagic world, the population growth and increases in wealth and trade that accompanied state formation did not go hand in hand with urbanization.[15] Scholarship on regional states often seeks to explain why a high degree of centralization was not possible. This has reframed the standard for judging the development of Southeast Asian states on their own terms: instead of political centralization, the standard is cultural integration.[16] What one commonly calls

---

[11] François Valentijn, *Oud en nieuw Oost-Indiën*, v. I (Dordrecht: J. Van Bram, 1724), 222.

[12] Cornelis Speelman, "Notitie dienende voor eenen corten tijt, en tot naeder last van de Hooge Regeringe op Batavia, tot naerrichtinge voor den ondercoopman Jan van Opijnen bij provisie gestelt, tot Opperhooft en Commandant int Casteel Rotterdam op Maccassar, en van den Capitain Jan France als hooft over de melitie mitsgaders die van den Raede," VOC 1276 (1669), p. 684v. Also see Cornelis Speelman, "Notitie ... ," typescript held by KITLV, Leiden, D H 802. The Dutch and their allies had to make one final push against Makassar in 1669. For more information on Speelman's manuscript, see J. Noorduyn, ed., "De Handelsrelaties van het Makassaarse Rijk Volgens de 'Notitie' van Cornelis Speelman uit 1670," *Nederlandse Historische Bronnen* vol. 3 (The Hague: Martinus Nijhoff, 1983), 1–3, 97–123.

[13] Jan Wisseman-Christie, "Trade and Early State Formation in Maritime Southeast Asia: Kedah and Srivijaya," *Jebat* 13 (1984/85): 44. See also Jan Wisseman-Christie, "State Formation in Early Maritime Southeast Asia: A Consideration of the Theories and the Data," *BKI* 151, 2 (1995): 235–88.

[14] Pierre-Yves Manguin, "The Amorphous Nature of Coastal Polities in Insular Southeast Asia: Restricted Centres, Extended Peripheries," *Moussons* 5 (2002): 73–99.

[15] Jan Wisseman-Christie, "States without Cities: Demographic Trends in Early Java," *Indonesia* 52 (October 1991): 23–40, esp. 24, 40.

[16] See: Hall, *A History of Early Southeast Asia*, 2; and Tony Day, *Fluid Iron: State formation in*

"kingdoms" may be understood as cultural and economic communities infused by networks of kinship.[17] This reframing has certain analytical advantages, since regional historiography has sometimes obscured the importance of kinship, as well as gender, in practice.[18] Yet at the same time, it begs the question of culture and its relation to politics. Many would say that conflict and competition lie at the heart of politics. However, anthropologists over the last three decades have reconceptualized culture as having at its heart not shared consensus but conflict. Cultural integration as a standard for judging the development of Southeast Asian states on their own terms is all well and good, as long as it does not sweep conflict under the rug. With accumulated research refining our understanding of states in the region, we gain a picture less focused on how they did not measure up to external standards, and more interest in, as well as a better sense of, how they actually worked.

Tiworo clearly had social hierarchy and leadership, a degree of autonomy, as well as substantive forts. Yet although those who lived there formed a polity of sorts, which is to say they had political organization and were collectively viewed as a substantive player, during the seventeenth century Tiworo was not the apex of a complex political structure. Nor did it have an entrepôt to which others flocked to buy goods. Nevertheless, many goods were indeed stored at, and moved through, Tiworo in its capacity as a staging area. This "realm," to adopt a term pragmatically, formed part of larger, flexible, segmentary political structures, with Makassar and then later with Boné, which were as much about lineage and alliances as they were about location.[19] Tiworo drew the interest of the VOC when it impinged on Dutch commercial agendas and consequently became a target of attack. Yet it was not big enough, and not perceived as having instrumental value to the Dutch, to attract much of their attention beyond this. Even as Tiworo shifted between the orbit of different political centers over time, as with other places in the region's history, when defeated, members of its ruling lineage were able to pick up and move. While this enabled them to put down their anchors elsewhere and forge new alliances, in later years, their descendants maintained ties with Boné, despite shifting among different locations at some distance away from it.

Received geographies form another factor that helped to render Tiworo and the networks of which it was a part historically inconspicuous. In this regard, the "oceanic turn" in the humanities usefully highlights how much historical knowledge has been organized according to places on land. Cartographic representations of political space mirror a misconception of the seas and shoals as uninhabited and uninhabitable: what is wet appears as "negative space," to borrow from the world of art, an area of shadows in-between the depicted figures. Maritime history sometimes challenges, and sometimes reinforces, this framework. When the maritime itself

*Southeast Asia* (Honolulu: University of Hawai'i Press: 2002).

[17] Barbara Watson Andaya, *To Live as Brothers: Southeast Sumatra in the Seventeenth and Eighteenth Centuries* (Honolulu: University of Hawai'i Press, 1993), 213.

[18] See: Tony Day, "Ties that (Un)Bind: Families and States in Premodern Southeast Asia," *Journal of Asian Studies* 55, 2 (1996); Day, *Fluid Iron*; and Barbara Watson Andaya, *The Flaming Womb: Repositioning Women in Early Modern Southeast Asia* (Honolulu: University of Hawai'i Press, 2006).

[19] Similarly, Thomas Keifer discusses how segmentary factions based on friendship and kinship lay at the heart of the Tausug-dominated Sulu Sultanate. It likewise relied on close alliances with maritime-oriented people. See Thomas Keifer, "The Sulu Sultanate: Problems in the Analysis of a Segmentary State," *Borneo Research Bulletin* 3, 2 (December 1971): 46–51.

forms an organizing concept, but still remains merely a space to be crossed, only, as it were, to get to the other side, the story of what happens in that space gets lost.[20]

Given this tendency to associate presence with land and absence with the sea, it comes as little surprise to find that later sources sometimes, without reference to the straits and those who lived there, locate Tiworo in the northwest region of Muna Island. The name "Muna" did not yet apply to the whole island in the seventeenth century, which period sources instead usually called Pangesane, or, in Speelman's prose, Pantsiano. Here wound a river, a source of fresh water whose channels through the mangroves provided fleets protection from enemies. Beyond its banks lay dry ground where forts had been constructed. Yet, although boats hid up these channels when under siege, this small river alone did not accommodate the regular comings and goings of Tiworo's vessels, as this was just Tiworo's landward southern margin. Other villages considered part of Tiworo were primarily found not further inland on Muna, but were located in and along the straits themselves, the main focus of the activities of Tiworo's inhabitants. Hence, in 1655, on board the yacht *Dromedaris* at Batoij, Arnold de Vlaming wrote to Governor Jacob Hustaert and the council in the Moluccas to report that, "We have fought the enemy's villages and the fortress at Tibore situated in the Straits of Pangesane," that is, in the Straits of Tiworo.[21] When later references to the historical realm of "Tiworo" simply assimilate it discursively to the large island of Muna, this effectively deletes the "Straits" from the geography of historical interactions and underwrites an amnesia about Tiworo's historically maritime-oriented population.

The knowledge that Tiworo's people were allied with Makassar and that Tiworo provided a haven for its fleets, served as a naval staging area, and was attacked for these reasons, sheds new light on regional maritime history. Certain details about events also make it possible to contrast Admiral Speelman's characterization of Tiworo with Sultan Hasanuddin's statement rationalizing his campaign of re-expansion by a need to avenge it. Without understanding details of the events, the geography, and Tiworo's role, it would not be possible to grasp that when Sultan Hasanuddin spoke of avenging "Pancana" (Pangesane/Pantsiano), he referred,

---

[20] A rather more mundane factor may also contribute to why Tiworo itself could escape the notice of readers or translators of Southeast Asian sources from Sulawesi. Readers and speakers of Indonesian (and Malay) who are able to read Bugis or Makassar language materials (a fairly rare occurrence), yet are unfamiliar with the place Tiworo (these days it seems only Sama people know of it), are likely to mistake the name for a direction: "east" or possibly "south." In European sources, Tiworo appears under the variations "Tioro," "Tibore," Tiboore," and "Tivora," which suggests an association with or derivation from the Makassar term *timboroq*. Cognate with the Malay/Indonesian term *timor* (east), *timboroq* is sometimes translated as "east," sometimes as "south," and appears to derive from the Proto-Malayo-Polynesian term for the southeast monsoon. On this derivation of the Makassar term *timboroq*, see Horst Liebner, "Indigenous Concepts of Orientation of South Sulawesian Sailors," *BKI* 161, 2 (2005): 269–317, especially pp. 272–75, and 300–1, notes 26 and 27. Winds are named for the direction from which they come, while ocean currents are named for the direction in which they flow. It seems likely that the place name "Tiworo" derived either from a Makassar reference to the location of its close subordinate ally toward the east, or from a cognate Austronesian or early Sama term referring to the southeast monsoon, with its ability to carry one back to Tiworo from areas east and south (e.g., Banda, Timor, Australia).

[21] Arnold de Vlaming and Willem Maetsuyker, Letter to Governor Jacob Hustaert and the Council in Molucco, with the Yacht *Dromedaris*, on February 2, written from Batoij, signed on the chaloup *Sumatra*, lying at anchor off the coast of Celebes opposite Chassea island, 1655, VOC 1211 book 2, p. 97. Batoij is presumably Batoei, in Central Sulawesi.

without doubt, not to the whole of Muna Island, but specifically to the Straits of Tiworo. This clarification, elaborated in chapter three, exposes that, like Admiral Speelman, he considered Tiworo and its people important historical actors in the seascape of seventeenth-century conflicts.

In later centuries, Tiworo was subject to changing maritime geographies of power, reflected in cartographic knowledge. While Speelman launched an early modern image of the Straits of Tiworo as notorious, the view of it as a place that harbored threats had completely changed by the nineteenth century, when warnings about its nonhuman navigational dangers supplanted its reputation for infamy. Cartographic history shows that while Europeans had no knowledge of Tiworo and precious little of Celebes in the sixteenth century, geographic knowledge of the straits was strongest in the maps and charts that followed on the heels of the seventeenth-century conflicts over spices. However, by the late eighteenth century, Tiworo seemed to hover, invisible, just beyond the edges of better known and more commonly represented waters, such as the Straits of Buton, which flowed by Tiworo's eastern entrance.

In the late-nineteenth century, Tiworo was portrayed as a place whose perilous waters were unknown to Europeans, a view that kept most outsiders away and minimized close scrutiny. While its physical geography, a zone of protected waters with two points of egress, made evasion and flight more viable options for its residents than, for instance, a location in the interior of a bay where the chances of getting cornered were higher, the lack of reliable knowledge about it in charts and navigation guides also produced incidental benefits for Tiworo's inhabitants. Habits of disregard during the late-nineteenth and early twentieth century *pax Neerlandica* bolstered the security that the straits provided to those who wished to keep would-be overlords at arm's length, and for those who engaged in unofficial trade.

Europeans knew precious little of Celebes in the early sixteenth century: only the very northern tip of Celebes, but none of the rest, appears in a map of 1537.[22] Cartographic knowledge expanded over the course of the sixteenth century, yet even as late as 1580, knowledge of the areas near Tiworo was restricted merely to the existence of Kabaena, which sits before the southwestern mouth of the straits. It appears as "Coboina" in Fernão Vaz Dourado's Atlas of 1580, but is absent from his earlier works.[23] This suggests, however, that the Portuguese, or some pilot they employed, likely had knowledge of the Tiworo Straits, since it sits so close to Kabaena. Dutch knowledge of the waters around nearby Buton date to Jan Corneliszoon May, who first surveyed the area in 1599, as noted in the journal of Jacob van Heemskeerk, with whom he sailed. May returned to the Indies in 1614 as a shipmaster with Joris van Speilbergen, and drew the map of Buton inset in plate 19 of *The East and West Indian Mirror*, the narrative about that voyage. He took careful soundings of the Buton Straits and also sailed by Kabaena and Kaledupa. Yet, although he drew the eastern mouth of the Tiworo Straits, the rest of it remained unrepresented.[24]

---

[22] Anonymous (but ascribed to Gaspar Viegas), "Atlas of Twenty-Four Charts," Archivio Stato, Firenze, Plate 52 D, in Armando Cortesão and Avelino Teixeira da Mota, *Portugaliae Monumenta Cartographica* (Lisbon: Coimbra University Press, 1960), hereafter *PMC*.

[23] Fernão Vaz Dourado, Atlas of 1580, http://www.wdl.org/en/item/8918/view/1/40/, accessed March 29, 2014.

[24] Joris van Speilbergen, *The East and West Indian Mirror, Being an Account of Joris van Speilbergen's Voyage Round the World (1614–1617), and the Australian Navigations of Jacob Le Maire*, translated,

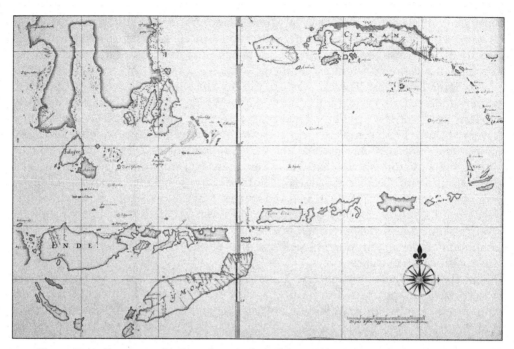

The central and eastern archipelago, from southern Sulawesi (Celebes) and Flores in the west, to the Tanimbar and Kei Islands in the east. From the Blaeu–van der Hem Atlas, 1665–1668.
Source: Austrian National Library

Tiworo makes its first cartographic appearance in the stunning Blaeu–Van der Hem Atlas in the mid-seventeenth century. Curiously, the name "Tivora" is found not on Muna at all, but, rather, in the east hook of the southeastern peninsula. Nearby, as noted in one of Admiral Arnold de Vlaming's reports, the map shows a *"waterplaets,"* a source of fresh water across from the island of Wowoni, information as dear to mariners as knowledge of hidden shoals and pirate haunts.[25] François Valentijn's eighteenth-century "Map [or chart] of the Governorship of the Moluccas" still presents the shapes of Muna (Pangesane) and the straits in a distorted manner. Yet here, with "Tibore" placed at Muna's north end, the map represents Tiworo closer to its actual location, along with the straits' many islands and depth soundings for its waters.

Despite all this eighteenth-century detail, late nineteenth-century piloting directions warn mariners off Tiworo for its dangerous and, it appears, supposedly

with notes, and an introduction by J. A. J. Villiers (London: Hakluyt Society, 1906), pp. xvi, xxvii–xxviii, xxx, xxxv–xxxvi, and the note by May accompanying plate 19 (between pages 128 and 129). Heemskerk would go on to play a pivotal role in the establishment of the VOC in Asia, not to mention providing key components of Hugo de Groot's *De Jure Praedae*. See: Peter Borschberg, "The Seizure of the Santa Catarina Revisited: The Portuguese Empire in Asia, VOC Politics and the Origins of the Dutch-Johor Alliance, 1602–c.1616," *Journal of Southeast Asian Studies* 31, 1 (2002): 31–62; Martine Julia van Ittersum, "Hugo Grotius in Context: Van Heemskerck's Capture of the Santa Catarina and Its Justification in De Jure Praedae (1604–1606)," *Asian Journal of Social Science* 31, 3 (2003): 511–48.

[25] "Map of the Southern Part of Celebes, Ceram and Timor," *Atlas Blaeu–van der Hem* (artist: Johannes Vingboons) (Vienna: Austrian National Library, 1665–1668). This *"waterplaets"* is noted by Admiral Arnold de Vlaming, inter alia, in VOC 1211 1656 book 2, p. 101.

uncharted waters. An 1878 guide for navigating the Indies, which credits the Rajah Sir James Brooke's single voyage around the island of Celebes with delineating the Gulf of Boné's extensive coasts, cautions: "Tioro [sic] Strait is intricate and unknown to European navigators. The shoals and islands are very numerous, and there are no inducements for taking it, especially in a large vessel."[26] No mincing words here: "no inducements" means "keep out."

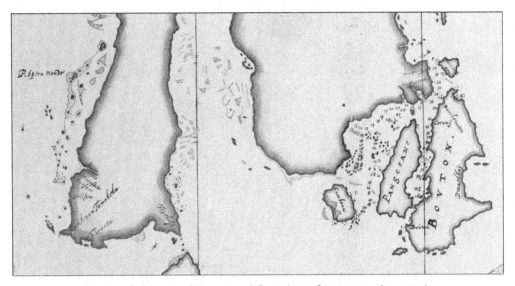

Southern Celebes detail (see upper left quadrant of map on previous page).
The name "Tivora" can be seen, written upside down, in the upper right corner of this image.
From the Blaeu–van der Hem Atlas, 1665–1668. Source: Austrian National Library

One needed reliable local knowledge or very good pilots, whether published or living, to navigate the Tiworo Straits. In fact, Brooke had had a pilot, and he was Sama. For his survey of the Gulf of Boné in 1840, conducted before he became the "White Rajah" in Borneo, Brooke had sent to Bajoé, the Sama settlement at Boné's harbor, expressly for a Sama pilot, whose name, unfortunately, we never learn. Although their journey round the gulf ended very close to Tiworo, the Sama pilot never took Brooke there, thus keeping Tiworo off of Brooke's otherwise remarkably well-delineated charts.[27] Whether it was intentional on the part of the pilot to keep knowledge of Tiworo from Brooke we will never know. But there is no doubt that a Sama pilot who knew his way around this area would have known Tiworo, for Sama people lived there at the time, a point noted by J. N. Vosmaer the previous decade.

While Brooke hoped to learn more about local politics in Celebes, to gauge the extent and depth of Dutch colonial rule there, and to survey coasts poorly known to the British, Vosmaer aimed to do something more ambitious and also similar, in its anti-piracy zeal, to what Brooke later attempted in Borneo. With the reluctant approval of the Dutch, Vosmaer sought to establish a trading post in Kendari Bay

---

[26] Alexander G. Findlay, *A Directory for the Navigation of the Indian Archipelago, China, and Japan*, second edition (London: Richard Holmes Laurie, 1878), vi, 815.

[27] Sir James Brooke and Captain Rodney Mundy, *Narrative of Events in Borneo and Celebes, down to the Occupation of Labuan: From the Journals of James Brooke, Esq., Rajah of Sarawak, and Governor of Labuan*, vol. 1 (London: John Murray, 1848): 150–51.

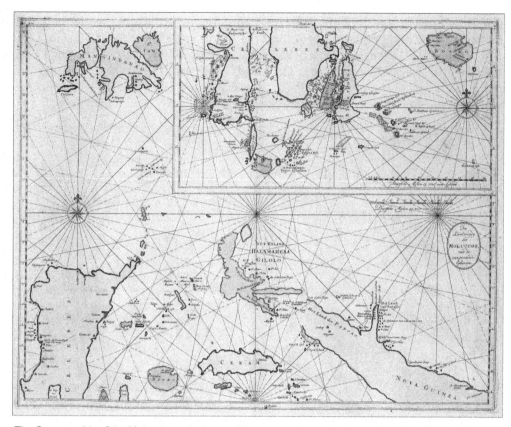

The Governorship of the Moluccas and adjacent islands, including an inset of South Sulawesi, with Buton, Bau-Bau, and Buru. Visible in the main map (bottom left) and the inset (top center) is "Tibore," at the northern end of Muna (Pangesane). From François Valentijn, *Oud en Nieuw Oost Indiën* (1724–1726), plate 37, reproduced in Johannes van Keulen, *De Grote Lichtende Zeefakkel* (1753) vol. 6, map 154. Source: Het Scheepvaartmuseum, the National Maritime Museum, Amsterdam

and to make honest mariners out of coastal raiders, particularly the Tobelo, whose raids had been depopulating the shores of eastern Celebes. Although Vosmaer did not set himself up as "rajah" as Brooke later did in Borneo, his efforts did result in drawing him in to local political dynamics.[28] The Sama in Celebes at this point were not the main focus of colonial concerns about "piracy" or raiding. Nevertheless, as gatherers of *trepang* (sea cucumbers), they held the key to the trade in this and other lucrative maritime commodities like tortoiseshell, and therefore Vosmaer needed them. Many of the Sama involved with Vosmaer's trading post came from the Straits of Tiworo. This is evident from the path laid down by his predecessor, Arung Baku; from remarks about the ethnicity of migrants to Kendari Bay; and from the name of its largest settlement.

---

[28] See: J. N. Vosmaer, "Korte Beschrijving van het Zuid-oostelijk Schiereiland van Celebes, in het bijzonder van de Vosmaers-Baai of van Kendari; verrijkt met eenige Berigten omtrent den stam der Orang Badjos, en meer andere aanteekeningen," *VBG* 17 (1839): 110; and Esther Velthoen, "Pirates in the Periphery: Eastern Sulawesi 1820–1905," in *Pirates, Ports, and Coasts in Asia: Historical and Contemporary Perspectives*, ed. John Kleinen and Manon Osseweijer (Singapore: Institute of Southeast Asian Studies, 2012), 206–9.

Vosmaer's success, albeit limited, came partly from following in the footsteps of a man known to the Dutch as Aru (or Arung) Baku (in Dutch: "Aroe Bakoe"), who most scholars call "Arung Bakung."[29] Vosmaer described "Aroe Bakoe" as a restless or seditious (*woelziek*) Boné prince, who brought upon himself the disfavor of his lord (athough he does not specify who that was), for which reason he made a timely departure from his homeland. Guided by coincidence, he visited the Laiwui coast, where, tired of wandering, he settled on the Sampara river in the region adjacent to Lepo Lepo. After spending a number of years there he left, and by marrying a "princess from Tiworo," the administration of that district fell into his hands. Although he lived in undisturbed tranquility, after a few years he got involved in an effort to make himself—which is to say himself and Tiworo—independent of Buton, which, since the end of the Makassar War, had periodically asserted claims to Tiworo that the Dutch eventually recognized in the early nineteenth century. Vosmaer relates that Arung Bakung was persuaded to exert independence from Buton by a "troublemaker" from Makassar named Sarib Alie, popularly known as Tuwanna I Dondang (probably from Sama: (*ahaq*) *toa*, "parent," meaning here "the father of I Dondang"), who had ambitions of his own on Muna.[30]

Originally from Labakkang, an area opposite many offshore islands north of Makassar, Tuwanna I Dondang estimated that the latter would help in a simultaneous attack on Muna. Arung Bakung eventually found him to be greatly inferior to the leading chiefs of the Magindanao pirates with whom he was said to be closely related by blood. Saddling himself with troubles by the methods he used on Muna, Tuwanna I Dondang was compelled to leave there, yet, returning to Tiworo, found it was also unsafe for him overnight, and thus he went back to Makassar. Arung Bakung, deprived of further help in his bid for independence from Buton, decided to leave Tiworo and, at the invitation of the Konawi prince in Laiwui, set out for Kendari Bay with a number of his most trusted people and about twenty boats of the Sama, who were united with Tiworo, thus putting distance between themselves and Buton. Their presence at Kendari Bay, which they reached in 1823 or early in 1824, drew other Sama people, and the Dutch war with Boné in 1824-25 drove many more Sama there from Bajoé. Traders from Makassar and a swarm of Bugis boats followed, seeking the products the Sama brought in, while people from other coastal towns and islands found a market for their produce there. Unexpectedly, in the middle of 1830 Arung Bakung left Kendari Bay, and the traders

---

[29] The title *Aru* or *Arung* usually appears with the name of a place. Hence "Arung Palakka" is the Arung of Palakka, and although only one is particularly famous, historically there have been many of them. In Bugis, with its consonant gemination, this is pronounced "Aruppalaka" (or with a glottal stop: "Aruq Palakka"). The "Arung of Baku" or "Arung of Bakung" would have undergone similar morphophonological changes among native speakers of Bugis. It would be helpful to know whether it was "Baku" or "Bakung" in order to narrow down the place to which the name refers. There is a Baku with a nearby "Tanjung Baku" (Baku Point) north of Palu on the west coast of Sulawesi; another Tanjung Baku sits south of Palu; a Baku lies not far from the coast near Wotu in the north end of the Gulf of Boné; and an offshore "Boné Baku" a few kilometers west of Makassar. One reason why so many coastal spots share this name may be its resemblance to cognate terms for "mangrove" in the region (Bugis: *bakko*, Makassar: *bangko*; Indonesian: *bakau*. A place named Bakung lies near Bulu Ponre in the landlocked interior of Boné. Another Bakung is found on the coast of Central Sulawesi very close to Batui, across from the Banggai Islands.

[30] Vosmaer, *Korte Beschrijving*, 129–31.

and Sama people followed suit, leaving only the saddest traces of its former prosperity.[31]

The following year, Vosmaer stepped into the place that Arung Bakung had occupied, minus the marriage to a Tiworo princess. Vosmaer got caught up in contests over the allegiances of the region's maritime populations and in the dynamics of competing claims over Kendari Bay, now called "Vosmaer's Bay."[32] Vosmaer's Bay and the protection provided by its temporary battery drew people from many different ethnic groups, including several families of Sama who erected houses there. The place again took on an air of life and prosperity and its largest settlement was called "Kampong Tiworo,"—Tiworo village, suggesting the importance of Tiworo to its migrants.[33]

Genealogical evidence from Sama sources in and beyond Tiworo suggest that this "Bugis prince," Arung Bakung, may not have been entirely Bugis, and if he came from Boné, he probably did not come across the Gulf of Boné to Tiworo on his own. Bugis language manuscripts about the Sama past, discussed in chapter four, strongly suggest that whoever Arung Bakung was, he probably was not simply Bugis. Like Sarib Alie, also known as "Tuwanna I Dondang," many people of the time were known by personal names in one ethnic context, and by different names, or titles that functioned as names, in another, and this was apparently the case for Arung Bakung. Such practices were also reflected in Sama genealogical memory and in the Bugis-language manuscripts concerned with the Sama past. The genealogical and political continuities of particular Sama lineages and their relations with Boné elites form the main focus of these manuscripts. They show that Sama people of high status lineages (*lolo*) maintained ties with and over Bajoé, in subservience to Boné.

The older, more detailed of these two manuscripts dates from the late nineteenth or early twentieth century, surviving by virtue of a recopying tradition of textual transmission in which new information was often added to the final section of a text over subsequent eras, as with south Sulawesi court diaries or chronicles. Among other things, it describes how, during the early nineteenth century, elder Sama relatives came together from scattered settlements along Sulawesi's east coast to choose a successor and install him as "the Lolo" (not just any *lolo*) in Kendari, as well as over Bajoé. In other words, they met to choose a paramount chief from among a chiefly lineage that was geographically dispersed. They chose a man named, in Sama, To Palettéi, or just Palettéi, yet he was also called Puwang Baringeng. Notwithstanding the Bugis honorific title, *puwang*, often used to address those with the title *Aru* or *Arung*, the Sama people who chose To Palettéi to be the next Lolo additionally addressed him as "my grandson," a genealogical relation, not just a polite term of reference. They told him, "You are the one to uphold the grandeur [protect the jewels/virtue] of Bajoé, to succeed the Lolo who died" (*Iko na Puwang Baringeng pallaq i arajanna tanaé ri Bajoé sulléi Lolo mallinrunggé.*)

Although in the Bugis language context *Aru lolo* means a "crown prince" or "viceroy" who rules on behalf of a sovereign (cf. Ind./Malay *raja muda*), among Sama

[31] Ibid., 131–34.

[32] See: Ibid., 129–33; A. Ligtvoet, "Beschrijving en Geschiedenis van Boeton," *BKI* II (1878): 88–89; and Velthoen, "Pirates in the Periphery." On the treaty history regarding Buton's claims to Tiworo, see chapter three in this book.

[33] Coenraad Jacob Temminck, *Coup-d'oeil général sur les possessions néerlandaises dans l'Inde archipélagique*, vol III (Leiden: A. Arnz, 1846–1849), 70–71.

people in the Sulawesi region, in Sama social contexts, "*lolo*" is both a Sama title and a term of reference that applies exclusively to individuals with descent through an elite Sama lineage. Palettéi thus had high-status Sama descent. He may well also have had elite or "aristocratic" Bugis descent. In choosing him to be the Lolo of the Sama, his relatives also chose him to be the Aru lolo or viceroy over the Sama "at Bajoé" and dispersed in networks of related kin.

What makes it extremely likely that Palettéi was, in fact, Arung Bakung is not the vaguely similar sounding pseudonym (Baringeng) coupled with the indications of ascribed high status. Rather, what clinches it is that his authority was bestowed by his Sama relatives while he lived among the Sama in Kendari, which created a formal connection to Boné. Moreover, there is the timing. In other words, although Palettéi was based in Kendari, he is said formally to have become the Lolo of Bajoé (in Boné), during the reign of the Boné ruler posthumously named Matinroé ri Laleng Bata, who ruled from 1812 to 1823.[34] The timing is crucial. Arung Bakung, according to Vosmaer, already long married to "a Princess of Tiworo," and having some authority over its governance, reached Kendari Bay with his Tiworo Sama followers in 1823 or early 1824, and left it in 1830, which, shortly thereafter, created Vosmaer's opportunity.

The point here is not only that European sources, like all sources, reveal partial perspectives, but rather to elucidate the view from Tiworo and regional Sama, along with their role in the politics between different coasts. Arung Bakung's marriage to a Tiworo "princess," whose name (like that of Brooke's pilot) we never learn from Dutch sources, had a variety of consequences relevant to my main argument. It provided him with a following in Tiworo and, combined with his selection as Lolo, a political connection to the Sama on coasts throughout the area. He was then able to benefit from the presence, abilities, and networks of Sama people when they relocated to Kendari Bay. The migration of substantive numbers of Sama from Tiworo to Kendari Bay was motivated not just by commercial interests, but by political ones as well, namely, to put distance between, on the one hand, Arung Bakung and his Sama followers, and on the other, Buton with its newly recognized claims over Tiworo. The kin connection between the Tiworo princess and Arung Bakung/To Palettéi maintained the longstanding ties between members of high-status Sama lineages in Tiworo, and the authority that emanated from Boné through Bajoé, serving as a bulwark against Buton. Buton's claims may have been recognized by the Dutch, but obviously did not hold much water with the Sama in Tiworo, who left. During this part of the early nineteenth century, at a time when more territorial structures of governance were gaining greater traction, such ties still provided an effective way to mobilize followings and, thus, to gain political power.

This sort of migration was neither a diaspora, a label applied with greater accuracy to people presumed to have a collective homeland, nor was it the mobility of wandering sea gypsies, an image that took on particular salience for the Bajo with

---

[34] *LB Lemobajo*, 92–93, 130–31, the Bugis language manuscript discussed above and in chapter four, photocopied with its inheritor's permission, photocopy in possession of the author. Apparently the original manuscript is now in tatters and exists only in fragments elsewhere. The full list of titles and names for the Bugis ruler of Boné mentioned here is: La Mappatunru To Appatunru' Paduka Sri Sultan Muhammad Ismail Muhtajuddin [Matinroé-ri Laleng-bata] (1812–1823). Puwang Baringeng was also called "La Palettéi." "*Puhawang*" is an old Austronesian term meaning "shipmaster." Personal communication with Pierre-Yves Manguin, July 17, 2015.

the *pax Neerlandica*, when mobile seafaring populations no longer posed a threat to colonial power.

## MARITIME PEOPLE

The Sama—the most numerous and widely dispersed of the region's sea people—were not known to come from any specific region, nor was any particular domain their taken-for-granted homeland. Hence, although scattered throughout much of archipelagic Southeast Asia, no singular place has provided them a reference point for diaspora. Similarly, no place name presupposes their relation to it in the way, for instance, one says Filipinos are from the Philippines and the French from France, regardless of histories of nation and subject formation. While no toponym stands in to signify their origin or sense of belonging, a wealth of evidence nonetheless illustrates that Bajo or Sama people have attached themselves to many places, where some anchored and others indeed settled. This dispersion of maritime-oriented settlements includes some long-standing places, such as the Sama settlement of Bajoé. Chapter four touches on how, during times of conflict, Sama people fled Bajoé, and while some later returned, others moved on, yet maintained allegiances to it.

Bajoé, which literally means "the Bajo" in the language of the locally dominant Bugis, was both the primary harbor for the Bugis realm of Boné and a settlement populated largely by maritime-oriented Sama people, familiar to Europeans by a host of similar sounding names: Bajow, Badjow, *Badjau,* Badjoo, *Badjos, Badjoers, baJuüs, baJus,* and the like.[35] As mentioned above, Brooke had sent "to Bajuè for a Bajow pilot" to guide him on his survey of the Gulf of Boné. When he first anchored off Bajoé in January 1840, near scattered shoals and amidst reefs topped with fishing stakes, he estimated—excluding boats—that it contained from 150 to 180 houses.[36] But Bajoé had been an even larger, bustling and multiethnic settlement early in the previous century.

Such settlements and their position in wider networks have often been overshadowed by outsiders' interest in Sama mobility and talk of them as nomadic or sea gypsies. For instance, while Brooke waited in Bajoé's offing for a reply to the message he had sent the ruler of Boné a few miles inland, a party of Bajo (i.e., Sama) people came aboard his vessel. The Bajo, he noted, "have no country, live in boats,

---

[35] For "Bajow," see Brooke, *Narrative,* inter alia 151, 163; for "Badjow," see Sir James Brooke and Henry Keppel, *The Expedition to Borneo of Her Majesty's Ship Dido for the Suppression of Piracy with Extracts from the Journal of James Brooke,* third Edition (London: Chapman and Hall, 1847), 126, 149, 199; for "Badjau," see H. von Dewall, "Aantekeningen omtrent de Noordoostkust van Borneo" (Medegedeeld door J. Hageman, Jcz.) *TBG* 4 (1855): 446–47; for "Badjoo" (adjective), "Oran Badjoo," and "Badjoos" (plural), see Thomas Forrest, *A Voyage to New Guinea and the Moluccas, 1774–1776* (London, New York, Melbourne, and Kuala Lumpur: Oxford University Press, 1969 [1780]), inter alia 372–73; for "Badjos," see Speelman, "Notitie," VOC 1276 (1669), ff. 871v; 865r–865v; for "Badjoers," see Speelman, "Notitie," f. 706v; for "BaJuüs," see Tomé Pires, *The Suma Oriental of Tomé Pires, an Account of the East, from the Red Sea to Japan, Written in Malacca and India in 1512–1515; and The Book of Francisco Rodrigues, Rutter of a Voyage in the Red Sea, Nautical Rules, Almanack, and Maps, Written and Drawn in the East before 1515,* trans. Armando Cortesão (London: The Hakluyt Society, 1944), 467; and for "baJus," see Pires, *Suma Oriental,* 400. This list of variations on the name is not exhaustive.

[36] Brooke first mentions "Bajuè" on page 33; see: Brooke, *Narrative,* 36, 135, 151; and Findlay, *Directory for the Navigation,* 815.

[and] carry on a trade in tortoise-shell, *bêche de mer* [sea cucumber]," and other marine goods. He could tell they spoke a language distinct from Bugis and Malay, and although they possessed no writing system of their own, they claimed to have books in the Bugis syllabary. Brooke hoped to see more of these Bajo people and, along with a vocabulary of their language, to "get some of their books," which were rumored to contain laws (*ondang-ondang*).[37] He wrote,

> It would be curious to obtain the maritime code of a maritime people—without a country, whose home is their *prahu* [boat], and whose livelihood is gained by collecting the produce of the sea and shores of distant islands. We may presume that laws made to suit such a state of society would be peculiar.[38]

Peculiar, indeed. So strong was the notion of them as nomadic or sea gypsies that Brooke's musings about them contradicted what he himself reported he saw. Brooke had sent "to Bajuè for a Bajow pilot," estimated the size of the settlement there, and explicitly noted the Bajo villages (*kampung*) on his month-long survey around the Gulf of Boné. Even so, his statement that the Bajo "have no country" glided all too easily into an image of them as always at sea. The Bajo in his eyes were so marked by the maritime and the "lack" of a homeland that he talked about them as though they lived only on boats.[39] In this, as in his use of them as pilots, he was not alone.

This discursive sleight of hand was not unique to the nineteenth century. Francisco Combés during the seventeenth century had a similarly uncanny way of disregarding evidence of settled life in the littoral even as he made a record of it. Combés described people in Mindanao, Jolo, and Baslian (in the southern Philippines) as "Lutao," since

> Lutao means, in those languages, "he who swims and goes floating over the water." Such is the nature of these people that they know no other house than the ship. In the villages which they have formed they well show the inclination

---

[37] Brooke, *Narrative*, 45–46.

[38] Ibid., 151–52. The "laws" he heard about likely refer to a Bugis commercial and maritime code often called the Amanna Gappa after the notable said to have set it down in 1676 (hijra 1087), although, as J. Noorduyn pointed out, his role as *Matoa* in Makassar did not begin until 1697. See "The Wajorese Merchants' Community in Makassar," *BKI* 156, 3 (2000): 476. C. C. Macknight and Mukhlis call the Amanna Gappa "a commercial and maritime code" in "A Bugis Manuscript about Praus," *Archipel* 18, 1 (1979): 272. On the position of the *matoa* of the Wajo community in Makassar, and on Amanna Gappa in particular, see Noorduyn, "The Wajorese Merchants' Community," 490–96.

[39] Brooke, *Narrative*, 150–51. It is interesting to note that for the east coast of the Gulf of Boné, Brooke divides the Menkoka people into coastal and interior groups, and remarks that: "The former have in some measure been *civilised* by their intercourse with the Bugis and Bajow people, and have nominally adopted the religion of Islam, without, however, rejecting their own barbarous customs and habits" (his emphasis; ibid., 163). What is striking about this is not the nineteenth-century European propensity to rank social taxonomies along a scale of civilizational attainment, but rather the inclusion of the Bajo among those with a civilizing effect. This contrasts sharply with later discourses that primitivize the Bajo. See Jennifer L. Gaynor, "Maritime Ideologies and Ethnic Anomalies: Sea Space and the Structure of Subalternity in the Southeast Asian Littoral," in *Seascapes: Maritime Histories, Littoral Cultures, and Transoceanic Exchanges,* ed. Jerry H. Bentley, Renate Bridenthal, and Kären Wigen (Honolulu: University of Hawai'i Press, 2001), 62–63.

with which they were born; for they are so fond of living on the sea that their houses are built in it, in places which the low tide leaves exposed ... When it is high tide the houses are very far from the shore, and the water in between is so deep that brigs and craft of heavier tonnage can sail there.[40]

Similar to Brooke's assertion that the Bajos' "home is their *prahu*," Combés stated they "know no other house than the ship," yet in his next breath he described the villages they made by building houses in the littoral.

The question is not whether the region's maritime people brought their families on boats and lived there with them. They did. Evidence for this exists.[41] In the early sixteenth century, Tomé Pires, a Portuguese apothecary who recorded his observations about the region, noted that maritime people of the central archipelago (BaJuũs/Celates) differed from others both by their distinct language and by the practice of bringing women on board their boats.[42] Yet even though this made them unique, he did not leave the impression that on-board living was all they knew. He characterized Celates in the western archipelago as "men who go out pillaging in their boats and fish, and are sometimes on land and sometimes at sea, of whom there are a large number in our time."[43] A century later, boat-dwelling gets more heavily emphasized while interaction with the land begins to drop away in descriptions. Passing through the Straits of Malacca, Pieter Floris wrote: "... the Salettes ... for the mooste parte keepe in the prawes with their wyves and children, living chiefly by fishing."[44]

---

[40] Francisco Combés, S. J., *Historia de las islas de Mindanao, Iolo, y sus adyacentes* (Madrid, 1667), reprint issued (Madrid, 1897) by Pablo Pastells, S. J., and W. E. Retana, in Emma Helen Blair and James Alexander Robertson, eds., *The Philippine Islands, 1493–1898* (hereafter BR), vol. 40 (1906), 99–182, esp. 104, http://www.gutenberg.org/files/30253/30253-h/30253-h.htm#pb104; page image at http://quod.lib.umich.edu/p/philamer/afk2830.0001.040/108?rgn=full+text;view =image;q1=blair, accessed May 5, 2013. Technically, Philippine languages include all the languages of the Philippines and northern Sulawesi, but do not include Sama/Bajo or what linguists call Samalan languages; see: Robert Blust, "The Greater Central Philippines Hypothesis," *Oceanic Linguistics* 30: 73–129; Robert Blust, "The Linguistic Macrohistory of the Philippines: Some Speculations," in *Current Issues in Philippine Linguistics and Anthropology: Parangal Kay Lawrence A. Reid*, ed. Hsiu-Chuan Liao and Carl R. Galvez Rubino (Manila: Linguistic Society of the Philippines and SIL Philippines, 2005), 31–68; and, on the linguistic position of Samalan, see pp. 41–53. Cognates in other Philippine languages north of this area do, indeed, mean "float" (e.g., Tagalog *lítaw*, "float"). From the verb *lítaw* one can form a stative adjective, *lutaw*, "in the state of floating," and, since an adjective can be used like a noun, it could be used to form a noun meaning "the floating (things)" (John Wolff, personal communication, February 9, 2014). In contemporary Sama (Southeast Sulawesi), the verb root for "float" is *lantuh* or *lantoh*; "floating" is *palantuh* or *palantoh* (Kamaruddin Thamzibar, personal communication, February 26, 2014).

[41] It is also clear that colonial powers later made efforts to settle them on land. James F. Warren, "The North Borneo Chartered Company's Administration of the Bajau, 1878–1909: The Pacification of a Maritime, Nomadic People" (master's thesis, Ohio University Center for International Studies, 1971).

[42] Pires, *Suma Oriental*, 226–27. See the next chapter for specifics on how Pires actually used the terms *BaJuũs* and *Celates*. Although we have come, through various secondary sources, to view these terms as applying to groups in different parts of the archipelago, a careful look at Pires shows that he himself did not draw this distinction, quite the contrary, in fact.

[43] Ibid., 232–38.

[44] Peter [Pieter Willemsz] Floris, *Peter Floris: His Voyage to the East Indies in the* Globe, *1611–1615, the Contemporary Translation of his Journal*, ed. W. H. Moreland (London: Hakluyt Society, 1934), 102.

Semporna Islands, Malaysia, 2009. Photo credit: Timothy Allen

The issue is not whether people really lived in boats, but rather the view that boat-dwelling was the *sine qua non* for a collectivity. Instead of noticing a range of dwelling practices that, subject to circumstance and historical change, people engaged in to pursue lives in the littoral and in relation with the sea, boat-dwelling came to be seen as a trait characteristic of sea people. Taken as a defining trait, boat-dwelling held a curious ideological power that obfuscated contradicting evidence that the very same groups of people also led settled lives in the littoral. Viewed as the quintessential feature of who they were, its "decrease," both real and imagined, was then read through the lens of nostalgia. Instead of historical change, this primitivized image of sea people substituted a set of evolutionary assumptions in which sea nomads came to be seen as either threatened with disappearance, or subject to existence as a kind of fallen version of their former selves. A late-twentieth-century example illustrates this well:

> It is obvious that many rather important places have been inhabited by Bajos [*sic*] for many decades. It is to be expected that the trend of becoming more sedentary, caused by intermixing with other tribes, interference of the government, new fishing devices, and more modernized living, will continue. These de-isolational influences will increase the disintegration of both Sama culture and the Sama language.[45]

---

[45] Jilis A. J. Verheijen, SVD, *The Sama/Bajau Language in the Lesser Sunda Islands*, Pacific Linguistics, Series D, No. 70, Materials in Languages of Indonesia, No. 32 (Canberra: Department of Linguistics, Research School of Pacific Studies, The Australian National University, 1986), 30. Subsequent chapters will make it clear that Sama cooperation with Makassar in campaigns across the Java Sea to the Lesser Sundas took place in the seventeenth

"Becoming more sedentary," "mixing," "modernized," "de-isolational," and "disintegration" are terms that portray people with an idealized past: nomadic, unmixed, not-modern, and isolated, and who now, supposedly, would come apart, despite centuries of social reproduction in dispersed communities of the archipelago. While addressing such discourse is not my main aim, readers will find in these pages ample means to counter this modern myth.

The focus here is primarily on the central archipelago, yet maritime-oriented people were also important to polities in other parts of island and peninsular Southeast Asia. For instance, to the north of Makassar, sea people in the southern Philippines were under Brunei's influence during the sixteenth century. Spanish relations with Manila and Sulu played a role in loosening this connection, yet sea people in this region remained subject to Brunei until near the end of the seventeenth century.[46]

During much of the eighteenth and nineteenth centuries, southern Philippines sea people were instead subject to the Sulu Sultanate. Among them, the Balangingi Sama and also the Iranun made raids across the archipelago. James Warren has argued that these raids provided slave labor for the procurement of marine and jungle products valuable to the China market. These products were traded for arms from European "country traders" (i.e., those who sought profits within Asia), who then exchanged them for tea. While Warren's work is extensively researched, reservations have been expressed about the tenuous basis for demonstrating that people who were taken in raids then participated in such goods-procurement as slave labor. In his explanation, the exchange of marine and jungle products, especially *trepang*, funded not only the purchase of firearms, but also enabled Tausug *datus* (aristocrats) to profit and display their resulting wealth. However, an alternative proposition points out that such patrons may instead have been interested in subjugating and humbling other human beings, as well as increasing their followings, which would, in and of itself, have marked their status and prestige.[47]

Regarding the Balangingi Sama, Warren makes a case for "ethnogenesis," since through their fearsome actions they distinguished themselves to such a degree that others wound up perceiving them as an ethnic group *sui generis*. Yet, as Charles O. Frake rightly pointed out, fellow speakers of what linguists call Samalan dialects continued to see the Balangingi as just another group of Sama.[48] This is an important point, for it means that what appeared to be ethnic differences from one

---

century. The history presents a very different picture than this nostalgic portrayal of potential linguistic and cultural death.

[46] D. E. Brown, "Brunei and the Bajau," *Borneo Research Bulletin* 3, 2 (December 1971): 55–58.

[47] James Warren, *The Sulu Zone, 1768–1898: The Dynamics of External Trade, Slavery, and Ethnicity in the Transformation of a Southeast Asian Maritime State* (Honolulu: University of Hawai'i Press, 2007). Warren's explanation is analyzed in greater detail in: Heather Sutherland, "*The Sulu Zone* Revisited," *Journal of Asian Studies* 35, 1 (2004): 133–57; David Henley, "Review of James Warren, *The Sulu Zone*: The World Capitalist Economy and the Historical Imagination" *Bijdragen tot de Taal- Land- en Volkenkunde* 156, 4 (2000): 834–38; and Jennifer L. Gaynor, "Piracy in the Offing: The Law of Lands and the Limits of Sovereignty at Sea," *Anthropological Quarterly* 85, 3 (2012): 840–44.

[48] Charles O. Frake, "The Genesis of Kinds of People in the Sulu Archipelago," in *Language and Cultural Description: Essays by Charles O. Frake*, selected and intro. Anwar S. Dil (Stanford: Stanford University Press, 1980), 311–32.

set of external perspectives did not always map onto how such distinctions were made in local social practice. Since Europeans sometimes ethnicized functional differences, and, without realizing it, lumped Sama people into groups at both ends of the piracy–nomad continuum, such classifications of Southeast Asian maritime people provide a cautionary tale about the limits of reading colonial sources against the grain.[49] Nevertheless, the archipelagic environment did put a premium on the abilities of maritime-oriented populations, and the usefulness of their skills was nothing new.

Southeast Asians with specialized nautical skills played a role in the trade, defense, and political legitimacy of regional coastal polities from the seventh to the nineteenth century. These included: Srivijaya, Champa, Majapahit, Brunei, Melaka, Johor, Makassar, and Sulu, as well as a host of lesser realms such as Patani, Banjarmasin, Bima, Boné, Buton, Ternate, Tidore, and Jailolo. Srivijaya, long unknown, and initially a mystery due both to its dispersed hub-and-spoke spatial structure and lack of durable remains, was prominent from the seventh to thirteenth centuries, as attested in foreign sources. It was based in southern Sumatra at the western end of what is now Indonesia. Champa, about which more is discovered every year, began around the same time along the central coast of what is now Vietnam, and reached its height in the ninth and tenth centuries. Majapahit, on the island of Java, rose from the end of the thirteenth century (c. 1293) and was in decline about 1500, around the same time as Melaka. Melaka, established circa 1400, lasted under Southeast Asian rule until 1511, when the Portuguese took it over, a situation that contributed to the rise of Johor. Johor flourished through alliances, particularly with the VOC, and saw its height in the latter sixteenth and much of the seventeenth century. Makassar, on the southwestern peninsula of Sulawesi, gained particular prominence during the sixteenth and first three-quarters of the seventeenth century, until its defeat by the VOC and its allies. Sulu, as mentioned above, gained importance during the late eighteenth and nineteenth centuries.

In most cases, it remains unknown how and why sea people shifted their allegiance from one center to another.[50] In this book I show how just such a process of allegiance shifting, from Makassar to Boné, took place for people from Tiworo. Boné may have had connections with the Sama before this, but it is clear that the advent and rapid expansion of the Sama settlement, Bajoé, followed the incorporation of dozens of Tiworo's men into Boné's sphere during the Makassar War. Bajoé's recent beginnings and impressive growth were noted by a Bugis trader who informed the Dutch in 1714 that a settlement had been established on the southern hook of Palette in Boné for the "Turijeners and Bajorese," Dutch renderings of Makassar and Bugis language terms for the Sama.[51] According to the report, the landward part was known as Cellu and the seaward part as Bajoé. Although the settlement was for the Sama, it drew many different sorts of people. It

---

[49] See, especially, Frake on "the pirate tribes" and other labels (ibid., 323–25). See also James Francis Warren, *Iranun and Balangingi: Globalization, Maritime Raiding and the Birth of Ethnicity* (Honolulu: University of Hawai'i Press, 2002).

[50] Brown makes this a central and unanswerable question in his brief piece on Brunei and the Bajau.

[51] "Turijeners" comes from *turijéqnéq*, formed by *tu* + *ri* + *jéqnéq*: people + on + water. *Turijéqnéq* is a synonym for *Bayo*, the Makassar equivalent of "Bajo."

had grown so much that "at present a great confluence of people had come to settle there, holding markets daily where all manner of nations come to do business, such as those from Johor, China, Malay, Wajo', Seram, Tambukko, Menado, Mandar, etc."[52]

Hence, in the early eighteenth century, the Bugis realm of Boné was fortunate to have at Bajoé a vibrant multiethnic market. Yet, Bajoé has also always been known as a Bajo place, and one cannot account for its advent and growth without acknowledging its predominantly Sama population and the complex networks of trade, kinship, and politics in which they participated. Littoral society at Bajoé, networked with other Sama and non-Sama communities, grew into a vibrant market town as a result of Sama relocation there.

While some Sama relocation and trade may have shifted to Boné as a result of Makassar's defeat, the latter alone does not account for Bajoé's growth, since Makassar neither stopped being an important center of trade, nor did the Sama cease to play an important commercial and military role there. Commercially, for instance, Makassar's tortoiseshell trade, in which the Chinese were crucial, increased during the early eighteenth century, in parallel with a China-focused boom in the *trepang* industry. Both appear to have been supplied by the Sama.[53] Militarily, although Makassar existed under a treaty regime that stripped its dual realms, Gowa and Talloq, of much power since its fall in 1669, Sama in the early eighteenth century remained a vital force for Makassar. One Dutch official remarked in 1733 that the Sama were the "muscles and sinews" of Gowa.[54] This rare glimpse of the position of Sama people in eighteenth-century Makassar is but a shadow of the role they played in, and in relation to, Makassar during the seventeenth century.

Usually conceived as peripheral to regional land-based states, maritime people, and particularly the Sama, were vital to Makassar's trade, its expansion to the south and east, and its support of those in the Moluccas who fought against the VOC. Their connections with Boné underwrote Bajoé's prosperity and Boné's political expansion in eastern Sulawesi. These aspects of the region's maritime past surfaced as a result of examining the dynamics and significance of connections that ran along and between the archipelago's littorals.

## ITINERARY

The preceding pages set this study of the archipelago's maritime-oriented people in comparative and historical context with respect to works on Southeast Asia and

---

[52] Makassar to Batavia, September 23, 1714, VOC 1853, p. 103; Leonard Andaya, "Historical Links between Aquatic Populations and the Coastal Peoples of the Malay World and Celebes," in *Historia: Essays in Commemoration of the 25th Anniversary of the Department of History, University of Malaya*, ed. Muhammad Abu Bakar, Amarjit Kaur, and Abdullah Zakaria Ghazali (Kuala Lumpur: The Malaysian Historical Society, 1984), 42. I have redone the translation. Bajoé appears on a "Map of Lands in the Northern Part of the Gulf of Bone," J. M. Aubert, 1752, NA Leupe collection 1298.

[53] See: Heather Sutherland, "Trepang and Wangkang: The China Trade of Eighteenth-Century Makassar c. 1720s–1840s," *BKI* 156, 3 (2000): 451–72; Heather Sutherland, "A Sino-Indonesian Commodity Chain: The Trade in Tortoiseshell in the Late Seventeenth and Eighteenth Centuries," in *Chinese Circulations: Capital, Commodities, and Networks in Southeast Asia*, ed. Eric Tagliacozzo and Wen-Chin Chang (Durham and London: Duke University Press, 2011), 172–99.

[54] Makassar to Batavia, May 21, 1733, VOC 2285, p. 119; L. Andaya, "Historical Links," 39.

maritime history. Intertidal history, a notion anchored in the sources, provides a way to think about the geography of interactions in the region's maritime past. It supports my main argument about the vital role that maritime people played in trade and war, particularly during the seventeenth century. Others forged connections with them in order to gain followings and to benefit from their skills, knowledge, and networks. The foregoing sections also introduced Tiworo, along with the historiographic challenges it presents, and discussed historical approaches to the region's maritime people, particularly the Sama.

Chapter two lays out the historical background for understanding the place of maritime people, particularly in archipelagic networks connected to Makassar, in order to illustrate precedents for Tiworo's place in the seventeenth-century nexus. An important ligament of these networks was the east–west route along the northern littoral of the Java, Flores, and Banda Seas. Along this route lay communities of mariners and boat builders. Knowledge of the northern littoral route remains underemphasized in the literature because Europeans and Javanese followed the southern littoral along the north Java coast to reach Moluccan spices. The northern littoral provided a more direct route to Malacca from Banda and the Moluccas, and also gave on arteries that led northward to the South China Sea. Both the vibrant port of Makassar, as well and the Straits of Tiworo, lay along this route. Makassar was a market for Chinese and Indian goods, a major rice exporter, and the main transshipment point for spices between the eastern and western archipelago. In addition, it attracted many different Europeans, including the Portuguese, whose principal haven it became after the Dutch took Malacca in 1641.

The early sixteenth-century Portuguese observer, Tomé Pires, described "the islands of Makassar" as an enormous swath of the central archipelago, raising questions about Makassar's relationship with this region's coasts and offshore areas. Sama who lived in the islands to the north of Makassar supplied it with valuable marine produce. During the seventeenth century they had politically subordinate ties with Makassar, and sources suggest these ties existed at least a century earlier. In addition to such tribute and trade with what one might call its hinterseas, seventeenth-century ties among Sama and Makassar elites in the port itself ran deep socially and politically, with the presence of Sama men and women in Makassar's royal inner circle, and top Sama leaders (*papuq*) who held the office of Makassar's harbormaster.[55] Vital to its defense and the projection of Makassar's power overseas, such figures of Sama leadership also co-commanded naval expeditions under Makassar's authority, indicating that Sama followers manned the fleets. Chapter two also explains how outsider's names for regional sea people derived from terms that referenced the ecological environments they inhabited. This included not only terms from Philippine and Malay languages, but also Iberian ones, suggesting that sustained interactions took place between sixteenth-century Iberian and Southeast Asian mariners.

Chapter three examines the attacks on Tiworo by the VOC and its allies in two seventeenth-century wars over the spice trade. Tiworo turns out to have been a key ally of Makassar in both the Great Ambon War and in the lead-up to the Makassar War. Its ruling family was tight with Makassar's ruler, and its people were

---

[55] On positions and titles in Makassar, see William P. Cummings, "Introduction," in Cummings, ed. and trans., *A Chain of Kings: The Makassarese Chronicles of Gowa and Tallok,* (Leiden: KITLV Press, 2007), 5–6.

demonstrably maritime oriented. Tiworo offered strategic advantages. During the Great Ambon War, it served as a staging area, with its boats transporting goods, supplies, and fighters to sites of conflict four hundred miles away. It also provided a haven for its own boats along with others sailing under Makassar. After its first defeat in 1655, three hundred of its women and children were captured and bestowed on the VOC's allies. The attack on Tiworo in 1655 became a rationale for Makassar's expansionary expeditions in the 1660s. This campaign of re-expansion bolstered Tiworo's rebound from its defeat in the Great Ambon War.

In conjunction with the Makassar War, Tiworo's forts were again razed and its settlements burned in 1667. However, this time Tiworo's "exquisite boats" were not destroyed. Instead, Arung Palakka, the VOC's principal ally, assumed control of them, prohibiting their acquisition by the VOC. At the same time, before he and his men set off with the VOC's forces to defeat Makasssar, Arung Palakka put together a "guard of prime commanders" from sixty of his own bonded men and sixty handpicked men from Tiworo, providing them each with firearms. He thus effectively severed the alliance of Tiworo's people with Makassar, and integrated these men from Tiworo into his own force with rank and responsibility. Although, as noted above, Admiral Cornelis Speelman, who led the VOC's forces, vilified Tiworo as a "nasty pirates' nest," the actions of his ally Arung Palakka bespoke a rather different disposition. Female kin of these sixty men of rank would not, as happened in 1655, be taken captive and distributed as spoils. On the contrary, the unmarried among them were likely candidates for negotiated marriages with Bugis matches, recognizing their status and cementing the loyalty of these handpicked mariners.

Although the VOC sources do not mention such unions, evidence of marital and other political connections between generations of Boné (i.e., Bugis) and Sama lineages are the focus of two rare Bugis-language manuscripts about the Sama past, considered in chapter four. One of these manuscripts was unearthed in a Dutch archive, while the other was inherited by a Sama woman. While in the latter manuscript the absence of dates and the use of titles rather than personal names present certain challenges, the former ascribes a partly Sama lineage to Arung Palakka. It claims he descended from the female Sama protagonist in the manuscripts' initial story. In this narrative about the daughter of a Sama *papuq*, her boat lands accidentally on the shores of Makassar and she marries into the royal line. The story, it is argued, reworks a widespread tale from Sama oral tradition, with versions set in diverse locations, about the capture of an elite daughter by ethnic others and her relocation among them. The capture so evident in those versions was effaced in the story's adaptation to Bugis-language manuscripts, which emphasize descent from this female Sama ancestress.

The effacement of capture in narrative, accomplished through the use of a literary device that euphemized an unsavory topic, brought the story in line with Bugis writing conventions that aimed to boost status. What made possible this capture-effacing adaptation of the story about a Sama woman's maritime relocation was a history in which Boné incorporated people from Tiworo into the ranks of its elites, and hence into its sphere of politics. This initial story in these manuscripts both orients the reader and is followed by less narratively driven writing about the Sama past and connections with Boné. Rather than see these cultural products as an effort to absorb and erase the differences between Bugis and Sama, such manuscripts, disseminated among branches of a high-status Sama lineage, served instead as a means to make a genealogically relevant history, and as a vehicle to express the mutual identification of their interests.

Chapter five examines the capture of a Sama woman from Tiworo, Hajjah Lawi, whom I introduced earlier. Lawi's capture and marriage to a Bugis regiment commander in the 1950s Darul Islam rebellion, and the capture of her brother, who became a smuggler for DI-TII, present an opportunity to examine in depth the qualitative dimensions of a land-based power's efforts to gain access to maritime people. That this example comes from a recent era underscores the durability both of capture as a tool of intergroup politics, and of efforts to access followings among people with skills, knowledge, and networks in the maritime world. Why Lawi was taken, what motivated her capture, emerged spontaneously in interviews with the commander to whom she had been wed. Interviews with Lawi herself, and with those who recalled events of the time, offer perspectives that other sources cannot, namely, a keen sense of the stakes involved. When juxtaposed with archival material from the time, they provide a sense of how little it seems the government knew about these events, and how strongly its agents imposed upon them a nationalist interpretation. Analysis of what participants recalled detail the wedding ceremony's curious letter-of-the-law legitimacy (conducted with the presence of guns), her family's retaliation, the structure of silences regarding her fate and that of her offspring, as well as how circumstances led to her brother's becoming a smuggler and the commander's adjutant.

In addition to the importance of access to maritime networks, this illustration of how Lawi's union to Jufri came about, and its ramifications, brings out the vulnerability of her capacity to reproduce socially. One can see this especially in how Lawi's first daughter was taken by the DI-TII regiment commander's sister and misled about her maternal parentage. This daughter's belated discovery of her Sama mother and maternal kin helps to underscore why, in an inherited story about Sama interethnic unions, passed down orally as well as in writing, the main figure exhorts her progeny to remember their Sama matriline. Such counsel echoes metaleptically beyond the boundaries of the narrative, among the audience of putative descendants. The Sama lineage in interethnic unions may be deemphasized or submerged in some social contexts, but when descendants do recall it, they engage in a practice of social reproduction. Foregrounding the importance of descent in the representation of the past, genealogical narratives provide a structure, a way to write and tell about the past, that is not centered on land. A portable past, this way of making "history" suits the ethos of movable polities, lineage-based elites, and networks of interaction in the maritime world.

CHAPTER TWO

# THE NORTHERN LITTORAL ROUTE
# AND MAKASSAR'S HINTERSEAS

Prior to the seventeenth century, there were regional networks already in place that tied maritime people to Makassar, to a range of littoral communities, and to other mariners within and beyond the region. Drawing on textual, cartographic, and linguistic evidence, this chapter elucidates who these maritime people were, where they lived, and the networks in which they interacted during the sixteenth century. The source materials illustrate the involvement of maritime people in broad archipelagic networks, and show how some littoral areas had special political and economic ties to Makassar. These ties suggest that it may be analytically useful to consider such areas as part of Makassar's hinterseas.

Textual sources, primarily *The Suma Oriental of Tomé Pires*, detail the maritime networks that linked Makassar to other parts of the archipelago. Pires reports on Makassar's regular contact with Malacca, and also shows, importantly, that Makassar's influence in a very broad swath of the region surrounding it was itself borne by maritime people. According to him, the movement of maritime people associated with Makassar extended from the Spice Islands, in the east, to Pegu, on the shores of the Indian Ocean, along Burma's (or Myanmar's) west coast. Cartographic evidence suggests that Sama people in islands north of Makassar, whom we know from VOC sources had ties with it in the seventeenth century, had similar relations with Makassar extending back at least through the sixteenth century.[1] The key to reinterpreting this evidence is the early modern Iberian term for "shoals" or "shallows"—*baixo/baxo*—that appears on period maps. As will be discussed later in this chapter, clarification of this term helps illustrate connections between Makassar and areas of nonurban littoral society. The same term also lies at the heart of a related matter. It was borrowed into other languages as an ethnic name. While this sheds light on the derivation of "Bajo," the important point, historically, given the lack of detailed period sources, is that such a process of linguistic borrowing implies regular sustained interactions between Iberian and Southeast Asian mariners.

Long before European involvement during the sixteenth and seventeenth centuries, spices and other goods from the eastern archipelago were shipped to and exchanged in the region's entrepôts. Cloves are indigenous only to parts of the eastern archipelago, while nutmeg, native to the Banda islands, has been exported from the area throughout recorded history. The export of cloves can be traced to Roman times. Pliny the Elder describes it in his writings from the first century, CE, and the South Asian Ramayana, written about 200 BCE, also mentions cloves. However, the trade may even be more ancient than this, as a single clove was

[1] Speelman, "Notitie," f. 706v.

discovered among charred plant remains at a Mesopotamian site in present-day Syria, dated to 1700 BCE.[2]

The Chinese were involved, during the Song and Yuan dynasties (c. 1000–1368), in networks of trade to the eastern archipelago, importing cloves from the Moluccas, nutmeg from Banda, camphor from Borneo, sandalwood from Timor, and tortoiseshell from various eastern archipelago sources. Chinese involvement moved mainly through three overlapping circuits. First, by the late thirteenth and fourteenth centuries, Chinese merchants, mostly sojourners in Southeast Asian ports, traded directly with the eastern archipelago. They joined seafarers of different ethnicities as intermediaries in supplying products from the eastern archipelago to the international marketplace. Second, the Yuan era's most important port in China, Quanzhou, drew on an alternate route to the Moluccas, and beyond them, via the Sulu and Celebes Seas. Third, in addition to sojourners who traded directly with the eastern archipelago, and the north to south route from Quanzhou, another circuit relied on the west coast of Borneo, which formed an especially prominent transshipment point for eastern archipelago products bound for Yuan-era Chinese ports. Locales on this Borneo coast of the South China Sea provided goods sourced not only from the eastern archipelago, but also from the Philippine region, which were then re-exported from Cham ports along the Vietnam coast. By the Ming era (1368), however, Chinese sojourners rarely traveled to the eastern archipelago, and the trade relied instead on the intermediary services of sojourners who had settled on the Borneo coast.[3]

In part a result of Ming-era prohibitions on private foreign trade, this pullback to the services of sojourners on Borneo's South China Sea coast implies a consequent increased role for other mariners, such as the Sama, in supplying this coast's ports with eastern archipelago and Sulu Sea goods. Evidence for this role of local mariners as intermediaries in trade circuits for eastern archipelago goods appears in the earliest European sources on the area. We know, for instance, that mariners came from nearby islands to trade with the Moluccas during the early sixteenth century, thanks to the Portuguese apothecary Tomé Pires, who noted that

[2] Paul Michael Taylor, "Introduction," in *F.S.A. de Clerq's Ternate: The Residency and Its Sultanate*, trans. Paul Michael Taylor and Marie N. Richards (Washington: Smithsonian Institution Libraries Digital Edition, 1999 [1890]), ii. The list usually includes mace, which is actually the lacy red covering around the nutmeg seed.

[3] See: Kenneth R. Hall, "Sojourning Communities, Ports-of-Trade, and Commerical Networking in Southeast Asia's Eastern Regions, c. 1000–1400," in *New Perspectives on the History and Historiography of South and Southeast Asia, Continuing Explorations*, ed. Michael Arthur Aung-Thwin and Kenneth R. Hall (Abingdon and New York: Routledge, 2011), 56–73, esp. 58, 66; Kenneth R. Hall, "Coastal Cities in the Age of Transition: Upstream–Downstream Networking and Societal Development in Fifteenth and Sixteenth Century Maritime Southeast Asia, in *Secondary Cities and Urban Networking in the Indian Ocean, c. 1400–1800*, ed. Kenneth R. Hall (Lanham: Rowman and Littlefield, 2008), 188–91; Roderich Ptak, "Some References to Timor in Old Chinese Records," *Ming Studies* 17 (1983): 37–48; "China and the Trade in Tortoise Shells (Sung to Ming Periods)," in *Emporium, Commodities and Entrepreneurism in Asian Maritime Trade, c. 1400-1750*, ed. Roderich Ptak and Dietmar Rothermund (Stuttgart: Franz Steiner Verlag, 1991), 195–222; Roderich Ptak, "The Northern Trade Route to the Spice Islands: South China Sea-Sulu Zone-North Moluccas (14th to Early 16th Century)," *Archipel* 43 (1992): 27–56; Roderich Ptak, "China and the Trade in Cloves, Circa 960–1435," *Journal of the American Oriental Society* 113 (1993): 1–13; and Roderich Ptak, "From Quanzhou to the Sulu Zone and Beyond: Questions Related to the Early Fourteenth Century," *JSEAS* 29 (1998): 269–94.

they traveled to the Moluccas—by which he meant the islands Ternate, Tidore, Motir, Makian, and Bachan along Halmahera's west coast—to buy goods in exchange for gold. The islands from which some of these local mariners came included: Morotai (*Mōr*), to the Moluccas' north; Siau (*Chiaoa*), off the north coast of Sulawesi; and, listed in a straight line from west to east just above two degrees south latitude, Tolo (either Tolo Bay or Tomori Bay),[4] Banggai (*Bemgaya*, the Banggai islands), Sula (*Çolor*), and Sanana (*Celebe*, labeled with variants of "Xula Bessi" on many maps). Besides conducting trade in the islands off Halmahera's west coast, local mariners also piloted Magellan's ships through the Sulu and Celebes Seas to the Moluccas. They may have done the same for the Chinese in previous centuries.[5] This evidence of local mariners' involvement in moving eastern archipelago goods supports the notion of a shift in who carried the lucrative trade from the eastern archipelago to northwest Borneo transshipment points between the late-fourteenth and early sixteenth centuries, following the pullback of sojourning traders to Borneo's northwest coast. Such a shift away from Chinese or sojourning transporters to more local intermediaries in this trade helps to explain the importance of the Sama in Brunei's rise during the period preceding Makassar's prominence.

## THE "ISLANDS OF MACASSAR" ALONG THE NORTHERN LITTORAL ROUTE

Tomé Pires was the first to give definitive news about the islands beyond Java. A fresh look at what he wrote contributes to a better picture of the Southeast Asian

---

[4] People in the Tomori Bay area, where the town of Kolonodale is located, normally call Tomori Bay "Tolo Bay" instead. Another "Tolo Bay" a bit farther up the coast is the site of a major Sama village, "Kolo Bawah" (Lower Kolo; "Kolo atas," viz., Upper Kolo, is in the hills). While there are small Sama villages throughout Tomori Bay, it is tempting to speculate whether the practice of calling both places "Tolo Bay" bears some historical connection with the Sama presence and the major settlement at Kolo.

[5] Pires, *The Suma Oriental of Tomé Pires*, pp. 221–22; Ptak, "The Northern Trade Route to the Spice Islands," 38; Antonio Pigafetta, *Primo Viaggio Intorno al Mondo* [First Voyage around the World], MS composed ca. 1525, of events of 1519–22, transcript of the original in the Biblioteca Ambrosiana, Milan, Italy, trans. James Alexander Robertson, in BR, vol. 33 (1906), 243–51, http://www.gutenberg.org/files/42884/42884-h/42884-h.htm, accessed June 20, 2014. Based on knowledge of seventeenth century cartography and on personal knowledge of place names from living and traveling in northern and eastern Celebes, I differ with Cortesão's interpretations of some of Pires's toponyms, particularly *Çolor* and *Celebe*. *Çolor* here is not the Sulu islands in the southern Philippines, but more likely "Sula" (Taliabu). In early maps, Xula or Xulla was applied to both Taliabu and Mangola to its east (as well as to other islands besides). Together with Sanana, these were known as the "Sula islands." Pires states *Çolor* is west of *Celebe*. Many seventeenth century maps show "Sula" or "Xula" (Taliabu) west of "Xula bessi" (Sanana). Hence, although Cortesão claims this as the first time "Celebes" is mentioned, it appears that he is wrong, or that, in any case, this name does not refer to the contemporary island of Sulawesi, which came to be called Celebes. "Xula" may be from the Latin "insula," or possibly from local language cognates of the term for "current," such as *suluk* (Sama), or *sulug* (Tausug). For an explanation of the derivation of "Jolo" from *sulug* (Tausug) or the cognate *suluk* (Sama), see Charles O. Frake, "The Cultural Construction of Rank, Identity and Ethnic Origins in the Sulu Archipelago," in *Origins, Ancestry and Alliance: Explorations in Austronesian Ethnography*, ed. James J. Fox and Clifford Sather (Canberra: Department of Anthropology, Research School of Pacific and Asian Studies, The Australian National University, 1996), 318, 325 (note 3).

littoral and its people during the sixteenth century.[6] In his *Suma Oriental*, written shortly after the Portuguese took Malacca in 1511, he advised Portuguese mariners starting from Malacca not to go to "the clove islands"—in other words the Moluccas—by way of the coast of Java. Instead, he suggested they go from Singapore to Borneo's south coast, from Borneo to Buton, and thence to the Moluccas.[7] Pires explained that the merchants of Malacca, with little capital and slaves for sailors, made use of the Java route—the route along the southern littoral of the Java Sea—taking their time to put in to ports on the north Java coast along the way. This made their journeys long and profitable, since they brought merchandise from Malacca "to sell in Java, and from Java to sell in Bima and Sumbawa, and from these islands they take cloth for Banda and the Moluccas."[8] There they would sell these goods along with cloth that they kept in reserve from Malacca, which is why, he tells us, "the people of Banda and the Moluccas adore them."[9] To obtain cloves, harvested in six crops a year, eight junks would travel from Malacca to Banda and the Moluccas, three or four originating from Gresik (*Grisee*) on Java's north coast, and the other half from Malacca, belonging, Pires says, to a Chetti merchant.[10] This was how they conducted their trade, "which they could not do along the way by Borneo and Buton and Macassar."[11] Pires reasoned that, since the Portuguese took on liberal supplies and good cloth when they set out, they had no need to add to their profits in this way, "and thus we make our way quickly."[12] With the monsoon winds one could sail this course along the northern littoral of the Java Sea to Banda or Ambon in a month and from there to the Moluccas in a day or two. In his estimation, it was convenient and not dangerous.[13] Hence, although traders starting from Malacca, and those from Java's north coast, traveled along the southern littoral of the Java and Banda Seas on their way to the Moluccas, Pires advocated that his compatriots not take this route, but instead follow the northern littoral route to cross the archipelago's latitudes.

The coasts along this route were by no means empty or dormant. They contained vibrant communities engaged in maritime endeavors, with skilled individuals who supported not only themselves and their families, but the maritime pursuits of others as well. In his descriptions, Pires used a simple principle to guide his decisions about which locales to speak of from among the "infinity of islands" that stretched from the Singapore Straits and the nearby Straits of Kampar, to the islands of Japan in the north and those of Banda in the east. He desired to remark on only "the few in this great abundance with which Malacca is in communication now, or was in the past."[14] In addition to sites along southern Borneo's littoral, Makassar

---

[6] Pires, *The Suma Oriental of Tomé Pires*, 200, note 1.

[7] Ibid., 213.

[8] Ibid., 220.

[9] Ibid.

[10] Ibid., 213–14. In other words, part of the diaspora connected to Tamil merchant guilds. See, inter alia, Geoff Wade, "An Early Age of Commerce in Southeast Asia, 900–1300 CE," *Journal of Southeast Asian Studies* 40, 2 (2009): 235–38.

[11] Pires, *The Suma Oriental of Tomé Pires*, 220.

[12] Ibid.

[13] Ibid., 219–20. Compare with page 212, "… two or three years from Malacca to Banda and the Moluccas, and many junks are lost."

[14] The Straits of Kampar lie at the southern end of the Malacca Straits. Pires, *The Suma Oriental of Tomé Pires*, 222–23.

was regularly in touch with the great emporium of Malacca, where "goods from all over the east are found [and] goods from all over the west are sold ... where you find what you want, and sometimes more than you are looking for."[15]

Following this northern course to the source of spices, from Malacca via Makassar, one passed a series of coastal locales and offshore islands along Borneo's south coast, "three or four days' journey from one another."[16] The people from these places regularly sailed to Malacca, as well as to Java. However, their importance to nautical activities went well beyond this journeying. Known as accomplished mariners, shipwrights, and raiders, the people along Borneo's southern littoral and offshore islands counted among their numbers skilled craftsmen who produced large vessels, "junks," which others were eager to buy. Pires explained, "the Javanese go and buy junks in these people's country, and these people sell the junks when they go to Java." They were, moreover, "great bowmen" and took "a great many slaves and gold."[17]

Some of the vessels in the archipelago during this era were huge. Portuguese sailors were surprised to find that the largest ships were often larger than their own. An average burden for these large ships was 350 to 500 metric tons; on occasion, they reached 1,000 tons and carried a thousand men. During the first quarter of the sixteenth century, the main builders of such ships of high tonnage could be found not only on the coasts of southern Borneo, but also in harbor cities on the north Java coast, as well as in Pegu (Burma). All these areas were close to teak forests, whose wood was "strong for junks."[18]

These large Southeast Asian ships of the late-fifteenth and early sixteenth century carried cargo that belonged to merchants of Malacca and other major trading cities of the region. They traveled chiefly to southern China, the Coromandel coast, and to the Moluccas. That is, on the one hand, they regularly ventured beyond what we currently take to be Southeast Asia proper, into the Indian Ocean and the South China Sea, and, on the other hand, they also played a role in trade within island and peninsular (or "insular") Southeast Asia. There were also boats under 100 tons, and an abundance of multipurpose vessels that could serve in either trade or war.[19] In contrast with this remarkably vibrant picture, about a hundred years further on, at the turn of the seventeenth century, Dutch and Portuguese sources only described ships of lesser tonnage. This left an impression that later scholars would interpret as

---

[15] Ibid., 228.

[16] Ibid., 222–25.

[17] Ibid., 225–26. On the etymology of "junk" from the Malay term *jong*, see Pierre-Yves Manguin, "The Vanishing *Jong*: Insular Southeast Asian Fleets in Trade and War (Fifteenth to Seventeenth Centuries)," in *Southeast Asia in the Early Modern Era: Trade, Power and Belief*, ed. Anthony Reid (Ithaca: Cornell University Press, 1993), 197–213.

[18] Manguin, "The Vanishing *Jong*," 198; Pires, *The Suma Oriental of Tomé Pires*, 151–52, translator's note 3. "Strong for junks" is in Pires, *The Suma Oriental of Tomé Pires*, 145. "Pegu," in the Martaban Bay region of the Bay of Bengal, lies on the eastern shores of the Indian Ocean.

[19] Manguin, "The Vanishing *Jong*," 198–99. Manguin goes on to state, "There are clear indications in Portuguese sources of late-fifteenth or early sixteenth century Indian Ocean trips leading them as far west as the Maldives, Calicut, Oman, Aden, and the Red Sea, and the Portuguese transcribed still vivid memories of earlier voyages to Madagascar" (page 199, with citations for this remark in note 4).

the lack of an ocean-going history on the part of Southeast Asian shipping.[20] The point to emphasize here is that, at this earlier moment during the sixteenth century, mariners on the southern Borneo margin of the Java Sea, perhaps among those Southeast Asians who plied the waters of the Indian Ocean and the South China Sea, were certainly active in trade to Malacca, Java, and the Moluccas. They also crafted ships that became the material instruments of conducting trade and war.

"Behind these islands," meaning beyond those along Borneo's southern coast, "is the route to the Moluccas via Macassar and Buton."[21] Tiworo, located between Makassar and Buton, lies among what Pires called "the islands of Macassar." The islands of Macassar included not just the offshore islands near the port city of that name, but also extended a great distance away from it. So large an area did these islands cover, according to him, that one must wonder about the political character of their relationship with, or as part of, Makassar. Pires noted these islands were numerous and he delimited their geographical extent this way: "It is a large country. One side [on the south end] goes up to Buton [in the east] and Madura [in the west] and the other extends far up north ... They say that these islands have more than fifty kings." This described an area of little land, which was brimming with coasts and bays, atolls and cays, in seas laced with island chains. Whatever characterized relations between Makassar and these places' people and numerous rulers, Pires understood this extensive speckled swath of the central archipelago to be politically connected with Makassar during the early sixteenth century.[22]

The people of these islands traded widely and plundered even further, for they had commerce "with Malacca and Java and with Borneo and with Siam and with all the places between Pahang and Siam"—that is, along the east coast of the Malay peninsula, including Patani, as well. "Their language is on its own, different from the others," he remarked, adding, "they are all heathens, robust, great warriors." Calling them this by no means ruled out a view of their pursuits as—in his eyes— piratical: "The men in these islands are greater thieves than any in the world, and they are powerful and have many *paraos* [vessels or boats]. They sail about plundering, from their country up to Pegu, to the Moluccas and Banda, and among all the islands around Java; and they take women to sea."[23] These were not people who simply shipped consigned cargoes for the rulers of major ports—although they may have done this as well. Rather, their language and the practice of women on board their vessels set them apart, while plunder by *paraos* suggests that at least to some degree they had designs of their own.

Like others in the region whom Pires called corsairs (pirates), those based in the islands of Macassar did not have to rely on the region's largest ports to sell their goods—whether ill-gotten or duly traded. Corsairs nearest Pahang made their trading ports there; those near the Moluccas and Banda traded in Bima, Sumbawa, and Sapeh; and those "nearest us"—that is, in Malacca—held a fair and traded in nearby Aru, Arcat, and Rupat. They brought countless slaves, which was why, Pires

---

[20] See: Ibid., 199–201; and Jennifer L. Gaynor, "Ages of Sail, Ocean Basins, and Southeast Asia," in *Journal of World History* 24, 2 (2013): 309–13.

[21] Pires, *The Suma Oriental of Tomé Pires*, 226.

[22] Ibid., 226–27.

[23] Ibid. Pires does not specify what role these women played. Regional Sama people are known for women's participation in fishing and other seaborne ventures. This contrasts with, for instance, the general proscription of women from Bugis ships.

reckoned, there were so many slaves in Malacca.[24] Corsairs who wished to shop their wares therefore had recourse to bring them to market in ports less impressive than the area's largest entrepôts, as well as at more temporary "fairs." This point shows that the geography of littoral society did not simply revolve around major ports and cosmopolitan centers in the early modern maritime world. Instead, the networks of maritime interaction were more diffuse, more geographically dispersed, and less urban-centered than is generally acknowledged.

As for Pires's use of the label "corsairs," it would be too reductive to regard this simply as a matter of his being Portuguese—in other words, to say that he called everyone "corsair" whose interests did not align with the crown to which he was loyal. Without a doubt, corsairs in *paraos* and cargoes in large junks interested Pires more than, say, fishermen did, and he was always careful to list how many *paraos* one or another ruler had at his disposal. He took note of their naval capacity. However, this association of boat-strength with a ruler or a given place did not necessarily clarify the character of what people did with them—that is, whether they were corsairs. For instance, when discussing the boats of Gilolo (Halmahera) just east of the Moluccan islands, he remarked in summary fashion: "Some of them go pillaging; some of them go trading—like all other nations."[25] Against this egalitarian, if phlegmatic, tone, it therefore seems a special distinction for people in "the islands of Macassar" to have garnered a particularly noteworthy reputation as "great warriors" and "greater thieves than any in the world … powerful … [with] many *paraos*," and who, from their bases in these islands, ventured to the Moluccas in the east, to Pegu in the west, and, perhaps, beyond.

Those from the islands of Macassar who did "not carry on this kind of robbery," noted Pires, "come in their large, well-built *pangajavas* with merchandise … many foodstuffs … very white rice … some gold," and from Malacca they take back South Asian textiles, quantities of black benzoin, as well as incense. Makassar's chronicle of Talloq records that the ruler posthumously known as Tunilabu ri Suriwa, who lived during the late fifteenth and early sixteenth centuries, traveled this northern littoral route. "It was this *karaeng* who went over to Melaka, then straight eastwards to Banda. For three years he journeyed, then returned." According to Pires, "these islands have many inhabitants and a great deal of meat, and it is a rich country. They all wear krises (daggers). They are well-built men. They go about the world and everyone fears them, because no doubt all the robbers obey these [men] with good reason. They carry a great deal of poison[ed weapons] and shoot with them. They

---

[24] Cortesão points out that Sapeh (or Sape) is an inhabited place on the east coast of Sumbawa that gives its name to the bay and the straits between Sumbawa and Komodo islands (Pires, *The Suma Oriental of Tomé Pires*, 228, note 1). In the early twentieth century (e.g., 1913 and 1914), the town of Sape was also a stop for steamers of the KPM (Koninklijk Paketvaart Maatschappij, Royal Packet Navigation Company). See, for example, *Straits Times*, October 3, 1913: 4; and *Straits Times*, November 6, 1914: 4. Current Google satellite maps show an area in town called "Badjo," the colonial Dutch spelling of the name, and reveal what are patently Sama settlements—stilt houses in the tidal zone, lots of boats parked in front— mostly on the bay shore but also opposite this at the sandy points and natural low tide causeway of the two small islands in the bay. These are typical late-twentieth–early twenty-first century Sama settlement patterns, both in terms of housing style and location. Positioned relative to safe anchorages, they offer access to, and keep a measured distance from, land-based authorities and amenities.

[25] Pires, *The Suma Oriental of Tomé Pires*, 221.

have no power against the junks which can all defend themselves, but every other ship in the country they have in their hands."[26]

## CELATES AND *BAJUŨS*

Who were these people from "the islands of Makassar" who were "mainly corsairs," but also traders, and who, apart from the junks, had every other ship in the country in their hands? Pires tells us: "The Javanese call them *BaJuũs*, and the Malays call them this and *Celates*."[27] Since scholars have sometimes misread this statement as support for the notion that the former were in Celebes and the eastern archipelago and the latter were in the western archipelago, it is important to be clear here that with this remark Pires laid out neither an ethnic distinction nor a geographic distribution. Rather, he simply stated that Javanese referred to the maritime-oriented people in the islands of Makassar as *BaJuũs*, while the Malays called them both *BaJuũs* and *Celates*. Pires himself also used "Celates" to refer to certain people, as well as an area, in the western archipelago. From the Malay word *selat* for "straits," the geographic—rather than the ethnographic—sense of the term indicated not the Malacca Straits per se, but rather the channels formed by the islands between Malacca and Java. Merchants from Malacca sailed along these passages to reach Java on their way to Banda and the Moluccas.[28] According to Pires, then, in addition to living in "the islands of Makassar," *Celates* also lived among these islands in the western archipelago.

Although Pires did not offer details about where *BaJuũs* or *Celates* lived in "the islands of Makassar," he did get specific about where they dwelt along the western archipelago's coasts. A look at his description of this area illustrates the kinds of relations that regional sea people had with land-based powers, and helps orient

---

[26] Ibid., 227 ("poison[ed weapons]" is in Cortesão's translation). See also: William P. Cummings, ed, and trans., *A Chain of Kings: The Makassarese Chronicles of Gowa and Tallok* (Leiden: KITLV Press, 2007), 84, 110.

[27] Pires, *The Suma Oriental of Tomé Pires*, 227. As with other scholars, such as Gene Ammarell and Clifford Sather, I follow Anthony Reid and Christian Pelras, inserting the terms from the original Portuguese, since all agree Cortesão mistranslated *baJuũs* as "Bugis." I have also capitalized the first letter of the term here, and likewise for *"Celates,"* which is lower case in the original Portuguese and sometimes marked with a cedilla. See: Gene Ammarell, *Bugis Navigation*, Monograph No. 48, Yale Southeast Asia Series (New Haven: Yale University Southeast Asia Studies, 1999), 242, note 79; Clifford Sather, *The Bajau Laut: Adaptation, History, and Fate in a Maritime Fishing Society of South-eastern Sabah* (Kuala Lumpur and New York: Oxford University Press, 1997), 6; Anthony Reid, "The Rise of Makassar," *RIMA* 17 (1983): 152, note 6, republished in Anthony Reid, *Charting the Shape of Early Modern Southeast Asia* (Singapore: ISEAS, 2000), 125, note 8; and Christian Pelras, "Célèbes-sud avant l'Islam, selon les premiers témoignages étrangers," *Archipel* 21,1 (1981): 165, note 16.

[28] Pires, *The Suma Oriental of Tomé Pires*, lxxix, 136. In note 2 on page 147, Cortesão cites Ferrand: "Cellates est un néologisme portugais formé avec le mot malais *selat* 'détroit.' Il a le sens de 'gens de détroit, population maritime vivant dans le détroit.'" See also: Gabriel Ferrand, "Malaka, le Mālayu et le Malāyur," *Journal Asiatique* XI (1918): 434. Dalgado says "Straits" in general and in particular those by Singapore, but Pires is much more specific. See Sebastião Rodolfo Dalgado, *Glossario Luso-Asiatico* (Hamburg: Helmut Buske Verlag, 1982 [reimpression of Coimbra 1919]), vol. I, 245. Linguistically, the terms Pires used both nominalize and pluralize, whereas Malay requires the term "people/person" plus the descriptor. Hence, Malay *"orang selat"* for "straits people," like the common term *"orang laut"* for "sea people."

readers to the social and geographic view from the waters. *Celates* could be found along much of Sumatra's east coast, particularly in "Arcat," north of Rokan, in Rokan itself, and in Bengkalis (*Purim*), which bordered on Siak. "*Celates* robbers" populated the sea coast of Arcat (*Arqat*), while those inland lived on their crops. Arcat had gold, wine, rice, and fish. Yet, Pires singled it out as a place where mariners loaded quantities of dried salt fish, indicating that it had a substantial maritime-focused population. It was also well-known for holding a slave market in certain months, "open to all," and to which "anyone who likes can go ... in safety." Its king was a Moor with many small *paraos* who did not do much trade, and was "a vassal" of nearby Aru.[29] Whereas Arcat was politically tied to Aru, the ruler of Bengkalis, "an important person and a great warrior," was, like those of Rokan and Rupat, "obedient to the king of Malacca," supplying the latter "with rowing men in great numbers." The market of Bengkalis had shad and other fish in large quantities, as well as some gold, rice, wines, meat, and other foodstuff. It was "almost entirely a country of *Celates*."[30] "Brought up on the sea,"[31] these robbers and great rowers with their many *paraos*, came there "to make a fair of the things they steal," including slaves.[32] The market for stolen slaves in Bengkalis was nearly the largest in the area, second only to the market in Arcat.[33] Pires's descriptions make clear that the allegiance of *Celates* under subordinate rulers brought not only economic benefits from their nautical pursuits, but also resulted in the ability to muster followings, particularly rowers with pluck, as well as boats.

*Celates* also populated the passages formed by the offshore islands and archipelagos between the Malay peninsula, Java, and Borneo. Pires carefully described the islands that formed the channel, beginning with Pulau Pisang, which, although he did not state it, signaled where to head due south to enter the navigable passage through the islands. This channel then ran between the islands at the mouth of the Kampar river and those situated further offshore, namely the Karimun islands, "the Selat[s]" (*dos celates*), and Kundur island (*Sabam*), all of which he indicates were inhabited.[34] The passage then flowed between the coast of Sumatra and Buaya island, and past the Lingga islands. The king of Lingga "is like a king of the *Celates*. He is feared and powerful—more than Kampar ... These islands must have four or five thousand men, and from the point of them opposite the islands of

---

[29] Pires, *The Suma Oriental of Tomé Pires*, 148.

[30] Ibid., 262.

[31] Ibid., 149.

[32] Ibid., 262.

[33] Ibid., 149, 262. The "area" that Pires discussed in this regard included Pedir and Pase (Pasai).

[34] Ibid., 156, 406. In this specific geographic context, "*dos çelates*" refers to the islands between Karimun Besar ("Great Karimun") and Kundur island in this cluster at the western end of the Riau archipelago. Elsewhere, Pires offers a list of the "islands of the *Celates*" that includes: *Çelağuym gum*, Kundur (*Sabam*), Buaya, Linga, Tiga (*Tigua*), Pulo Berhala (*Pullo Baralam*), Bangka (*Bamca*), and *Monomby* (Ibid., 136). The mouth of the Kampar River itself devolved into straits between nearshore islands, opposite which, just south of Karimun Besar, lies a passage to the Singapore Straits. Although the Kampar River lay north of Srivijaya's main centers at Palembang and later Jambi, this was once an important region, with a Buddhist temple site upstream at Muara Takus, and a "Kan-pa" anchorage at the mouth of the Kampar River familiar to Chinese mariners in the early fifteenth century. See: Ma Huan, *Ying Yai Sheng Lan: The Overall Survey of the Ocean's Shores*, trans. and ed. J.V.G. Mills (New York and London: Cambridge University Press, 1970 [1433].

Buaya lies the channel to Pahang and Bintang and to Siam and all these other parts."[35] In other words, at the northern point of these islands, one could opt to sail east through a channel that fed into the South China Sea, and thence to the Gulf of Thailand or the coasts of China.[36] If, instead of heading east here, one continued south past Lingga, the passage then flowed between Palembang and Bangka. Beyond these one could either bear south out of the channel toward Java, or, by turning east and passing south of Belitung, one could make for Borneo's south coast, the route to the Moluccas that Pires advocated.

Pires also discussed the *Celates* when he related the story he had heard of Malacca's fifteenth century beginnings, in which sea people formed the entourage of Paramesvara, the royal claimant from Palembang. When Paramesvara fled from, or was driven out by, Javanese forces, these *Celates*, sometimes fishermen and sometimes robbers, functioned as his protectors (though perhaps those he opposed might have called them his henchmen). Ennobled by him, their descendants intermarried with his own, including his son, "Xaquem Darxa," who was later "married to the principal daughter of the mandarin lords who had formerly been *Celates*."[37] Pires says nothing about where this son's mother came from, but he does indicate that the son was born during the five-year period that Paramesvara had been in Singapore, before moving on to Muar and finally settling in Malacca.[38] Some hundred-odd years later, in Pires's own time, the Singapore channel had "a few *Celates* villages; it is nothing much."[39] The timing suggests the possibility that this son's mother may also have been from the *Celates*. In any case, the marriage of Paramesvara's son to the principal daughter of ennobled *Celates* allied their lineages. The son's descendants could theoretically trace their lineage to *Celates* nobles, through a maternal line. What happens to the history and memory of such matrilineal descent concerns us here, because even as there is room to question the details of his story about Paramesvara, this pattern of alliance with maritime people crops up again in other contexts, such as the seventeenth century dynamics examined in the next chapter.

At one point in the text, Pires actually conjoins the terms *Celates* and *BaJuũs*, and at another he presents them together in a dynamic opposition. He conjoins them when he tells the story of Malacca and Paramesvara: "These *celates bajuũs*—men who lived near Singapore and also near Palembang—when *Paramjçura* (Paramesvara) fled from Palembang they followed his company and thirty of them went along together protecting his life."[40] However, when he described Malacca's longstanding conflict with Aru across the straits, Pires painted a picture of internecine conflict conducted through maritime raiding, which resulted in redistribution to the ruler and in support of the fleet. He characterized the dynamic by invoking a maxim about

---

[35] Pires, *The Suma Oriental of Tomé Pires*, 156–57.

[36] The northernmost of these islands is presently called "*Pulau Pintu,*" "Gate" or "Gateway Island."

[37] Ibid., 233–38. This appears to refer to Malacca's second ruler, who, according to official national histories, was named Megat Iskandar Shah. The third ruler was Muhammad Shah, while Paramesvara was also posthumously known as "Iskandar Shah."

[38] Ibid., 232–33.

[39] Ibid., 262.

[40] Ibid., 233 (see page 467 for the original Portuguese).

rivalries in the region, set out in a series of social oppositions. The king of Aru, he says,

> ... is always in residence in his kingdom. His mandarins and his people go robbing at sea, and they share with him because some part of the armada is paid by them. Since Malacca began, he has always been at war with Malacca and has taken many of its people. He pounces on a village and takes everything, even the fishermen; and the Malays always keep a great watch for the Arus, because this quarrel is already of long standing and it has always remained, whence comes the saying, "Aru against Malacca, Achin against Pedir, Pedir against Kedah and Siam, Pahang against Siam on the other side, Palembang against Linga, *calates* [*sic*] against *baJus* [*sic*], etc."[41]

This pairing of *Celates* and *baJuũs*, although it presents them in opposition, also says much about their intertwined complementarity since it appears in a list of often closely related neighbors and rivals in the western archipelago. Although the source of the saying is unclear, it nevertheless indicates that for some, the term *baJuũs* or *baJus* not only saw use in that broad area known to Pires as the islands of Macassar, but also applied to the social geography of the western archipelago. Just as *"Celates"* applied, in Pires's time, not only to maritime people in the western archipelago but was used by Malays to refer, as well, to people in "the islands of Makassar," the maxim above, which clearly Pires did not make up, similarly illustrates that *"baJuũs"* was used in the western archipelago and did not only apply further east.

The Dutch Admiral Cornelis Speelman a century and a half later also equated the two terms. He referred to "the people of *Zalette* or *Badjos*" and elsewhere used *"Zaletters"* interchangeably with *"Badjos."*[42] The spelling shift and inversion of the vowels (*Celates* to *Zaletters*) can be traced through late-sixteenth and early seventeenth century sources.[43] Although at present all variants of the term *Celates* are now defunct, the history of how these terms were used shows that, far from referring to two different groups of maritime people in different parts of the archipelago, *Celates* were both associated with, and equated with, *baJuũs* or *Badjos*. Looking at how Pires and others used these terms also portrays a view from the waters, illustrating a world in which maritime alliances and allegiances were

---

[41] I have replaced the erroneous translation "Bugis" with *"baJus"* from the original Portuguese. The original reads: *"calates com baJus &c"*; ibid., 147, 400.

[42] Speelman, "Notitie," f. 871v, f. 865r/v. See also the Dutch variant "Badjoers," ibid., f. 706v.

[43] Pires himself sometimes wrote *calates*, but, like his more commonly rendered *Celates*, João de Barros (1553) wrote *Cellates*. Then we find: *"Seletes"* by Pedro Teixeira in 1610; in the same year, *"Selletes,"* in Carta Regia; *"Celetes,"* by Diogo do Couto, in 1616; and *"Salettes,"* in Pieter Floris. See: Dalgado, *Glossario Luso-Asiatico*, vol. I, 245. Floris, born in east Prussia, considered himself a Dutchman and wrote in Dutch by preference. He had previously worked for the Dutch, but was hired along with a compatriot, under pseudonyms, to work for the English East India Company. He died two months after his return to London in 1615, and his journal was shortly thereafter translated into English, apparently by a native speaker of Dutch, although by whom is not known. The original Dutch journal has never been traced. Perhaps Speelman had access to it, or to the French translation that became available in 1650. Did Speelman pick up "Saletters" from Floris in the Dutch or the contemporaneous English translation? We cannot be sure, but this spelling in the Floris was nearly identical with Speelman's "Zaletters." See: Floris, *His Voyage to the East Indies in the Globe*, 102; and Moreland (ed.), "Introduction," in Floris, supra, xlii, xliv, xlix, lix, lxii.

organized through lineage connections and subordinate rulers. These networks of kinship and politics made it possible to muster followings in nautical endeavors that also resulted in redistributing wealth and people.

## LITTORAL NAMES, "PIRATES," AND PILOTS

Where, then, does the name *Badjos* come from? If it is clear that Speelman's seventeenth century terms *Zalette* and *Zaletters* come, like Pires's sixteenth century *Celates*, from the Malay term for "straits" (*selat*), the derivation of *Badjos*, as in "the people of *Zalette* or *Badjos*," is still a mystery. Solving it helps to clarify more than just a linguistic puzzle, for the answer sheds light on the place of these maritime people and the character of their interactions in the early modern archipelago.

An instructive paradox about the Sama is that scholars were not aware until the 1970s that the people who throughout the region were called "Bajo" (and similar variants) called themselves, in their own language, "Sama." While the literature on the region contains many examples of names that outsiders used for the "hill people" of one or another part of Southeast Asia, outsiders applied these labels, such as "Dayak" in Borneo and "Igorot" in Luzon, in ignorance of linguistic and cultural diversity and internally perceived ethnic affiliations. To find, at such a late date, that the people who live scattered on the coasts of Borneo, Indonesia, and the Philippines, called "Bajo" by their neighbors and by Western observers, actually call themselves "Sama," and speak a distinct subgroup of languages that linguists call "Samalan," was surprising, and, as Charles O. Frake has pointed out, seems to vindicate the ecological application of an ethnic label by outsiders.[44]

His remark was prescient, for the name "Bajo" and its variants, applied by outsiders, appears to come from the early sixteenth century Iberian term for "shoal" (*baixo/baxo*) or "shoals" (*baixos/baxos*). Before explaining this derivation and what it tells us about interactions in the maritime world of the sixteenth century archipelago, some attention must first be paid to a widespread but apocryphal folk etymology. This inaccurate etymology associates the name with the Malay word for "bandit," *bajak*. The idea is that since the compound "*bajak laut*" (sea bandit) effectively means "pirate," the exonym "Bajo," or, as often seen in print, "Bajau," must have come from the Malay *bajak* or a cognate term in another language. However, when one looks at how other terms for pirates came into regional languages, this particular etymology for *bajak* is unconvincing. The names historically applied to maritime people in the southern Philippines illustrate how, instead, the process went the other way, with ethnic names becoming the sources of terms for "pirate."

Over the centuries, many names have been applied to Sama people in the southern Philippines. Some, such as the Balangingi Sama, merely became associated with piracy, while the names of others actually came to mean "pirate." As we saw earlier, "Lutao," which referred to people in Mindanao, Jolo, and Basilan who lived on boats or built their houses over the water, derived from some local non-Sama

---

[44] See: Charles Frake, et al., "Conference Report: The Muslim Peoples of the Southern Philippines," *Current Anthropology* 14, 3 (1973): 326–29; and Frake, "The Genesis of Kinds of People in the Sulu Archipelago," 319–20. Frake goes on to note that not all who call themselves *Sama* have been called "Bajao," and not all speakers of Samalan languages call themselves *Sama*, but "so far as I know, all people called 'Bajao' by their neighbors and Western observers are Samalan-speaking Sama" (p. 320).

language in which it meant a thing or person that floats. According to Combes, while some Lutao had been Christianized, most were Muslim, described as "Moros," but were different (ethnically) from the kings of Sulu and Mindanao, to whom they were apparently subject. Although the Spanish adopted the term "Lutao," it fell out of use in the nineteenth century. Since historical linguistic work shows that speakers of Samalan languages had already lived in the southern Philippines for centuries by the time of Combés's description, and since, during the following century, the coasts and islands of Mindanao, Jolo, and Basilan were dense with Sama populations, it seems safe to say that the Lutao were Sama. Others came to call them "Lutao" from references to how, or where, they lived.[45]

The Spanish also used the names "Camucones" and "Tidong" in the sixteenth and seventeenth centuries to refer to especially fierce, non-Muslim pirates. Although the Spanish apparently considered such pirates to be different groups, descriptions of them and of their fate are indistinguishable. They made raids throughout the Philippines from bases in western Sulu and northeastern Borneo and met their demise at the hands of Spanish and Sulu forces. These notorious pagan pirates then disappear as an ethnic identity. Although variants of "Bajo" do not appear in early Spanish accounts, English and Dutch visitors freely used the name "Bajao" to label Sulu populations.[46] In addition, parallel terminology in Brunei and Spanish documentation of southern Philippines sea people from 1599 shows that the Spanish referred to "Camucones" as the translation of the Brunei term "Bajau."[47] Hence, the Camucones appear to have been Sama, and this may also be the case for the Tidong, who were identically described.

The name "Tidong" no longer applies to maritime people in the southern Philippines.[48] However, *"tidong"* survived as a term for pirates in several central and northern Philippine languages.[49] The term *"lanun"* similarly was used for pirates throughout much of the region. It arose from the eighteenth century maritime raids of the southern Philippines's Iranun (or Ilanun).[50] These examples of *tidong* and *lanun* illustrate regional semantic equivalents for "pirate" that started out as ethnic names and then lost that identification. The folk etymology for "Bajo" would have it the other way around, with the term for pirate, *bajak laut*, as the source for that name. However, this seems unlikely, given the instances above, in which terms for "pirate" came from ethnic names. Indeed, one might make a case, in light of the sixteenth- and seventeenth-century reputation of *baJuūs* and *celates* as corsairs, that *bajak* may have come from a variant of *Bajo*.[51] Where "Bajo" and its variants—such as *baJuūs*, *baJus*, *Badjo*, bajau, badjao, and bajaw—come from is a separate matter.

---

[45] See: Frake, "The Genesis of Kinds of People in the Sulu Archipelago," 322–23; Warren, *The Sulu Zone*, 60–61; James Francis Warren, "Who Were the Balangingi Samal? Slave Raiding and Ethnogenesis in Nineteenth-century Sulu," *Journal of Asian Studies* 37, 3 (1978); and A. Kemp Pallesen, *Culture Contact and Language Convergence* (Manilla: Linguistic Society of the Philippines, 1985), 245ff.

[46] Frake, "The Genesis of Kinds of People in the Sulu Archipelago," 321–23.

[47] Brown, "Brunei and the Bajau," 56.

[48] Jennifer L. Gaynor, "Piracy in the Offing: The Law of Lands and the Limits of Sovereignty at Sea," *Anthropological Quarterly* 85, 3 (2012): 847–48.

[49] Frake, "The Genesis of Kinds of People in the Sulu Archipelago," 311–32.

[50] Warren, *Iranun and Balangingi*, 141.

[51] Or, the similarity could just be a coincidence.

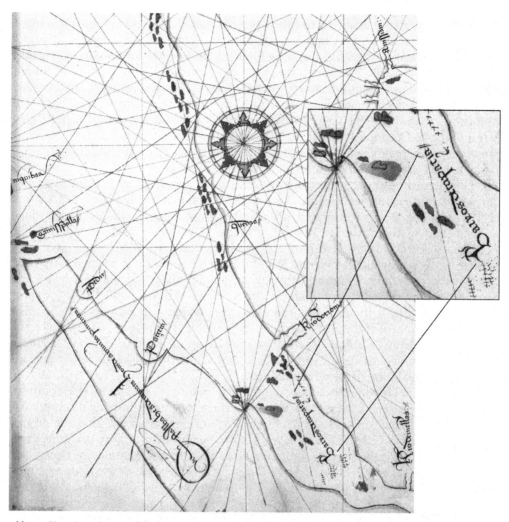

Map, with enlarged inset of "Baixos de capaçia," c. 1513, from *The Book of Francisco Rodrigues* (Roïs), folio 34. Rodrigues was a pilot and cartographer under the Portuguese in the Indies. Source: Library of the French National Assembly

Since Pires associated *Celates* with *baJuũs/baJus*, and Speelman associated *Zalette/Zaletters* with *Badjos/Badjoers*, it seems clear that either the latter derives from the former, or both come from a common source. Although those from outside the region sometimes applied ethnic names in a way that ran roughshod over internal differentiations, the use of ethnic names derived from environmental referents was actually fairly common in the region. For instance, with the Tausug people of the Sulu archipelago, *"tau"* comes from "people/person," and *"-sug"* from the word *su(l)ug*, meaning "current." The name of the Subanun of Zamboanga's mountainous interior similarly has roots in the ecology of their lifeworld: a Subanun's place is *suba'*, "upstream."[52]

---

[52] These examples may be found in Frake, "Cultural Construction of Rank, Identity and Ethnic Origins in the Sulu Archipelago," 318; see 325, note 3, for an explanation of how the place names "Sulu" and "Jolo" also derive from *sulug* (Tausug) or the cognate *suluk* (Sama).

Like other exonyms for Sama people, such as "Lutao" from the word for "float" and "Turijéqnéq" from "people on the water," the name "Bajo" apparently derives from references to the environment, or to a lifestyle, that served to identify them socially. Whether living on boats at anchor or in houses on stilts, the people called "Bajo" had a predilection for life in the intertidal zone, an environment comprising not only littoral habitats along the shore, but also offshore shoals exposed, or nearly so, at the lowest low tides, the spring tides, during the new and full moons. Even today, Sama people build settlements or sometimes just a fishing hut or two, atop such shoals. At low tide, people pick their way across the tidal flats to dig up crabs, snare shrimp or lobster, catch fish in tidal pools, and gather sea cucumbers and mollusks. When the tide rises, people fish their shallows.

On sixteenth century Portuguese charts, the term *"baixos"* designates inshore shallows as well as sandbanks or shoals.[53] Later mapmakers sometimes carried over this usage in the names on their maps and charts. For instance, a 1664 Dutch map primarily of Southeast Asia shows *"Baixos de S. Barthólome"* by Micronesia, and near the Maldives and Chagos archipelagos one finds *"Baixos de padua,"* as well as *"Baixos dos peros dos banhos."*[54] However, on some early sixteenth century Portuguese charts, one also finds the term written as *baxos*. *Baixos* and *baxos* were interchangeable, something seen in two particularly apropos maps of the southern Straits of Malacca. Created c. 1513 by Francisco Rodrigues, a contemporary of Tomé Pires and a pilot with Abreu's fleet in the Indies, the maps show the "Shoals of Capaçia" as *"Baixos de capaçia"* on one and as *"os baxos de capaçia"* on the other.[55]

---

[53] In contemporary Portuguese it is *baixios*.

[54] Willem Janszoon Blaeu (dedicated to Laurentius Real), *India quae Orientalis dicitur et Insula Adiacentes* (Amsterdam, 1664), held, among other places, at the Nederlands Scheepvaartmuseum; accessible through http://www.geheugenvannederland.nl by searching "India Orientalis" (accessed February 5, 2015). Laurentius Real was presumably the Amsterdam lawyer and art collector Laurens van der Hem (1621–78) who compiled the fifty-volume Atlas Blaeu-van der Hem, https://rkd.nl/en/artists/419399, accessed February 10, 2015.

[55] Pires, *The Suma Oriental of Tomé Pires*, lxxix, xcv. In "the Paris codex," as Cortesão calls it, the maps are at folio 34 and folio 29, viewable at http://archives.assemblee-nationale.fr/bibliotheque/manuscrits/002/index.html, accessed May 8, 2013. In the Cortesão and Teixeira da Mota facsimiles (citation below), the relevant maps are Plates XVII an XV, opposite pages 96 and 88, respectively. On the "Shoals of Capaçia," see J. V. G. Mills, *Eredia's Description of Malacca, Meridional India and Cathay* (Kuala Lumpur: Malaysian Branch of the Royal Asiatic Society, 1997 [1613]), 123. Pires himself spelled the word for shoals *"baixos"* ("Baixos Chilam," also known as "Adam's Bridge" and Rama's Bridge (*Ram setu*), between Ceylon and the South Asian mainland"; see Pires, *The Suma Oriental of Tomé Pires*, 76), but other sixteenth century Portuguese maps use both variants. *Baixos* and *baxos* were both commonly used to refer to areas of shoals or shallows with small islands. See *"Baixos das Chagos"* and *"Baixos de S. Miguel"* in the Indian Ocean area of the map ascribed to Bartolomeu Lasso–Arnoldus Florentius van Langren of 1596. This particular map was used by Linschoten in his *Itinerario*. See Vol. III, Plate 384, in Cortesão and Teixeira da Mota *PMC*. "Baxos" appears in other maps as well. For instance, in a map of "South Africa and the Southwest Indian Ocean Islands," anonymous but ascribed to Bartolomeu Lasso–Petrus Plancius, 1592–94, one finds *"Baixos de Judea"* (or *"Baixos de Iudea"*) west of Madagascar, and, to its north, *"Baxos de Patram"* (see Vol. III, Plate 382B, in Cortesão and Teixeira da Mota, *PMC*). One finds both *"c. dos baxos"* (on the seaward side) and *"c. dos baixos"* (on the landward side) of the chart of Terranova and the Azores, the seventh chart of "The Atlas of Seven Charts," by João Freire, 1546, Vol. I, Plate 76, in Cortesão and Teixeira da Mota, *PMC*; original in The Huntington Library, San Marino, California; digitized at http://dpg.lib.berkeley.edu/webdb/dsheh/hehbrf?Description=&Call Number=HM+35, accessed February 27, 2014.

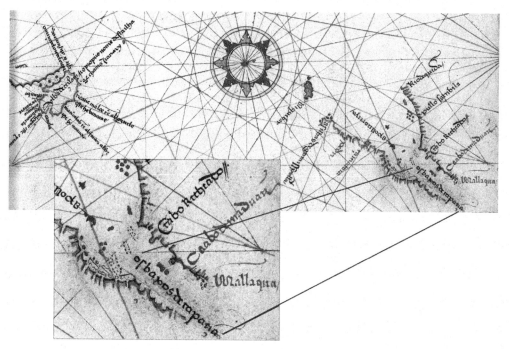

Another Rodrigues map from *The Book of Francisco Rodrigues*, folio 29,
with enlarged inset of "os baxos de capaçia." Source: Library of the French National Assembly

The contemporary Portuguese term for "shoals," *baixios*, like the current Spanish word *bajíos*, underwent pronunciation and spelling changes over the centuries. While in the sixteenth century the Portuguese used both *baixos* and *baxos* (in the plural), seventeenth century Spanish sources used both *baxio* and *baxo* for "shoal," which by the nineteenth century became *bajío* and *bajo*.[56] "*Baxos*" for shoals had thus been known in both Spanish and Portuguese, although it later fell out of use. During the sixteenth and seventeenth centuries, Iberian dialects as a whole

---

[56] "*Bajo*" was defined in 1817 this way: "The same as *bajío* for sandbank" (*Lo mismo que bajío por banco de arena*); and *bajío* was similarly defined: "a dangerous sandbank, which is found in some parts of the sea. An accumulation of sand in the sea, shallow places, shoals" (*Banco de arena peligroso que suele haber en algunas partes del mar* [Sp.]; *Arenae cumulus in mari, loca vadosa, brevia* [Lat.]). Real Academia Española, *Diccionario de la Lengua Castellana por la Real Academia Española* (Madrid: Imprenta Real, 1817), 114, http://archive.org/details/5eddiccionariode 00acaduoft, accessed May 9, 2013. "*Baxo*" was defined in 1726 as: "It is also called sandbank, and the same as *Baxio*" (*Baxo. Se llama tambien el banco de aréna, y lo mismo que Baxio*). The 1726 dictionary cited seventeenth century attestations: "Sailing the armada over some shoals, which are between the port of Trinidad and the Cape of San Anton [...]" (*Navegando la armada sobre unos baxos, que estan entre el Puerto de la Trinidad, y el Cab de San Anton* [...]), from Don Antonio de Solís, *Historia de Nueva España* (Madrid: Bernardo de Villa-Diego, 1684), vol. I, ch. 12; and "Between which and the southern land are many shoals (*baxos*) and reefs" (*Entre la qual, y la tierra austral hai muchos baxos y escollos*), from Padre Alonso de Ovalle, *Historia del Réino De Chile* (Rome: Francisco Caballo, 1646), 25. See also: Real Academia Española, *Diccionario de la lengua castellana, en que se explica el verdadero sentido de las voces, su naturaleza y calidad, con las phrases o modos de hablar, los proverbios o refranes, y otras cosas convenientes al uso de la lengua* [...] *Compuesto por la Real Academia Española* (Madrid: Imprenta de Francisco del Hierro, 1726), vol. I, 580. For a page image, see: http://books.google.es/books?id=PrxKAAAAcAAJ&printsec= frontcover&hl=es#v=onepage&q&f=false, accessed May 5, 2013. My thanks to Bruce Mannheim for translation assistance.

underwent a patchy process of phonological shifts. In the wider picture, this process created dialectal alternations among the sounds /sh/ (written x in Spanish); /zh/ (as in "rouge," written j in Portuguese); and the velar spirant—a German or Scottish "ch" (written j in modern Spanish).[57] Since neither Sama, Makassar, nor Bugis, nor the regional lingua franca of Malay, have the sounds /sh/, /zh/, or a Scottish sort of "ch," Southeast Asians who spoke those languages would not have been able to pronounce *baxos* as a native Iberian language speaker did, which is to say, as "bashos." The pronunciation would have changed in a systematic way familiar to linguists and demonstrated in loanwords. For instance, Portuguese loanwords with /zh/ or /z/, sounds that native Malay words do not have, became /dzh/ (as in "judge" or "Fiji") in Malay. Some "s" or sibilant sounds from Portuguese also became /dzh/.[58] Hence, *baxos* was altered in local pronunciation to *bajos*, with the /dzh/ of "judge."[59]

For the term *"bajos"* to move in this way through different languages, a social context had to exist that brought Iberians into regular contact with people who lived in or were familiar with the littoral. Before the development of more-or-less reliable published pamphlets, called "pilots," European ships often required the help of local human pilots, some of whom helped voluntarily and were sometimes paid, while others were taken aboard by force. This use of local mariners created a situation in which the kind of cultural contact existed that could promote the adoption of the term *bajos* as a name.

During his 1611–15 voyage, Pieter Floris relied on the advice and direction of the earlier voyager Linschoten, but nevertheless also took aboard a local pilot in the southern Straits of Malacca, quite likely to navigate the "Shoals of Capaçia." A number of boats came alongside his ship, "being of the Salettes under the King of Johor." From them he learned news of the then-positive relations between Johor and

---

[57] The variation in the Spanish spelling from *baxio/baxo* to later *bajío/bajo* reflected the variation in the sounds. The phonological shifts involved a number of different dialects. One of the shifts at play entailed a series of paired voiced and voiceless sibilants (such as /s/ and /z/, /sh/ and /zh/), which over time became devoiced and merged. Hence, it is possible that what was represented by the "x" in "baixos/baxos" had earlier been voiced and still was so in some Iberian dialects, making a sound like the /zh/ in "leisure." This is suggested, though not proven, by the existence of *"baizos"* in a portolan chart, where other charts have *"baixos"* designating the shoals off northwest Sumatra. Bartolomeo Olives(?), *Portolan Atlas* (Majorca?), created after 1580. Held at the Huntington Library, HM32, folio 14. (NB: Question marks indicate probable provenience as noted by the Huntington Library.) On the relevant phonological changes in sixteenth century Spanish, see: Bruce Mannheim, *The Language of the Inka since the European Invasion* (Austin: University of Texas Press, 1991), 153–76; and D. Lincoln Canfield, "Spanish American Data for the Chronology of Sibilant Changes," *Hispania* 35, 1 (February 1952): 25–30. Charles O. Frake has also noted that when the Spanish wrote down "Jolo," the "j" was pronounced as /sh/. See Frake, "Cultural Construction of Rank, Identity and Ethnic Origins," 325, note 3. Thanks to Bruce Mannheim for helping me make sense of the sound shifts in sixteenth century Iberian dialects.

[58] Malay /jendela/ (from Port. *janela*, with /zh/) "window"; Malay /gereja/ (from Port. *iglesa*, with z) "church"; Malay /meja/ (from Port. *mesa*, with z) "table." Many thanks to John Wolff (personal communication, May 20, 2013) and Robert Blust (personal communication, February 14, 2014) for guidance on the phonological changes from Portuguese to Malay. Bruce Mannheim explained that "mesa" could have been a voiced, or voiceless apical (or retroflex) sibilant, with some leaning toward voiced for Portuguese and Galician (personal communication, May 20, 2013, February 17, 2014).

[59] The sixteenth century Portuguese variant *baxio*, pronounced with that Scottish sort of "ch," is a likely source for *"bayo,"* the Makassar language version of "Bajo."

Aceh—meaning both affinal (i.e., through marriage), as well as political connections. "Heere wee tooke a pilott to bring us thorough the Straighte of Sinca Pura." The editor of this source notes, "Since there is no mention of any intercourse with the shore, it seems that the pilot must have been one of the Saletters; and the rest of the party would be 'they' who marked the dangerous places with 'beacons.'"[60]

The enormous potential for damage to ships in unfamiliar waters, and worse, the loss of cargo and lives, produced a need for local knowledge; in other words, pilots familiar with safe routes through the shoals were useful and valuable. Earlier Iberian travelers would likewise have needed pilots. Some early Portuguese maps make explicit note of areas with safe harbors and pilots, as those who read them were keen to know where pilots could be found. For instance, on an early seventeenth century map, at the northeast point of Ende (called *"Cabo dos flores,"* from which the island gets its present name of Flores), the mapmaker marked: "Inner (protected) harbor for ships, go there until you arrive at the pilots."[61] Picking up pilots in the areas around this particular point enabled safe travel onward to Banda or the Moluccas for spices, or southward through the passage between the islands toward Timor for sandalwood, which attracted the Portuguese as it had the Chinese earlier.[62] Portuguese ships looking for "pilotos" may have cared less about the social affiliations of potential pilots than about where they could be found. Although the logbooks of European ships in Asian waters show that they commonly took on native pilots when needed, in many cases the identities of these local pilots, and the groups from which they claimed descent or ethnic affiliation, remain unclear. Rather than note to which group of people the pilots belonged, ships' records refer instead to locations where the pilots were picked up or, as sometimes happened, chased down.[63]

Louis-Antoine de Bougainville hired local pilots near Tiworo. In an effort to avoid heavy seas on his westward journey across the archipelago from the Pacific in 1768, he was assisted first by a stowaway French soldier previously in the employ of the Dutch, who had snuck aboard when they stopped at Buru. He guided them to the calmer waters of the Straits of Buton, right past the entrance to Tiworo. To continue south in the Buton Straits, Bougainville took on a local pilot, whom he paid for his service, and after this he was aided by the latter's father. These two men returned to Bougainville's ships the following day to warn that the winds would pick

---

[60] Floris, *Peter Floris: His Voyage to the East Indies in the Globe*, 100, 102, 102 (note 2).

[61] *"Sorgidorodenaos atichegar os pilotos."* Alternatively: "... there the pilots arrive (to you)." Anonymous and Manuel Godinho de Erédia, c.1615– c.1622 (collection of Dr. C. M. C. Machado Figuera, Lisbon), Vol. IV, Plate 418 A (Fol. 59 r.), in Cortesão and Teixeira da Mota, *PMC*. My thanks to Hal Langfur (personal communication, September 26, 2014) and also to Bruce Mannheim (personal communication, March 2, 2014) for help with the phrase, which also appears off the same cape in another chart by Manuel Godinho de Erédia, 1613 (at the Royal Library of Brussels), Vol. IV, Plate 412 L (Fol. 48 v.), in Cortesão and Teixeira da Mota, *PMC*. Some maps embellished by Manuel Godinho de Erédia and said to be based on Javanese models were taken by Admiral Heemskerk. See Vol. IV, p. 47, *PMC*. They may have been taken from the captured Portuguese carrack, the *Santa Catarina*, in 1603.

[62] Maumere Bay to the west of this point has long been known to have Sama settlements, though whether it did in the sixteenth century is a question that at this point cannot be answered. The main Sama settlement on Maumere Bay, known locally as "Wuring," is called "Buré" in Sama, a name familiar to Sama people in Southeast Sulawesi, although most of them have never been there. Hence, it is part of broad-based Sama geographical knowledge.

[63] Pires, *The Suma Oriental of Tomé Pires*, lxxxi.

up swiftly at noon. Many canoes came to sell their wares at the French ships and promptly dispersed before this time. Bougainville also mentions learning about the passage from Tanakeke in southwest Sulawesi to Java from reading, in the journal of the circumnavigator Woods Rogers, the route by which a local pilot had guided his ships. The ongoing need for local pilots was inadvertently fostered by the Dutch, who carefully guarded their navigational knowledge from other Europeans so as to maintain a competitive advantage.[64]

Sometimes, however, Europeans in need of pilots left no room for negotiating terms. Antonio Pigafetta, who accompanied the ships that set out under Ferdinand Magellan, yet completed the first circumnavigation of the world (1519–22) without him, recorded one such incident. After their ships cruised between Cagayan, Jolo, and Mindanao (now in the southern Philippines), they entered a harbor "between the two islands" of Sarangani and Candighar, anchoring near a settlement at the former where gold and pearls were found. The explorers stayed one day in that harbor, where they "captured two pilots by force, in order that they might show us where Malucho lay"—in other words, to guide the ships to the Moluccas (which the Portuguese had earlier reached from the other direction, in 1512). One of these captured men, said to have been the brother of the king of Magindanao (*Maingdanao*), had his small son with him. Although this pilot escaped in the night by swimming to an island near Sangir (*Sanghir*), his son, unable to hold tightly to his father, drowned.[65] Pigafetta recorded the names of this island's four kings, which suggests that the information came from the remaining captive. This man, caught while in the harbor near Sarangani, knew details about local political society on Sangir (part of an archipelago north of Sulawesi, Indonesia), which lay, according to Pigafetta, twenty-seven leagues—about ninety-three miles—to the south. He may or may not have been Sama, but he was certainly familiar with the social makeup of communities on far-flung islands. Pigafetta does not indicate how they communicated, but as a pilot, the man likely knew the regional lingua franca of Malay, and may even have had some familiarity with Portuguese, since its speakers had been present in the archipelago at least since Malacca's conquest in 1511.

Portuguese was spoken not only on Portuguese ships, but also on Spanish ships of the Indies fleets. Despite Spanish efforts, at least one in five crewmen was not Spanish, and of these "foreigners," 50 percent were Portuguese. Even Magellan, who sailed on behalf of Spain, but who, after all, was Portuguese, swore before a notary that he had made efforts, albeit unsuccessful, to obtain Spanish rather than foreign mariners. Aspiring Portuguese pilots found it easy to pass themselves off as Spaniards, and for common sailors it was far easier. Moreover, with the help of complicit or indifferent shipmasters, many Portuguese were clandestinely passed off as Galicians, replacing Spaniards who had signed up but who were not, in the end, required to sail. As a result, during the sixteenth century, many non-Spanish Iberians, but in particular Portuguese, had so populated "all the Indies" that, as one captain commented, it was "a marvel to find there a boatman, small innkeeper, grocer, doctor, or apothecary who is not Portuguese."[66]

---

[64] John Dunmore, ed. and trans., *The Pacific Journal of Louis-Antoine de Bougainville, 1767–1768* (London: The Hakluyt Society, 2002), 153–63.

[65] BR, vol. 33, 243–51. The islands were almost certainly contemporary Sarangani and Balut islands.

[66] Pablo E. Pérez-Mallaína, *Spain's Men of the Sea: Daily Life on the Indies Fleets in the Sixteenth Century*, trans. Carla Rahn Phillips (Baltimore and London: Johns Hopkins University Press,

Southeast Asian pilots who came aboard sixteenth century Portuguese or Spanish ships were responsible for a vessel's safety and had to communicate where danger lay in the waters ahead. Unless such pilots had somehow gained substantial experience sailing on European ships, they would not have been likely to take the helm directly, for Southeast Asian ships at this time, still chiefly rigged in the Austronesian fashion, maneuvered differently from European ships. A rudimentary grasp of shared nautical terms regarding hazards was necessary in order to shout alarms such as "sandbank!" or "shoals!" As Iberian mariners gained greater experience in Southeast Asia, such communication may well have taken place in the regional lingua franca of Malay. However, before this point, Southeast Asian pilots entering the Iberian linguistic setting of the ship would likely have picked up some Iberian words useful in recurring circumstances, to direct the helm in swift and unmistakable terms to navigate away from impending danger. Some pilots may even have gained prior knowledge of Iberian terms through experience with the Portuguese in the Bay of Bengal, or elsewhere in the Indian Ocean, before the Portuguese took Malacca in 1511.[67]

While in the early sixteenth century one could expect Southeast Asian mariners who came aboard as pilots to accommodate themselves to the predominant Iberian dialect on deck, by the early seventeenth century it was actually common for Southeast Asians to be aboard Portuguese ships. The linguistic contact was intense and regular enough to result in a good deal of linguistic borrowing in both directions, from Southeast Asian languages (particularly Malay) into Portuguese, and from Portuguese into local languages. The Portuguese, one observer wrote in 1615, took an astonishing profit in every part of the Indies they entered, and they also associated with the natives, who accompanied them on their voyages: "even their sailors and pilots are entirely natives of the Indies, heathens or Moors."[68]

Shipboard life provided the type of new and repeating context of interaction that favors the adoption of a term of reference. Through well-understood processes of how particular sounds change when terms are borrowed between languages, the Iberian *baxo/baxos* ("shoal"/"shoals") became the name *baJuũs/baJus* in Portuguese, the name *Badjos/Badjoers* in Dutch, and also entered local non-Sama Southeast Asian

---

1998), 55–59, 62. Moreover, the Iberian dialects at play aboard these ships were not limited to Spanish and Portuguese, but included (in addition to Galician) Judeo-Iberian or Ladino. Judeo-Iberian was a koine or dialect used as a trade language in the Mediterranean in the fifteenth and sixteenth centuries. Hence, as with Portuguese, its linguistic history gives us a sense of how seafarers' vernacular sounded. Bruce Mannheim, Personal communication, February 18, 2014.

[67] See, for instance, Pires's references to mariners from "the islands of Makassar" sailing to Pegu. Pires, *The Suma Oriental of Tomé Pires*, 226–27. Although archaeological remains generally do not reveal ship rigging, visual representations even well into the seventeenth century, such as on this book's cover and in the Blaeu–van der Hem atlas, offer evidence that the archipelago's ships were still rigged in the Austronesian manner. For further references and discussion of Southeast Asian ships and shippers in the Indian Ocean, see: Gaynor, "Ages of Sail."

[68] "*Associam-se com os naturals, que os acompanham em suas navegações, e ate todos os seus marinheiros e pilotos são indios, ou gentios ou mouros.*" Francisco Pyrard de Laval, *Viagem de Francisco Pyrard de Laval*, ed. Joaquim Heliodoro da Cunha Rivara (Nova Goa: Imprensa Nacional 1858–62), vol. I, 363. Cited in the introduction to Sebastião Rodolfo Dalgado, *Glossário Luso-Asiático* (Hamburg: Helmut Bushe Verlag, 1982 [1919]), xii–xiii. My thanks to Bruce Mannheim for assistance with the translation.

languages, for instance, as *Bajo* in Bugis, and as *Bayo* in Makassar. This linguistic borrowing most likely occurred in one of two ways. When Portuguese or other Iberian dialect speakers looked for people, particularly for pilots, who lived in the littoral or on the shoals, they would have used the term *baxo* or *baxos* (with /sh/, /zh/ or "ch" pronunciation) in interactions with Southeast Asians. These Southeast Asians then used this term as an exonym in non-Sama language settings to refer to Sama people who dwelt in boats or houses in the shallows. In the process the pronunciation was altered to the /dzh/ of "judge"), resulting in "Bajo" or "Bajos." The Portuguese (as well as the Dutch and English) then picked up the exonym from these Southeast Asians. The Portuguese sound system, however, altered /dzh/ to the /zh/ of "leisure," written with a "j" (*baJuũs* and *baJus*).

Alternatively, speakers of Malay, Sama, or another local language, used their knowledge of the Iberian term for "shoal" or "shoals" (*baxo* or *baxos*) to explain who they were or from where they (or others) came. However, in doing so, they altered the pronunciation through the sound system of their own languages, reproducing "shoal" or "shoals" as *bajo* or *bajos*, with the /dzh/ of "judge." European mariners then adopted that reference with the altered pronunciation, *bajo*, as an ethnic name. Iberian mariners, hearing neither the /sh/, /zh/, nor "ch" of the word they knew to mean "shoal" or "shoals," borrowed the term *back* into Portuguese as an exonym, converting the /dzh/ of *bajo* into the /zh/ of "leisure," written by Tomé Pires as *baJuũs* and *baJus*.[69]

While these scenarios may explain the derivation of Pires's *baJuũs/baJus* and Speelman's *Badjos/Badjoers*, showing how, as with other regional ethnic names, they derive from references to the ecology of people's lifeworlds, the underlying point warrants emphasis here. Such a process of borrowing, in which the sixteenth century Iberian term for "shoals" became a widespread ethnic name for the Sama, entails recurrent and structurally similar interactions between Iberian and Southeast Asian mariners in the early modern archipelago. Some of those mariners were undoubtedly Sama. The knowledge that such regular interactions took place is particularly valuable in view of the lack of other, detailed sources.

## MAKASSAR'S HINTERSEAS

While maritime people's skills made them valuable to Europeans as pilots, they maintained a variety of more complex relations with other Southeast Asians. What do we know about these relations in Celebes? Although sparse, early sources from the period before Gowa and Talloq's rise to prominence as the dominant powers of Makassar offer glimpses of how rulers along Celebes's west coast relied on people

---

[69] In other words, a local person's /dzh/ sound was heard or reproduced by his Iberian interlocutors as /zh/ and recorded by Pires as the "j" of "*Junkos*" (junks) and "*jemte*" (Portuguese *gente*, people). From evidence in Pires's own text, it appears that the final vowel may well have been /o/, since, for the place called "Baros," we see in his text the same type of spelling variation (*barus* and *baruũs*). Pires, *The Suma Oriental of Tomé Pires*, 409. Or, he may just have been representing regional allophonic variation on a final vowel: cf. "*pulau*" and "*pulo*," both still widely encountered, for "island." As for the capital "J" in *baJus* and *baJuũs*, it appears to have been capitalized to signal syllable stress. Although in Pires's *Suma Oriental*, "J" regularly appears in the initial position of words such as "*Juncos & Jemte*," "Junks and people (*gente*)," it is also capitalized in "*aJunta*" ("gather") and "*beiJoym*" (beijoim), meaning benzoin; similarly, "D" in "*marcaDarias*" (*mercadorias*) meaning "goods" (ibid.). Unlike Spanish, there were no efforts to standardize Portuguese orthography before the twentieth century.

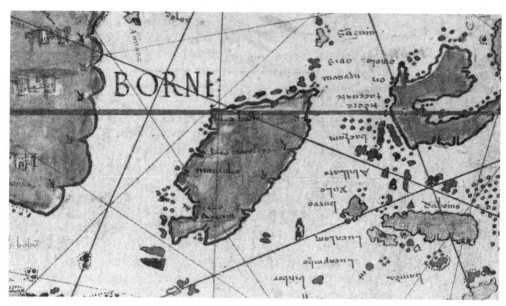

Pierre Desceliers, world map, 1546, Celebes detail. Copyright, University of Manchester

with maritime skills. They were in command of large numbers of vessels manned by sailors and oarsmen. For instance, Suppa's nautical resources are mentioned by Antonio de Paiva in a 1544 letter about his second trip to the west coast of Celebes (the first had been in 1542). When Suppa's ruler sought out Paiva to meet with him again, he approached Paiva's vessel with about twenty boats, each carrying seventy to eighty men. Making for Paiva's junk, they struck their sails and approached by oar. Understandably wary about the approach of 1,400 to 1,600 men, albeit apparently friendly, Paiva made clandestine defensive preparations, just in case.[70] Although the Suppa ruler's intentions turned out not to be aggressive, he signaled his power and importance, like figures in literary texts of the region, through an unmistakable show of strength in men and boats.[71]

Paiva explicitly mentioned the offshore islands in his letter. In one passage, after describing how rich the land was in rice, meat, and fish, he stated: "In this island *and in the other little islands close to it* are the following: sandalwood, gold, ivory, seed pearls, iron, and white cloth; and there is more slave labor for rowers than anywhere else in the world and very cheap. They are sturdy men and strong-limbed, bred for the oar from birth until death," and skilled archers, as well.[72] The above list of goods found at nearby small islands suggests a world in which people actually lived in such places and for whom trade was of primary importance, since gold and iron were not mined locally, and neither were tusks grown there. Moreover, the impressive abundance of rowers implies a stratified society, and one that was strongly maritime-oriented.

---

[70] Brett Baker, "South Sulawesi in 1544: A Portuguese Letter," *Review of Indonesian and Malaysian Affairs* 39, 1 (2005): 71. The date for the first trip appears in information in the Italian version. See Hubert Jacobs, "The First Locally Demonstrable Christianity in Celebes, 1544," *Revista Quadrimestrial Studia* (1966): 260–61, cited in Baker, "South Sulawesi in 1544," 82, note 10.

[71] Manguin, "The Amorphous Nature of Coastal Polities," 78–81, 98.

[72] Baker, "South Sulawesi in 1544," 63. My emphasis.

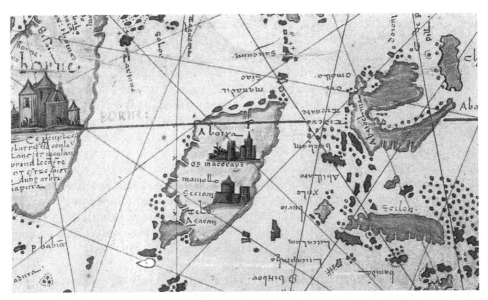

Pierre Desceliers, planisphere, 1550, Celebes detail. Copyright, British Library Board, Add. 24065

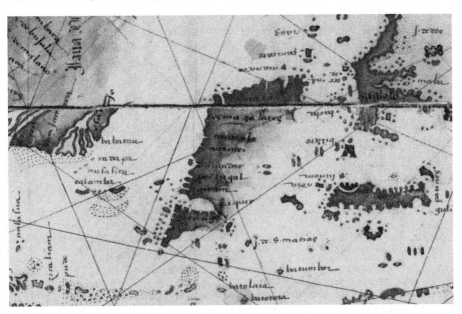

Lopo Homem, planisphere, 1554, Celebes detail. Source: Museo Galileo, Firenze

The earliest maps showing Celebes date from shortly after Paiva's 1544 letter, and most likely used information derived from his 1543–44 trip to its west coast.[73] They offer additional insights on a time and place for which the historical record is source-poor, but it is important to analyze carefully how previous scholars read their

---

[73] E. C. Abendanon, *Midden-Celebes Expeditie. Geologische en Geographische Doorkruisingen van Midden-Celebes (1909–1910)*, vol. 4 (Leiden: Brill, 1917–18), 1775. In Paiva's original, Suppa and Siang were written "*Supa*" and "*Sião*," respectively. Baker, "South Sulawesi in 1544," 82, notes 12 and 15.

clues. These maps place "*os macocays*" (Desceliers, 1550) and "*os magasares*" (Lopo Homem, 1554), in other words, "the Makassars," surprisingly far north of the port we associate with this name. The words "*a baixa*" also appear above this on the 1550 Desceliers world map. The contemporary scholar Christian Pelras wondered what this term signified and why it appeared with "Makassar" so very far north.[74]

Paiva himself applied a similar term to Siang: "*o Macaçar de baixo*." Yet curiously, Siang, like Makassar to its south, lies nowhere near the very northward placement of either "*a baixa*" on Desceliers's map (1550), or of "*os magasares*" on Lopo Homem's (1554) and Vaz Dourado's (1570, 1580) maps. Dutch scholars of the late-nineteenth and early twentieth century interpreted Paiva's "*o Macaçar de baixo*" as "low Makassar." According to P. A. (Pieter Anton) Tiele, Paiva and his men sailed from Suppa to Siang, "which (land) is called low Macassar (*o Macaçar de baixo*)."[75] Likewise, drawing on a Spanish translation from the early seventeenth century, E. C. (Éduard Cornelius) Abendanon stated that Paiva and his men sailed first to Suppa and then to Siang "… *donde llaman el Macaçar de abaxo*"[76]; "thus," he declared, "*laag Macaçar*" (low Macassar).[77]

Abendanon went on to dismiss the reference to Siang as "low Macassar" as an error that reflected geographical ignorance. He assured his readers that use of this term was obviously mistaken since the placement of similar names on period maps is much farther north than the region where we know Siang had been.[78] Yet, Abendanon may have been too quick to dismiss this as an error. Precisely the same phrase, "*o Macasar de Baixo*," was used a few years later by Manuel Pinto, who, after traveling to the Banda Sea, tells us: "And after I went to *Macasar de Baixo*, here I went to a city that is called Siang, which was of a Christian king, our good friend, and many [poor quality?] Christian people."[79]

Pelras, who was less dismissive of Paiva's geographic knowledge (after all, Paiva had previously spent several months there), sought an alternative explanation. Rather than just treat this as an error, Pelras revisited the question of translation.[80]

---

[74] Ibid., 1775, and images 296 and 297 in plate 178; and Christian Pelras, "Les premières données occidentales concernant Célèbes-sud," *BKI* 133, 2 (1977): 246. Pierre Desceliers planisphere (map), 1550, British Library, Add. MS 24065; and Lopo Homem, 1554 (map), Museo Galileo, Florence. The far northern placement of "*os magácares*" also appears on later maps, such as Vaz Dourado, 1570, from "The Atlas of Twenty Sheets," Huntington Library, San Marino, California, in Vol. I, plate 271, *PMC*, in addition to his atlas of 1580; see http://www.wdl.org/en/item/8918/view/1/40/, accessed February 27, 2014.

[75] "Van Supa voer Payva naar de havenplaats 'Siam, 50 mijlen afstands van Supa waar men (het land) laag Macassar heet' (*o Macaçar de baixo*)." P. A. Tiele, *De Europeërs in den maleischen archipel*, vol. III (The Hague: Nijhoff, 1880), 328. Note that Tiele adds "the land" (*het land*).

[76] Ioan de Lucena, *Historia de la vida del P. Francisco Xavier*, trans. Alonso de Sandoval (Seville: n.p., 1619), Vol III, 151, in Abendanon, *Midden-Celebes Expeditie*, 1774, 1767.

[77] Abendanon, *Midden-Celebes Expeditie*, 1774.

[78] Ibid., 1767 (note 9).

[79] Manoel Pimto (Manuel Pinto), letter of December 7, 1548, from Malacca, quoted in "Fr. Melchior de Melo S. I. Sociis conimbricensibus, Goa 27 November 1552," *Documenta Indica II* (Rome: Monumenta Historica Soc. Iesu, 1950), 421. My thanks to Bruce Mannheim for help with the translation.

[80] It is not clear whether Pelras had been familiar with the 1546 world map Desceliers made for Henri II of France, where the original Portuguese, presumably the same as "*a baixa*" on his 1550 map, was translated as "*La basse*." For Henri II, see https://rylandscollections.

It would seem at first contradictory for both placements, so distant from each other, to be correct, especially since it remained unclear where "upper Makassar" (*Makassar du haut*) might be. Pelras wondered where these terms came from, since he did not know of any practice in Portuguese that used such terms as "high" and "low" to indicate direction. Turning to a senior specialist on Celebes, Jacobus Noorduyn, he discovered that in the Makassar language "*rirawa*" [*sic*] means both "low" and "north." Thus equipped with input from the eminent Noorduyn, Pelras reasoned that "*a baixa*" would indicate the northern part of the west coast, where, he parenthetically remarked, perhaps a colony of ethnically Makassar people had been established. "*A baixa*," he also surmised, would indicate the northern extent of the area covered by this population, where he put the current linguistic border between the Bugis and Makassar languages, in the area of present-day Pangkajene.[81]

One might take issue with this view of linguistic borders, which, in reality, do not map onto discrete geographic spaces or polities, but instead are socially organized.[82] A more pertinent point, however, concerns the geography of coastal and offshore Pangkajene, reflected in its current name *Pankajene Kepulauan*, meaning "archipelagic Pangkajene" or "Pangkajene and the islands." The early seventeenth century Spanish translation, "*donde llaman el Macaçar de abaxo*," could have meant "from below it is called Makassar," indicating Makassar's geographic extension.[83] Yet, rather than geographic extent, or a "northerly" colony of ethnically Makassar people, a more plausible explanation attends to two aspects of linguistic practice at the time. The first entails the use of place names that specify a topographical relation. The second embraces the meaning of the terms *baixo* and *baxo*, discussed earlier, namely, the shallows along the shore, and the littoral zones created by shoals offshore.

Had Pelras considered topographical relationships rather than direction, he might have noted that "upper" (*alto*) and "lower" (*baixa*) distinguish neighborhoods of Lisbon (Bairro Alto, and Baixa Pombalina or Baixa de Lisboa). One finds a similar usage in present-day Sulawesi with paired place names, for instance, "Kolo *bawah*" ("Lower Kolo") and "Kolo *atas*" ("Upper Kolo"), two villages, one on the coast and one in the hills, respectively. Kolo Bawah happens to be a large, overwhelmingly Sama village, located on central Sulawesi's Tolo Bay (see photo, next page). According to Pires, during the early sixteenth century, local mariners from Tolo Bay

---

wordpress.com/2014/03/17/a-rare-outing-for-pierre-descelierss-1546-world-map/, accessed August 18, 2015.

[81] "Ce pourrait etre la region la plus septentrionale de population indigene makassar." Pelras, "Les premières données," 246.

[82] Nor can we be sure what language they spoke here. Scholars assume that Paiva, who said he could speak their language, meant the Makassar language. However, he nowhere specifies what language he conversed in with the kings of Siang and Suppa. Multilingualism in Makassar, Bugis, Malay/Indonesian, Sama, and other languages, depending on location and patterns of social interaction, is still fairly common among coastal communities in Sulawesi, particularly for men who have spent time as laborers on boats.

[83] Thanks to Bruce Mannheim for suggesting the possible "from below" reading, as well as for the impression that the Spanish may instead express a moiety distinction. In other words, it could refer to a social segment or grouping rather than a place. Personal communication, August 15, 2015.

exchanged gold for goods in the Moluccas.[84] *Bawah*, here, signifies lower topographically, and it applies to the littoral.[85]

Kolo Bawah, North Bungku, Central Sulawesi, Indonesia, 2009. Credit: Dave Carr

"*Rawa*" in Makassar does mean "low." "*Irawa*," cognate with Indonesian "*di bawah*," literally means "under, beneath," as well as "below," and because it expresses this quality or state in relation to something or someone in a higher position, "*duduk di bawah*," "to sit below," effectively means "to sit on the floor." This sense of "below" or "lower," applied to locations in the littoral, is attested in sixteenth century Makassar language sources. For example, the Talloq Chronicle notes that before Karaéng Pattingalloang became ruler of Talloq in the early 1540s, "he destroyed [the] Tidung below in Majene" (*nanaropu Tidunga irawa ri Majeneq*), in other words, the group of Tidung people located in littoral Majene.[86]

To understand what such terms meant, it is essential to present evidence of local usage from the sixteenth century, as shown above. However, since this discussion also concerns the translation of such terms into sources written in Iberian languages—particularly Portuguese—their  Portuguese meanings remain relevant, as well. "*Baixa*" in Portuguese has many uses. It is not only an adjective, as

---

[84] As noted earlier in this chapter, this may refer either to Tolo Bay or Tomori Bay.

[85] Compare to "upstream" and "downstream," discussed below.

[86] Cummings, *A Chain of Kings*, 85, 98. The translator appears to render this as a place name, that is, without the definite article (*-a*), which, I think, indicates that "Tidung" refers to a group of people (the Tidung), residing "below" (*irawa*) viz., on the tidal flats or littoral, in Majene (*ri Majeneq*). Karaéng Pattingalloang ruled from 1540/3 to 1576. I describe the Tidung further in "Sama at the Center" in chapter three. It should be mentioned that in Indonesian, "*rawa, rawah*" also means "swamp" or "marsh," including salt marshes, perhaps related to the word "*rawa*" in the Makassar language.

in *"baixa-mar"* (low tide) and *maré baixa* (ebb tide), but may also stand on its own as a noun, with the singular definite feminine article, *"a,"* meaning "the low place." (Similarly, *"planta baixa"* means "floor plan.")

When tides ebb, the water around small islands and shoals recedes, exposing tidal flats in this "low place," while at high tide such flats once again become shoals or shallows. In contemporary Portuguese, "tidal flats" are *"baixios de maré"* or *"regiões de baixios,"* and "mud/sand flats" are *"baixios lodosos/arenosos."* During the sixteenth century, as discussed in the previous section, the Iberian terms *baixo* and *baxo* referred to such flats, or shoals and shallows. Given the geographic expanse to which Pires (and Paiva, as discussed below) applied "Makassar" in the sixteenth century, *"de baixo"* in *"o Macaçar de baixo,"* translated this sense of the flats or shoals and their relative topographic placement with an unmarked *"Macaçar"* above sea level.[87] Hence, on Desceliers's 1550 map, *"a baixa os macocays"* meant that one found at "the low place, the Makassars," emphasizing the people who lived there, whereas Paiva's *"o Macaçar de baixo"* stressed the place, "low/lower Makassar," or simply "Makassar shoals." There would have been no contradiction in applying these terms of reference to people who, despite living in locations distant from one another, shared an association with the polity of "Makassar," and who also shared the practice of residing in the intertidal zone.

This argument puts contemporaneous information in a new light. Hubert Jacobs, the Jesuit who brought Paiva's writing to our attention, underscored the fact that Siang was located on a small island: "everything suggests that the configuration of the terrain has been modified since the sixteenth century, as the French and Italian versions of Paiva's narrative situate [Siang] on an islet."[88] Yet, where was this islet located? One explanation holds that the plains of Pangkajene, still quite marshy, first must have been a bay deeply set in karst hills, which then transformed into a delta with numerous channels, within one of which would have been an island boasting the Lord of Siang's residence. Pelras suggested that "during Paiva's visit in 1544 a process of silting must have made this channel less accessible and the sea less deep, since the Portuguese had to anchor their junk a league from the shore."[89]

A former branch of the Pangkajene River may once have given easier access to the coast from the location of present-day Kampungsiang, and a considerable process of silting may have shifted the coastline farther west over the centuries.[90] However, the region's mariners are familiar with other reasons for having to anchor a league from shore in this area. The Makassar Straits's impressive tidal range—that is, the vertical difference between high and low tide—reaches up to three meters (almost ten feet). This presents challenges at low tide, and would be especially forbidding for European deep-keeled ships, in contrast to Southeast Asian craft, many of which used outriggers for stabilization and hence had shallow draughts.

[87] "Unmarked" in the linguistic sense. Compare to "scissors" and "left-handed scissors."

[88] *"...tout suggère que la configuration du terrain s'est modifiée depuis le XVIe siècle, puisque les versions italienne et française du récit de Paiva situent [Siang] dans un îlot."* Hubert Jacobs, "The First Locally Demonstrable Christianity in Celebes, 1544," 303; Hubert Jacobs, *Conversions in the Country of Macassar in a Paris Imprint of 1546* (Rome: Pontificia Università Urbaniana, 1968), 523, cited in Pelras, "Les premières données," 243.

[89] Pelras, "Les premières données," 243.

[90] Campbell Macknight's explanation with no citation in footnote 12 of Baker, "South Sulawesi in 1544," 82 (note 12).

Approaching the Pangkajene coast, or an island in the offshore shallows, a ship with a deep draught would run aground at low tide, requiring that its crew walk over the tidal flats to reach shelter and hospitality.[91]

Paiva depicts another scenario in which conditions prevented his anchoring near shore. On his return to Siang, "As soon as I arrived in the port ... the king came to the sea in person to see me, [for I was] toiling a league beyond the bar."[92] This means that Paiva had trouble contending with the current on the outer side of a sandbar. He does not say how far from land this sandbar was. "Toiling" suggests that he was trying to approach or go through a cut in the bar to reach calmer waters on the shore side, but was prevented by a current, most likely a rip current, which commonly form in such spots. It was gracious of the king to come out past the bar to Paiva's boat, thus relieving him of a Sisyphean task. Although the silting of a channel offers one possible explanation for Siang's location on *un îlot*, another possibility is that Siang, or part of it, as Paiva's description of the west coast in general suggests, was located on one or more small islands offshore.

To take in and acknowledge evidence of life, trade, and politics conducted in the littoral and on small offshore islands, whether it applies to Siang or elsewhere, may require bracketing previous assumptions about such places, which the historian John Gillis calls *islands of the mind*.[93] Small islands and the littorals in which they sat were not only inhabited, but also had political, economic, and social ties to similar places, as well as to commercial and political centers. Indeed, they may themselves have constituted such "centers," not unlike the forms taken by coastal polities in the western archipelago.[94]

In this case, comparing the cartographic notations with textual sources from the period suggests that offshore areas, such as the small islands Paiva mentioned, made up part of a loose political configuration associated with "Makassar." When, for instance, Paiva referred to the ruler of Suppa as "one of the principal kings of Macassar," he did so in the same manner that Pires, a few decades earlier, spoke of "the islands of Macassar" and its "more than fifty kings." Both Pires and Paiva used "Macassar" during the sixteenth century to refer to a region much broader than the vicinity of Gowa and Talloq, expressly including a large area with myriad islands. Whether this implied a direct political connection to the port we now call "Makassar" is uncertain.[95] However, such a connection between this port and the

---

[91] "Spring tide ranges are a metre or less on the south west coast of Sumatra, but they increase to more than three metres in the narrows of the Straits of Macassar." See http://archive.unu.edu/unupress/unupbooks/80197e/80197E02.htm, accessed June 28, 2013. Three meters is similar to the tidal range in Boston harbor. For comparison, Nova Scotia's famous Bay of Fundy has a tidal range of seventeen meters (almost 56 feet). Running aground on the shoals at low tide and walking the rest of the way to a residence on a small island was a fairly common occurrence during my fieldwork.

[92] Baker, "South Sulawesi in 1544," p. 65.

[93] John R. Gillis, *Islands of the Mind: How the Human Imagination Created the Atlantic World* (New York and Hampshire: Palgrave Macmillan, 2004).

[94] See John Miksic, *Singapore and the Silk Road of the Sea, 1300–1800* (Singapore: NUS Press, 2013).

[95] Baker, "South Sulawesi in 1544," 62; Pires, *The Suma Oriental of Tomé Pires*, 226–27. It is also not certain whether, at that point in time, the name "Makassar" applied to the port. A polity with a loose confederations and a shifting center was nothing new in the maritime world; Srivijaya is a shining example. Also see Baker, "South Sulawesi in 1544," 84 (note 43), on

islands off Pangkajene did exist during the following century, providing one example of Gowa and Talloq's political ties with maritime people in noncontiguous littoral zones—the subject of the following chapter.[96]

In the seventeenth century, Speelman noted that "Badjos live on the islands before Labaccan," in other words, off the Pangkajene coast. They traveled, he tells us, to the islands far out at sea, where they gathered tortoiseshell, which they were obliged to deliver to the King of Makassar. They also served as *"amba raja,"* slaves or servants of the king, ready to go in their vessels wherever he might see fit to send them.[97]

Makassar in the seventeenth century could therefore muster from among the Sama in this location many men with nautical skills, thus reaping the economic and military benefits of their labor. Ethnically Makassar people may well have lived among them, and even intermarried with them. Yet, rather than a colony of ethnically Makassar people, these were "Badjos" or Sama people who had affiliations with Makassar: political, economic, and social. Did this same sort of arrangement, offshore Sama communities with ties to Makassar, hold true for people in the same place some hundred years earlier, in Paiva's time? Something likes this seems to have been the case, since the predecessors of those who Speelman knew as the Badjos of Makassar lived in what Paiva had called "Makassar shoals" (*o Macaçar de baixo*).

Although not contiguous with the area around the port of Makassar, this coastal littoral, along with its associated shoals and islands, supplied seventeenth century Makassar with maritime products and people who might serve its leaders. Working what could be called Makassar's hinterseas, these littoral-dwelling people formed economic and political relations with rulers of the port like those that Makassar maintained with surrounding terrestrial polities. As the next chapter shows, these relations were often sealed through marriage, and by the conferral of title and office.

"Hinterseas" may be conceptually useful for thinking through the geography of similar instances in which social and political structures tied maritime-oriented people to centers of politics and trade. The idea of hinterseas builds on such well-known metaphors as O. W. Wolters's "mandala polities," with their interlinked hub-and-spoke patron-client ties, common to the region's amorphously structured coastal polities, and on Bennet Bronson's well-known dendritic imagery of "upstream–downstream relations."[98] Usually discussed with regard to the western archipelago, political systems structured spatially along the branches of a river were also structured socially by alliances among different segments of descent group lineages. They drew on the language of relative geographic orientation to express the relations between polities upstream (*hulu*) and those downstream (*hilir*), recorded in Malay literary texts set down after the fifteenth century. Terms such as *anak sungai*, "confluents," and *teluk rantau*, "bends and reaches," encapsulated

---

Gowa at this time, curiously referred to as "Lontar," particularly interesting given the rise of writing there (*lontaraq* manuscripts) around or shortly after this time.

[96] Speelman, "Notitie," f. 706v.

[97] Ibid.

[98] See: O. W. Wolters, *History, Culture, and Region in Southeast Asian Perspectives*, rev. ed. (Ithaca: Southeast Asia Program Publications, 1999), 27–40; Manguin, "The Amorphous Nature of Coastal Polities," 78–81; and Bennet Bronson, "Exchange at the Upstream and Downstream Ends," in *Economic Exchange and Social Interaction in Southeast Asia*, ed. K. L. Hutterer (Ann Arbor: Center for Southeast Asian Studies, University of Michigan, 1977), 39–52.

relations between subordinate, or at least compliant, upstream political entities, and presumably dominant downstream ports.[99] "Bends and reaches" is Pierre-Yves Manguin's elegant translation of *teluk rantau*. It conveys not only a sense of the riparian geography that structured relations between upstream and downstream polities, but also orients one to the view from the port, as *rantau* represents movement to another place, away from one's usual stomping—or fishing—grounds, in order to make a living.

*Teluk rantau* can also signify the "bays of a shoreline" or the "bights of the coast." Because similarly structured interactions did not just stop at the downstream port, I suggest transposing this riparian imagery to understand the organization of political relations that ran along and between the region's coasts. In other words, take that dendritic form of a river and its branches, and pivot it from its riparian geographic context so that it now reaches up and down coasts and across stretches of seawater to touch other littorals. Whether the bends and reaches belonged to river systems, or formed the bays of a shoreline on shared or opposing coasts, maintaining connections with *teluk rantau* meant stepping into a boat. "Hinterseas," then, translates the concept of *teluk rantau* to a saltwater environment. In doing so, it preserves how *teluk rantau* reflects the geographic underpinning of social relations, and retains how flexibly it applies to people in either contiguous or noncontiguous spaces who may have viewed their ties to the center differently than did those located in the center. Hinterseas offers a way to conceptualize the confusing coast-skipping, straits-crossing, and island-hopping array of allegiances that one finds across the historical maritime world of Southeast Asia. Transposing the dendritic structure of political and social relations from a riverine to an intertidal geography provides a model for grasping how the connections, and the continuity of relations, reached across maritime space.

"Hinterseas" may also help to focus analysis on questions about the dynamics of alliances and political maneuvering among polities along the region's coasts and archipelagos. This might have been hard to grasp decades ago. However, scholars have drawn on new sources and methodologies to look afresh at such apparently impressive Southeast Asian land-based capitals as Angkor, Funan, and Majapahit, and to reevaluate them as polycentric societies in fragile and temporary coalitions.[100] The maritime-oriented Cham polity on the central Vietnam coast provides an even more apropos comparison, as it was less like its mainland wet-rice plain neighbors to the west and north, and more similar to the Malay riverine states.[101] Building on such advances, the notion of hinterseas merely opens for greater scrutiny how archipelagic geography anchored nautical pursuits, and with those pursuits a political economy that depended on social relations between maritime people and those who wanted access to, and benefits from, their networks, knowledge, and skills.

---

[99] Manguin, "Amorphous Polities," 74ff. In fact, downstream polities did not always call the shots. As Barbara Andaya shows for Sumatra, through connections along the mountain range linking different river valleys, upstream producers had access to other downstream outlets of trade on other river systems. Barbara Watson Andaya, "Upstreams and Downstreams in Early Modern Sumatra," *The Historian* 57, 3 (1995): 537–52.

[100] Reid, *Charting the Shape*, 49.

[101] Kenneth Hall, "Economic History of Early Southeast Asia," in *The Cambridge History of Southeast Asia, From Early Times to c. 1800*, Vol. I, ed. Nicholas Tarling (Cambridge: Cambridge University Press, 1993), 253, cited in Reid, *Charting the Shape*, 54.

Like the shoals off Pangkajene, Tiworo—with its shallows, reefs, and small islands, and its maritime-oriented population—was similarly situated at some remove from Makassar, yet politically connected with it. Makassar, however, was not the only major power in the region interested in Tiworo.

CHAPTER THREE

# "THAT NASTY PIRATES' NEST": TIWORO AND TWO WARS OVER THE SPICE TRADE

Ternate and Makassar, rivals that competed for coastal dominance, maritime superiority, and influence in the central and eastern archipelago, both laid claim to Tiworo during the seventeenth century. Ternate had been allied for a time with the Portuguese, but threw them out in 1575 and went on an expansionary campaign in 1580 that nearly reached Makassar. Makassar, which had originally been of little interest to Europeans, became, like Ternate, a force to contend with in the spice trade. As Makassar's role in trade expanded and grew in importance, it posed a threat to the VOC's efforts to monopolize the trade in Moluccan cloves and nutmeg. While Makassar became a prosperous entrepôt during the seventeenth century, it also undertook its own expansionary campaigns in the eastern archipelago, actively supporting Moluccan resistance against the Dutch. Tiworo played a vital role in Makassar's nautical pursuits, which led the VOC and its allies to attack Tiworo twice when Tiworo–Makassar ties were strongest, first in 1655 (with Ternate) and again in 1667 (with Boné).

In the mid-seventeenth century, hinterseas such as Tiworo were not the only places that connected maritime people with Makassar. Sama people moved among Makassar's royal elites and held significant positions in its political and military structures. The legendary beginnings of Makassar's royal lineages are well known to scholars, with genealogies that ascribe descent, in part, from a Bajo prince or king (*Karaeng Bayo*). Yet, beyond this legendary Bajo presence in Makassar's founding genealogies, the Sama figures who moved in Makassar's elite circles during the seventeenth century have somehow been overlooked. These included a respected older Sama woman who was consulted on matters of history by one of Makassar's most learned sultans. Crucially, it also included harbormasters. While the office of harbormaster may conjure the image of an official who merely oversees the comings and goings of boats at a busy port, Sama leaders based at Makassar did more than this, leading part of Makassar's expansionary campaign in the eastern archipelago during the 1660s and later expeditions across the Java Sea.

Tiworo, which had been crushed during the 1655 attack, was reinvigorated by the resuscitation of its role in Makassar's naval endeavors, including its support of Moluccan resistance against the VOC. When, finally, the Dutch formed a new alliance with Makassar's erstwhile Bugis enemies from Boné, the VOC again moved against Tiworo before attacking Makassar itself in 1667. The VOC leveled Tiworo's forts (there were two at this point, compared to just one in 1655), and its villages were again razed. Also, as in 1655, Tiworo's second defeat at the hands of the VOC and its allies severed some of its connections with Makassar and impelled a number of Tiworo's survivors to forge new connections with Makassar's enemies. However, the fate of those who survived this second incursion on Tiworo was markedly different from the outcome a dozen years earlier.

## TERNATE, MAKASSAR, AND THE GREAT AMBON WAR

Tiworo's geographic location had long affected the structure of its relationships with outsiders. It was able to maintain some distance from prominent centers, yet was also subject to the rivalries among competing powers. During the late sixteenth century, the most significant powers it had to contend with were Ternate, in the Moluccas, and the rising power of Makassar, in south Celebes. Ternate had initially benefited from the presence of the Portuguese, who built a fort there that was completed in 1523, shortly after the death of Sultan Abu Lais, who had first welcomed them. Both Ternate and the Portuguese profited from the absence of the Spanish, who departed from the Moluccas in 1565 to devote more energy to their efforts further north.[1] Over the half century following the establishment of friendly relations between Ternate and the Portuguese, a series of tensions and conflicts eventually led to outright military hostilities and the murder of Sultan Hairun by the Portuguese in 1570.[2]

After a five-year siege, the Portuguese were expelled from Ternate in 1575 (following which the Portuguese built a new fortress in nearby Tidore and made Ambon the primary center of their activities in the eastern archipelago). With the Portuguese gone, in 1580 Ternate's Sultan Baabullah (r. 1570–83) went on an expansionary campaign. Baabullah's boats were joined by boats under the command of Cappalaya from Sula, just east of central Celebes. The joint fleet sailed first to north Celebes, then south to Tobungku on Celebes's east coast, on to Tiworo, and then west as far as Salayar, stopping short of Makassar. Ternate then concluded a treaty with Gowa, ending hostilities.[3] In disputes concerning Tiworo during subsequent centuries, this campaign apparently served as the basis for Ternate's claims to Tiworo.

The polity around the port of Makassar had formed from an alliance between Gowa and Talloq in the mid-sixteenth century. At the time of Baabullah's 1580 campaign, Makassar had only recently emerged from a bitter war against the Bugis realm of Bone. Talloq appears to have been oriented to the sea from its founding. Although scholars agree that the Bajo played some role in the beginnings and early

---

[1] Leonard Y. Andaya, *The World of Maluku: Eastern Indonesia in the Early Modern Period* (Honolulu: University of Hawai'i Press, 1993), 115–18. "The Moluccas" originally referred only to the islands just to the west of Halmahera, including Ternate. The name has come to refer to a much broader area that includes Ambon and surrounding islands as well as the Banda islands. While Gerrit Knaap uses the "Great Amboinese War" to differentiate the geographic and period referent from the contemporary place name "Ambon," in accord with a trend to drop "-ese" and to avoid confusion, others, such as Hans Hägerdal, simply call it the "Great Ambon War." I follow the latter practice here.

[2] At this point, the Portuguese had the support of their allies from Jailolo, one of the four main Moluccan kingdoms, which had been subordinated by the Portuguese earlier in the century. Ibid., 130–31; and Merle Calvin Ricklefs, *A History of Modern Indonesia Since c. 1200* (Stanford: Stanford University Press, 2001), 28.

[3] Valentijn, *Oud en nieuw Oost-Indiën*, vol. I, 222, and vol. III, 124; Taylor and Richards, trans., *de Clerq's Ternate: The Residency and Its Sultanate*, 109; Andaya, *The World of Maluku*, 134, 162; and Leonard Andaya, "Cultural State Formation in Eastern Indonesia," in *Southeast Asia in the Early Modern Era*, ed. Reid, 38.

successes of Makassar, the particulars of this involvement have been very hard to come by.[4]

Traders from beyond the surrounding regions were also important to Makassar's rise, particularly those from the Malay peninsula. For instance, in the 1540s the Portuguese found that the principal traders in Siang, not far up the coast from Makassar, had come from Ujung Tanah in Johor, as well as from Patani and Pahang, also on the Malay peninsula. According to Anthony Reid, these Muslim Malay merchants had probably been established originally in Melaka before its 1511 conquest by the Portuguese, and had followed the route pioneered by "the Bajau" to south Sulawesi.[5] That the Bajau did this, and how they did so, is left unclear. As for the traders, they may have come from Malacca, or they may have traded at Malacca and been based elsewhere. The Portuguese did not grasp that Malacca was little more than an agreed upon marketplace for the commodities of other centers, so that when they seized it, "the sedentary and migratory merchant communities responded by shifting their trade to other equally acceptable and mutually inter-changeable regional ports: Aceh, Johor, Java, Ayuddhya, Bago (Pegu), etc." As a result of Malacca's seizure, while sixteenth century international trade still focused on Southeast Asia, it once again became multi-centered.[6] Hence, when Malacca was seized, some of these sedentary and migratory merchant communities shifted their base of operations. Some may have moved as far east as Siang, to join other traders from the Malay peninsula, who we know from Antonio de Paiva's important letter of 1544 had already relocated to south Celebes prior to the Portuguese capture of Malacca in 1511.[7]

Whether the Sama pioneered the route from the Malay peninsula to south Sulawesi depends, in a sense, on where one thinks they started out, and on the assumption (reasonable, but not a foregone conclusion) that these traders from the peninsula did not include, or were not themselves, Sama. Pires understood the islands off the Pangkajene coast where Siang lay to be part of the "islands of Makassar." He described how the *Bajuũs* or *Celates* from these islands traded widely, plundered farther, and had commerce with, among others, "all the places between Pahang and Siam," a stretch of the Malay peninsula that included Patani.[8] If he was correct, then Sama traders from the central archipelago had already been accustomed to traveling to the Malay peninsula and western archipelago, just as traders from the Malay peninsula had already come, before his time, to Celebes.

Merchants who came to Makassar around the mid-sixteenth century were apparently not particularly interested in procuring spices from the Moluccas. Instead, they came for other south Celebes exports, notably sandalwood, sea produce (especially tortoiseshell), rice, and slaves. This changed as Makassar made itself a major collecting center for exports from a wider region, instituted a uniform

---

[4] Reid, "The Rise of Makassar," 109–17; F. David Bulbeck, "The Politics of Marriage and the Marriage of Politics in Gowa, South Sulawesi, during the 16th and 17th Centuries," in *Origins, Ancestry and Alliance*, ed. Fox and Sather, 285; and Cummings, ed. and trans., *A Chain of Kings*, 1.

[5] Reid, "Rise of Makassar," 117.

[6] Kenneth R. Hall, "Local and International Trade and Traders in the Straits of Melaka Region: 600–1500," *Journal of the Economic and Social History of the Orient* 47, 2 (2004), 252–53.

[7] Baker, "A Portuguese Letter," 73, 84 (note 45).

[8] Pires, *The Suma Oriental of Tomé Pires*, 226–27.

system of weights and weighing, and accorded special residential permission and certain guarantees of freedom, in writing, for the Malay community that settled in Makassar. By the first decade of the seventeenth century, the Makassar ruler Karaeng Matoaya kept an agent in Banda, and the trade of Makassar rice and cloth for Moluccan spices was well established.[9]

Rice was already one of south Celebes's main products during the sixteenth century.[10] In the early seventeenth century, it was carried not only eastward to the Moluccas, but also transported to the western archipelago. The quantity of rice traded westward from Makassar was substantive enough to be a factor in diplomatic calculations. In 1607, the sultan of Johor asked his Dutch allies to intercede with Makassar to suspend their supplies of rice to Malacca.[11] This implies that Portuguese Malacca had been receiving sizable supplies of rice from Makassar. It also implies that Johor, whose alliance with the Dutch was only four years old at this point, thought that the Dutch had the ability, if successful inducements were applied, to stop those rice shipments.[12] Johor's sultan may have expected that the Dutch would welcome the chance to deliver such a blow against Portuguese Malacca, and hoped to reap the benefits of those rice shipments for Johor, and perhaps to shift some of its other trade away from Malacca. However, at this point, the Dutch had no power over Makassar, which maintained an open port, and Johor's request was unsuccessful.

Although the Dutch had been interested in spices from the start, they were not initially interested in Makassar, except as a provisioning station. For instance, in July 1616, Joris van Speilbergen noted, "In the island of Selebes the town of Macassar was abandoned by young and inexperienced [Dutch]men who did not take into consideration the great trade that this place gave us in rice and sago, which we use instead of bread, and in other necessaries of life; but we have again begun to make alliances."[13] Only later, in the 1650s, during the Great Ambon War, would the Dutch come to see Makassar as a strategic entity, particularly its position as a lucrative transshipment point and its defense of Moluccan spice growers. These would later lead the VOC to seek to control Makassar's port in the Makassar War.

Makassar's role in the spice trade expanded substantially during the first quarter of the seventeenth century, in part due to the welcome it extended to traders of all stripes. In 1625, a Dutch report estimated that the Malays from Patani, Johor, and other places, who lived in Makassar in the thousands, sent forty junks a year to the

---

[9] Reid, "Rise of Makassar," 117–18.

[10] Pelras, "Célèbes-sud avant l'Islam," 156.

[11] Paulus van Soldt, "Verhael ende Journael van de Voyagie gedaen van Bantam, naer de Custe van Choromandel, ende andere quartieren van Indien, door den Opper-Coopman Paulus van Soldt, a subpart of "Beschrijvinghe van de tweede Voyagie, ghedaen met 12 schepen, onder den Heer Admirael Steven van den Hagen," in *Begin ende Voortgangh van de Vereenighde Nederlantsche Geoctroyeerde Oost-Indische Compagnie*, ed. Isaac Commelin (Amsterdam: J. Janssonius, 1646) II, 40–91, cited in Pelras, "Célèbes-sud avant l'Islam," 157.

[12] Their "alliance" dates from Jacob van Heemskerk's seizure of the Santa Catarina. See van Ittersum, "Hugo Grotius in Context"; Peter Borschberg, "The Seizure of the Santa Catarina Revisited"; and Markus Vink, "Mare Liberum and Dominium Maris: Legal Arguments and Implications of the Luso-Dutch Struggle for the Control over Asian Waters, ca. 1600–1663," in *Studies in Maritime History*, ed. K. S. Mathew (Pondicherry: Pondicherry University, 1990), 38–68.

[13] Van Speilbergen, *The East and West Indian Mirror*, 157–58.

Moluccas.[14] Makassar's growing importance vis à vis Ternate as a source of spices, and as a market for Chinese and Indian goods, attracted others as well. The English set up a factory there in 1613, as did the Spanish in 1615, the Danes in 1618, and the Chinese in 1619. In addition to such pull factors, there were also push factors that increased the significance of Makassar: as the Dutch made it harder for the Portuguese to trade directly with the Moluccas, the number of Portuguese traders coming to Makassar rose. A Dutch estimate in 1625 reckoned that between ten and twenty-two Portuguese frigates a year visited Makassar, and up to five hundred Portuguese might be present at one time in the port. After Portuguese Malacca fell to the Dutch in 1641, Makassar became the archipelago's principal haven for the Portuguese, with as many as three thousand living there. However, the influx of foreign traders was due to more than just trade. English and Portuguese dispatches frequently remarked on the freedom and security of foreigners and their property in the city, which made it a refuge for prominent figures, including a Portuguese merchant diplomat, an uncle and a sister of the queen of Patani, and an Indian merchant who became one of the city's leading financiers and traders.[15]

In 1605, as part of its endeavor to maximize its share of the world trade in Moluccan spices, particularly in cloves, the first fleet that the VOC sent out captured the Portuguese fort and dependencies in Ambon. Thereafter the VOC took on the role of a state.[16] In areas not under its control, the VOC entered into "contracts" or treaties with local authorities that stipulated delivery of all cloves to the VOC for a fixed price. In newly acquired territories, the VOC dispensed with the pretense of a contract or treaty and simply paid a certain amount for the cloves that it demanded its subjects hand over. In return, the VOC promised to protect their subjects from renewed Iberian aggression. The producers, however, both individually and collectively, were dissatisfied with the VOC's prices and attempted to sell to the highest bidder rather than to the Dutch. The VOC proceeded to enforce its treaties with violence. The resulting series of armed conflicts, from 1624 to 1658, are referred to as "the Amboinese Wars," "the Great Amboinese War," or, simply, "the Great Ambon War."[17]

---

[14] Sihordt, *Dagh-register* 1624–29 [*Dagh-register gehouden in't Casteel Batavia*, 31 vols. (Batavia and The Hague: Nijhoff, 1887–1931)], 125, cited in Reid, "Rise of Makassar," 118.

[15] Reid, "Rise of Makassar," 118.

[16] Gerrit Knaap, "Headhunting, Carnage, and Armed Peace in Amboina, 1500–1700," *Journal of the Economic and Social History of the Orient* 46, 2 (2003): 166. The VOC had been preceded by what are called the *voorcompagnieën*—the precursor companies. They had already begun to take on the role of a state, as seen particularly in the writings of Jacob van Heemskerk, whose decisions and justifications of his capture of a Portuguese carrack, the *Santa Catarina*, became part of the argument made by Hugo Grotius in his *Mare Liberum*. Grotius framed Heemskerk's deeds as actions that only states could perform, thus trying to obviate the possibility that the capture of the *Santa Catarina* could be seen as piracy. See: Martine Julia van Ittersum, *Profit and Principle: Hugo Grotius, Natural Rights Theories, and the Rise of Dutch Power in the East Indies, 1595–1615* (Leiden: Brill, 2006); and Jennifer L. Gaynor, "Piracy in the Offing," 833–40.

[17] See the note, above, on its naming conventions; and Knaap, "Headhunting, Carnage, and Armed Peace," 168. This broad rubric includes the Hituese war (on Hitu), 1641–46, and the Hoamoalese War (on the clove-rich Hoamoal peninsula of Ceram), 1651–56/58. The latter's outbreak was marked by the surprise capture of eight minor VOC strongholds and the subsequent massacre of 150 people who lived in them by the "Amboinese" of Hoamoal and the islands to the west of it, formally Ternatan territory. Knaap, "Headhunting, Carnage, and Armed Peace," 178–80.

During the 1640s and 1650s, the VOC finally subdued the independent states of the Amboina (Ambon) islands, as well as other nearby "rebellious dependencies" of its ally, the sultan of Ternate. In addition to conducting its campaign along the eastern and southern littoral of Celebes during the late-sixteenth century, Ternate had also extended its reach to the western part of the Amboina Islands, including the Hoamoal peninsula on Ceram, as well as to the independent petty states both on the island of Ambon itself and to its east, including Hitu. The Dutch campaigns in these areas, often characterized by total warfare, effectively left in their wake a VOC monopoly on clove production, whose continuation was secured by an armed peace.[18]

Most scholarly work on cloves and colonial conflict rightly focuses on the Moluccas, especially Ternate and the vicinity of Ambon. Yet the conflict over cloves went beyond this, and was an abiding concern to Makassar. Makassar's expanding role in the spice trade was not limited to the function of its port as an entrepôt or a transshipment point; Makassar aimed to control the trade routes as well. For instance, Makassar's constant struggle to establish its supremacy in the region around Buton, against the claims of Ternate and later of the Dutch, was part of its push to dominate the spice route.[19] Makassar furthermore played an active role in protecting its sources of supply in that part of the conflict known as the Hituese war, which lasted from 1641 to 1646. In 1641, a fleet of more than twenty-six Makassar vessels approached the coast of Hitu carrying men, a great deal of rice, and some eight thousand pounds of English gunpowder to assist the VOC's adversaries.[20]

Similarly, Asahudi on the Hoamoal peninsula of Ceram received supplies, as well as reinforcements, from Makassar's forces. The VOC initially made staunch adversaries in Hoamoal when, early on in the conflict in 1625, it burned deserted Hoamoal villages on a massive scale, destroyed a few hundred canoes and other vessels, and felled tens of thousands of clove trees and other economically valuable species.[21] With the arrival of an expeditionary force from Batavia in 1652, the VOC began to lay siege to the fortifications on the Hoamoal peninsula's east coast—first at Loki. After the VOC cut off supply lines to Loki and destroyed villages and sources of livelihood in the vicinity, the people of Hoamoal regrouped with reinforcements from Makassar. These reinforcements arrived during 1653–54 and numbered a few thousand men. They made Asahudi on Hoamoal's northwest coast their headquarters, but also proceeded to erect a double fortress at Laala, on the peninsula's east coast. Laala was eventually overwhelmed in 1654 by a force of eight hundred VOC soldiers and several hundred Amboinese in a fierce battle that left seven hundred of Hoamoal's and Makassar's people dead. In addition, although sixty people apparently got away, more than four hundred people—mostly women and children—were taken captive, a matter I return to in the following section.[22]

---

[18] Gerrit Knaap, *Kruidnagelen en Christenen: De Verenigde Oost-Indische Compagnie en de bevolking van Ambon 1656–1696* (Dordrecht and Providence: Foris, 1987), 22–27; Knaap, "Headhunting, Carnage, and Armed Peace," 168.

[19] Reid, "Rise of Makassar," 118.

[20] Knaap, "Headhunting, Carnage, and Armed Peace," 178.

[21] Ibid.

[22] Ibid., 180–81; and Livinus Bor, *Amboinse Oorlogen, door Arnold de Vlaming van Oudshoorn als superintendent, over d'Oosterse gewesten oorlogaftig ten eind gebracht* (Delft: Arnold Bon, 1663), 236–41.

The focus of the conflict then shifted to Asahudi, which had one of the most formidable strongholds in the area: an impressive complex of seven small fortresses ascending the seaward side of a mountain slope, plus two more fortresses on the landward side, as well as a battery on a small island off the coast. To counter those installations, from early in 1655 the VOC erected temporary strongholds to forestall enemy movements. The VOC also destroyed enemy vessels with artillery from its large "east Indiamen" ships in order to cut off their adversaries' communications. These attempts to blockade Asahudi weakened it. Then, on July 29, 1655, the VOC launched a frontal attack on the main fortress at Asahudi with seven hundred VOC soldiers, seventy sailors, and about eight hundred Amboinese, capturing all the fortresses within four hours. In the weeks that followed, the one remaining stronghold in the interior was taken. At this point, many Hoamoal people and those from islands to the west, such as Boano and Kelang, asked for and obtained pardons from the VOC. Makassar fighters who fled north into Ceram were hunted down and killed. Out of more than a thousand men who had fought for Makassar, only about a quarter of these were taken prisoner. Although violent actions continued on Buru into 1658, the assaults on the Hoamoal peninsula mark the end of the Great Amboinese War.[23]

## TIWORO DURING THE GREAT AMBON WAR

The military engagements in the Hoamoal peninsula and surrounding islands, such as Hitu, demonstrate Makassar's efforts to support those who grew and transported spices bound for its port. Makassar's stake in this set of conflicts establishes the context necessary to understand Tiworo's involvement and why it, too, was attacked by VOC forces: the VOC viewed Tiworo, a large region of protected waters between Makassar and the Moluccas, as subject to "the Makassars."[24]

Tiworo served as a haven for Makassar's fleets, yet the people there also had ships of their own, which were destroyed by the VOC in the 1655 attack. Lest one take for granted the presence of ships in archipelagic places, it is worth remembering how carefully Tomé Pires had noted the number of boats belonging to each realm or ruler he discussed. Ships were materially vital to early modern archipelagic polities, and a polity's fleet signified its strength. Rather than a "ship of state," likening governance, as Plato did, to the command of a naval vessel, in Southeast Asia "fleets of state" metaphorically stood for polities. An array of archipelagic texts depict fleets of state: for instance, a seventh century Srivijayan inscription; the Malay Chronicles' description of the thirteenth century establishment of Singapore; and a sixteenth century Javanese text about Sunda. Each portrays the gathering of a fleet around a leader, either for war or to make an impression on a momentous occasion. Malay texts alluded not only to center and periphery but also to the movements of a polity's fleet, which symbolized a whole social group.[25] As with the story of Paramesvara's relocation from Palembang to

---

[23] Bor, *Amboinse Oorlogen*, 288–98, 301–3; and Knaap, "Headhunting, Carnage, and Armed Peace," 180–81.

[24] "Originele generale missive," 12 July 1655, VOC 1208 book 4, 538–48, esp. 543r.

[25] Manguin, *The Amorphous Nature of Coastal Polities*, 78–81, 98.

Malacca at the latter's founding, the portrayal of such fleets surrounding a ruler and relocating the polity's center explicitly included maritime people.

Many of Tiworo's vessels were probably built locally. As mentioned above, major boat-building centers in the region have historically been located close to teak stands, since teak was known to be good for ship construction. Shipwrights who built large vessels during the sixteenth century were found primarily in southern Borneo, Java's north coast harbor cities, and in Pegu (Burma), all of which lay close to teak forests. Timber suited for building boats also grew on Tiworo's southern margin, on the island of Muna. Although the Dutch found teak forests on Muna in 1727, they did not begin to exploit them until after they established direct rule in 1910. Dendrochronology researchers, however, have found that tree ring samples for the oldest teak trees in Indonesia, which happened to grow in Muna, date back to 1565, and the forests themselves may predate this time.[26] Since at least the mid-sixteenth century, then, shipwrights would have had access to the teak stands on Tiworo's margin.[27]

Tiworo's sheltered waters lay just off of the northern littoral route that Tomé Pires favored, from Malacca to the Moluccas. Had the Portuguese taken Pires's advice, it is likely that the area would have been mapped better at an earlier date.[28] Nevertheless, even those who traveled from the Moluccas to Java used a route that passed by Tiworo or went through nearby waters. In July 1616, Speilbergen abandoned—with no regrets—a stone fort at Buton, "between the Molucques and Java, because we considered it unnecessary," suggesting that Buton lay on a path or common route between the Moluccas and Java.[29] In the eighteenth century, as we saw above, an experienced European pilot took Bougainville from Banda to the Buton Straits, where local pilots then brought him right past the eastern entrance to Tiworo and set him on a course for south Celebes and thence to Java. During the mid-nineteenth century, the most highly traveled commercial route between the Moluccas and the Java Sea passed through these waters. "Between Boeton and the archipelagos of Toekang bessi and Wangi-wangi, is found the strait most frequented as [a] trade route between the Java Sea and the Moluccas; some ships also come through the Strait of Boeton."[30] For mariners bound instead for Makassar, the passage through Tiworo and from it across the Gulf of Boné was, for those who knew how to navigate it, safer during the west monsoon than going around the southern point of Buton, due to its calmer waters. It was also a considerably shorter route. If one had family in Tiworo, a stopover could, moreover, be replenishing. Tiworo was off the main route, but not by much. For mariners, even those based

---

[26] E. H. B. Brascamp, "De ontdekking van djatibosschen op Pangesana in 1727," *Tectona* 11 (1918): 723–43; Valentijn, *Oud en nieuw Oost-Indiën*, v. I, 228–29; and Satria Bijaksana et al., "Status of Tree-ring Research from Teak (*Tectona grandis*) for Climate Studies," *Jurnal Geofisika* 2 (2007): 2–7.

[27] Knowledge of boat-building remains a tradition passed on among Sama people in Tiworo, near Kendari, and in other areas, many of whom are descendants of Nakoda Manting. I have seen many cargo boats typical of the region in various stages of construction in the shallows of the Sama village at Pulo Balu. In 1990, a large ship of around 200 tons burden was built there, and shipwrights from Ara (not Bugis, and not from Bira) oversaw the construction. The location was close to the source of teak and had a ready supply of skilled Sama labor.

[28] Pelras, "Les premières données," 246.

[29] *The East and West Indian Mirror*, 157–58.

[30] Temminck, *Coup-d'Oeil Général sur les Possessions Néerlandaises*, vol. 3, 73–74.

elsewhere, it was not far out of the way; that said, one would be unlikely to go there without a reason.

During the seventeenth century, in addition to providing Makassar with ships and men (although exactly how many of each remains hard to determine), Tiworo provided Makassar with at least two other forms of support during the Great Ambon War. First, it was literally a haven for forces under Makassar; second, Tiworo served as a staging area for the conduct of the conflict farther east.

A letter brought by envoys from the King of Buton on April 5, 1654, and copied that day into the daily register of Superintendent Arnold de Vlaming, commander of the VOC forces, clearly illustrates Tiworo's role as a haven for both Makassar's fleet and for those who fought on Makassar's behalf. The letter reveals that Tiworo was a defensible place to which Makassar's forces could retreat and still guard their position. It also clarifies where Buton stood at the time vis à vis Makassar and the VOC, as the King of Buton entreats de Vlaming to help defend Buton from Makassar's fleet, and apologizes for not being able to do more. The apology followed an incident at sea, explained in the letter, in which the VOC's adversaries took advantage of a tactical opportunity when a small VOC boat, a *chialoup*, ventured too far from the protection of its mother ship. The *chialoup* had been pursuing five of Makassar's vessels off the coast of Celebes. But when it got rather far from the main ship, the five Makassar boats turned around and overpowered it, beating to death all but five of the Dutchmen, who were taken captive. In retaliation, the VOC then burned fifteen of Makassar's junks. Of the five hundred men who had sailed on these junks, 150 were said subsequently to be at Tiworo, while the rest fled into the forests.[31]

The king of Buton sent two boats with envoys and slaves over to Tiworo to try to free the five Dutchmen, who were apparently held there. However, once the boats arrived, the Makassars did not want to let them in. It is not quite clear whether "the Maccassars" here means those who fled from the junks, or others in Tiworo subject to Makassar; Buton's ruler and his VOC allies may not, in any case, have cared particularly much about the distinction. That the Makassars "did not want to let in" the envoys and slaves from Buton most likely means that they blocked the entrance to the straits, or to the river channels through the mangroves on Muna's northwest coast, which led to the main settlement of Tiworo. The envoys from Buton, for their part, neither wanted to just drop the matter, nor did they wish to attempt to take the five Dutchmen by force, since Tiworo was full of Makassar's supporters and the envoys were outnumbered. "My realm," added the King of Buton, "is also not strong enough, save by the force of the Company [VOC], and we have not enough boats (*praauwe*) with which we would have been able to get the Dutchmen with guns."[32]

---

[31] "Letter from the King of Buton to Arnold de Vlaming and Governor Willem Van der Beecq, Dachregister bij d'Hr. Arnold de Vlamingh van Outshoorn," April 5, 1654, VOC 1205, 1655, book 2, 892r–894r.

[32] Ibid. In this letter of April 5, 1654, the king of Buton mentions that he had heard that Makassar's king had died. But the king, Pattingalloang, is said to have died on September 15 of that year, not in April. Either Buton's ruler reports a rumor here, or the date in the Gowa and Talloq chronicles is incorrect, or the letter does not mean the actual ruler of Makassar. The letter does not discuss the circumstances or location of the death. Yet Pattingalloang's posthumous name records his death as having occurred at Bontobiraeng, also known as the Bira peninsula, a common stop-off for mariners traveling between Makassar and Tiworo.

To help protect their ally Buton, and also to monitor and try to prevent Makassar's forces from heading for the Moluccas, the Dutch erected two small forts on the beach below Buton. At the beginning of January 1655, de Vlaming stopped to visit one, and outfitted the other with twenty-two Dutchmen and twelve Ternatans, in addition to laying up stores of food for five months, along with powder, lead, fuses, five cannon, and two "metal balls." Then he traveled north up the Buton Straits to where it meets the Pangesane Narrows—another name for the Straits of Tiworo. There, at the northeast confluence of the two straits, he was joined by Vice Admiral Roos. Roos had come from a location around the east side of Buton, where he had met with the enemy at the village of Kumbewaha, and, in "a truly efficient achievement," burned and rendered useless all the ships found there, among which were three Makassar junks, full of rice and *padi* (unthreshed rice).[33]

Meanwhile, five or six days previously, the Ternaten king and VOC ally, Mandarsyah, had gone on ahead about five or six miles into the straits to the enemy's small town of Tiworo. This motivated de Vlaming to urge Roos to take eleven row yachts and three hundred Dutchmen to Tiworo to find and join Mandarsyah in order to look for the Makassar fleet together. He advised Roos, if it were not too dangerous, to undertake something violent on Tiworo.[34]

With the permission of the Ternatan king (who, it is implied, still asserted a claim over Tiworo stemming from Sultan Baabullah's 1580 campaign), Roos undertook an attack on the villages and fortress of Tiworo. After rowing into a river on the northwest side of Muna (Pangesane) for about a mile, the Dutch landed and, guided by two Tiworo captives, without being discovered, burst into the village at around noon (when things in tropical villages tend to move slowly), surprising its inhabitants. Frightened, the people fled hither and thither, some to the fortress, into which the Dutchmen followed and, after scant resistance, overpowered them. De Vlaming himself admitted that the VOC had a great deal of luck on its side in this exploit: around three hundred of Tiworo's "most courageous men" were away from home at war, subduing (*te debelleren*) neighboring areas. A second troop, around 150 strong, had gone off to hunt buffalo. Thus, the way was clear for the VOC, whose success would otherwise have been less certain and more costly, as their own complement had only "150 white and as many Ternaten" men, the rest remaining with the ship. "In such cruel mayhem," the Dutch had only three casualties and some lightly wounded, mostly from accidents caused by their own recklessness.[35]

---

[33] Bor, *Amboinse Oorlogen*, 259. A small littoral settlement—out in the tidal zone as opposed to up on the beach, and presumably Sama, currently sits on the shores of Kumbewaha. It is one among a few others on the contemporary east coast of Buton.

[34] Ibid., 260; and "Letter of January 9, 1655, from Arnold de Vlamingh van Outshoorn aboard the *Erasmus*, delivered express to the Authorities before Tiworo (*Tibore*)," VOC 1211, book 2, 76–77.

[35] Bor, *Amboinse Oorlogen*, 260–62; "Letter of January 9, 1655, from Arnold de Vlamingh van Outshoorn," 76–77; and "Arnold de Vlamingh to Simon Cos," VOC 1211, book 2, 88–89. Although Livinus Bor, as de Vlaming's personal secretary, had access to de Vlaming's records—indeed, may have written and at the very least recopied many materials—the original reports have more detail than Bor's narrative. The three hundred Tiworo men Bor stated were off making war elsewhere were, according to the original report, in neighboring *negerij* (the precise translation of which is elusive in this context—it could mean village, district, region, or country). "*Te debelleren*" meant to fight, to combat; to subdue, to suppress; to conquer, to defeat, or to vanquish ("*bestrijden, bedwingen, overwinnen*"), according to Petrus Weiland, *Kunstwoordenboek* (Rotterdam: D. Bolle, 1858), 165, http://www.dbnl.org/arch/

On January 3, 1655, the VOC took Tiworo's fortress, some six miles from the river. A sturdy stone structure reinforced with distinct bulwarks and walls five fathoms high, they dismantled it before they departed, leveling it to the ground. De Vlaming sent the news to Jacob Hustaert, the governor in the Moluccas, in a letter cosigned by the merchant Willem Maetsuyker, the governor-general's nephew. They declared, "the name and weapons of the Company will without doubt gain a reputation in these parts, since the oft-mentioned fortress was reputed to be very strong and the capital place of Pangasane Island."[36] This remark illustrates the importance of Tiworo and its fortress over and above any other places on the island of Muna. The event was commemorated by de Vlaming's secretary, Livinus Bor, in a stanza of verse:

| | |
|---|---|
| *Daer sie ik Tyboors vesting branden.* | There I saw Tiworo's fortress set ablaze. |
| *Is dit haer moed op eige landen?* | Is this what they call courage in their own realms? |
| *Dat sterke fort, in korten stond,* | That mighty fort, in an instant, |
| *Geraekt ten puinhoop en te grond.* | Turned to rubble on the ground.[37] |

As a result of the attack, around two hundred people were killed at five places in Tiworo, and "a vast number," around three hundred people, were taken alive. Moreover, huge amounts of provisions, including rice, as well as merchandise (such as clothing and other goods), lay ready to be shipped—according to the report—apparently to Asahudi. In other words, these provisions and merchandise appeared ready for transport to the VOC's adversaries fighting in the Hoamoal peninsula. The VOC forces stole or destroyed these stockpiles. At least fifty "exquisite ships" were also destroyed by fire: junks, galleys, and kora-kora.[38] Tiworo thus provided a nautical staging area, a place where sailors and shippers gathered, and where stores of food and other supplies were collected, loaded onto boats, and transported elsewhere, in support of Makassar's military and trade endeavors.

Just three days later, on January 6, as some VOC boats lay at the mouth of Tiworo's main river taking on fresh water, a Makassar fleet appeared, some fifty ships strong. Those that sailed upriver were sure to discover the bodies of the slain,

---

weil004kuns01_01/pag/weil004kuns01_01.pdf, accessed July 13, 2015.

[36] "Letter of 16 January 1655, to Marten Doane, Skipper of the *Concordia*, sent with the Post to Het Haesjen, from Arnold de Vlaming van Outshoorn, in the ship *Erasmus* at anchor by the (fresh) waterplace in the Buton Straits," VOC 1211, book 2, 79–81"; "Letter of 17 January 1655, to Simon Cos, Provis. President in Ambon, from Arnold de Vlamingh van Outshoorn in the ship *Erasmus* lying at anchor by the east end of the Buton Straits," VOC 1211, book 2, 87–94, esp. 88; "Letter to Governor Jacob Hustaert and the Council in Molucco, with the Yacht *Dromedaris*, on February 2 [1655], written from Batoij, signed on the chaloup *Sumatra*, lying at anchor off the coast of Celebes opposite Chassea island, by Arnold de Vlamingh and Willem Maetsuyker," VOC 1211, book 2, 97–111, esp. 97, 100; and Bor, *Amboinse Oorlogen*, 262. The latter says, rather than "bulwarks," that it was "reinforced with seven round towers." Maetsuyker's uncle, Joan Maetsuyker, was governor general from 1653–78. Aside from the mere value of the description in establishing Tiworo's historical importance, my hope is that these details about the fortress may be useful for future archaeologists. Two other fortresses in Tiworo recorded in archival papers a dozen years later, and probably built after this one's dismantling, appear to have been smaller and closer to Muna's northwest coast.

[37] Bor, *Amboinse Oorlogen*, [no page number].

[38] "Arnold de Vlamingh to Simon Cos"; and "Gen. Mis.," 12 July 1655, VOC 1208, book 4, 543r.

"among whom were also many Macassars."[39] As de Vlaming wrote, had the Makassar fleet come a few days earlier, it would have been impossible for the Dutch "to have been there alone to carry out the job and our people undoubtedly would have perished and been beaten."[40] Things undoubtedly would have turned out very differently for Tiworo, too.

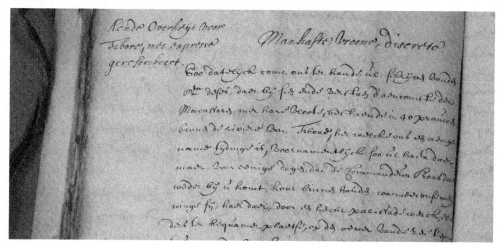

Arnold de Vlaming letter, written on the *Erasmus,* January 9, 1655
(source: National Archives of the Netherlands, VOC 1211, p. 76):

To the authorities before
Tibore, express
delivery.

Courageous, Righteous, Discrete.

Just now we were handed your letter of the 8th, whereby we see and understand the arrival of the Makassars with their fleet consisting of 40 prauwe within the rivers of Tibore, which is a joyous tiding ...

Delighted by this new development, de Vlaming urged the vice admiral to use caution to evade them, "since they may be too strong for you." At the same time, he devised a plan whereby his men would build a palisade on the shore and then attack the Makassar forces upriver, driving them downstream to "extrude" them—a word that suggests he intended to force them through a narrow exit where they might be picked off one by one.[41] It was a clever plan, given the numerically stronger Makassar force, yet it ran up against environmental realities for a variety of reasons: the river's shallow depth at low tide, the presence of underwater mangrove roots, and the fact that fresh water would then only lay behind enemy lines. These problems eventually led the Dutch to abandon any plans to deal with the Makassar fleet at Tiworo itself.[42]

---

[39] "De Vlaming to Simon Cos," VOC 1211, book 2, 87; and "De Vlaming and Maetsuyker to Jacob Hustaert," VOC 1211, book 2, 97. In VOC 1211, page 77, the estimate was forty vessels, although this was based on the earliest intelligence, received on January 8. Forty is also the number given by Bor, *Amboinse Oorlogen*, 263.

[40] "De Vlaming to Simon Cos," 88.

[41] "Arnold de Vlaming to the Authorities before Tiworo," VOC 1211, book 2, 76–77.

[42] "De Vlamingh to Simon Cos," 91.

Nevertheless, deciding to remain in this area of Celebes for a while, de Vlaming placed outlying ships in strategic locations: four (the *Teryeer, Sandijck, Coutchien*, and *De Haringh*) close to the eastern mouth of the Tiworo Straits, and beyond this two others (the *Erasmus* and the *Pool*) on moorings, filled with available personnel.[43] Since the VOC was unable to occupy Tiworo, it was feared that the Makassar fleet would try by any means possible to break through and proceed with its trek to the Ambon region, by sailing a route between Buton and Wowoni, which it commonly took eastward across to the Sula (*Xoula*) islands. De Vlaming, on *Erasmus*, thus sent two sturdy and well-provisioned ships, the *Pool* and the *Haesjen*, off to Sula, along with "all the small vessels," instructing them to remain continuously sailing in the waters back and forth between Buru and Sula to its north.[44] Buru, quite a large island, lay just west of the Hoamoal peninsula, with Manipa and Kelang interposed between them. De Vlaming also conveyed orders from Batavia for the *Pool* and the *Haesjen* to find the yacht *Concordia* on the south side of Sula and to stick with her there, in order to keep watch "for Macassars or other unfree strangers and not to let anyone pass there." The ships' captains were told "to try to take under fire anyone they notice going hither and yon, not in possession of the correct pass papers, and to take in tight security and transfer goods keeping a good inventory on your ships."[45] The placement of these patrols in the waters off Buru were meant primarily to catch ships in support of Makassar on their way to or from the Hoamoal peninsula.

To prevent VOC enemies from exiting Tiworo and heading east in the first place, ships were also posted in the channels on the north and south side of Wowoni, one straight across from it at "the waterplace." This blocked boats in Tiworo either from taking the direct route eastward, or from heading north up the coast to Tobungku and then skirting the Banggai islands to arrive at Sula. In addition, a ship was placed straight in front of the town of Buton to protect the Dutch and their allies there, and another stationed "in order to have good oversight so the enemy cannot go unnoticed south of the land of Buton."[46] In other words, should the enemy's ships double back to exit the Tiworo Straits via its southwest end, they would have to divert their route far to the south of Buton to evade its notice.

De Vlaming and Willem Maetsuyker wrote to Governor Jacob Hustaert and the Council in the Moluccas vehemently expressing the hope to see the whites of their eyes, intending to "infest their coasts relentlessly ... until they beg the Company for peace," which, he stated in the same breath, "those folks will just not understand ... whatever and however good and beneficial preference we have granted them." Moreover, de Vlaming imagined that his foes were "egged on by the Portuguese,"

---

[43] Bor, *Amboinse Oorlogen*, 260; "Letter from Arnold de Vlamingh van Outshoorn," January 9, 1655, VOC 1211, book 2, 77.

[44] "Letter of 16 January 1655, to Marten Doane, Skipper of the *Concordia*." This communiqué also mentions the company's continuing friendship with Buton despite the deposing of its king, Ali, and the reinstatement of his judge, or "Houcoum" (*hukum*).

[45] "Letter of Arnold de Vlamingh van Outshoorn, on board the *Erasmus*, January 16, 1655," VOC 1211, book 2, 78.

[46] "Orders for Commander Gerrit Roos, in order to instruct him further, from Arnold de Vlamingh van Outshoorn in the ship *Erasmus* at anchor by the waterplace in the Buton Straits, January 17, 1655," VOC 1211, 1655, book 2, 81–86, esp. 81–82; "Originele generale missive in dato 24 Dec 1655," VOC 1209, 1656, book 1, 6v.

not aware, it seems, that they had their own motives for waging war, regardless of European rivalries.[47]

Arnold de Vlaming, Order for Gerrit Roos, written on the ship *Erasmus,* in the roads at the waterplace in the Buton Straits, January 17, 1655 (source: National Archives of the Netherlands, VOC 1211, p. 81):

Order for the Commander Gerrit Roos, to instruct him further.

Having deliberated more deeply and gone back and forth over the opportunity as it is before us and we deem it so important that we changed our first plans, it was advised to let Your Lordship come over here in order to command both on land and at sea in our name and to serve as our compass.

Beyond our initial plans to keep the four bottoms, namely, Terveere, Sandijck, Coetchien, and De Haringh, here to occupy the shipping channels, it seems advisable, if and when the Makassar fleet comes through [the strait's eastern exit] from the Tiworo rivers, to add to them the ship Hulst, in order to place Terveere and Hulst on the short side of the coast, straight across from the Island Wawonij ...

---

[47] De Vlaming and Maetsuyker to Jacob Hustaert," VOC 1211, book 2, 97–111, esp. 102.

On April 6, departing from Ambon narrows, de Vlaming met the yacht *Hulst* with the news, from Roos, that the Makassars continued to stay put in Tiworo's river.[48] Within just a few weeks, however, the Makassar fleet slipped out of their sanctuary in Tiworo, eluding the Dutch in an unusually dense fog. "Absolutely disheartening," wrote de Vlaming's personal secretary. Nevertheless, he added, it could not be undone, and de Vlaming again dispatched some boats to try to find the Makassar fleet near Buru.[49]

The foregoing makes it clear that Tiworo was a haven for Makassar's fleet, in addition to a staging area for its endeavors further east, particularly in the Hoamoal peninsula. This is fairly remarkable given that the Hoamoal peninsula lay nearly four hundred miles (about 630 kilometers) away. Here, then, the colonial archives illuminate the politics of connection and distance in the archipelago's maritime world, and the dynamics of trade and war in which Tiworo played a vital role as a nonurban maritime hub.

## WOMEN OF RANK AS SPOILS OF WAR

The connections between Tiworo and Makassar included more than just ties of trade and military considerations. They also involved political and social connections between ruling families. The extent of these ties between Tiworo and Makassar are reflected in the VOC's interest in who had been killed at, and who had been taken from, Tiworo prior to the appearance of Makassar's fleet in its river. Among those killed in the attack on Tiworo were its king, along with the greater number of his entourage or notables, as well as his sons.[50] De Vlaming viewed this as a serious blow to Makassar, "to lose their friend, the king, with most of his peers," as he was "a man on whom a lot was riding and in this region was greatly esteemed."[51] VOC reports also made particular note of the fact that the three hundred women and children taken alive at Tiworo included most of the king's wives and daughters.[52]

People captured by the VOC and its allies in this mid-seventeenth century conflict did not have a uniform fate. At Asahudi, for instance, the VOC captured two hundred of Makassar's reinforcements and spared their lives. These people were then sent to Batavia, probably to be sold as slaves. On occasion, captured people also made surprising escapes. For instance, about six hundred people, among them elites and some women and children, slipped passed the fort of Seborg due to the recklessness of an officer-in-training. If he had acted wisely, the people would not have escaped, and while the hope—de Vlaming's hope—would have been to kill the escapees, in the end "it cost only thirty of their lives, to the great dissatisfaction of

---

[48] Bor, *Amboinse Oorlogen*, 273.

[49] "*Middelerwijl sijn de Makassaren, uit haer wijk plaets aen Tyboor, onze besettingen in een dijs onslipt* ..." Ibid., 274. "Within just a few weeks" because, on page 276 of Bor's narrative, the next date mentioned is May 17.

[50] "De Vlamingh and Maetsuyker to Jacob Hustaert," VOC 1211, book 2, 99–100; and "Originele generale missive," 12 July 1655, VOC 1208, book 4, 543r. Makassar's practical reliance on and kin connections with prominent Sama, such as the family of a number of its harbormasters during the seventeenth and eighteenth centuries, are discussed in the following chapter. It is not clear, however, what connections those Sama may have had with Tiworo.

[51] "De Vlamingh to Simon Cos," VOC 1211, book 2, 89.

[52] Ibid., 89; De Vlamingh and Maetsuyker to Jacob Hustaert, VOC 1211, book 2, 99.

the Superintendent."[53] In the 1654 storming of Laala on the Hoamoal peninsula, when the VOC's forces killed seven hundred people capable of bearing arms, both locals and Makassar's reinforcements, four hundred people, as mentioned in the previous section, were taken captive. Rather than being sent to Batavia to be sold as slaves, these women, children, and the indigent elderly were granted as spoils to the victors (that is, to the VOC's allies), to foster or stimulate bravery among them in the future.[54]

The women and children taken as part of the *"buijt"* (plunder/loot/booty/spoils) at Tiworo were dealt with in the same way. According to the *Generale missiven* sent from Batavia to the heads of the VOC, hence based on earlier descriptions of events, "the king's real wife and daughters as well as a good number of concubines were left to the conquerors."[55] They were bestowed on those who fought for the Dutch, "amounting to a good number of them falling into the hands of the Ternatans and Mardijkers [freemen]." This was done, de Vlaming and Maetsuycker explained to Governor Hustaert, "in order to get them off our hands, of which Your Lordship will respect the special nature," alluding, perhaps, to the mayhem that could result if three hundred women and children were to come aboard the VOC's vessels. De Vlaming elaborated that allowing him, the governor's delegate, "to please them [their allies] to be treated," was a way to keep those combatants calm and contented to continue with the work." In short, he suggests, these spoils were a payoff to keep the fighters amenable to engaging in further combat.[56]

The loyalty of their allies could not be taken for granted. Quite a few people fled impressment. At Tobungku (*Tabouko*), formally under Ternate, "if they did not want to yield to the proposals of their lawful monarch," then, to gain compliance and "prepared to win with weapons," soldiers were ordered "to put two bullets in their muskets and two in their mouths, which caused great astonishment among them."[57] Some people who had lived in areas under Mandarsyah's control, despite being cajoled with sweet talk and promises from the VOC, simply refused to come back. They ended up residing in the river at Kayeli on Buru, expressly stating that without any opinion against the VOC or intention to initiate enmities against it, they no longer wished to endure Mandarsyah's ruthlessness.[58] De Vlaming was nothing if not pragmatic about creating the expectation of war spoils among local fighters.

Why were these captives not sold as slaves? Southeast Asia constituted the largest circuit of Dutch slavery in the world of the seventeenth century Indian Ocean. Of the nearly ten thousand slaves brought to Batavia by Asian vessels between 1653 and 1682, many of them after Makassar's defeat in the late 1660s, over half came from, or through, southern Celebes. More than four thousand (about 42 percent) came from southwest Celebes, primarily Makassar, and almost twelve hundred (12 percent) came from Buton. The demand for slaves was mostly urban centered.[59] However, despite the regional traffic in slaves, not all captives were

---

[53] Bor, *Amboinse Oorlogen*, 300–1.

[54] Ibid., 236–40.

[55] "Originele generale missive," 24 December 1655, VOC 1209, book 1, 5v-6r.

[56] "De Vlamingh and Maetsuyker to Jacob Hustaert," VOC 1211, book 2, 99.

[57] Bor, *Amboinse Oorlogen*, 265.

[58] "Originele generale missive," 12 July 1655, VOC 1208, book 4, 543v.

[59] Markus Vink, "'The World's Oldest Trade': Dutch Slavery and Slave Trade in the Indian Ocean in the Seventeenth Century," *Journal of World History* 14, 2 (2003): 143–44, 146–49.

shipped off to urban slave markets, as shown by the above examples of the four hundred taken at Laala on Hoamoal in 1654, and the three hundred taken from Tiworo in early 1655.

This should not be surprising, as the practice of capturing people in maritime raids long predated the European presence in the region.[60] In light of this long history of raiding in the archipelago, it is clear that the VOC's bestowal of captives on local fighters as war spoils did not initiate, but rather built on, earlier practices of obtaining captives in raids. However, understanding why some captives, especially women and children, were not shipped off to be sold as slaves, but instead were transferred to the victors in conflicts, goes deeper than simply the imperative to increase followings. Negotiation of, and competition over, rank and status gave capture social consequences, cultural significance, and material ramifications.

Rank and status in Southeast Asia were not inflexible, but were instead constantly renegotiated and redefined.[61] While genealogy and ascribed descent from high-status forbears was important, rank was also negotiated in part through the conduct of relations between groups, particularly through marriage. For instance, during the sixteenth and seventeenth centuries, high-ranking chiefs in outlying districts of Ternate's sultanate provided the court with hundreds of royal wives, and it was not uncommon for a sultan to have a wife in every major settlement under his rule.[62] Giving women in polygamous marriages to rulers or other high-ranking elites at a polity center was an act of fealty from which one might expect a return flow of elevated status and bridewealth valuables. In contrast, the daughters and sisters of rulers were married to men of similar rank from neighboring polities, such as those in Sulawesi and Sulu, securing alliances with them.[63]

Similarly, in Makassar, transfer of control over outlying districts was usually legitimized by marriage between the daughter of a subjugated king and the Gowa king or one of his sons. Gowa's increasing monopolization of power in the late-sixteenth century was visible in, among other things, a poorly reciprocated pattern of local aristocratic women marrying into Gowa circles, while Gowa appointed its own aristocrats as the lords of territories that had previously been under the jurisdiction of neighboring kingdoms. A more balanced pattern of aristocratic marriages was restored when Talloq recovered its throne and brought the entire Makassar coastal strip under its control. These actions enabled Talloq's Karaeng Kanjilo (Sultan Abdullah) "to summon Makassar's talent for the thrust into Eastern Indonesia."[64]

Ethnographic and historical evidence from across the region suggests that, while marrying within social class (rank-endogenous marriage) was weakly proscribed, both individuals and whole kin groups could move vertically within the social

---

[60] Junker, *Raiding, Trading, and Feasting.*

[61] Ibid., 143.

[62] L. Andaya, *The World of Maluku,* 37.

[63] Barbara Watson Andaya, "Political Development between the Sixteenth and Eighteenth Centuries," in Tarling, ed., *The Cambridge History of Southeast Asia,* 419.

[64] David Bulbeck, "New Perspectives on Early South Sulawesi History," *Baruga* 9 (September 1993): 10–18, esp. 14, in which the author provides a summary of his PhD thesis, "A Tale of Two Kingdoms: The Historical Archaeology of Gowa and Tallok, South Sulawesi, Indonesia" (Australian National University, 1992).

hierarchy through a single fortuitous or ill-advised marriage.[65] However, to have high-ranking daughters and wives simply taken during conflicts posed a flagrant disregard of the process of negotiating a union, which, whether fortuitous or ill-advised, was nevertheless a concerted effort to bring together spouses as well as kin groups, and served as an avenue by which mutual acknowledgement was achieved in social practice. The capture of women precluded negotiations over gift exchange commensurate with rank and obviated reciprocal prestations that could lead to or cement politically strategic alliances. Instead, there was simply conquest. This subordination brought about through the violent acquisition of dependents did not just affect those captured, but also redounded to the social status of their kin.

The capture of women of rank in this manner was no less a part of the dynamic of power and politics among groups in the archipelago than the more commonly discussed marital unions negotiated between members of high-status lineages. Like two sides of the same coin, the significance of one practice—negotiated marriages as part of alliance-making—made meaningful the other—the capture of women of rank as both sign and means of conquest. This facet in the workings of political economy and social geography also illustrates, beyond mere trade and war, how the politics of connection and distance in the archipelagic world cut across ethnic differences. The capture of women of rank, and their dependents, helps illustrate how divisions of rank were remade across the boundaries of ethnic or descent groups. Colonial conflict built on and exploited these dynamics, underscoring the need to recognize and overcome the false analytical separation between, on the one hand, colonial conflicts, and, on the other, the relations among groups in the archipelago. The boundaries of rank and ethnicity, remade through the capture of women, formed a part of both intergroup relations as well as colonial conflict.

## THE SEASCAPE OF THE MAKASSAR WAR

Despite the attack on Tiworo in 1655, when two hundred men were killed, three hundred women and children were taken, and its fort was razed, Tiworo bounced back. However, a dozen years after the first attack, the VOC subdued Tiworo again in connection with the "Makassar War," sometimes called "Speelman's War." In this conflict, the VOC, under Admiral Cornelis Speelman, and its allies, primarily under the Bugis leader Arung Palakka, eventually defeated Makassar itself.[66]

As in the 1650s, the desire to exert control over the spice trade guided the VOC's endeavors. Likewise, the competition and rivalry between Gowa and Ternate again played a crucial structuring role. In addition, within the peninsula of south Celebes, Gowa's history of war with the Bugis, especially the Bugis of Boné, fed the

---

[65] Junker, *Raiding, Trading, and Feasting*, 142.

[66] In fact, although the VOC defeated Makassar in 1667, it subsequently viewed Makassar as abrogating treaty provisions, and took the citadel of Sombaopu, reconquering Makassar in 1669. The name "Speelman's War" comes from a seventeenth century manuscript titled *Sja'ir Sipelman* (viz., Speelman), MS no. XVI in the Leiden Juynboll catalogue. Cyril Skinner collated, transcribed, translated and edited the two previously known London and Leiden manuscripts, ascribed authorship to Encik Amin ("the Sultan of Gowa's Malay secretary"), and renamed it the *Sja'ir Perang Mengkasar*, viz., *Sya'ir* (rhymed chronicle) of the Makassar War. English translation is published in *VKI* 40 (1963). J. C. Bottoms, "Some Malay Historical Sources: A Bibliographical Note," in *An Introduction to Indonesian Historiography*, ed. Soedjatmoko (Ithaca: Cornell University Press, 1965, 2007; and Jakarta: Equinox, 2007), 186 (note 120), 193.

flames of resentment and enmity between the two, fueling Arung Palakka's rise. Rather than give a detailed account of his rise, the lead-up to the war and its progress, for which there are more thorough treatments, I offer enough historical background below to clarify Boné's role and to contextualize Tiworo's involvement.

During the first decades of the seventeenth century, Gowa's efforts to spread Islam, "by conquest if necessary," led to the subjection of Boné, its most powerful political opponent in the peninsula. Gowa was then able to claim overlordship of the entire peninsula of south Celebes, with the exception of Luwu, which professed to be the first realm on the peninsula to embrace Islam, and which Gowa never tried to subdue.[67] The alliance between the VOC and the Bugis enemies of Gowa would spell Makassar's downfall.

Earlier in the century, during the early 1640s, a conflict between the Bugis realms of Boné and Wajo eventuated in Gowa backing Wajo. Gowa and Wajo joined forces with the Bugis realm of Soppeng (or one of its factions) to attack Boné, whose leader fled to Luwu. When Gowa forcibly brought this ruler, La Ma'daremmeng, the defeated Arumponé (Arung of Boné) from Luwu to Makassar, his brother secretly returned to Boné and raised an army against Gowa. Gowa assembled its troops and, calling on the support of Luwu, Soppeng, and Wajo once again in 1644, vanquished Boné with a superior army. Having reasserted its overlordship, Gowa reduced Boné's status from "vassal" to "slave," withdrew previous privileges, placed it at Gowa's service, and, to prevent rebellion in Boné, brought its nobles to Gowa.[68]

Despite Makassar's strong position in the south Sulawesi peninsula, the VOC hoped to gain a toehold in its vicinity. It was encouraged in this by revolts in Boné and in Mandar in 1659, and bolstered by news that Gowa's mercenary troops from Banda were willing to assist the VOC in any attack on Makassar. In 1660, a VOC expedition did, in fact, manage to occupy one of Makassar's forts, located at Paqnakkukang. In response to this, and to contain the VOC, Gowa summoned ten thousand Bugis to dig a canal that cut off the fort from the Gowa mainland. These corvée laborers were put in groups to minimize desertions, each group under a Bugis leader from Boné or Soppeng. Eventually, they refused to continue working and fled back to their homelands, where they assembled a large enough army to cause Gowa serious concern. By October, however, the Dutch, still in the fort at Paqnakkukang, heard the returning Gowa troops' celebratory shots announcing their victory, once more, over the Bugis.[69] Arung Palakka had been one of the leaders who oversaw the laborers. According to local tradition, he had originally been brought to Gowa in 1644 at the age of eleven with his family and other hostage nobles. In 1660, after Gowa defeated these rebels, Arung Palakka fled into exile on the island of Buton with his family and other Bugis leaders.[70] Given that Arung Palakka departed for Buton from Boné, he is likely to have passed through Tiworo.

---

[67] Leonard Andaya, *The Heritage of Arung Palakka: A History of South Sulawesi (Celebes) in the Seventeenth Century* (The Hague: Martinus Nijhoff, 1981), 1; and J. Noorduyn, "Origins of South Celebes Historical Writing," in Soedjatmoko, ed., *An Introduction to Indonesian Historiography*, 146–47.

[68] L. Andaya, *The Heritage of Arung Palakka*, 39–43.

[69] Ibid., 48–52.

[70] Ibid., 59, 66; on the discrepancy concerning which year it was, late 1660 or early 1661, see page 316, note 17. Dutch sources say 1661, and Cummings says 1660: "1660 25 December— The day of Tunisombaya's [Arung Palakka's] journey from Campalagi [in Boné] east to Buton." Cummings further notes: "Like several later entries about Arung Palakka, this entry

The first years of his exile on Buton, within easy reach of Gowa's fleets, were followed by a move to Batavia (accomplished with Dutch assistance) where things were less tumultuous. Gowa repeatedly expressed its preference to the VOC that the Bugis rebels either be returned to south Celebes or exiled to Ceylon, reflecting its fear of the threat they posed. Yet such requests remained unfulfilled. In 1666, Arung Palakka and his followers distinguished themselves in a campaign with the Dutch against the Minangkabau on Sumatra's west coast, a mission whose success he was led to believe held out the possibility of a war with the VOC against Gowa.[71] In Makassar, it was widely believed that Arung Palakka had been killed while fighting in this campaign. Hence, when he returned from exile and was seen on December 19, 1666, aboard Speelman's ship anchored off Makassar, it caused a fright among the messengers from Gowa, who had been sent by Gowa's ruler with reparation payments to avoid open conflict over an incident with the Dutch.[72] This incident and how it came about explain a good deal about the state of Gowa's maritime relations at the time.

Back in 1660, after the Dutch had taken the fort at Paqnakkukang, treaty negotiations were held in Batavia between the VOC and Sultan Hasanuddin's representative. When the Dutch envoys came to Gowa on October 13, 1660, to deliver the signed treaty, the sultan welcomed them and asked when they would be giving back his fort at Paqnakkukang. The Dutch noticed on this visit that major defensive preparations were underway in Makassar. They did not realize, however, that this was as much a precaution against a rumored Buton-Bugis-Ternate invasion, as it was preparation for the possibility of hostilities with the Dutch.[73] The 1660 treaty between Gowa and the VOC contained provisions in which Gowa was made to acknowledge that Buton (in Article 1) and Manado (in Article 2) belonged to Sultan Mandarsyah of Ternate. Nevertheless, the treaty was ignored by Sultan Hasanuddin, who continued to have pretensions to, or claims over, these lands.[74] By the end of 1661, there had still been no progress in the treaty's implementation. Instead, it was said that Makassar's harbor region was being fortified, large quantities of gunpowder were being stockpiled, and it was evident that even more defenses were being built. Moreover, twelve- to fifteen-hundred boats in different areas were said to be in a state of readiness.[75]

Then, in 1662, sixteen cannons and other items were seized from a Dutch ship that foundered in Makassar's waters. Although eight of the cannons were later

---

must have been interpolated into the annals after he had conquered Makassar with the VOC in 1669 and subsequently became the preeminent figure in South Sulawesi for the remainder of the century." William Cummings, trans. and ed., *The Makassar Annals* (Leiden: KITLV Press, 2010), 90 (note 233). It is also quite possible that Arung Palakka left Gowa in late 1660 and arrived in Buton in 1661.

[71] L. Andaya, *The Heritage of Arung Palakka*, 65–68.

[72] See F. W. Stapel, *Het Bongaais Verdrag* (Groningen: J. B. Wolters, 1922), 101 (note 2), on the belief in Makassar that Arung Palakka had been killed in Sumatra. See also: L. Andaya, *The Heritage of Arung Palakka*, 73–74; and "Summary of the actions of His Lordship who set sail with the fleet the 24th [November] 1666 from the harbor of Batavia till today the 23rd of January of the year 1667," VOC 1264, book 3, 25r–26r.

[73] L. Andaya, *The Heritage of Arung Palakka*, 59–61.

[74] *Corpus Diplomaticum Neerlando-Indicum*, ed. J. E. Heeres (The Hague: Martinus Nijhoff, 1931), vol. II, 168–77, esp. 171, cited in ibid., 65.

[75] L. Andaya, *The Heritage of Arung Palakka*, 60.

returned, this was managed only through negotiations and concessions. Another Dutch shipwreck occurred at an island off the coast of Makassar, and the Dutch were angered by the sultan's refusal to allow them to send a boat out to recover its valuables. When it was rumored that the sultan sent his own people to retrieve the ship's money chest, the Dutch, not surprisingly, considered this piracy. Then, making matters worse, the members of the Dutch party sent out to the island to investigate the incident were murdered.[76] Subsequent efforts to resolve this situation broke down, and the entire Dutch post in Makassar sailed to Batavia on June 23, 1665. Sultan Hasanuddin himself seemed entirely nonplussed by the prospect that the Dutch might wish to start a war. The VOC, for its part, tried to dispel the impression that this was its aim, and to this end, in November 1665, decided to send a mission to Makassar. However, its envoy was not permitted to land and had to continue on to Ambon.[77]

Rumors reached Makassar, probably via merchants from England, which was at war with the Dutch in Europe, that the English had seized seventy to eighty VOC ships, that Batavia suffered scarcities, and that, due to losses caused by plague and other illnesses, the VOC had to recruit natives. In addition, it was rumored that the English had blockaded the Netherlands and taken Banda, and that Batavia would soon follow.[78]

These rumors may have encouraged Gowa to believe that the time was right to reestablish its authority in areas of the archipelago to its east.[79] In 1665, Gowa's forces invaded the Sula islands east of Celebes with more than two hundred ships, and took the cannon from the fortress at Ternate, along with more than two thousand people. This, according to Admiral Cornelis Speelman,

> ... put all the eastern provinces in turmoil, and not without reason, since, certainly encouraged by this booty, one saw with what incredible power they equipped and furnished [a fleet] the following year under [Karaeng] Bontomarannu, consisting of, according to musterings done in the Bay of Boné, more than 700 vessels and 20,000 people, no doubt with the intention to bring Buton to her fealty, and then subsequently to concentrate first on Maluku, or closer, on the island of Sula. In this they have with God's help been prevented by the High Government in Batavia in a timely manner.[80]

The VOC sent a new mission to Makassar after the previous one was barred from landing, apparently to preserve the peace, despite Makassar's military maneuvers, and to seek satisfaction from Gowa for the Dutch murders. Commissioner van Wesenhagen arrived in April 1666 and learned that the *sabannaraq*, or harbormaster (Malay/Indonesian: *syahbandar*), Daeng Makkulle, of Gowa, had just returned home after two months away. He had been part of a fleet sent to the Sula islands, Tambuku (Tobungku) on Celebes's east coat, and to the Banggai islands northeast of there. English, Portuguese, and Indian Muslim

---

[76] Ibid., 62–63.

[77] Stapel, *Bongaais Verdrag*, 83–85, cited in Ibid., 63.

[78] L. Andaya, *The Heritage of Arung Palakka*, 63–64; and "Gerwits, bearer of the Company's letter to Sultan Hasanuddin, January 22, 1666," VOC 1257 1667, 504.

[79] L. Andaya, *The Heritage of Arung Palakka*, 64.

[80] Speelman, *Notitie*, 684r–684v.

merchants in Makassar told van Wesenhagen that the reason for this expedition was to assert Gowa's suzerainty over lands contested by Ternate, many of which had been seized by Gowa in the first half of the seventeenth century, including, in addition to the aforementioned, Gorontalo and Muna—where Tiworo was located. Makassar's fleet also attacked Ambon and Buton, but was unable to conquer them. Hence, it was rumored that a second fleet of three hundred boats was being prepared for an expedition aimed at Buton and Ternate—both allies of the Dutch.[81]

Rather than the rumored three hundred boats, however, Speelman, as mentioned above, later recorded an impressive seven hundred boats. Although Speelman seems to have thought that Gowa's ability to muster this impressive force was motivated by people's expectation of acquiring spoils, whether in goods or persons, this was not the sole motive. Sultan Hasanuddin offered another rationale. Just as the VOC took the defense of its allies, Ternate and Buton, as justification for a combat-ready posture, Makassar, for its part, rationalized reexpansion to the east as rectifying the attack committed by the VOC and Ternate on Tiworo in 1655. As Commissioner van Wesenhagen reported, the sultan would be inclined toward peace with the Dutch if the rebel Bugis leaders who had fled from Buton to Batavia were returned, and also if the Dutch would condone his occupation of the lands disputed by Ternate. Sultan Hasanuddin explained "that he would never have had to maintain his rights to these lands in question if Ternate had not attacked the Makassar territory of Pancana."[82]

"Pancana" (or "Pantsiano," as Speelman called it; earlier sources referred to it as "Pangesane") is the island now called Muna. In the seventeenth century, it was the site of three local realms. The northwest was under Tiworo. The second "head king" of Pantsiano was "the Radja of Woona, others call him Oona [*Oena*]," in other words, Muna. The third and last was Lohia (*Loeija*). The king of Buton laid claim (typically not well-received) to "the upper powers," that is, overlordship, over the last two, but apparently, in Speelman's time, not over Tiworo.[83]

In terms of naval force and trade, Tiworo was by far the most powerful, and also the most heavily fortified, of the three. It may be recalled from the above section on the Great Ambon War that, in January 1655, the VOC forces dismantled Tiworo's fortress, an imposing stone structure. De Vlaming was effusive over the VOC's good fortune at taking Tiworo when most of its own fighting men were away, and just before Makassar's fleet showed up. Yet, although Tiworo's defeat was due to considerable luck, Speelman still opined that: "the name and weapons of the Company will without doubt gain a reputation in these parts, since the oft-

---

[81] "Report of Commissioner van Wesenhagen on mission to Makassar and Ternate," 16 July 1666, VOC 1257, 1667, 511, 514; Stapel, *Bongaais Verdrag*, 1922, 86, cited in L. Andaya, *The Heritage of Arung Palakka*, 64. Speelman says on the first page of his *Notitie* that Makassar invaded the Sula islands in 1665. Speelman, *Notitie*, 684r.

[82] "Report of Commissioner van Wesenhagen on mission to Makassar and Ternate," 521; L. Andaya, *The Heritage of Arung Palakka*, 65.

[83] "Letter from Speelman to Governor General Joan Maetsuijker and the Council of the Indies," 18 August 1667, VOC 1264, book 3, 44–61, here: 52r–52v. The initial consonant of "Muna" as pronounced by contemporary speakers of the Muna language, phonologically quite different from most of the other Austronesian languages in the area, sounds to my unschooled ears something like a mix of /m/, /b/, /v/, and /w/. Hence, the spelling variation in seventeenth century Dutch sources is not at all surprising.

mentioned fortress was reputed to be very strong and the capital place of Pangasane Island."

When, therefore, Sultan Hasanuddin pointed to the attack on "the Makassar territory of Pancana," he was referring to the attack on Tiworo in 1655. This was his rationale for undertaking a campaign over places Ternate disputed in the eastern archipelago. In that attack, as discussed above, Ternate's men, followed by the Dutch, entered the Pangasane narrows, also known as the Straits of Tiworo; leveled Tiworo's fort and settlement at the northwest end of the island; killed two hundred of its men; and captured three hundred women and children. Sultan Hasanuddin's explanation specifically invokes Ternate's role as the attacker. Taking spoils may well have been one aim of Makassar's initial raids on the Sula islands and Ternate, before the immense mustering of Makassar's forces in the Bay of Boné. However, it is also clear that Makassar's intent was retaliation. The vivid symbolism of seizing a cannon from Ternate's fortress showed that Ternate not only failed to get off a shot but that Makassar rendered it unable to defend itself, an unmistakable insult.

## SAMA AT THE CENTER

Sultan Hasanuddin was not the only one who considered Tiworo significant. Admiral Speelman later made his condemnation of Tiworo clear in the opening to his voluminous "Notitie" about the Makassar War, where he singled out "... the recalcitrant Pantsiano and particularly that nasty pirates' nest, Tiboore [Tiworo]."[84] Before taking a closer look at this "nasty pirates' nest" in the Makassar War, a digression may help to allay misconceptions about the Sama as peripheral to regional states. Without a doubt, hinterseas such as Tiworo contributed to Makassar's ability to muster extremely large followings with nautical skills, demonstrating that nonurban littorals—some, like Tiworo, hubs in their own right—were vital to trade, politics, and military endeavors in the archipelagic world. However, the remote overtones of "hinterseas" should not obscure the fact that important Sama people moved among Makassar's social and political elites.

Scholars are familiar with the legendary beginnings of Makassar's royal Gowa lineage, which include a Bayo or Sama figure as an apical ancestor. Gowa's rulers are thought to descend from a special pair, one of whom "came down"—which is popularly understood to mean from the heavens, but sometimes is just taken to mean from the mountains.[85] The other appeared from the sea and was called *Karaeng Bayo*, the title *karaeng* signifying "royal" or high-status lineage in the Makassar language.[86] Yet, apart from this legendary Bajo presence in the founding of Gowa's

---

[84] Speelman, "Notitie," VOC 1276, book 4, 684v. I translate *wederhorige* as "recalcitrant," (viz., *weerspannige*), following G. J. Van Sterkenburg, *Een Glossarium van Zeventiende-Eeuws Nederlands* (Groningen: Wolters-Noordhoff, 1981).

[85] At the notion that any apical ancestors actually came down from the heavens, the scholar Daeng Mangemba chortled. He was seventy-six years old at the time and nearly blind, but still spry of wit. His opinion was that someone had just come down from the mountains. Personal communication, Makassar, September 14, 1999.

[86] Popularly, as well as in the scholarly literature, the "One who descended" is taken to be female, and the Bayo person of "royal" or chiefly descent is understood to have been male. However, the terms themselves are not gender specific. A male *Karaeng Bayo* fits with "stranger king" narratives, while a female *Karaeng Bayo* fits with narratives of high-status Sama women relocated by strategic marriage or capture, like those examined in the next chapter.

royal lineage, Makassar language sources also mention other Sama figures, historical ones. Scholars have mostly overlooked these Sama people, who, during the seventeenth and eighteenth centuries, moved in Makassar's inner circle.[87]

The cause of this disregard seems to be threefold: limited access to the relevant sources, the need for cultural competencies to recognize the significance of certain terms, and the expectation that those involved in Makassar's politics would be ethnically Makassar. It is therefore fortunate for generations of scholars to come that William Cummings has translated and edited *The Makassar Annals* and the Chronicles of Gowa and Talloq.[88] Among many other things, they reveal the presence and importance of high status Sama figures at Makassar's "court." They show, for instance, that Sama and Makassar elites intermarried, and that the *papuq*, the title for a paramount Sama leader, sometimes held the important post of Makassar's harbormaster (*sabannaraq*).[89]

It is hard to overemphasize the significance of finding a *papuq* (indeed, more than one) along with his kin, in these materials from the elite political and social center of Makassar's seventeenth and eighteenth century life. The scholarly literature says little about this title, where or when any person who bore it may have lived, or what being a *papuq* entailed.

The existence of an actual historical *papuq* has heretofore relied almost entirely on the merest wisp of textual evidence in an eighteenth-century colonial report. This report, a Dutch letter of 1725, mentions "Bajau Laut [viz., sea Bajau] from the domain of Papoek" in connection with another contemporaneous report regarding the sighting of ninety-one people: men, women, and children, aboard "seven small Bajau Laut or Makassarese fishing vessels." The ruler of Lamakera on Solor, along with an interpreter, ordered that they be taken captive.[90] James J. Fox, who brought attention to this letter, suggests they were taken captive because the people of Solor, among the first to ally themselves with the Dutch in the seventeenth century, were obliged to report and refuse entry to foreign vessels in their waters.[91] That may be, although these reports also mention places just east of Flores, whose straits historically led to the sandalwood of Timor, along whose north coast lies "Makassar Beach" (*Pantai Makassar*). The name hints at the area's long history of traffic and settlement from Sulawesi, and hence, how "foreign" the people aboard these vessels were may be open to debate. Sixteenth century maps of this area direct Iberian mariners to find pilots around Cape Flores, at the eastern end of the eponymous island. While pilots could be found locally at settlements along the Cape Flores shore, whether they were Sama remains unknown. Despite the long history of interactions involving mariners from Sulawesi in Timor, and the availability of boat pilots in eastern Flores since at least the sixteenth century, neither Dutch reports nor Iberian maps offer clues as to where "the domain of Papoek" might have been.

---

[87] Exceptions, touched on below, may be found in the work and notes of A. A. Cense and in William Cummings's edited translations.

[88] Cummings, trans. and ed., *The Makassar Annals*; and Cummings, trans. and ed., *A Chain of Kings*.

[89] Some scholars have written "papu," however, the correct Sama-language pronunciation of this title ends with a glottal stop, hence: "papuq."

[90] James J. Fox, "Notes on the Southern Voyages and Settlements of the Sama-Bajau," *BKI* 133, 4 (1977): 460.

[91] Ibid., 459–60.

For this, Fox drew on the work of Christian Pelras, according to whom *Papu* [*sic*] was the hereditary title of "'the sovereign of the Sama' whose seat, if one can employ that expression in speaking of someone who dwells at sea, was at the base of the Gulf of Boné, in the region of Luwu."[92] Pelras got the idea that the Luwu region of the Gulf of Bone was the "seat" of the Papuq from the stories told by his research subjects in Sulawesi. Prominent among them was a Sama family in Kambuno, an island in the Pulau Sembilan group off Sinjai, that claimed to have had a manuscript about the Sama past much like the *LB Lemobajo* manuscript discussed in the next chapter. The family turned out not to have such a manuscript, or at least did not reveal one. Instead, they had some familiarity with oral versions of the story at the beginning of *LB Lemobajo*, or from a related manuscript about the Sama past. Insofar as documents were concerned, this Sama family in Kambuno apparently possessed only a single-page testimonial from the Bugis queen of Boné, Fatimah Banri (r. 1871–95), which declared that whoever came to the aid of the person possessing it came to the aid of the ruler of Boné.[93]

In fact, the *LB Lemobajo* manuscript does state that the *papuq* and his daughter lived in Mangkuttu, which is, indeed, in the Luwu area of the Gulf of Boné. However, their emplacement near Luwu in this text has less to do with demonstrable historical fact and rather more to do with emplotment—with being able to tie them narratively to other, patently mythological, elements of the story. The historicity of the Luwu location for the "domain of Papoek" is therefore doubtful. Their association with this area is nevertheless an important element of the opening story, which establishes claims about precedence vis à vis other lineages and offers an interpretive frame for information in the sections that follow it.[94]

The term *papuq* only ever comes up in relation to Sama connected with Sulawesi or encountered on the opposing coasts of the surrounding region where the influence of its realms were felt. "*Papuq*" may well come from *papuwangeng*, a title that in Mandar was equivalent to *gellareng*, a lower title of rank given to vassals by more powerful south Sulawesi rulers.[95] The connection between the two terms is

---

[92] Ibid., 460 (Fox's translation); and Christian Pelras, "Notes sur Quelques Populations Aquatiques de L'Archipel Nusantarien," *Archipel* 3 (1972): 164–65.

[93] Pelras, "Notes sur Quelques Populations Aquatiques de L'Archipel Nusantarien," 153–54. Pelras's subjects in Kambuno, with whom I stayed more than thirty-five years later, also showed me this royal letter, joined now by an offprint of Pelras's article. The family descended from branches of the same prominent Sama family that had left Bajoé and settled in Tiworo and in Lemobajo (among other places in southeast and eastern Celebes) during the nineteenth and early twentieth centuries. The mother, Hajjah Kuaq, elderly when we met, was literate in Bugis, which she used to keep a ledger in her *kios* (sundries stand).

[94] On the importance of precedence and texts as a vehicle for identity, see Henk Schulte Nordholt, "The Invented Ancestor: Origin and Descent in Bali," in *Texts from the Islands: Oral and Written Traditions of Indonesia and the Malay World*, ed. Wolfgang Marschall (Bern: Institute for Ethnology, 1994), 245–64. On the importance of precedence as discourse and practice in Austronesian societies see, in Fox and Sather, eds., *Origins, Ancestry and Alliance*: James J. Fox, "Introduction" and "The transformation of Progenitor Lines of Origin: Patterns of Precedence in Eastern Indonesia," 1–17, 130–53; and Peter Bellwood, "Hierarchy, Founder Ideology and Austronesian Expansion," 18–40.

[95] B. F. Matthes, *Boegineesch-Hollandsch Woordenboek* (The Hague: Nijhoff, 1874), 149. *Papuwangeng* nominalizes the root *puwang*, an honorific term of address or reference in Bugis for "sovereign," "lord," "mistress," and the like. The noun is formed by adding the prefix *pa-* and the suffix *-eng* to *puwang*. If "*papuq*" is related to "*papuwangeng*," it seems the sort of abbreviation or alteration that only a nonnative speaker of Bugis would be likely to make. The

strongly suggested not only by the semantic overlap and the phonological similarity, but also by Mandar's strong association with the sea. The Mandar ethnic group inhabits the coastal strip around Majene point and the hilly areas above it along south Sulawesi's northwest coast. Like the Sama, Mandar people are regarded as having lifestyles related to maritime pursuits, primarily fishing. Unlike the Sama, though, the present-day Mandar are strongly identified with this one area and are not scattered throughout the region.

However, historically, Majene was not only associated with Mandar people. The town of Majene and nearby coasts on Majene point, which sit across from southeast Borneo, apparently had settlements of "Tidung" people in the sixteenth century. As mentioned in the previous chapter, the Talloq Chronicle notes that before Tumenanga ri Makkoayang became ruler of Talloq in the early 1540s, "he destroyed [the] Tidung below in Majene."[96] The Spanish used the term Tidung, or "Tidong," during the sixteenth and seventeenth centuries for especially fierce non-Muslim "pirates" in western Sulu and northeast Borneo. The term also appears in Makassar language poetry and in Sama oral histories, where it refers to maritime people who had high-ranking lineages. In other words, they had a class of *"karaeng."* The Tidung in this Makassar and Sama intertextual context were comparable, if not equivalent, to the Bajo or Sama. In the Borneo context, at times it appears that the Tidung were a distinct group, while at other times they appear to have interacted so closely with Sama people as to be indistinguishable, cooperating, along with other groups, to establish coastal polities together.[97] Although the Talloq Chronicle does not specify whether Tumenanga ri Makkoayang, after "destroying" them at Mandar, made any "Tidung" into *papuwangeng*, that is, into ranked vassals of Makassar, one would expect some relationship of vassalage or servitude for the survivors as a result of their defeat. This, at least, is what often occurred with land-based vassals.

Much of our understanding of the structure of south Sulawesi polities comes from tributary and domain lists. Such lists, dating from around the late-seventeenth century and after, are known for all the Bugis kingdoms, some of Makassar's, those of several Massenrempulu-speaking realms, and the Bugis-ruled kingdom of Luwuq. Each demonstrates an expression of the tributary tie and a list of settlements with this designation, and also indicates which domains or cluster of villages were, in contrast, supervised directly by a member of the center's ruling family or by a subordinate who reported to the polity's head. Whether already allied in confederations or not, each tributary named in particular tributary and domain lists remained an independent political unit ruled by its own paramount noble chosen

---

term *puwang*, moreover, is not restricted to Bugis, and its pronunciation varies among Bugis dialects and other area languages, reflecting its broad use. The Sama equivalent of Bugis *"puwang"* is *"puah."* As noted in chapter one, *"Puhawang"* is an old Austronesian term meaning "shipmaster." Personal communication, Pierre-Yves Manguin, July 17, 2015.

[96] Tumenanga ri Makkoayang ruled from 1540/3 to 1576. Cummings, trans. and ed., *A Chain of Kings*, 85, 93, 98, 110.

[97] It is possible that *"tidung"* was at times simply applied as another exonym for the Sama. Cummings, for instance, cites Rahim and Ridwan: "Tidung on the east coast of Borneo was known for its seafarers, who often voyaged to settle along the littorals of South Sulawesi. People from there were known as *turijeqneq* or *bayo.*" *Sejarah Kerajaan Tallo'* (*suatu transkripsi lontara'*) (Ujung Pandang: Lembaga Sejarah dan Antropologi, 1975), 30–31, cited in Cummings, trans. and ed., *A Chain of Kings*, 93 (note 19). *Turijéqnéq* and *bayo* are common Makassar-language exonyms for Sama. For further Tidung references, including linguistic studies, see Gaynor, "Piracy in the Offing," 847–48.

from among its own ruling family. Although they had substantial autonomy over governance, they were expected to participate in war when called upon, or face military reprisal. Tributaries defeated in war would often be forced to swear an oath renouncing their earlier tributary relationship and establishing a new one with the victor.[98]

Two matters about these tributary relationships stand out as relevant here. First, knowledge about who was tributary to whom was organized largely by place; and, second, they had relative independence to choose their leaders from among their own kin networks. Although alliances were maintained in practice through members of particular lineages, since knowledge about them as tributaries was structured by noting their locations, when tributaries shifted their allegiance, the lists reflected this by places dropping in or out of a list. In contrast, the switch in allegiance by people from Tiworo, discussed at the end of the next section, did not follow the logic of place in the same manner.

When people from Tiworo, which clearly had been allied with Makassar, shifted their allegiance to Boné after Tiworo's second defeat, this shift did not result in an occupation of Tiworo or a claim by Boné over its waters and shores. Rather, after Tiworo had been leveled and disbanded in 1667, dozens of prominent people from it were given rank in a special guard and they rearranged their loyalties to Boné and accompanied Arung Palakka. Hence, they shifted their allegiance after defeat, much as tributaries on the peninsula did. Yet, rather than take over Tiworo or claim tribute from someone in that place, this shift in allegiance resulted, as shown below, in relocations. While other powers later bickered over claims to Tiworo itself, Boné's connections with the Sama were maintained primarily through memorializing, in writing and historical memory, how the two were linked through lineage alliances, confirmation of status, and the conferral of rank. For this reason, and not because they supposedly followed Bugis traders, Sama in eastern Sulawesi claim a history of political ties with Boné, even in areas where Boné had no claims over land. In the nineteenth and early twentieth centuries, Sama descendants of these lineages carried manuscripts substantiating these connections with Boné, as well as memories about them and their renewal, in their migrations from Bajoé to southeast and eastern Sulawesi. The bestowal of rank and formation of kinship connections could, then, create strong ties between a more powerful realm like Makassar or Boné, and subordinate polities or lineage segments, without their organization into tributary "lands." Hinterseas may not appear in tributary or domain lists for just this reason.

However, the Sama paramount noble who bore the title *papuq* does appear in the *Makassar Annals*. To be mentioned in *The Makassar Annals* at all was a mark of social status and potential significance. One particularly telling detail, however, starkly reveals how Makassar's relations with the *papuq* and Sama resembled relations between powerful south Sulawesi centers of rule and their tributaries. Like the lineage elites in land-based tributaries, Sama people at the polity's center similarly

---

[98] See: Stephen C. Druce, *The Lands West of the Lakes: A History of the Ajattapareng Kingdoms of South Sulawesi 1200–1600 CE* (Leiden: KITLV Press, 2009), 26–29; and Rahila Omar, "The History of Boné A.D. 1775–1795: The Diary of Sultan Ahmad as-Salleh Syamsuddin," (PhD thesis, University of Hull, Centre for South-East Asian Studies, 2003). At times the leadership of tributaries was imposed from the center, as, for instance, by Gowa during the late sixteenth century (see Bulbeck, "New Perspectives on Early South Sulawesi History," 13).

had the relative independence to choose their leaders from among their own kin networks. Hence, we find that after the death of Papuq Daeng Numalo, on March 12, 1703, the *Makassar Annals* records that, on June 12, 1703, I Daeng Makkulle Ahmad was "installed as Papuq by his family." This remarkable line alerts us to the important point that he was not installed as *papuq* by any of Makassar's rulers or councils, but rather by "his family," in other words, his Sama kin. Even though the *papuq* and his kin interacted closely with Makassar's ruling family, and, as was common with tributaries, apparently became in-laws, they were still able to choose their own leader, the *papuq*.[99]

Papuq Daeng Numalo is also mentioned in other Makassar language manuscripts. For instance, he is referred to in an example that A. A. Cense offered to illustrate a kind of Bugis and Makassar historical writing that he described as "brief historical overviews" and sometimes simply called "notes." The example relates that when Karaeng Bontosunggu (1643–1726), wishes to know about the origins and history of the Turijéqnéq or Bajos,

> he turns to I A(m)bo(ng) [sic, i.e., Mboq], mother of the *papuq* (head of the Badjos) Daeng Numalo, who then tells him about the initial establishment of the people on the west coast of South Sulawesi, the emergence of their subjection to the prince of Gowa, and the rights acquired by a former *papuq* at the place called Pota on Sandao (Manggarai) [viz., Flores]. Since this statement about the Badjos in the manuscripts is usually preceded by a part about Gowa's intervention in Sandao, and, in the time of Karaeng Bontosunggu, expeditions to this part of the island of Flores occurred several times, the interest shown in the Badjos must be seen in relation to Gowa's political aspirations toward Manggarai [the region in which Sandao lay].[100]

---

[99] Cummings, trans. and ed., *The Makassar Annals*, 7, 176. Cummings explains that "*Papuq* was a title of the head of the Bajo community that traditionally had been loyal to the rulers of Gowa" (176, note 483). On "in-laws," see below.

[100] A. A. Cense, "Eenige aantekeningen over Makassars-Boeginese geschiedschrijving," BKI 107, 1 (1951): 50–51. In note 26 on page 51, Cense cites the source for this brief overview or historical note, "found, among other places, in Mak. en Bug. Hss. Ned. Bijbelgen. No. 17, 97–99 and No. 208, 62." Viz., *Makassaarsche en Boeginesche handschriften van het Nederlandsch Bijbelgenootschap*, Makassar and Bugis language manuscripts of the Netherlands Bible Society. For how the note typically precedes a section about Gowa's intervention in Sandao, he cites (in note 27 on page 51) Mak. en Bug. Hss. Ned. Bijbelgen., No. 17, 95–96 and No. 208, 61. In Cense's own archived notes, he describes the appearance of the same passage on page 12 of Hs 193 of the colonial Matthes Foundation (Matthes Stichting, hereafter MS). Most of Hs 193 was recorded in the period 1677–1709 (although some parts were copied from an earlier source). "Aantekeningen over de Badjo's" (unpublished), KITLV Or 545 18. My own notes indicate that this manuscript, MS Hs 193, was not in C. C. Macknight's 1973 list of the manuscripts remaining in Makassar (then called Ujung Pandang). Readers of the Bugis syllabary must often interpret written words in context to determine unrepresented sounds. Cense did not know that in Sama, /ᵠᵐboq/, written "Mboq" here, is a respectful term of reference or address for elderly Sama men and women. Not knowing this, when he read ᴧ𝅘𝅥ᴧ, representing /a/ + /bo/, he supplied letters in parentheses for the sounds he presumed "missing" in the Bugis transcription. He mistakenly arrived at the name "A(m)bo(ng)," instead of the common Sama-language honorific for elders, "Mboq."

The passage was likely set down between the 1660s and 1690s.[101] Papuq Daeng Numalo's mother, I Mboq, certainly witnessed a great deal during her own lifetime and could have conveyed details of Sama–Makassar relations during the sixteenth century from what she had heard from participants and eyewitnesses. She also may have gained such knowledge from reading early manuscripts, or from hearing others read them aloud. This appears possible in light of the fact that the brief historical overview discussed above is also found in another manuscript, Hs 193, some of whose details were taken from "the black leather-bound manuscript" of the prince Tumamenang ri Papambatuna (r. 1639–53).[102] Recopying was part of this manuscript tradition. I Mboq may even have read the manuscript herself, for although we know little about literacy in her time, we do know that, in the nineteenth century, some elite Bugis women were highly literate readers of South Sulawesi texts. Moreover, since manuscripts were important to the elite Makassar society in which she moved, it is possible that knowledge transmission could have gone from I Mboq reading to speaking with Karaeng Bontosunggu; that is, from a written mode to an oral one. Then, after consulting her on the history of Sama interactions with Gowa, the Karaeng himself, or someone else, set this information down in writing, moving knowledge from an oral interchange into manuscript.[103]

The fact that Karaeng Bontosunggu consulted I Mboq says a good deal about how he viewed her as a source of knowledge. These brief overviews were often based on information obtained from recognized experts in the field of history and *adat* (customary practice). According to Cense, in Makassar, certain people descended from the rulers were consulted as a kind of "oracle" or walking encyclopedia, such as the Talloq ruler Karaeng Tumamenang ri Agamana. Also known as Karaeng Matoaya (1573–1636; r. 1593–1623, advising his son Kareng Kanjilo to 1636), he is credited with uniting the diarchic rulership of Gowa and Talloq. Another fount of knowledge was his son, Karaeng Pattingalloang Tumamenang ri Bontobiraeng (1600–54; r. 1641–54), known in Holland for his great command of languages and his comprehensive interests, about which the Dutch poet Vondel wrote: "the whole world before long [became] too small for his brain." His son, Karaeng Bontosunggu Tumenanga ri Taenga (1643–1726), was also highly regarded as knowledgeable. He, in turn, apparently consulted with those he regarded as particularly well-informed, including I Mboq.[104] This rare example of an interaction between a Sama woman of rank, and an erudite royal son of Makassar, offers a fascinating glimpse into the interplay between written and oral modes of

---

[101] The date range is reckoned based on when Karaeng Bontosunggu would have been of an age to engage the *papuq*'s mother in such a conversation—he was born in 1643—and before Papu Daeng Numalo's death in 1703, as the reference to him apparently presumes he is still alive. Cummings, trans. and ed., *The Makassar Annals*, 176.

[102] Cense, "Eenige aantekeningen over Makassars-Boeginese geschiedscrijving," 50. I have conformed dates and the spelling of names (where available) with those in Cummings's *A Chain of Kings*.

[103] On the porosity of the oral–written divide in Sulawesi, see chapter four.

[104] Cense, "Eenige aantekeningen over Makassars-Boeginese geschiedscrijving," 50. Not to be confused with another Bontosunggu. See also Cummings, trans. and ed., *The Makassar Annals*, 74–75. On Matoaya and Pattingalloang, see Anthony Reid, "A Great Seventeenth Century Indonesian Family: Matoaya and Pattingalloang of Makassar," in Reid, *Charting the Shape of Early Modern Southeast Asia*, 126–54.

producing history in early modern Celebes. It also suggests the high regard in which Sama women of rank were held.

I Mboq's response to Karaeng Bontosunggu's inquiry suggests that the divisions acknowledged among Sama in the region had been at least provisionally tied to specific places: "As regards the groups in which the Badjos are divided, there is one group of Badjos from Katingang, one group of Badjos of Barasa', one group of Badjos from Sitawa (?) [sic] to the west of Barrang (!) [sic]." Notwithstanding Cense's own question and surprise, indicated by his parenthetical punctuation marks, I Mboq's response suggests that the Sama were organized into groups with ties to particular places, even if those places might, for various reasons, change.[105] More to the point, as Cense underscored, the passage and its placement in manuscripts implied a relation between Karaeng Bontosunggu's interest in the history of Gowa's subjection of Sama on Sulawesi's west coast, and Gowa's political and military aspirations in Flores.[106]

Barasaq, one place I Mboq mentioned as having a group of Sama, was, according to the Talloq Chronicle, twice conquered jointly by Tumamenang ri Makoayang (r. 1540/3–76) and the Gowa ruler Tunijalloq (r. 1565–90).[107] Apparently once was not sufficient. Yet, what is most striking about this is that it took place during a period of relative peace following Gowa's defeat of a number of realms in the south Sulawesi peninsula. In particular, Gowa's victory over the realms of Suppaq and Sawitto radically changed the balance of power along Sulawesi's west coast, paving the way for its dominance in the peninsula.[108] With Gowa's subjection of realms that littoral populations may previously have partnered with along the west coast, if Sama people were to remain in the area after defeat rather than flee, then it behooved those in Barasaq, as it would have the Tidung "destroyed below in

---

[105] It is also possible that I Mboq was invoking a version of the allied seven brothers in seven places, a common trope about west coast polities before their incorporation into Gowa, or within its network of alliances. William Cummings, *Making Blood White: Historical Transformations in Early Modern Makassar* (Honolulu: University of Hawai'i Press, 2002), 152–53.

[106] I Mboq's response was set down in Hs 193 and copied into Cense's notes, which stop there. MS Hs 193, 12, in A. A. Cense, "Notes on the Badjo's," KITLV, Or 545 18. "Barrang" probably refers to islands off the port of Makassar. There is a "Barasa" to the south of Makassar, as well as in Pangkajene to the north; the latter is the more likely reference. About "Sitawa," I am as stumped as Cense. The only "sitawa" I know of is "*sitawa sidingin,*" a medicinal plant, *Kallanchoe pinnata,* widely distributed, including in areas with Austronesian-speaking populations. "Katingang" here probably does not refer to the mouth of the Katingan River on Borneo's south coast—it is remarkably well protected by an isthmus, an ideal anchorage, but the name is also mentioned among other Sulawesi names in the Chronicle of Gowa as a place conquered by Gowa's ninth ruler, Tumaparisiq Kallona (r. 1510 or 1511 to 1546). On the subject of writing, the latter was also said to be the ruler who made written laws and written declarations of war. Moreover, "The *sabannaraq* of this *karaeng* was Daeng Pamatteq—he was *sabannaraq,* he was *tumailalang,* he made Makassarese manuscripts." *Tumailalang* was a title for a minister who acted as a go-between; see: Cummings, trans. and ed., *A Chain of Kings,* 32, 107, 109; *Makassar Annals,* 233; Cummings, *Making Blood White,* 42, 216 (note 17). It is noteworthy that the *sabannaraq* wrote Makassar-language manuscripts. This shows that the *sabannaraq,* or at least this early one, was literate. As some *sabannaraq* were Sama, this increases the likelihood of literacy in their households, including among elite Sama women.

[107] Cummings, trans. and ed., *A Chain of Kings,* 85.

[108] Druce, *Lands West of the Lakes,* 241–45.

Mandar" by this same Tumamenang ri Makoayang, to form new alliances with Makassar's overlords. As subordinate allies, their valuable nautical skills and numbers would then enable Makassar to push out from the peninsula to gain allies and subordinates across the waters.

Precisely this sort of capacity became part of the "portfolio" of Makassar's *sabannaraq*. Papuq I Daeng Makkulle Ahmad, chosen "by his kin" in 1703 to succeed Papuq Daeng Numalo, was then also installed in 1710 as Makassar's *sabannaraq*, replacing I Daeng Buraqne in that post. A Makassar insider, *The Makassar Annals* record the death of Daeng Makkulle Ahmad's grandparent in 1710 at the ripe age of 102 (an *mboq*, and perhaps the I Mboq mentioned above), as well as the births of his children and a few major events in their lives. For instance, his daughter, I Saenaq, married Daeng Manassaq on March 14, 1721, and the birth of a daughter from this marriage in 1722 was also noted. He wielded considerable power, sharing the prerogative to punish transgressors—for instance, in 1712 Papuq Daeng Makkulle Ahmad ordered someone confined to his house, and a week later this same person "was ordered brought east to Sandao" (actually south across the Flores Sea). He also led military expeditions. Two months after I Saenaq married Daeng Manassaq, "I Daeng Manassaq and I Papuq went over to Sandao, sent to advance against Toring [on Flores]." The following year, this son-in-law jointly led another expedition to Sandao with a different commander.[109] Expeditions against Sandao show that Makassar's defeat in the seventeenth century did not keep it from launching military expeditions well into the eighteenth century, and that the Sama allied with Makassar continued to play a role in them.[110]

Given the relative independence that the *papuq*'s kin had in choosing their leader, and the fact that the important position of harbormaster was at times filled by someone Sama, as well as the military leadership that such figures clearly

---

[109] Cummings, trans. and ed., *Makassar Annals*, 196, 198, 203, 204, 233, 234, 236, 237.

[110] Both in the time of Karaeng Bontosunggu (who died in 1726) and afterward, Sandao was targeted by Makassar, and at times became a place of exile from Makassar. With regard to Sandao, the *Makassar Annals* (ibid.) record: a failed expedition in 1693 (164, note 445); an expedition to make war on Sandao in 1699 (169); a joint expedition with the people of Boné to sail to the east to make war on Sandao in 1704 (179; a cooperative venture that raises more questions than it answers, for example, did it include Sama contingents based in Bajoé? Was it authorized by Boné's rulers?); an individual "ordered brought east to Sandao" in 1712 (204); the death of someone "across on Sandao" in 1718 (222); a relative of the writer arriving from exile in Sandao in 1720 (232); in 1721, "I Daeng Manassaq and I Papuq went over to Sandao, sent to advance against Toring [on Flores]" (233); in that same year (1721), Daeng Manassaq married I Saenaq, a child of the Papuq (233), hence they went to Sandao as father and son-in-law (Daeng Manassaq returned later that year); in 1722, again "war leaders sailed eastward to Sandao to make war, Karaeng Batupute was commander with I Daeng Manassaq" (237); in 1723, Karaeng Batupute landed, arriving from Sandao, and he warred and conquered Toring and Wangka [on Flores] (238); in 1729, Sandao also appears as a place to which one might go when circumstances on the peninsula leave one feeling unwelcome (262); in 1730, "the [royal] banners were smeared with blood as people [warriors] went over to Sandao" (265); in 1730, Karaeng Bontomajannang sailed with Karaeng Bontotannga over to Sandao to make war (266); in 1731, Karaeng Bontomajannang arrived from Sandao and conquered Poma [on Flores] (268); and on August 25, 1749, Karaeng Mannyiori, [Karaeng] Balloq, Papuq Daeng Manggappa, Daeng Maqruppa, and a wife of Daeng Malliongang arrived from Sandao (301, note 756). This is apparently the same Daeng Manggappa who was also a *sabannaraq*. At times there were simultaneously two *sabannaraq*, e.g., in 1644 and in 1735. Cummings notes that it is not clear whether they had different duties or were responsible for different communities (63, note 141; 278).

provided, one must at least ask the question, who was the *papuq*, the leader of the Sama, leading, if not Sama people? In view of the jointly led expeditions and the fact that they involved naval contingents, it is reasonable to conclude that some of these naval forces were made up of Sama people.

*The Makassar Annals* explicitly mention three people who held the title of *papuq*. In addition to Daeng Numalo and Daeng Makkulle Ahmad (discussed above), there was Daeng Manggappa, born in 1688, also known as "Mommiq." Like Daeng Makkulle Ahmad, Papuq Daeng Manggappa had served as Makassar's *sabannaraq*. Although the writer of the *Annals* is usually unknown, one section is known to have been written by Karaeng Lempangang, a noble, and later ruler, of Talloq. He used "grandparent," probably as a way to express the respect in which he held Daeng Manggappa, when he noted in 1731, the death of "I Dandung, a wife of my grandparent I Daeng Manggappa."[111] Other figures in *The Makassar Annals* may have been Sama, but these three are the only ones specified as having been the *papuq*.

One *sabannaraq* who almost certainly was Sama, but is not mentioned along with the title of *papuq*, was I Daeng Makkulle, presumably the father of I Daeng Makkulle Ahmad.[112] Installed as *sabannaraq* in 1661, the *Annals* also record I Daeng Makkulle's marriage and the birth of a child, showing that he, too, was part of the inner circle of Makassar's ruling families.[113] Shortly after his installation as *sabannaraq* he would have played a large role in fortifying Makassar's coastal defenses. As discussed in the previous section, by the end of 1661 there had still been no progress in implementing the treaty between the VOC and Makassar's representative over the incidents of the previous year, namely, the murder of those sent out to investigate the Dutch boat that ran aground on an offshore island, and the VOC's taking the fort at Paqnakkukang. Instead of treaty implementation, the commissioner sent by the VOC to investigate its progress found instead that Makassar's harbor region was being fortified, large quantities of gunpowder were being put by, and even more defenses were being erected. Moreover, twelve- to fifteen-hundred boats in different areas were said to be in a state of readiness, a concern for the VOC, yet also a precaution against a rumored offensive by an alliance among the Bugis, Buton, and Ternate.[114]

As with later *sabannaraq* (and particularly his son), this Daeng Makkulle took part in leading military expeditions across the waters. In April 1666 he returned home after two months on a mission to Buton, where he went after accompanying the fleet sent by Makassar to the Sula islands to force them to accept Gowa's suzerainty. In addition, the fleets went to Banggai and Tobungku on Sulawesi's east coast.[115] One expects that Daeng Makkulle passed through Tiworo with the fleet

---

[111] Cummings, trans. and ed., *Makassar Annals*, 156, 211 (note 558), 268 (note 669), 301 (note 756). Cummings notes that this was probably but not necessarily the same Daeng Manggappa as the *sabannaraq*.

[112] "Presumably his father" and "presumably the son and successor" according to Cummings. Ibid., 139 (note 358), 176, 196. This first Daeng Makkulle was apparently also called "I Daeng Makkulle I Mappaq" (234).

[113] Ibid., 91, 122, 126.

[114] L. Andaya, *The Heritage of Arung Palakka*, 60.

[115] Ibid., 65; "Report of Commissioner van Wesenhagen on mission to Makassar and Ternate," VOC 1257, 511.

from Makassar, as did Makassar's expeditions to the eastern archipelago in the previous decade, when Tiworo served as a vital ally and naval staging area.[116]

Makassar cultivated connections with maritime-oriented people in noncontiguous littoral zones, which allowed it to draw on their unique skills and to make strategic use of littoral and maritime geography for the purposes of trade and to support its interests in "overseas" conflicts. Yet, in addition to its important ties with these hinterseas, prominent Sama people moved in Makassar's inner circle. Linked to the heart of Makassar's politics by ties of kinship, rank, and office, they nevertheless chose their own leaders to be *papuq* from among the kin of Sama lineage elites. They undoubtedly also had Sama relatives scattered in other littoral locations. Sama figures who became Makassar's *sabannaraq* were responsible not only for matters in the port, but also led nautical endeavors across the waters.

The vital nautical roles played by Sama people so tightly connected with Makassar's center would have mattered to Tiworo. Tiworo could, theoretically, have become the object of punitive expeditions, or, to the benefit of its own trade and prestige, it could support Makassar's endeavors, as well as those of Sama people who were likely linked to its own elite kin networks. Makassar's ties with Tiworo would only have been made more reliable, strengthened by its recognition of prominent Sama people and the nautical power that they bore on behalf of, and along with, Makassar. Until, that is, the combined forces of the VOC and Arung Palakka persuaded people from Tiworo to relinquish and remake its ties.

## THE VOC RETURNS TO TIWORO

Makassar's campaign to reassert its claims in the eastern archipelago provided the VOC with a justification for defending its allies and protecting its economic interests. Eventually the company also became resigned to the fact that future hostilities with Makassar were unavoidable. On November 2, 1666, the Council of the Indies in Batavia resolved to send an expedition to Makassar and the Eastern Quarters (i.e., the Sula Islands, Buru, the Moluccas, Ambon, Banda—basically everything east of south Celebes) to demonstrate how quickly they could be in war-readiness and to announce the war to the Makassar people. They made Cornelis Speelman "Superintendent, Admiral, Commander, and Commissioner to the Eastern Quarters." Nevertheless, sober reassessment of the situation led the Council of the Indies on November 23 to instruct Admiral Speelman to be prepared to receive messengers from Gowa asking for peace, as the council hoped to avoid extremes, if that were possible. The council expressly forbade Speelman from landing at or attacking the well-defended port city of Makassar, which they regarded as too hazardous an undertaking. However, they were not averse to a bombardment of Makassar from the water. Speelman's position of command gave him a chance to redeem his name, which had been sullied by his suspension from VOC service some years earlier in Coromandel for engaging in private trading. The desire to vindicate himself may have propelled Speelman to "reinterpret" his instructions, as Leonard Andaya diplomatically put it, and launch an all-out war against Gowa. Arung

---

[116] The *sabannaraq* Daeng Makkule also distinguished himself in battle on land: "Goa's successful campaigns in the interior were a marked contrast to the difficulties it faced against Arung Palakka and the Dutch in the west. The Makassar forces under Syahbandar Daeng Makkulle, joined by a thousand men from Wajo and Lamuru, marched through Soppeng burning as they went …" L. Andaya, *The Heritage of Arung Palakka*, 126.

Palakka similarly had a personal axe to grind, as victory would restore his self-respect and honor—his *siriq*—so burdened by the Gowa overlords of Makassar. The two of them, in other words, may have been itching to prove themselves.[117]

To situate events in Tiworo in relation to the rest of the Makassar War, one has to back up chronologically to when the combined fleet of the VOC and its allies assembled under Admiral Speelman and Arung Palakka at Buton. Admiral Speelman and the rest of the VOC fleet had been scattered farther east to load and unload goods, including slaves. The VOC forces came together again with the rest of the combined fleet in June 1667 at Buton, whose forces had also been prepared. The Sultan of Ternate joined them as well, and additional men were sent from Tidore and Batchan. In the months before their departure, "that nasty pirates' nest, Tiworo," was "mostly purged" by the Bugis under Arung Palakka, with the assistance of some Dutchmen under Captain Lieutenant David Steijger.[118] Two days before the Dutch contingent headed across the Gulf of Boné, the men under Arung Palakka set off from Tiworo and nearby Kabaena, where they had been sent to gather bamboo—probably for use as weapons. During the fleet's passage across the gulf, the many Bugis, Butonese, and Ternatans aboard *prauw* and *kora-kora* met with storms and got separated from the rest. As a result, only the VOC's troops, with the Tidorese, Batchans, and Ternatans who had been accepted into the company's own militia and had therefore been divided among its ships, came together again at Bantheyn (Bantaeng). The Sultan of Ternate, with four sloops and nineteen *kora-kora*, met up with Speelman, while Arung Palakka, whose temporary disappearance caused no small amount of hand-wringing, eventually rejoined them. Ultimately, in November 1667, Gowa signed the Treaty of Bungaya. However, even this was not quite the end, as the VOC's declared position was that the treaty was subsequently violated and a land campaign was carried out to enforce it. Finally, the Makassar stronghold of Sombaopu was "taken by pure violence of fire and sword on 24 June 1669."[119] Tiworo, then, had been taken care of by a detachment even before the fleets sallied forth en masse toward Makassar in June of 1667.

---

[117] Ibid., 68–70, 74; F. W. Stapel, *Cornelis Jansz. Speelman* (The Hague: Martinus Nijhoff, 1936), 32–36; 196–198, 214–16.

[118] Speelman, "Notitie," VOC 1276, 684v. Speelman neglects to mention that many had fled Tiworo in February, forewarned about the impending arrival of VOC forces by Daeng Mangaga, whom they were chasing. Nor does Speelman mention the escape in May by the Raja of Tiworo, discussed below.

[119] Ibid., 684r–685v. Steijger expressly asked for the command to deal with Tiworo. In addition to spices, slaves were also gathered by the VOC ships before Ambon and Banda: "In respect to aforementioned slaves, it was deemed correct to recommend that the women, amongst whom quite a few nice ones were spotted, in first rendition could very well be sold and we can be sure that the Chinese also would be eager for others and would give quite a lot for them." "Letter from Speelman to Joan Maetsuijker and the Council of the Indies," 18 August 1667, VOC 1264, book 3, 44v. On the Bugis troops "from Tiworo" landing at Pattiro, three to nine miles east of Boné, and soon rallying thirty thousand Bugis men, see "Speelman to Maetsuijker and the Council," 56r. Given the outcome of things at Tiworo, discussed below, these Bugis troops coming from Tiworo would have included sixty Tiworo men handpicked by Arung Palakka. On the Bugis fleet setting off from Kabaena and the hand-wringing over Arung Palakka's temporary disappearance in the storm, see L. Andaya, *The Heritage of Arung Palakka*, 81–83; H. MacLeod, "De onderwerping van Makassar door Speelman, 1666–1669," *De Indische Gids* (1900), 1275–77. Speelman sent Poolman out to look for Arung Palakka in the Gulf of Boné, and eventually found that he had made land at Kassi (in Bulukumba). He had started a march independently from Pattiro (Boné), but then

At first, the VOC seemed once again extraordinarily lucky to be able to take Tiworo without a fight. Near the end of January 1667, word got around that a fair number of VOC boats had been "hauled in" in the Straits of Buton, in other words, it was rumored that VOC boats had been waylaid there. On January 29 and February 2, the VOC sent some men out to investigate, and they returned with two of Makassar's boats. In addition to fifty-three men, women, and children from Buton, the VOC detained thirty-one men who reported that they had been sent off with part of the Makassar fleet under Daeng Mangaga to pillage the outer coast of Buton, where they seized booty that included some twelve- to thirteen-hundred people. Seven days earlier, this sixty-boat squadron under Daeng Mangaga lay midway in the Straits of Pantsiano (viz., of Tiworo), still unaware of the VOC's advance. Daeng Mangaga was thinking of moving his ships back to Buton, but Lohia, reporting on the situation with the Dutch, warned him against such a move. At this point, the Makassar squadron turned around and with all of its might headed west to retire to Tiworo. However, two Makassar ships—the ones eventually detained by the VOC men sent to investigate—had some problems en route at night and lost their way. Come daylight they then mistook the enemy's ships for their own and fell into the hands of the VOC and its allies. Speelman sent the Buton people to their king, and, in addition to the guns found on the two ships, he gave the Makassars over to the Bugis and Butonese, who "helped them exit their lives."[120]

In order that this Makassar squadron not slip out of the hands of the VOC and its allies, Arung Palakka was urged to go around the south side of the island (Muna) and to approach Tiworo from the west end of the Straits. He was instructed to find out whether the enemy had sought refuge in the river there and to "sniff out" the salt marshes of the Pantsiano (or Tiworo) Straits. While he did this, other VOC boats were sent to crisscross the Buton Straits and to take up positions before Wowoni, blocking egress to the east and north. From their positions there, near the eastern end of the Tiworo Straits, the VOC boats were to await news from Palakka and his group. The latter's boats suffered considerable difficulties due to low tides and slow winds—much to the amusement of the locals, who apparently followed them. When Palakka and his group reported back on February 12, it turned out that, after all their searching, Daeng Mangaga's ships were found neither off the coast by Wowoni and "the waterplace" (where at least the winds were better), nor, once they finally reached it, in the river at Tiworo.[121]

In Tiworo's fortress they also found no occupation or resistance, just a couple of infirm old ladies, from whom they learned that, a few days before, the Makassars had, indeed, entered the river there, but that Daeng Mangaga had only come with two or three light vessels. Apparently, while the rest of his ships continued to fall back westward from the Tiworo Straits with the VOC and Arung Palakka bent on pursuit, Daeng Mangaga diverted from his withdrawal, and with a few quick, light boats he entered the river to alert Tiworo's people of the VOC advance, just as Lohia had warned him. After that almost everybody sailed off, including the ruler of

---

Speelman unexpectedly met up with him and Poolman by boat, and, having in July already taken some actions at Bantaeng, they landed troops on August 1 to take Makassar (MacLeod, "De onderwerping," 1275–79). For an excellent piece on the land campaign, see F. David Bulbeck, "The Landscape of the Makassar War" *Canberra Anthropology* 13, 1 (1990): 78–99.

[120] "Speelman to Maetsuijker and the Council," VOC 1264, 45r–45v.

[121] Ibid., 45v.

Tiworo with his family, and those who remained, whether high-born or commoner, had fled into the hills.[122]

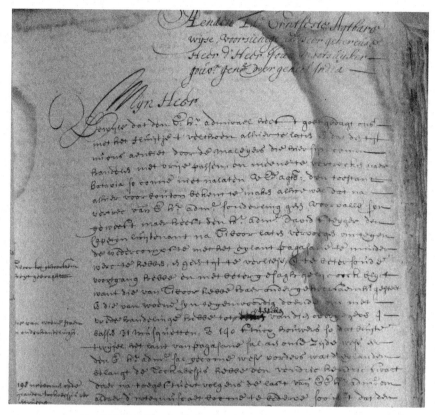

Jan Hendrichz ten Haege, Seles Pietersz ten Zuijderstont in the ship
*The Pheasant* ('t Velthoen), April 16, 1667
(source: National Archives of the Netherlands, VOC 1264, p. 28r):

[Marginalia] *Tiboor tot gehoorsaem-
heyt gebracht* [Tiworo brought to subservience]

To the noble, esteemed,
wise, foreseeing and very generous
Lord, Sir Joan Maetsuijker—
Governor-General of all of India—

My Lord,

As it pleased the Noble Lord Admiral [Speelman] to leave us here with the ship The Pheasant, the time offers us, courtesy of the Malays (*Maleijers*) who have come here to do commerce with free passes and are about to leave for Batavia, so could (we) not neglect to acquaint your Lordship with the situation here before Buton, even though, oddly enough, no events have occurred, but the Admiral, not to lose any time and to have better progress, sent ahead the Captain Lieutenant David Steijger to Tiworo in order to have less work upon his return to the island of Pangesane, and with more authority as it also appears, for those of Tiworo have been put under obedience, and those of Muna (*Woena*) are currently busy negotiating... Pangesane will be on our side before the Lord Admiral will have come, what is more, the deputy officer Hendric Swart was sent over to the Tukangbesi Islands (*de Tochabesjis*) in order to damage the nutmeg trees, spoiling 204 old and 456 young ones and placing Wanci under the authority of the admiralty of their statuory ruler, the king of Buton.

---

[122] Ibid., 46r. Flight, clearly an option in the 1660s, as it remained in the 1950s.

This was how Tiworo initially fell into the hands of Arung Palakka, who, finding some food stored in the fortress and in the village, left the better part of his men inside the "occupied territory" to receive orders from the VOC regarding what he should do next. Speelman sent a resolution on February 13 that they try to keep Tiworo in their hands by sending all of Palakka's power to Tiworo except for thirty ships, which, the plan was, would "infest Pantsiano from the east side," to purge the straits of Makassar's men.[123]

To calm the people of Tiworo, Speelman wanted to work toward having Arung Palakka and his men retreat, while issuing special directions to David Steijger to become, in effect, a kind of local governor. To this end, Steijger expressed his willingness to defer the position of captain lieutenant, with the provision that he handle the various tasks on Tiworo and that he may, on occasion, have command over other tasks in Buton, as well as "govern the site of the Pantsiano Straits," inspect the lands more thoroughly and deeply, and make a correct map, or chart, to serve the company.[124]

On February 27, Arung Palakka arrived at Buton from Tiworo, and wound up bringing along all but a few of the Bugis ships with him. Although both the Bugis and Butonese were allies of the VOC, there had previously been scant friendship between them. One nameless representative of Buton declared he neither trusted Boné nor liked Arung Palakka, who, he said, the kings of Tiworo and Buton and Muna would agree, would do better to mind his own business and not get mixed up in the affairs of others. Shortly thereafter Arung Palakka left Buton with his people and, following a brief expedition to the Tukangbesi islands, departed on March 10 with his orders from the admiral's ship, the *Velthoen*, plus a sergeant, ten soldiers, and two masters, to take over the watch in the fortress at Tiworo. He left only ten boats to guard Buton.[125]

This was, undoubtedly, a great relief to both the king of Buton as well as the Dutch, since, if Arung Palakka and the King of Buton reached an accord, the VOC would not have to contemplate any action to intervene between them. The King of Buton insisted that two or three Dutch ships come to stay nearby and wanted the *Velthoen* itself to be visible. He had been worried about the newly arrived Bugis, and he also had concerns that, in the absence of the VOC fleet, either new ships might be sent from Makassar, or Daeng Mangaga might return with his sixty boats to try to occupy Buton, to "impart evil on him" again. This worry was not assuaged by the fact that "on Pantsiano, the enemy, primarily the Tiworese, does not subjugate himself," a concern the VOC shared with its allies, who viewed the Tiworo ruler as thus too risky. Such fears led Buton to hope for a Dutch return—that is, after their expedition to Makassar—"in order to have less work to guard the islanders adequately."[126]

Six days after Arung Palakka returned to Tiworo from Buton, on March 17, Steijger arrived in Tiworo with ships and supporters, and found its ruler in his fortress in a wooded area on elevated ground situated six miles from Tiworo's settlement.[127] On March 23, Commander van Voorst came to assure Arung Palakka

123 Ibid.
124 Ibid., 47v.
125 Ibid., 51r.
126 Ibid., 45r.
127 Ibid., 51v–52r.

that Daeng Mangaga would only be capable of mobilizing a few of his sixty vessels, since his squadron had been in a fight and many of the boats fled in different directions without heeding their commander. He himself had reportedly reached Makassar. This, therefore, eliminated any real threat that Daeng Mangaga might return to Tiworo with a substantial force.[128] Now it would be easier to put pressure on Tiworo's ruler.

While Arung Palakka was in Buton, the *raja* of Tiworo sent a delegate, who, despite delays, communicated Tiworo's inclination to subjugate itself to the VOC—if it could be done by the delegate. Then, as he communicated, the *raja* would expect the follow-up of a messenger sent to call on him, and he would agree in person, on receipt of a gift of two krisses, fifteen machetes, and fifteen spears.[129] However, when the *raja* held back with various excuses not to have his subjects disarm, on April 18, "a considerable troop" of Bugis men, assisted by ten Dutchmen, marched on the walls of the fortress and occupied them, disarming about one hundred men. Steijger recommended that the *raja* do the same with his entourage, that is, disarm them, but the *raja* deemed it unnecessary. In what ensued, many took flight, and although some "lost their heads" (literally), the majority escaped.[130]

The pursuers, namely, "his Highness," meaning Arung Palakka, with three thousand Bugis, and accompanied by ten Dutchmen and twenty Dutch soldiers, pushed forward until under the fortress named Ollenbaca, thinking to overrun it. However, he was stopped: easily one hundred of his men were injured by stone-throwing, a few by spears, and himself with an arrow. One Dutchman was killed and two wounded, and, were it not for the presence of the Dutch, Arung Palakka might have been killed. "After this shock he trembled," wrote Speelman in his letter to the governor-general. It is not entirely clear whether he trembled from physical shock after being struck by an arrow, or from his close brush with death. Had Arung Palakka been killed in Tiworo, it would surely have changed the course of the Makassar War.[131]

Steijger advised against attacking with grenades, which some of the men had begun to prepare, and instead recommended that they approach the fortress, and issue orders under threat of opening fire. There was some talk of a treaty, and then twenty-eight people came out, surrendering very few arms, and swearing submission of eternal obedience to the VOC. However, at the neighboring fortress of Lapadacca, this truce was apparently disregarded, as the very same day, "without listening to anything," a Bugis was stuck (i.e., impaled) high on its walls. Over the course of the following days, Tiworo reentered the accord. Yet, entirely against what had been intended, they were left with their possessions—in other words, they were not disarmed. "Captain Lieutenant Steijger reproached him"—that is, reproached Arung Palakka—for allowing them to keep their arms. The latter replied, "It could go wrong for us in Makassar, and here we still have a safe retreat. If we killed the

---

[128] Ibid., 51v.

[129] *"Hasegai,"* or assegai, is a light wooden spear or javelin pointed with iron. The term is of African origin.

[130] "Speelman to Maetsuijker and the Council," 51v–52r. According to Dirk Geirnaert, a lexicographer at the INL–Treasury of the Dutch language, the figurative meaning of "lost their heads" is not found in Dutch before the nineteenth century. Personal communication to Martijna Briggs and forwarded to the author, June 13, 2014.

[131] "Speelman to Maetsuijker and the Council," 52r.

people, who would grow our food, for from the Butonese we can expect nothing, they do not trust the Bugis, and this is now the Company's land, as we tried to be the Company's own and just subjects."[132]

Arung Palakka was thinking strategically about Tiworo's possibilities as a safe haven to retreat to should things go poorly in Makassar. It could provision food. Its naval capacities also had not escaped his notice. One need only be reminded of how the locals followed his boats, for amusement, while his own mariners struggled against slow winds and low tides, to understand why this would be important. Arung Palakka's comment to Steijger shows how well he grasped the fact that access to such resources, skills, and benefits relied on good relations with the people in Tiworo.

His view of Tiworo as a place of potential retreat, and therefore as a potential ally, offers an explanation for why the Raja of Tiworo and his men had been allowed to keep most of their arms after being pursued to the Tiworo fort of Ollenbacca, and why those who surrendered at the neighboring fort of Lapadacca had also been allowed to keep their arms. It seems that, in addition to trying to convince Steijger of the need for a fallback position, Arung Palakka may have been engineering a future quid pro quo, a return of the favor, from Tiworo.

Is it possible that Arung Palakka had been thinking along such a strategic vein long before, on his flight in late 1660 (or early 1661), when he was a less threatening Bugis noble on the run from Makassar to exile in Buton? Given how lousy his relations were with Buton's ruler, one wonders where in Buton he could have stayed. A line in *The Makassar Annals*, clearly interpolated later, after he gained authority in Makassar, stated that "Tunisombaya," that is, Arung Palakka, had journeyed "from Campalagi [in Boné] east to Buton."[133] Tiworo lay along the shorter of two possible routes from Boné to Buton, so it is likely that he passed through Tiworo. Did his entourage back then, which must have had nautical skills and would have been helped by a knack for clandestine travel, include Sama people, with whom one might expect to stop among the settlements of the straits? Could he have laid the groundwork for future relations even then?[134] In 1667, before departing Buton for Makassar with the VOC, Arung Palakka first made a side trip in the opposite direction, to the Tukangbesi islands. The sources are not clear on why, but he may well have been shoring up support among local mariners, with whom he may have had contact earlier in the decade while apparently in Buton. In any case, negotiations with the Tiworo *raja* in 1667 show him to be working rather hard to convince his Dutch ally to compromise, rather than on getting concessions from Tiworo.

For the time being, the *raja* of Tiworo was detained in the fort, along with "the goegoegoe." This would seem to be Ternate's *jogugu*, a kind of prime minister second only to the ruler, whose own authority in Ternate had been weakened, apparently because he was fired from his post. On May 19, after Steijger left for Buton as ordered by Commander van Voorst, the detainees were released, with Arung

---

[132] Ibid., 52r.

[133] Cummings, trans. and ed., *The Makassar Annals*, 90.

[134] It is hard to resist drawing the parallel with the previous era's Paramesvara in the western archipelago, and his entourage of sea people, first taking refuge at Temasik (now Singapore), before settling at Malacca. The reader may recall that his entourage included maritime people, his protectors, whom he later ennobled.

Palakka's approval, so that they could wash themselves. This took place without an adequate guard and thus they escaped. His Highness (Palakka) followed with one thousand men, but, unable to catch the Tiworo *raja*, Palakka had to be satisfied with a promise from the *raja* of Woona (Muna) that he would soon conquer the Tiworo *raja*, dead or alive.[135] The *raja* of Tiworo escaped, then, on the pretext of needing to bathe.[136]

Subjecting Tiworo had been Arung Palakka's task. He did not deny that carelessness on his part during Steijger's absence resulted in the escapes. Yet he also insisted that the escapees remained hidden partly out of fear of the Ternate ruler, and that, had it not been for Buton's interference, he would have recaptured them with the *raja* of Muna's help. Arung Palakka's complaint about Buton's interference referred to the actions of Buton's *capita laut*, the commander of its modest naval force. It took several warnings by the Dutch Lieutenant Jan van Haerlem (aka "Te Hage") before the *capita laut* pulled back on May 17, when Muna (*Woona*) appeared more inclined to subjugate itself to the Dutch than to Buton. Arung Palakka was not the only one to complain about the actions of Buton's *capita laut*. On May 29, Arung Palakka and Steijger received a declaration of Tiworo's willingness to put itself in a position of obedience to the company and surrender all its guns, *if only the Butonese were ordered to let them pass in that direction*. In other words, Tiworo wanted the VOC to command Buton to let Tiworo's ships pass eastward. The envoy was summarily sent off with an escort, while Buton's *capita laut* was admonished not to cause further discord among the VOC, Buton, and the Bugis.[137]

Tiworo clearly maintained an interest in preserving the mobility of its mariners to regions east of Buton. For his part, Arung Palakka would have taken note that Buton could not automatically rely on Dutch support. At the same time, Tiworo's own position remained somewhat ambiguous. Arung Palakka may well have sought ways to edge aside Buton's incipient inroads on Tiworo. Indeed, few were willing to swallow the king of Buton's claims about the division of authority on Pantsiano (now "Muna Island"). Although Buton's king professed to have the "upper powers," or overlordship, over Muna and Lohia, Speelman noted that Muna (the polity, not the whole island) was more inclined to admit Dutch authority over itself than to recognize Buton's claims. The Buton king's relationship with Tiworo was even more tenuous. After all, Makassar and Ternate previously each maintained claims to

---

[135] "Speelman to Maetsuijker and the Council," 52r. On the weakening of the Ternate *jogugu*'s authority, see L. Andaya, *The World of Maluku*, 168; on Ternate's "*gugugu*" fired, see "Speelman to Maetsuijker and the Council," 53v–54r.

[136] This showed that he was clever, not a coward. Speelman's *Notitie* mentions that Aru Mabiring, "honored by the Raja of Buton to this name" (meaning the latter bestowed it on him), was ordered to embark on a boat with the "Tiworese King of Wawouw," who murdered him and his followers, six people strong, and again returned home. Speelman, "Notitie," book 4, 717v–718r. Since the Tiworo ruler's name is nowhere else mentioned, and "Wawouw" might refer to a place name (though not one current in Tiworo), it is hard to be certain whether this was the name of the same Raja of Tiworo, mentioned above, who escaped; or, perhaps a Raja of some nearby area called "Wawouw." Both examples illustrate instances of escape from enemies by a Tiworo ruler. In either case, as we will see in chapter five, one does not want to get into a boat with strong men unless one is sure of their friendship.

[137] "Speelman to Maetsuijker and the Council," 52v, 53v, my emphasis. In nineteenth century copies of Bugis manuscripts, Arung Palakka is portrayed as having conquered Tiworo. See Nederlands Bijbelgenootschap Collection, University Library, University of Leiden, NB 181, part 9, 156–59, and NB 182, 74.

Tiworo. Muna purportedly wished to put off recognizing Buton's claims until Tiworo and Lohia might join it. This move was intended to strengthen Tiworo's hand, and Muna's own position. As for Tiworo, it never submitted to Buton, either before or after the attack on Makassar.[138]

If Makassar should lose when confronted by the combined forces, Tiworo might face the prospect of Buton trying to press the issue, asserting its claims vis à vis Ternate. In such a scenario, expressing fealty to the Dutch might be a better option, if something else could not be figured out. Arung Palakka knew the contours of these power dynamics intimately. He understood that Tiworo wished to stave off claims of overlordship both by Buton and by Ternate, at whose hand it had suffered severely in 1655. Arung Palakka, with his own eye on the future, was likely to bear such considerations in mind when dealing with the Tiworo *raja* on behalf of Steijger and the VOC.

Before departing for Makassar across the Gulf of Boné, Speelman drew up the contract or treaty with Buton, following discussions between Sultan Mandarsyah of Ternate and Buton's king. The sultan of Ternate made the claim that all the kings of Pantsiano (meaning those of Tiworo, Muna, and Lohia), of Tollensusu (viz., Kalisusu—the northern regions of the island of Buton), and Tambuco (Tobungku, along Celebes' east coast) were his subjects. This claim, it is worth pointing out, concerned hierarchies of human relations rather than territories per se. The king of Buton did not dispute Tiworo, yet also would not agree with the rest. Speelman, when he had heard enough, stopped the discussion without much protest from either side, and drew up the treaty, which he seemed pleased effectively tied Buton not only to the VOC but also closer to Ternate.[139]

As the VOC's various ships arrived in Buton from the east, Captain Poolman was sent to Tiworo to evaluate the situation there before the fleets' departure to Makassar. Everyone agreed that it was high time that the company's ships as well as Buton's vessels get organized for a procession, in order to have everything ready for the combined fleet's impending departure. As a consequence of this order, the captain tore down most of the overgrown fortress in Tiworo, and Arung Palakka set fire to the village, leaving on June 2 with all the people. The land of Pantsiano did not, according to Steijger, produce all that much food, and although it was rich in timber, the wood was difficult to harvest. The arms captured and goods acquired on Tiworo included hundreds of "Tambuco swords," 60 machetes, 450 spears, 230 muskets, and 12 *krisses*, as well as 140 slaves, some cash, rice, and obligations signed by the King of Buton.[140]

The people of Tiworo, said Speelman, "disloyal, treacherous, evil-minded people who lived off kidnapping, strange as can be are now once and for all stripped of their prauws." This was the pot calling the kettle black, considering that in the previous conflict the VOC did not show itself to be averse to capturing people, and its

---

[138] "Speelman to Maetsuijker and the Council," 52r–52v, 53v.

[139] Ibid., 54r. In 1677, Ternate relinquished the greater part of Pantsiano to Buton: "Only the small realm of Tibore, to the north of Pantsiano, remained under Ternate." *Daghregister van Batavia*, 1677, 235–36, In "CCCLXXXII. Molukken-Boeton. 11 Mei 1677," *BKI* 91, 1 (1934, Documenten): 54–55. With the removal in 1682 of Kaitsjili Sibori (Prins Amsterdam, viz., Sultan Mandarsyah's son) to Batavia, the king of Buton thereby made use of the opportunity to make himself master of Tiworo. Ligtvoet, "Beschrijving en Geschiedenis van Boeton," 66–68.

[140] "Speelman to Maetsuijker and the Council," 52v–53r, 54v–55r.

amassed ships had just returned from the eastern archipelago, where they loaded disparate "goods," including slaves. Tiworo was thoroughly divested of its boats, a turn of events seen ("strange as can be") as a bit of a marvel. They were brought to Buton, floated there to Arung Palakka over several shipments, "with the description: all of which your Lordship [the governor-general] may not hinder."[141] In other words, Tiworo was stripped of all its boats, but Arung Palakka was not about to hand them over to the company. Why the boats he retained from Tiworo had to be "floated" to him, rather than sailed or rowed, in "several shipments," is not specified. Yet it suggests that Arung Palakka was short of skilled mariners. Having gone to such trouble to preserve these vessels, one wonders who he got to captain and crew them.

The answer may lie, in part, with what happened to Tiworo's men. Before taking off to do battle in south Sulawesi, Arung Palakka put together a "Guard of Prime Commanders," with sixty of his bonded men and sixty handpicked men from Tiworo. He armed them with, among other things, 120 guns.[142] So Arung Palakka not only integrated these sixty handpicked men into his forces, but also gave them prominent positions. His earlier leniency may have paid off, helping to gain their loyalty. Their shift of allegiance, following defeat, was not unusual for the course of conflicts in Sulawesi.[143] In the wider picture, looking at the Great Ambon War and the Makassar War together makes it possible to grasp the dynamics of archipelagic interactions in each, and how the allegiance of superior mariners was not a resource to be squandered.

---

[141] Ibid., p 52v–53r, 54v–55r.

[142] Ibid., 55r.

[143] See discussion of tributaries in the section "Sama at the Center," above. See also: Druce, *Lands West of the Lakes*, 21–22, 26-29; and Omar, *The History of Boné A.D. 1775–1795*.

# CHAPTER FOUR

# SAMA TIES TO BONÉ
# AND NARRATIVE INCORPORATION

Although Admiral Cornelis Speelman vilified Tiworo as "a nasty pirates' nest," the actions of his ally Arung Palakka, who integrated sixty men from Tiworo into a special "Guard of Prime Commanders," reflected a different attitude. Arung Palakka may have set fire to Tiworo's main settlement and then fled with all the people. However, because he gave positions of rank, as well as weapons, to those sixty men, their female kin were not distributed as spoils, as they had been in 1655. To do so would have invited retaliation from people he had just armed. On the contrary, unmarried female kin of these men were more likely to become candidates for negotiated marriages with Bugis men. Such marriages would not only expand the number of Arung Palakka's followers, but also recognize their status claims and cement their loyalties. Marriages would strengthen the commitment of each mariner to Boné, as something each shared with his kin and, potentially, passed on to future generations.

VOC sources do not mention any such unions. However, evidence of marital and other political connections between generations of Boné and Sama "noble" lineages can be found in two rare Bugis-language manuscripts about the Sama past.[1] This chapter analyzes some of the important features of these manuscripts, which, on the one hand, sit squarely within the traditions of south Sulawesi writing about the past. They are part of the large corpus of primarily Bugis and Makassar language *lontaraq* manuscript writing that emerged from a tradition of inscribing palm leaves, bound together not in booklets as elsewhere in the region, but rather sewn end to end and wound in reels.[2] On the other hand, Bugis-language manuscripts about the Sama past incorporate and adapt a Sama story with many variations in different parts of the archipelago. Rather than address collective origins, these stories form a class of narratives built around the structure of a high-status Sama woman's maritime relocation and her arrival among ethnic others. Invariably the child of a Sama ruler or chief, in versions from Sulawesi she appears as the daughter of a *papuq*.

The adaptation of this Sama narrative to Bugis *lontaraq* manuscripts was part of the colonial transformation. Although the Dutch had nothing to do with this adaptation directly, it was a consequence of the defeat of Makassar and Tiworo by the VOC and its allies. Before its defeat in the second conflict, Tiworo had been allied with Makassar. The Makassar War did not eradicate the role of Sama people in

---

[1] "High-status," "elite," and "noble" are used interchangeably here. In the archipelagic context, rulers were paramount nobles.

[2] The origin of "*lontaraq*" is debated. See Andi Zainal Abidin, "Notes on the Lontara' as Historical Sources," trans. The Editors, *Indonesia* 12 (October 1971): 161–63.

relation to the port.[3] However, the war not only caused Tiworo to disband, but also drove a substantial contingent of its people over to Boné. This new political relationship and the expansion of Bajoé, Boné's harbor and littoral settlement zone, occasioned the conditions for addressing Sama relations with Boné in Bugis-language manuscripts.[4] Amidst interethnically shared practices of oral and written narrative production, the reformulated Sama narrative became part of a story in a cluster of contested traditions about the past, and about lineages. How the narrative was transformed in the Bugis-language context offers insights on the social and political world in which the Sama participated. This story about a *papuq*'s daughter and her coming to live among others got reinscribed and adapted anew in an early twentieth century Dutch rendition that both built on earlier changes, yet also reflected the late-colonial circumstances of the *pax Neerlandica*. This was a time when serious nautical threats had been eliminated and the Sama could safely be viewed as quaintly exotic sea nomads.

While Bugis-language *lontaraq* about the Sama past addressed a history in which the Sama had lineal and political ties to Makassar, they placed primary emphasis on a legacy of Sama ties with Boné. This record of links with Boné sits in relation to the initial story containing the adapted Sama narrative, which establishes the interpretive frame for subsequent parts of the manuscript. Claims to genealogical precedence form an important component of this frame. In effect, these claims concern which lineages had "inherent" reason to be highly regarded, and which were the progenitors of certain famous figures. When Sama people who inherited these manuscripts carried them in flight eastward from south Sulawesi in later years, they became part of a portable past.[5] These writings recorded the periodic renewal or recommitment of Sama ties with Boné, both from Bajoé and, through it, from explicitly mentioned scattered coastal locations in southeast and eastern Sulawesi. Like most *lontaraq*, they order information for the most part sequentially according to the reigns of particular rulers.[6] Yet, they are shot through with the importance of lineages, and for this reason they are genealogical rather than structured territorially—that is, by a logic that orders things according to connections with places on land. The land-based kingdoms of south Sulawesi tended to trace their bilateral genealogies in a manner that deemphasized Sama lineages, making the latter, in anthropological terms, "submerged."[7] However, what in that context may

---

[3] The "muscles and sinews" of Makassar, Sama people continued to carry on military expeditions for Makassar and to serve as harbormasters for its ports. See the section "Maritime People" in the Introduction, and the eighteenth-century campaigns described in the previous chapter's section on "Sama at the Center."

[4] On Bajoé's establishment and impressive growth noted in the early eighteenth century, see "Maritime People" in the Introduction.

[5] The phrase "a portable past" comes from a remark once made by Janet Hoskins about these manuscripts, which I gratefully acknowledge.

[6] Abidin, "Notes on the Lontara as Historical Sources," 164.

[7] Discussed in "Sama at the Center," in the previous chapter, *The Makassar Annals* give evidence that the lineage of the *papuq* was intermarried with Makassar "royalty." On the politics of Gowa's genealogical ties to the ruling lineages from other parts of the south Sulawesi peninsula, see Bulbeck, "The Politics of Marriage and the Marriage of Politics in Gowa." The author thanks an anonymous Wenner-Gren reviewer for mentioning the rarely discussed but useful concept of submerged lineages. The Sama, like most (but not all) groups in the region, reckon kinship bilaterally (through both parents). This holds especially for the central archipelago up through the Philippines. However, in practice, for a variety of reasons,

be submerged, these manuscripts instead emphasize, underscoring descent from a Sama lineage, in particular a Sama matriline. A genealogical past, carried across the waters, these manuscripts incorporate the seas and reveal the connections of an intertidal history.

## LONTARAQ MANUSCRIPTS

Bugis and Makassar *lontaraq* manuscripts include a variety of different kinds of texts: mythological and legendary traditions; brief historical overviews or fragments from oral histories; heroic poems about historical events; short poems and riddles; treaties, law codes, and tributary and domain lists; court annals and diaries; as well as some chronicles.[8] One of the greatest differences between Bugis and Makassar written and oral traditions is that the Bugis *La Galigo* "epic," reckoned by some to be the world's longest, is unknown in the Makassar traditions.[9]

The *La Galigo* cycle begins with the origins of the Bugis people, but its main hero is the mythical Sawerigading, while his son, La Galigo, also a great sea captain, is the cycle's namesake. If all the episodes were taken together, the *La Galigo* would be about one and a half times the length of the Indian *Mahabarata*. Transmitted in manuscripts, each usually contains only one or two episodes. There is no "complete" *La Galigo* anywhere, and it appears unlikely that there ever was. Unique in its use of a strict pentasyllabic meter, the *La Galigo* also uses many words and phrases absent from everyday spoken Bugis, but known in poetic works and in the liturgical songs of the *bissu*, transvestite ritual specialists at the former courts of the Bugis.[10] Variations of *La Galigo* are widely distributed among different people in the region, some of whom claim Sawerigading (under different names) as a culture hero of their own. Versions are known in central Sulawesi, southeast Sulawesi, and Gorontalo (north Sulawesi), as well as in the Malay peninsula and Riau islands of the western archipelago, where the Bugis played a prominent role during the eighteenth century.[11]

Although the Makassar tradition does not have anything that quite compares, it does share notions of mythical genealogical beginnings from a "white-blooded" person who "came down" (Mak. *tumanurung*, Bug. *tomanurung*), usually taken to mean from the heavens.[12] The *tumanurung*'s marriage with Gowa's other apical ancestor, Karaeng Bayo, who appeared from the sea, produced rulers who inherited this white blood. Ideologies of white blood underwrote claims to rule in south Sulawesi from at least the sixteenth century and acquired greater authority when

---

people may emphasize one or another line of descent.

[8] Some of the items in this list are mentioned by Druce, *The Lands West of the Lakes*, 5–6.

[9] Cummings, *Making Blood White*, 42.

[10] Sirtjo Koolhof, "The Sleeping Giant: Dynamics of a Bugis Epic (South Sulawesi, Indonesia)," in *Epic Adventures: Heroic Narrative in the Oral Performance Traditions of Four Continents*, ed. Jan Jansen and Henk J. Maier (Munster: LIT, 2004), 99, 106.

[11] Andi Zainal Abidin, trans. and adapted by C. C. Macknight, "The I La Galigo Epic Cycle of South Celebes and Its Diffusion," *Indonesia* 17 (October 1974): 160–69.

[12] However, see Daeng Mangemba's comment in the previous chapter, in the section "Sama at the Center."

incorporated into written chronicles (Bug. *attoriolong*, Mak. *patturioloang*, Mandar *pattodioloang*), such as Makassar's chronicles of Gowa.[13]

The term translated as "chronicle" literally means "about the people of former times," or "that which is about the ancestors." As often happens, the translation misses the mark, since these chronicles encompass a wide range of texts of an historical nature. For the most part, they contain genealogies and fragments of narratives about a ruling family or kingdoms' origins. Yet they may also include stories about war, treaties among two or more kingdoms, agreements between a kingdom and a tributary, stories that set out a border, and, sometimes, they include tributary and domain lists.[14] Since they focus on a particular lineage and the stories pertinent to it, south Sulawesi chronicles may be grouped among a wider regional category of literary-historical writing known as "genealogical narratives."[15]

Noted for their matter-of-fact and often quite reliable historical character, chronicles from Sulawesi have a relatively unembellished style that, compared with other somewhat similar forms of writing elsewhere in the region, employ fewer elements of the fantastic.[16] Even so, they can be hard to pin down chronologically. One of the two manuscripts considered here contains an accompanying paratextual note about when and by whom it was recopied, but, like most South Sulawesi manuscripts, neither one indicates a date of composition for the work, nor assigns the work itself a name, nor identifies authorial responsibility for it.[17] Frequent use of titles, and in some cases pseudonyms instead of personal names, compounds the difficulty of determining when and where manuscripts were inscribed. Beyond such issues of inscription and nomenclature, at the level of textual reproduction, Bugis *lontaraq* manuscripts generally belong to a tradition of copying and intergenerational transmission. Hence, texts often exist in more than one version, and dating them can present insurmountable challenges, which can sometimes be overcome by pinning their composition, or recomposition, to, or after, particular events through oblique references in the text.[18] However, almost nothing is known from direct

---

[13] Cummings, *Making Blood White*, 100–104.

[14] Druce, *The Lands West of the Lakes*, 65; *The Makassar Annals*, 350.

[15] C. C. Macknight, "The Concept of a 'Work' In Bugis Manuscripts," *Review of Indonesian and Malaysian Affairs* 18 (1984), 103–14; C. C. Macknight, "Notes on the Chronicle of Boné," in *Living through Histories: Culture, History and Social Life in South Sulawesi* ed. Kathryn Robinson and Mukhlis Paeni (Canberra: ANU's Dept. of Anthropology, Research School of Pacific and Asian Studies; and National Archives of Indonesia, 1998), 45–55; C. C. Macknight, "South Sulawesi Chronicles and their Possible Models," in *Vasco da Gama and the Linking of Europe and Asia*, ed. A. R. Disney and E. Booth (New York: Oxford University Press, 2000), 322–32. Here, Macknight discusses Sulawesi's (court) chronicles as squaring with A. Teeuw's category of genealogical narratives. A. Teeuw, "Indonesia as a 'Field of Literary Study': A Case Study— Genealogical Narrative Texts as an Indonesian Literary Genre," in *Unity in Diversity: Indonesia as a Field of Anthropological Study*, ed. P. E. de Josselin de Jong (Dordrecht: Foris Publications, 1984), 38–62; Abidin, "Notes on the Lontara' as Historical Sources," 159–72.

[16] Macknight, "The Concept of a 'Work'"; Noorduyn, "Origins of South Celebes Historical Writing," in *An Introduction to Indonesian Historiography*, ed. Soedjatmoko, 140–41; Abidin, "Notes on the Lontara' as Historical Sources," 165–67; and Cense, "Eenige aantekeningen over Makassaars-Boeginese geschiedschrijving," 42–60.

[17] Macknight, "South Sulawesi Chronicles and their Possible Models," 324; see also Macknight, "The Concept of a 'Work.'"

[18] Macknight discusses one way to figure the timing of their composition by just after the last reign discussed. See: Macknight, "Notes on the Chronicle of Boné," 48, 50–51; and "South Sulawesi Chronicles and their Possible Models," 324. However, recopying can take place in

evidence about the concrete circumstances in which manuscripts were actually written and reinscribed. In the process of recopying *lontaraq*, people sometimes added interlineal or marginal notes, or made simple additions to or omissions from a text, resulting in considerable variation. Variation also resulted from the porous boundaries between oral and written transmission.[19]

Writing in Sulawesi appears to have developed initially to set down the genealogies of the ruling elite, beginning about 1400 among the Bugis in the eastern half of the peninsula.[20] There is little evidence to suggest that written texts of a historical nature played much of a role in Sulawesi before the seventeenth century.[21] During that century in Makassar, however, the influence of texts was thoroughly transformative.[22] While social stratification preceded the use of writing in Sulawesi, writing institutionalized the power of genealogical hierarchies. It is clear that the use of writing expanded dramatically among the elite during the seventeenth century. One is tempted to think that literacy must have been restricted to elites, but how broad a class this was and at what times is impossible to say. Against such presumptions about writing's limited extent stand well-informed statements about the "radically manuscript oriented" cultures of the south Sulawesi peninsula, especially the Bugis.[23]

Statements about "radically manuscript oriented" cultures only hint at the great variability in how people from different walks of life engaged with manuscripts, creating histories of practice in which written texts and oral modes of knowledge built off each other through readings and references. As elsewhere in the archipelago, oral modalities and written texts shaped each other, circulating in shared traditions whose forms were pushed and prodded by social structures, ideological investments, and historical contexts.[24] Part of what made oral versions

---

different locales, or by different people who may not be court scribes, and these people may also add to a "work" or add sections to parts of codices. This generally accords with Macknight's explanation of the Chronicle of Boné, for instance, as not a single narrative, but rather a series of accounts of successive reigns; see Macknight, "Notes on the Chronicle of Boné," 48.

[19] On the porosity of the oral-written divide in Bugis literature, see: Christian Pelras, "L'oral et l'écrit dans la tradition Bugis," *Asie du Sud-Est et le Monde Insulindien* 10 (1979): 271–97; Sirtjo Koolhof, "The 'La Galigo': A Bugis Encyclopedia and its Growth," *BKI* 155, 3 (1999), 362–87; Roger Tol, "Een Haan in Oorlog: Toloqna Arung Labuaja, Een Twintigste-Eeuws Buginees Heldendicht," *VKI* 141 (Dordrecht: Foris Publications, 1990): 2–3; Druce, *The Lands West of the Lakes*, 40–56, 72–80, 249–50; on Makassar: William Cummings, "Rethinking the Imbrication of Orality and Literacy: Historical Discourse in Early Modern Makassar," *Journal of Asian Studies* 62, 2 (2003): 531–51; Ian Caldwell, "Form Criticism and Its Application to Bugis Historical Texts," in *Language and Text in the Austronesian World: Essays in Honor of Ulo Sirk*," ed. Y. A. Lander and A. K. Ogloblin (München: Limcom Europa, 2008), 301–12; Sirtjo Koolhof, "*Sureq* versus *lontaraq*. The Great Divide?" in *Language and Text in the Austronesian World: Essays in Honor of Ulo Sirk*," ed. Lander and Ogloblin, 327–33.

[20] Ian Caldwell, "South Sulawesi AD 1300–1600; Ten Bugis Texts" (doctoral thesis, Australian National University, 1988); and Macknight and Caldwell, "Variation in Bugis Manuscripts"; and Druce, *The Lands West of the Lakes*, 56–66.

[21] Druce, *The Lands West of the Lake*, 250.

[22] Cummings, *Making Blood White*.

[23] Koolhof, "The 'La Galigo,'" 363.

[24] Kenneth M. George, "Felling a Song with a New Ax: Writing and the Reshaping of Ritual Song Performance in Upland Sulawesi," *Journal of American Folklore* 103, 407 (1990): 19; Cummings, "Rethinking the Imbrication of Orality and Literacy," 534; Kenneth M. George,

important lay in what a spoken or sung representation might provide where literacy was not widespread. It could broaden an audience, create a public effect, and make it possible to propagate a message.[25] Yet, while many types of writing in south Sulawesi are commonly known in oral versions, this holds more for some types of writing than for others.

Not all texts appear likely to have lent themselves to oral rendition. Certain characteristics of some texts suggest that they were meant to be read, versus spoken or performed, such as the annals (or as they are sometimes called, diaries) of Sulawesi's courts and nobles. As Druce argues, the terse and matter-of-fact style of the chronicles, which have few characteristics of texts associated with oral performance, suggests they were also primarily meant to be read, or would have demanded major transformations by a performer if they were to entertain an audience.[26]

Remarks echoing earlier scholars about the matter-of-fact and unembellished style of Sulawesi annals and chronicles suggest that such texts did not traverse the interchange between writing and oral modes with ease. Yet such statements speak as much to the matter of orality as they do to the question of whether such *lontaraq* contained mythological materials. How much chronicles convey the factual as opposed to the fantastic has, of course, been a primary concern of historians. Noorduyn, for example, writes: "The Bugis and Makassar chronicles ... reveal tendencies quite the opposite to the ones in Java. Their writers have clearly tried to disassociate themselves from the mythological and legendary elements that they had to include because they found them in their sources."[27]

Bugis chronicles nevertheless commonly contain in their opening sections the *tomanurung* myth and portions of, or references to, the *La Galigo* epic. The narration sometimes makes it clear that the chronicles' authors or scribes disavowed any responsibility for the veracity of the *tomanurung* material, the "tale of the first kings," yet they still included that content.[28] The gist of such remarks in the narration shares the basic approach that historians take to *lontaraq*. Most historians view the opening stories in such works as myth and largely disregard them, although they commonly acknowledge that elements of the supernatural justify the assumption of rule or the social status of elite lineages.[29] For many in Sulawesi, however, the stories at the beginning of such chronicles—often portions of *La Galigo*—are much like those about the hero Odysseus in Greek mythology. Not only do both have narrative episodes that revolve around a seafaring protagonist, but references to

---

*Showing Signs of Violence: The Cultural Politics of a Twentieth Century Headhunting Ritual* (Berkeley, Los Angeles, and London: University of California Press, 1996); Laurie J. Sears, *Shadows of Empire: Colonial Discourse and Javanese Tales* (Durham and London: Duke University Press, 1996); Laurie J. Sears and Joyce Burkhalter Flueckiger, "Introduction," in *Boundaries of the Text: Epic Performances in South and Southeast Asia*, ed. Laurie J. Sears and Joyce Burkhalter Flueckiger (Ann Arbor: Center for South and Southeast Asian Studies, University of Michigan, 1991); and Amin Sweeney, *A Full Hearing: Orality and Literacy in the Malay World* (Berkeley: University of California Press, 1987).

[25] Macknight, "Notes on the Chronicle of Boné," 46.

[26] Druce, *The Lands West of the Lake*, 250.

[27] Noorduyn, "Origins of South Celebes Historical Writing," 138; on "businesslike-ness," see Cense, "Eenige aantekeningen over Makassaars-Boeginese geschiedschrijving."

[28] Abidin, "Notes on the Lontara' as Historical Sources," 166.

[29] Macknight "Notes on the Chronicle of Boné," 48.

these stories appear ahead of textual matter regarded as non-mythical. Moreover, with both, some episodes are well known among popular and scholarly audiences, they remain vitally important as cultural heritage, and they are often viewed themselves in some sense as historical.[30] Few Sama people in Sulawesi actually owned *lontaraq* and could read them. Yet, quite a few had a little familiarity with the contents of the two Bugis-language manuscripts discussed here. Invariably, if people knew anything, they were familiar with the beginning story about a Sama woman, the daughter of a *papuq*, relocated by sea, or a short Makassar-language poem usually quoted or referenced in that story.[31]

## PROVENANCE AND TRAJECTORIES OF *LONTARAQ* ABOUT THE SAMA PAST

This chapter's primary concern is how this Sama narrative changed in its adaptation to *lontaraq*, and why. Yet before delving into how it transformed in the Bugis-language context, it may be helpful to know a bit about the production and circulation of these two manuscripts. The two *lontaraq* have quite different recopying histories. One is lodged in the archives of the KITLV.[32] The other was kept by its owners in the village of Lemobajo, at Lasolo Bay, north of Kendari on Sulawesi's east coast. I refer to the latter as *Lontaraq Bajo Lemobajo*, or "LB Lemobajo," in order to specify both the focus of its content and where it came from, although Lemobajo is not where it was inscribed.

The history of the distribution and circulation of these manuscripts both clarifies their import in the present and provides clues to the social relations they were part of in the past. As with other Bugis-language manuscripts, these are obviously known in more than one version, and there were rumors of three other untraceable "sibling" manuscripts of *LB Lemobajo*. Also, like other Bugis manuscripts, the contents of *lontaraq* about the Sama past are known in oral version as well. However, unlike other Bugis manuscripts, the Sama-focused contents of these *lontaraq* do not appear in the rest of the Bugis corpus, and, moreover, according to Muhamad Salim, their oral versions are basically unknown among Bugis people. After gaining familiarity with *LB Lemobajo*, Salim, whose work was central to a major project to microfilm and catalog both privately and publicly held manuscripts in South Sulawesi, emphasized that he had never before heard of, nor read, what the manuscript conveyed about Sama people.[33] Salim had very broad knowledge of the Bugis corpus, and his observations deserve serious consideration.

---

[30] Sirtjo Koolhof, "The *La Galigo* as Bugis History," in *The Indonesia Reader*, ed. Tineke Hellwig and Eric Tagliacozzo (Durham: Duke University Press, 2009), 115–20; and Koolhof, "The 'La Galigo': A Bugis Encyclopedia and Its Growth," 362–87.

[31] This pattern of familiarity through oral versions was the case during my own fieldwork as well as for other researchers. For example, see Horst H. Liebner, "Four Oral Versions of a Story about the Origin of the Bajo People of Southern Selayar," in *Living through Histories*, ed. Robinson and Paeni, 107–33.

[32] A. Djamali, copyist, "Geschiedenis van de Badjo's van Zuid Celebes" (History of the Bajos of South Celebes), KITLV, Or 545/262, March 7, 1940 (previously number 260 in the Matthes Foundation catalog).

[33] Muhamad Salim, personal communication, July 22, 1998. Salim added that he had been unaware that the Bajo had *bangsawan*, in other words, that they had a class of people with "noble" or "royal" lineages.

Lontaraq Bajo Lemobajo, photographed in 1990 by the author

His remark underscored that, although the contents are set in a context strongly marked culturally and geographically by Makassar and especially Bugis reference points, they have been reproduced by and passed on through communities of Sama people, both via inherited manuscripts as well as orally. Transmission has taken place primarily among people who reckon their descent through the Sama lineage with which the contents are connected. In particular, knowledge of the story about the maritime relocation of the *papuq*'s daughter was shared even among those who only traced Sama descent from one side, and regardless of whether they themselves could speak, or read, some Bugis. This female figure in the framing story at the manuscripts' beginning is a putative Sama ancestor, and its message about her own position and her progeny's has remained relevant to subsequent generations. Hence, the result is the story's reproduction and dispersion among an audience primarily of descendants of this Sama lineage.

Written in a practiced and consistent hand, the KITLV manuscript has a cover sheet stating that it is a copy of a manuscript from Kolonodale, a town on Central Sulawesi's east coast. This fifty-six page copy was made in Makassar by A. Djamali, and completed on March 7, 1940, for the colonial Matthes Foundation (*Matthes Stichting*).[34] The Matthes Foundation was named after B. F. Matthes, who was sent

---

[34] The designation "Or" marks the KITLV archive's Cense collection. A. A. Cense was a twentieth century Dutch colonial scholar of, among other things, Sulawesi. Or 545/263 is an eighty-page typescript Indonesian translation of Or 545/262. Lodged with Or 545/263 (and, curiously, not with the one in Bugis) is a letter of authority and testimonial for the *lolo* Bajo from the ruler and council (*hadat*) of Boné, with a hand-drawn rendition of the seal of the Boné ruler that says (in Arabic): "Sultan Ahmad al-Salih Syamsuddin, may God immortalize his realm and dominion [of] Boné." This sultan reigned from 1757 to 1812. Annabel Teh Gallop and Bernard Arps, *Golden Letters: Writing Traditions of Indonesia* (London: The British

by the Netherlands Bible Society (*Nederlandsch Bijbelgenootschap*) to Makassar in 1848, and who laid a most impressive foundation for the study of the languages and literatures of South Sulawesi. The Matthes Foundation was the colonial precursor to Indonesia's Institute of South and Southeast Sulawesi Culture (*Yayasan Kebudayaan Sulawesi Selatan dan Tenggara*).[35] Comparison of the manuscript holdings listed in the catalogs for collections in Indonesia and the Netherlands suggest that this manuscript was probably moved to the Netherlands shortly after World War Two.[36] The copy that A. Djamali made in Makassar in 1940 was based on an "original" brought there from Kolonodale, in Tomori (or Tolo) Bay. Numerous Sama villages dot the bay, as well as areas up the North Bungku coast at Tokala Bawah and Kolo Bawah.[37] Presumably, the manuscript belonged to someone from the Sama lineage who had migrated to the Kolonodale area from Bajoé, or who had inherited the *lontaraq* from a relative who had come from there.[38]

Locally prominent families in many parts of south Sulawesi possess chronicles that document important events in the history of their lineage, diaries of events covering varying periods of time, or anthologies containing information and transcriptions from assorted other manuscripts—all of which fall into the category of *lontaraq*. Written by one generation and bequeathed to the next, which may recopy and add to it, events recorded might address more than purely local matters. *Lontaraq* are therefore appealing documents for historians, who want to draw comparatively on numerous *lontaraq* from a range of places to write the history of a given area.[39] Although a laudable goal, it can be frustrated by the challenges of dating these documents, as well as by the difficulty of connecting decontextualized bits of information that mark passages in a life, or in the prestige of the lineage, to other events.

Still, historians can make use of *lontaraq* in other ways, by understanding changes in them at the level of the text, and situating those changes within their historical context, including the paths they traced on journeys with those who carried them from one place to another, and how they were transformed along the way. Rather than gather a collection of texts in an area to investigate a place, one may instead follow textual itineraries. First, one may examine how narrative

---

Library; and Jakarta: Yayasan Lontar, 1991), 108–9. Many thanks to Annabel Teh Gallop for helping to identify and translate the central portion of the seal. The fact that the page with the testimonial is also translated and contains a hand-drawn seal suggests that there may have been a Bugis-language page with the original seal along with Or 545/262, or, perhaps, a copy in Bugis of a page with a hand-drawn seal. The seal suggests that portions of the *lontaraq* were inscribed during his reign.

[35] On his life and work, see, inter alia, H. Van den Brink, *Dr. Benjamin Frederik Matthes, zijn leven en arbeid in dienst van het Nederlandsch Bijbelgenootschap* (Amsterdam: Nederlandsch Bijbelgenootscap, 1943).

[36] Cense brought other manuscripts originally from Sulawesi to the Netherlands in 1948. See Roger Tol, "A Royal Collection of Bugis Manuscripts," *BKI* 149, 3 (1993): 613.

[37] Tokala Bawah and Kolo Bawah were visited by the author in 2011, and the many Sama villages in Tolo Bay were noted then. Beyond Bungku Utara, in the Banggai islands and Tomini Bay, are many more Sama communities.

[38] Attempts to trace the "original" or any similar manuscripts in the Kolonodale-Kolo Bawah-Tolo Bay area in 2011 turned up some very interesting "dead ends," but dead ends nonetheless.

[39] Abidin, "Notes on the Lontara' as Historical Sources," 167. More people claim to have *lontaraq* than can back up such claims.

components move from one discursive context to another—a process of entextualization—to become part of different kinds of literary or historical production. Second, one may also follow textual itineraries at the level of physical texts, tracing how objects moved through time and space, as well as how they were withheld from circulation, both of which reveal information about their significance, social relations, and history.

Who produced *LB Lemobajo*, and the circumstances under which it was written, are matters left unaddressed in the text—as is the case with most *lontaraq*. However, a forensic assessment of *LB Lemobajo*'s paper, along with certain features of the content, support a date for its production in the late-nineteenth or possibly the early twentieth century.[40] A dating in the late-nineteenth century, however, only indicates roughly when this particular manuscript may have been copied or inscribed. It says nothing about when materials in it may originally have been composed or set down. Like many other *lontaraq* containing more than one text, and more than one genre, or type, of writing (as previously explained), this manuscript or codex comprises different kinds of texts.[41] About half of this manuscript's three-hundred-odd pages are narrative and much of the rest consists of materials related to Sufi or "mystical" Islam, including diagrams and calligraphic designs that have astrological and divinatory intent. These *kutika*, as they are called, are beyond the scope of this study. However, it is worth emphasizing that people would not have continued to reproduce such materials had there been no interest in doing so.[42]

While both *LB Lemobajo* and OR 545/262 clearly draw connections with Boné and bear some relation to its chronicle, the aim here is not to enumerate those claimed connections in each "work." Instead, by examining such manuscripts about the Sama past in relation to the wider context of south Sulawesi manuscript production, and then analyzing this crucial story at the beginning and a few other choice portions, we may gain from these Southeast Asian source materials a better sense of what, from their point of view, was significant in the historical contexts that generated them and in which they circulated. The story of the highborn Sama woman who, after a passage at sea, winds up at Gowa and marries into royalty there, only takes up, in the longer version, the first fifteen pages of the manuscript. What makes this story so important is not only how it adapts a narrative from Sama oral traditions, but also that in its adaptation to the Bugis-language context, it sets an

---

[40] Russell Jones kindly offered his professional forensic estimation of two fragments of paper from *LB Lemobajo*, to which he gave a probable date in the latter half of the nineteenth century. Other evidence for its dating, in relation to migration histories of the owners, is discussed below.

[41] Tol, "A Royal Collection of Bugis Manuscripts," 618; and Macknight, "The Concept of a 'Work' in Bugis Manuscripts," 103–14.

[42] See Macknight, "The Concept of a 'Work' in Bugis Manuscripts." Some pages of the manuscript were too critter-eaten to read, a few were entirely missing. Kenneth George notes in his review of *Living through Histories* that Kathryn Robinson's refreshing discussion of such astrological and divinatory lontaraq called *kutika*—a manuscript genre usually neglected by scholars—addresses a crucial source for understanding the historical interplay of writing, material culture, and Islamization in south Sulawesi. Kenneth George, *Journal of Asian Studies* 6, 1 (2002): 332–33 (review of Robinson and Paeni, eds., *Living Through Histories*). Matthes mentions a Malay *kotika* dealing with wind and weather used by the "Badjo's" or *turijéqnéq*. B. F. Matthes, "De Makassaarsche en Boegineesche *kotika's*," in Van den Brink, *Dr. Benjamin Frederik Matthes*, 477.

interpretive frame for understanding the sections of the manuscript that follow. In a sense, this first section holds the key to the manuscript's significance.

Based both on content and on what its owner, Molana, and her husband, Haji Mahmud, related about its migration history, *LB Lemobajo* was brought by their parents from the Boné region of South Sulawesi. According to Haji Mahmud, who was born in Lemobajo in 1920 and was Molana's first cousin through their fathers, the manuscript had been brought from Bajoé by his father, Tanjéng. Molana, however, inherited it through her maternal line. It passed to the youngest child in each generation of her family, who happened to be a woman, and other heirloom objects were kept by her as well. Both Tanjéng and Molana's father, Aco, had been born at Bajoé. They left Bajoé, as did other Sama people, with their extended family for points east.[43]

The families of Tanjéng and Aco reportedly left Bajoé because it "didn't agree" (*tidak cocok*) with them. After leaving Bajoé, this extended family, which collectively had an interest in the *lontaraq* and what it represented, moved from place to place a number of times, and did not all settle in the same location.[44] These relocations should not be confused with trading ventures or types of fishing trips.[45] The latter are categorically different from residence shifts in which people "moved villages" (*pindah kampung*), in this case, first from Bajoé to Boépinang, then to Tinobu, and then settling finally in Lemobajo. Given that Haji Mahmud was born in Lemobajo in 1920 and that these moves took place over the course of ten or fifteen years, the extended family's departure from Bajoé most likely came in connection with the Dutch assault on Boné in 1905.

According to Haji Mahmud, the manuscript had been written by his "grandparent" Puah Rukka. It is possible that by this he meant La Singkeruq Rukka, the ruler of Boné from 1860 until his death in 1871, and the father of La Pawawoi Karaeng Segeri, the Boné ruler sent into internal exile by the Dutch in 1905.[46]

---

[43] Fieldnotes, Lemobajo, Southeast Sulawesi, September 27, 1990. Molana's mother, Hindong (a.k.a. Nindong), may also have been born at Bajoé. Molana was already hard of hearing when we first met. Attempts to communicate with her in future years were very difficult, and Haji Mahmud generally did not mind representing himself as an owner of the manuscript, given his position and knowledge about it. Hajjah Sitti Alang, another of Hindong's daughters, said that Hindong died at Pulo Maginti in the Tiworo Straits. She also said that Hindong's father was Jémulong, and her husband was Hamba Daeng Baco, a likely source for the nickname "Aco." Fieldnotes, Hajjah Sitti Alang, Boépinang, Southeast Sulawesi, April 11, 2000; and Haji Mahmud, Lemobajo, Southeast Sulawesi, March 3, 2000. Haji Dunde and his son Mohamad Jamil Yusuf, respectively the great-grandfather and grandfather of people I spoke with in Central Sulawesi's Tolo Bay area, traced their lineage to Bajoé as well. Likewise, Haji Umar Nanga, head *imam* of the main mosque of Poso during the 1990s, a Sama man, also traced his lineage to Bajoé. (For those unfamiliar with the term "*imam*," an *imam* leads communal worship and often delivers a Friday sermon at the mosque.) He himself was born in Kaléroang in the Salabangka islands. He had relatives on his mother's side in Tiworo at Pulau Katéla, and traced one of his Bajoé Sama kin connections to Haji Abdul Rahim, who he said was "Lolo Bajo from Bajoé."

[44] Fieldnotes, Lemobajo, Southeast Sulawesi, March 3, 2000.

[45] Jennifer L. Gaynor, "Flexible Fishing: Gender and the New Spatial Division of Labor in Eastern Indonesia's Rural Littoral," *Radical History Review* 107 (Spring 2010, issue on "Transnational Environments: Rethinking the Political Economy of Nature in a Global Age"): 74–100.

[46] "Grandparent" (*nenek*, Indonesian; *mboq*, Sama) can simply mean "antecedent," prior to the parental generation. Two "Rukka" figures should be mentioned in this connection. First,

However, no evidence of authorship or copyist exists in the manuscript itself. Given its ownership and migration history, to say nothing of its contents, it is fair to say that the manuscript was almost certainly produced in Boné, by a highly literate person related to the ruling elite. A woman, or women, may have been involved in its composition, its recopying, or possibly even readings of it. B. F. Matthes, in his studies of Bugis writings during the nineteenth century, found elite Bugis women to be the most knowledgeable—and therefore his best teachers—about *lontaraq*. Hence, one should not assume that this manuscript or others were written or recopied solely by male hands; we simply do not know.

*LB Lemobajo*, carried from Bajoé, was said to be one of four "sibling" manuscripts. A second one was rumored to be in Southeast Sulawesi's provincial capital, Kendari, but proved untraceable.[47] A third manuscript had been held at Bontu Bontu, a Sama village that straddles the intertidal zone between two small islands at the eastern entrance of the Tiworo Straits. Lo Kadér, who recalled much of its contents and retold what he remembered of them over the course of a few hours, said it was burned in the 1950s during the conflict between the Darul Islam movement and the central government's armed forces. A fourth version had been held by Kalabeq ("Puah Habeq") at Pulo Balu in the Tiworo Straits. It, too, appears to have been burned during the 1950s, along with about two hundred houses at Boné Boné, where people had fled to take refuge, across the water from Pulo Balu on Muna's northwest coast. However, a portion of this fourth manuscript, a genealogy, survived, and acquired its own history of borrowing, discussed below. Like *LB Lemobajo*, these other manuscripts, copies, or recensions were probably also carried from Bajoé. What drove people to leave Bajoé, and to take the manuscripts with them?

## FLIGHT AND SOMETIMES RETURN

Relations between the Dutch and Boné, the two former allies, had been deteriorating over the course of the nineteenth century. Although Boné, by the end of the seventeenth century, had become the most powerful political entity in the south Sulawesi peninsula, as early as 1825 the Netherlands East Indies authorities felt it necessary to send a military expedition to sign a renewed Treaty of Bungaya—the treaty that spelled out the settlement of the late-1660s Makassar War. Boné signed the treaty in 1838, but, according to the Dutch, did not fulfill its

---

Cense identified one: "In a genealogical note about the ancestors of a certain Rukka in a Macassarese diary of the year 1836 it is said, 'this is the reason why I record this; I do this in case posterity should ask about it.' If one came up against certain difficulties, then." A. A. Cense, "Old Buginese and Makassarese Diaries," *BKI* 122, 4 (1966): 424. On the other "Rukka," Ahmad Singkeruq Rukka, see Tol, "A Royal Collection of Bugis Manuscripts," 617. Although there is no proof that either is the "Rukka" intended by Haji Mahmud, the possibility should not be ruled out. After all, prominent Sama people in Makassar were closely intermarried with Gowa elites in the eighteenth century.

[47] This second version had supposedly been bequeathed to Lo Mariama (Hajjah Mariama), a descendant of Pabitte (former Lakina Tiworo, and brother of Lolo Wawo or Wawona ["Puah Basar"]); see below, in this chapter. For a while I thought that it might be held by Alimaturahim, a former journalist who has sometimes promoted himself as a Sama leader. But if he had had it, then he would not have bothered to acquire photocopies of photocopies of portions of the one in Lemobajo. Also, he was prone to bragging and secret sharing in order to impress, yet never mentioned it. "Sibling manuscript" was a term used locally.

commitment. Over the next twenty years a series of incidents increased tensions, resulting in the Dutch sending a punitive expedition. Among the proximate causes of the intervention, the Dutch claimed that Boné treated other kingdoms as its subjects, and the new queen, Bessé Kajuara, did not appear in Makassar to sign the treaty until after she ascended the throne in 1857. However, the Dutch may have been most irritated by Boné's rulers having ordered that ships entering its waters fly the Dutch flag upside down. In 1859, a Dutch fleet anchored at Bajoé, whereupon most of the military forces went ashore to conquer the capital at Watamponé, a few miles inland. A small squadron also surveyed the Cenrana River and took punitive actions against villages on its banks—events that were recorded in verse in the "Toloqna Musuq Boné" (Poem on the Boné War) shortly after they took place.[48]

The Dutch authorities continued to have problems with what they viewed as Boné's transgressions after the turn of the twentieth century, evident in the counsel given by Christiaan Snouck Hurgronje. A renowned Dutch Islamologist better known for his role in the Aceh War, Christiaan Snouck Hurgronje also had a hand in shaping colonial policy toward Boné in his capacity as the governor-general's Advisor for Native Affairs. In his memorandum of November 5, 1904, nine months before another Dutch action against Boné, he offered his assessment that the most pressing problem with Boné's opposition, disloyalty, and disobedience was that it increasingly made the Dutch an object of mockery in South Celebes. He proposed a number of recommendations aimed in large part at following through on admonishments, trying at the same time not to give the impression that the Dutch wished to establish direct rule. He explained that if native rulers thought that the aim was to establish direct rule, then the threat of abolishing the relative independence that these leaders had under indirect rule would only increase their opposition. However, to "bring Boné to reason" would, he felt, discourage rebelliousness among others.[49]

The Dutch were also after the taxes collected at Pallimek harbor at the mouth of Boné's Cenrana River. This was not the only place that the Dutch made efforts to capture revenue. Indeed, the 1905 Boné campaign was part of a larger effort of consolidation that extended to parts of the peninsula beyond Boné. Earlier the same year the Dutch had occupied the harbor of Paré-Paré on the west coast of the peninsula, with an eye to transferring the levy of toll duties from Sidénréng to the Dutch government. The Dutch thus had reason to suspect that alliances were forming against them, centered around Boné, Gowa, and Wajo, and possibly also including Sidénréng and Soppéng. When the harbormaster at Pallimek handed over

---

[48] The coast of Kajuara, an area of Boné just north of Sinjai, sits opposite the Pulau Sembilan archipelago. Sirtjo Koolhof and Roger Tol, "The Delight of the Dutch *Compagnie*: On the *Toloqna Musuq Boné* by Daéng ri Aja," *Jambatan* 11, 3 (1993): 99–100. See also Christiaan Heersink, *The Green Gold of Selayar: A Socio-Economic History of an Indonesian Coconut Island c. 1600–1950s, Perspectives from a Periphery* (Amsterdam: Vrije Universiteit, 1995), 76; and Elsbeth Locher-Scholten, "'Een gebiedende noodzakelijkheid': Besluitvorming rond de Boni-expeditie 1903–1905," in *Excursies in Celebes*, ed. Harry Poeze and Pim Schoorl (Leiden: KITLV, 1991), 147.

[49] *Ambtelijke Adviezen van C. Snouck Hurgronje, 1889–1936*, vol. 3, Rijksgeschiedkundige Publicatiën, Kleinen Serie 35 (The Hague: Martinus Nijhoff, 1965), 2106–13. Shades of George Orwell's 1936 essay "Shooting an Elephant," nothing threatens the bearers of imperialism more than to be the object (real or imagined) of derisive laughter.

the refusal of the Arumponé—the ruler of Boné—to the Dutch waiting in the harbor, the war machine was then not to be stopped.[50]

The "Tolok Rumpaqna Boné," another Bugis history in verse, tells of the 1905 Dutch attack, the Bugis defense, and the exile of Boné's ruler, La Pawawoi. Among other things, it relates the arrival of Dutch ships "that carried thousands of soldiers and hundreds of *marechaussé* [police]" to Boné's harbor at Bajoé.[51] The poem's repetition and description of the troops disembarking, and the formulaic numbers, although stylized, give an impression of how many were involved that is not far off the mark. In the regulation for the transport of the troops, around twenty-four hundred military men were mentioned along with about a thousand other personnel.[52]

The military action against Boné at Bajoé in 1905 was not the first time that attacks on Boné caused those who lived at Bajoé, the settlement on the seaward side of Cellu, to flee for safer beaches. For instance, Vosmaer noted how the Dutch war with Boné in 1824 and 1825 led to an exodus from Bajoé, and that Sama people took refuge in, among other places, Luwu, particularly in the Palopo region at the north end of the Gulf of Boné. Although Vosmaer was assured that at the time more than two hundred houses had been erected there at the mouth of the Pasalui (Baliase) River, the occupants had slowly dissipated until, by the time he visited in 1833, not even a decade later, not a single house remained. Some of these people, according to Vosmaer, had moved to Kendari.[53] However, quite a few people must have returned to Bajoé over the next few years, for when Brooke first anchored off the littoral settlement at Bajoé in January 1840, he estimated that it contained somewhere between 150 and 180 houses.[54] According to *LB Lemobajo*, Sama people did at times return to Bajoé, for instance, during the rule of La Singkeruq Rukka (r. 1860–71) in Boné.[55] The population of Bajoé, like that of Tiworo in the face of seventeenth-

---

[50] Roger Tol, *Een Haan in Oorlog: Toloqna Arung Labuaja, een Buginees Heldendicht* (Leiden: KITLV, 1990), 101.

[51] Muhammad Salim, trans., *Transliterasi dan Terjemah Lontarak Tolok Rumpakna Bone* (Ujung Pandang: Departemen Pendidikan dan Kebudayaan Propinsi Sulawesi Selatan, 1991). This version of the *Tolok* is based on the manuscript in the old manuscript collection of the Kantor Yayasan Kebudayaan Benteng Ujung Pandang. Unfortunately, Salim did not provide the manuscript number, but it is probably the one Roger Tol describes as ms 2963 in the same Yayasan ("oude signatur is Mak., 123"), inscribed in the same hand as most of another manuscript that was, by Cense's request, written in the thirties and likewise deposited in the Yayasan (Tol, *Een Haan in Oorlog*, 37–38). Tol himself used a manuscript version of the *Tolok Rumpakna Bone* from the University Library in Leiden: ms cod.or. 6773. He subjects the *Toloqna Arung Labuaja* to extensive comparison with it because it treats much the same material, in some cases seems to lift whole sections of pages from the former, and appears to be written—which is not to say "invented"—by the same figure: I Mallaq Daeng Mabela, Arung Manajeng. The Leiden manuscript of the *Tolok Rumpakna Bone* was apparently inscribed by Mallaq in 1908. Tol, *Een Haan in Oorlog*.

[52] Tol, *Een Haan in Oorlog*, 101. For further resources on the 1905 campaign against Boné, see "De expeditie naar Zuid-Celebes in 1905–1906," *Indisch militair tijdschrift*, Extra bijlage (supplementary issues) 35, 37 (Batavia [Jakarta]: Kolff, 1915–16).

[53] Vosmaer, "Korte Beschrijving van het Zuid-oostelijk Schiereiland van Celebes," 73, 132–33. He reckoned that "Arung Bakung" reached Kendari around 1823 or 1824. (As shown in the section on Tiworo, in the Introduction, Arung Bakung was probably the same person as To Palettéi.)

[54] Brooke and Mundy, *Narrative of Events in Borneo and Celebes*, 36, 135.

[55] *LB Lemobajo*, 70.

century conflicts, waxed with favorable conditions and waned in the face of danger. In their dispersion from Bajoé, more than just the memory of the Sama connection with Boné lived on. According to the manuscripts, the link, through this lineage, was periodically reaffirmed.

## FEALTY FROM AFAR

Beyond the matter of dispersals and returns, the *lontaraq* about the Sama past show the recommitment of Sama people to Boné over the course of generations. From the reign of one ruler to another, they expressed the loyalty and subservience of the *lolo*, and implicitly their followers, through a paramount Sama "noble."[56] In *LB Lemobajo*, declarations of loyalty appear in different contexts, such as when a particular individual was selected to become, as it were, the top *lolo*. This was the case, for instance, when I Palettéi (To Palettéi) was selected by various *lolo* of the southeast and eastern Sulawesi coasts. Although reportedly installed in Kendari, Palettéi was made the Sama leader "at" Bajoé. While the leader was associated with Bajoé, the communities that had dispersed from Bajoé maintained their fealty from afar. At least they did so for a while, until, it appears, they ran up against the enormous changes in political economy of the late-colonial period.

Perhaps the more familiar European history of vassalage as a relationship that involves tenancy on land makes it difficult to conceptualize such intertidal political relationships. "Hinterseas," therefore, is useful here, too, as a way to describe the links political centers maintained with subordinate satellites on the "bends and reaches" of other coasts. These connections were organized as much through relations between elite lineages as through trade and taxes, titles, and testimonials.

One thing these manuscripts have done is to substantiate the status claims of this Sama lineage, making such *lontaraq* a valuable and socially productive resource in the present.[57] This kind of "proof" of descent carries political weight, not least for demonstrating membership in a class of people from whom leaders are usually chosen. The *lontaraq* "proves" such membership on one level simply by its status as an heirloom object. One need not be able to read Bugis—few Bugis these days do— to appreciate that merely having a *lontaraq* in the family implies the high-status significance of the lineage. At another level, this status is explicitly recognized throughout the manuscript. A rare literary-historical artifact, produced in the language of another ethnic group, it seems to vouch in the specifics of the text what possession of it stands for—the clout of the lineage. That the manuscript retains such importance roughly a century after it was carried from Bajoé speaks volumes, less to the importance of the *lontaraq* in the past than to its past uses and its enduring significance in new social and political contexts.

---

[56] For a discussion of *lolo* as a Sama honorific for descendants of elite Sama lineages; of *lolo* as a Sama paramount noble; and *aru lolo* as a viceroy of the Bugis, see the section on "Tiworo" in the Introduction.

[57] Jane Drakard comments on Malay royal genealogies, including *hikayat*: "That these chronicles should be preserved by the descendants of the royal families of Barus is not surprising in view of their contents, since both deal directly with the relationship between the two families, and explain their position vis-a-vis each other." Jane Drakard, *A Malay Frontier: Unity and Duality in a Sumatran Kingdom* (Ithaca: Cornell Southeast Asia Program, 1990 [2004]), 56.

Yet the significance of such *lontaraq* is not only about asserting high-status descent or substantiating it through claims of connection to important political centers. The political relationship that Boné, like other centers before it, had with the lineages of maritime oriented groups mattered to Boné, too. These were people who fished and traded; people who, because of their broad dispersion, could travel long distances and still find ways to connect socially on other coasts; and who, at least in their association with Gowa, had clearly been involved in martial affairs.

More than just substantiating this lineage's status claims, Sama *lontaraq* attested, even as its members dispersed, to their relationship with Boné and its ruling elite. This testament to their long relationship is clear through much of the manuscript, but is perhaps most obviously exemplified by a list of "Bajo *puwang*" that follows a list of Boné rulers.[58]

| Mula puwanna Bajoé | The Lords of Bajoé begin |
|---|---|
| 1. Manurunngé ri Ussuq riasenngé I Papuq | 1. The One who Came Down in Ussuq named I Papuq |
| 2. Anakna sulléi riasenngé Puang ri Pasana | 2. Succeeded by his child, Puang ri Pasana (ruler of Pasana) |
| 3. Anaknasi sulléi riasenngé Toappa, Sultan ri Bonératé, taro adeq na rilantiq | 3. Succeeded then by his child, Toappa, sultan in Bonératé, (who) maintained customs and was then installed |
| 4. Anaknasi sulléi riasenngé I Galimbo | 4. Succeeded then by his child, I Galimbo |
| 5. Anaknasi sulléi riasenngé Puang Toa, makkunrai | 5. Succeeded then by his child Puang Toa, female |
| 6. Anaknasi sulléi riasenngé I Pallettéi | 6. Succeeded then by her child, I Pallettéi |
| 7. Anaknasi sulléi riasenngé I Makku, ri Kandari taro tudang, narilaba | 7. Succeeded then by his child, I Makku, (who) lived in Kendari (and) was then installed |
| 8. Nappasi eppona riasenngé I Wawo makkukkué tettong Lolo ri Bajoé[59] | 8. And then his grandchild named I Wawo is now Lolo in Bajoé |

At least two in the list were women, including the last, named Wawo. Molana, who had inherited this manuscript, was a close relative of I Wawo through her mother, Hindong (a.k.a. Nindong). Wawo, a figure in living memory, thus represents the direct relationship between this manuscript and those who kept it. Haji Mahmud, Molana's husband, stressed that I Wawo had been the last one "installed as *Datu* in Bajoé," "*datu*" being an equivalent title for a paramount noble. But, he explained, she was not installed (in the position) because Bajoé disbanded.[60] Not only did Bajoé disband at this time, but the man who ruled Boné, La Pawawoi, as mentioned above, was sent to internal exile in Batavia.[61] In contemporary Tiworo

---

[58] "*Bajo puwang*" is a Bugis honorific title; see the section on Tiworo in the Introduction. Also see the discussion of *papuwangeng* in the section "Sama at the Center," in Chapter Three.

[59] *LB Lemobajo*, 91.

[60] Fieldnotes, March 3, 2000.

[61] The similarity between "I Wawo" and "La Pawawoi" is, of course, striking, if one

and the surrounding areas, many Sama people trace their lineage to, or through, a man named Pabitté, or Lolo Pabitté, whose sister, Wawo, appears to be the same person. She was usually referred to as Lolo Wawona, with the title *Puah Basar*, where "*puah*" is the Sama equivalent of "*puwang*," and "*basar*" (cognate with Indonesian "*besar*") literally means "big," indicating that she was paramount among Sama entitled to be called *puah*.[62] Pabitté himself was known as Sapati Tiworo (the Sapati of Tiworo), a title that reflects Buton's creeping claims and influence.[63]

Vosmaer never mentioned the use of texts by Sama people, or any "*papuq.*" However, during the 1830s he did mention that, during his time, different groups of Sama people claimed ties to Gowa and to Boné, and that the latter used to appoint people to titled positions:

> Up to the present day they still consider themselves, when not residing in Government territory, subjects of Gowa or Bone. Those who, in the Sumanap [Sumenep], or as the Makassarese say, Kangiang [Kangean] Islands are known under the name of Sadoelangs, as well as those who live in the Makassar Straits, acknowledge the Raja of Gowa as [their] patron. While those belonging to this clan and wandering about elsewhere mostly want to have themselves considered subjects of Bone. One still nowadays finds leaders among them appointed by Bone under the designation of Lolo, Glarang [Mak. *gallarang*, Bug. *gellareng* ], Poengawa [*punggawa*], and Kapitein [*kapitah*]; but being for the most part now also gone from that land and scattered here and there, so it is presently the heads chosen by themselves, without the intervention of Bone, to whom they hold. They choose the aforementioned by succession from those among them who on account of birth are entitled to it under the names of Lolo, Glarang, or Poengawa, in popular parlance often combined under the, for them, deferential title of respect, Elders (*Orang Toewa*).[64]

It is not certain whether Vosmaer was correct that Boné had directly appointed Sama people with these titles. While the leadership of tributaries on the south Sulawesi peninsula had sometimes been imposed, for instance, as discussed in the previous chapter, by Gowa during the late-sixteenth century, tributaries on that peninsula were more-or-less independent political units that commonly chose their own leaders. As shown above with Gowa, for Sama dispersed in the hinterseas who expressed loyalty to a particular center, their leader, the *papuq*, had been chosen by "his kin." A similar arrangement with Boné was likely. In other words, choosing

---

understands that *pa-* and *-i* are typical Austronesian affixes.

[62] Lolo Wawona, a.k.a. I Wawo, the Puah Basar, was married to Daeng Pabetta, not to be confused with her brother, Pabitté.

[63] He was also known as Kapitah (Negeri) Lakara, and Kapitah Labolong. Pabitté was married to "Lolo Bessé."

[64] The Kangean Islands are off the east end of Madura. (Chalk one up for Tomé Pires, whose earlier description of the geographic range of "the islands of Makassar" included these islands and the Selates or "Bajuus" who—but for the junks—had all the boats in their hands. Particularly since some scholars may be apt to dismiss Pires's description, this kind of passing mention of later ties between Sama in the Kangean Islands with Gowa suggests Pires may have been observant and informed about his information on "the islands of Makassar.") Vosmaer, "Korte Beschrijving van het Zuid-oostelijk Schiereiland van Celebes," 27.

their own leader may not have been, as Vosmaer seems to assume, a result of distance having forced them to decide on their own, absent Boné's input.[65]

Genealogies gathered from people in the Straits of Tiworo and their Sama relatives show that many people could also trace their lineages, in part, to non-Sama descent groups, as well. These included Boné and Gowa, as well as people now known as "Tiworo," or "Muna Tiworo." In contemporary Muna, those called "Tiworo" generally speak a Tiworo dialect of the Muna language, a language that phonetically is extremely different from Sama, Bugis, Makassar, and many other languages in the region. These Muna Tiworo are not maritime oriented, and generally settle on land, but sometimes form mixed communities with Sama people (and a few Bugis) on the northwest shore of Muna. Along that coast, the picture is one of multilingual communities, and which language is used in a given interaction depends very much on the context, abilities, and proclivities of those involved. In contrast, Sama people dominate the villages on islands and shoals in the straits, and also live in littoral settlements along its encompassing shores. Muna Tiworo only occasionally live in the predominantly Sama villages, and a few mixed Bugis and Sama villages, in the straits. While all can speak the national language, Indonesian, Sama is the lingua franca of most villages in the straits, with some Bugis here and there.

Hence, what "Tiworo" means now and what it meant historically are different things. At present, "Tiworo" is viewed as an ethnic and linguistic subgroup of "Muna." Historically, Tiworo was a polity that encompassed the settlements of the straits, with a strongly maritime-oriented population. It may have been a predominantly Sama polity; the evidence points in that direction. In any case, the successes of its resident maritime-oriented population and the growth of the polity appear to have drawn in the participation of Muna people who migrated to the island's northern shores bordering the straits.

In addition to tracing descent partially from Bugis, Makassar, and Muna Tiworo antecedents, people in Tiworo who identified as Sama sometimes also traced genealogical ties to Buton (Wolio) and even to a *sayid* (descendant of the prophet) of indeterminate ethnicity (perhaps Malay) who had come to Tiworo from east Kalimantan. As a result, the titles people employed a few generations ago commonly varied, depending on social and linguistic context, a matter reflected in genealogies and oral history. People known as Sama kin among their Sama families were referred to, in other contexts, with titles commonly in use in those settings. For instance, in Bugis or Makassar contexts, they were "*Daeng*" so-and-so; in Tiworo-Muna or Buton, they were "*La Ode*" (or just "*La*," for males), and "*Wa Ode*" (or just "*Wa*," for females); while among the Sama, they were "*Lolo*" or "*Lo*" so-and-so. Names or nicknames could also vary along with (and sometimes without) titles, and teknonymy—referring to parents by the names of their children—is also common throughout the region (e.g., "Ibu Erna" for "Erna's mother"; "Tuanna I Dondang" for "Dondang's parent"). In addition, certain titles combined with place names (e.g., "*Arumponé*" for "the Arung or ruler of Boné") also referred to particular persons, in place of a name.

"Arung Palakka" is an example of these naming conventions. His many names are, of course, in part, a reflection of his stature. Arung Palakka, that is, the Arung

---

[65] See: "Sama at the Center," above; Druce, *The Lands West of the Lakes*, 21–22, 26–29; and Omar, "The History of Boné A.D. 1775-1795."

of (the place) Palakka, pronounced in Bugis, *Aruppalakka*, was also known as "La Tenri Tatta," where "La" indicates high status; and "La Tenri Tatta To Unru," that is, person from Unru (or "To Appatunru"). While there have been many Arung Palakka's, he is the most famous one. He was also known as "the long-haired one," *malampéqé gemmeqna*, which is usually preceded by the title *"Petta."* *"Petta"* also often precedes his title *"To Risompa-é"* (*Torisompaé*), which means "He, to whom homage is paid," a name by which this particular Arung Palakka is generally known among the Bugis.[66] The Makassar language version of this term is *"Tunisombaya."* Like other Bugis and Makassar rulers, he also had a posthumous name that states where he died, in his case, at Bontoala: *"Matinroé ri Bontoala."* There are still more, not the least of which is Sultan Sa'adduddin.

Although the list of Boné rulers in *LB Lemobajo* that precedes the list of Bajo *puwang* includes Arung Palakka, and mentions that "he attacked Gowa," it does not call him "Arung Palakka." Nor does it use his personal name, La Tenritatta. Instead, it lists him as "Sultan Almarhum Asaduddin [*sic*] Abdullah, Petta Torisompaé, Malampéqé Gemmeqna." In other parts of the manuscript he is usually referred to simply as "Torisompaé." The Sama people who had some familiarity with the manuscript or oral versions of its contents, as far as I could tell, did not recognize this as Arung Palakka. This is ironic, since both *lontaraq* manuscripts (*LB Lemobajo* and Or 545/262) set out genealogical claims of descent for Arung Palakka from the daughter of the "first *papuq*," supposedly from Ussuq.[67]

### POETIC ALLUSIONS, COLONIAL ILLUSIONS

Although few Sama people owned *lontaraq* or could read them, some older Sama men and women had basic literacy in Bugis, and Bugis reportedly had been used in letters for the purpose of trade during the 1950s in Tiworo. Although no such letters have survived, Hajjah Kua, an elderly Sama woman on Kambuno, in the western Gulf of Boné's Pulau Sembilan archipelago, who fled Tiworo with her family during the conflict of the 1950s, still used Bugis writing in 1999 to keep track of goods sold in her kiosk.[68] Despite the fact that few Sama people owned *lontaraq* or could read them, many knew part of the initial story about the Sama "princess" who winds up in Gowa and marries royalty, or some version of the Makassar-language poem usually quoted or referenced in it.

Little evidence exists to show that the contents of *lontaraq* about the Sama past were performed publicly in the theatrical manner common to a number of traditions

---

[66] Cense, "Old Buginese and Makassarese Diaries," 427 (note 10).

[67] In a discussion of how the importance of genealogical ties has led some Bugis and Makassar individuals to fabricate elaborate genealogies with ties to prominent people, Cummings cites a personal communication (no date) with Leonard Andaya, explaining that "among the Bugis, powerful families throughout South Sulawesi incorporated childless Arung Palakka into their genealogies, thereby enhancing their social status by enhancing their descent." See Cummings, *Making Bood White*, 106, 225 (note 33). This claim to descent from Arung Palakka contrasts with what I describe here, namely, that a genealogy is provided *for* Arung Palakka, establishing the genealogical precedence of his (supposed) Sama forebears.

[68] Hajjah Kuaq was the wife of one of Pelras's subjects. Her daughter, Julla, used Indonesian, and thus neither could read the other's writing, which I found an amusing way to keep the books. This family had lived in Tiworo, but during the 1950s Darul Islam conflict fled Tiworo for the Pulau Sembilan cluster off Sinjai. Fieldnotes, Pulau Kambuno, South Sulawesi, September 30, 1999.

in Southeast Asia.[69] Nevertheless, like some other *lontaraq* in Sulawesi, those about the Sama past have, in places, a style that in many respects seems obviously related to oral modes of discourse, for instance, containing repetitive passages, filled at times with dialogue. Like many other literary and historical products of southern Sulawesi, Bugis-language manuscripts about the Sama past exist in more than one version, and have their counterparts in oral versions. The only truly elaborated oral version I heard clearly derived directly from a manuscript. This was the telling delivered by Lo Kadér, in Tampo at the eastern end of the Tiworo Straits, who was intimately familiar with the third of the sibling manuscripts mentioned above. He confirmed that even when the manuscript had been accessible, this narrative about the Sama past had neither been performed in the grand sense, nor read to the general public. However, parts of it were told, and sometimes read aloud, generally just among members of the family.[70] In some cases, people remembered hearing their grandmothers tell the story or parts of it. In other cases, people mentioned hearing their elders read parts of the manuscript aloud. For instance, although people said that *LB Lemobajo* had not been read publicly, they did recall that the father of Molana, the woman who inherited it, read aloud from it to his family and when others requested to hear it.[71] Just as *LB Lemobajo* primarily had relevance to a particular Sama lineage, access to its narrative contents was more-or-less restricted knowledge that a person would not be likely to know without some family connection.[72]

Some people recalled hearing part of the story sung, in particular the short Makassar-language poetic verse in it, known as a *kelong* (Bugis: *élong*). A teller would, in effect, perform that part as a direct quotation in the story. A friend from Bontu Bontu at the eastern end of the Tiworo Straits remembered her grandmother singing the part with the *kelong*.[73] Across the Gulf of Boné in Kambuno, an elderly man recalled small gatherings in which the *kelong* was sung as one of multiple stanzas.[74] An elderly Bugis woman, who spent a good deal of time when she was young at the Bugis court of Palopo, also claimed to have heard songs there that included bits about the Sama past.[75] Finally, a man in Ara, South Sulawesi, whose

---

[69] Druce (*The Lands West of the Lakes*, 250) similarly found little evidence that texts of a historical nature had been performed.

[70] Fieldnotes, Lo Kadér, Tampo, Southeast Sulawesi, April 16, 2000.

[71] Fieldnotes, Lemobajo, Southeast Sulawesi, September 27, 1990; and author interview with Hajjah Erna and Hajjah Lawi, Wawo, North Kolaka, June 22, 2011.

[72] When I asked an elderly Sama woman whether her family had any manuscripts, and described them by referencing the story at the beginning, she voiced her curiosity about whether I had any Sama ancestors.

[73] Nuhba, a.k.a. Céq, who later married and lived on Pulo Tasippi (also in Tiworo), referring to her grandmother Lolobaco. Si Céq's own beautiful singing when I lived in and was socialized to Sama ways in Bontu Bontu brought to mind the descriptions in H. Arlo Nimmo, *The Songs of Salanda and Other Stories of Sulu* (Seattle: University of Washington Press, 1994).

[74] Fieldnotes, Kambuno, November 8, 1999.

[75] Whether she heard the *kelong* in question is unclear. This woman, Puang Lebbi (Puaq Lebbi), whom I chanced to meet at an elite Bugis wedding in Malili, was one of the very few Bugis people I ever met who was aware of "*lolo*" as a Sama-related term, and not just as a word in Bugis, where it means "young," and is associated with the term Aru lolo (cf. Malay/Indonesian: *raja muda*), "viceroy/vicereine." The way she used it, *loloku*, she explained, explicitly referred to someone Sama, and meant something like the Indonesian *tanteku*, (my "aunt"). Lebbi's use of *loloku* may be related to Bugis "*lolong*," to be bonded, connected, or to

mother was not Sama, recalled his father singing the *kelong*, dispelling the impression that only women sang it.[76]

Near the beginning of KITLV's "History of the Bajos of South Celebes," the *kelong* mentioned above is merely alluded to by invoking its last line.[77] The narrative relates that when the ruler of Gowa sent his envoy to find out who has just arrived with his fleet, the protagonist's father refers to the *kelong* to clarify his identity. He tells the envoy to say to his liege: "Know that we come with good intentions to appear before Karaéng Torisompaé, and our name is I Papuq, the leader of these many Bajo people—'Tidung are princes so Bajo are paid homage, too' [*Tidung karaéng manna Bajo nisomba tonji*], meaning more or less: 'Although [he is] Bajo, [he is] still paid homage.'" The speaker, I Papuq, tosses off this last line of the *kelong*, practically making the allusion another part of his title. In this manner, the poem is invoked with the presumption that the audience is already familiar with it. Yet the reference also includes a brief and rather casual refresher explanation of what it means, for those not in the know, since the *kelong* is neither in Bugis nor Sama, the languages presumably most familiar to the audience.

A version of this *kelong* appears in a "children's song," recorded by B. F. Matthes. Matthes refers to it in one of his dictionaries to explain that the "*Toe-rijéqnéq*," or *Bayo* people, were also called *Tidung*.[78] The children's song itself appears in his compilation of Makassar-language literature. Often only lines resembling the second half of this song get cited in stories about the Sama past. Matthes's Dutch translation, on which the English translation here is based, comes with a curious interpretation, discussed below.

| | |
|---|---|
| ᨕᨗᨊᨕᨗ ᨕᨊ ᨆᨆᨗᨔᨙ, ᨆᨄᨚᨈᨚ ᨀᨙᨅᨚ. <br> Inai ana mamisé, maponto kébo? | Who are those people with white bracelets, whose oars cut through the water over there? |
| ᨕᨊᨊ ᨅᨐᨚ, ᨊᨕᨘᨊᨑᨘᨊ ᨈᨘᨑᨗᨆᨙᨉᨙ. <br> Anana Bayo, naunrunna Turidjéqnéq. | They are the children of the Bajos, the descendants of the Turijéqnéq. |
| ᨆᨊ ᨅᨐᨚ ᨈ ᨅᨐᨚᨊᨘ, ᨆᨊ ᨈᨗᨉᨘ ᨈ ᨈᨗᨉᨘᨊᨘ. <br> Manna Bayo ta Bayonu, manna Tidung ta Tidunnu. | But even though you are Bajo, nonetheless you do not belong to yourself anymore. Even if you are Tidungers, nonetheless you do not belong to yourself anymore, |
| ᨈᨗᨉᨘ ᨀᨑᨕᨙ, ᨍᨑᨗᨊ ᨈᨘᨊᨗᨔᨚᨅᨐ. <br> Tidung karaéng, jarinna Tunisombaya.[79] | because the king of the Tidungers is a descendant of Tunisombaya.[80] |

---

belong with something (see Matthes, *Boegineesch-Hollandsch Woordenboek*, 602). However, this would not explain what she said was a specifically Sama reference, and with the sense of *tante*.

[76] Fieldnotes, Johari, Ara, South Sulawesi, October 27, 1999. This *kelong*, and the *kelong* form, appears to be unrelated to the Sama lamentations known as *iko-iko* songs (a kind of Sama genre of the blues, often accompanied by a *gambus*, and sometimes libations).

[77] "Geschiedenis van de Badjo's van Zuid Celebes," OR 545/262, KITLV.

[78] B. F. Matthes, *Makassaarsch-Hollandsch Woordenboek* (Amsterdam: Frederik Muller, 1859), 40.

[79] B. F. Matthes, *Makassaarsche chrestomathie: Oorspronkelijke Makassaarsche geschriften, in proza en poëzy* (The Hague: Nijhoff, 1883 [1860]), 223, 431. On page 431, r. 16, the transliteration from "Koerroe-koerroe djangang" reads: ANaNa BaYo. NaNuRuNa TuRiJéNé. MaNa BaYo TaBaYoNu. MaNa TiDu. TaTiDuNu. TiDu KaRaE. JaRiNa TuNiSoBaYa.

Matthes inserts a long note, first elucidating that Tunisombaya is Arung Palakka, "who, in the time of Speelman rendered such important services to the government." He then tries to help the reader by explaining that, "To understand this *kelong* well, one has to know that according to tradition [*overlevering*] the son of one of the kings, of either Boné or Gowa, was married to the daughter of *Lolo-poléyang*, or the king of the Tu-ri-jéqnéqs, and that, because of that, really, the government would have come into the hands of strangers."[81] This explanation needs to be unpacked on a number of levels: first, addressing "*Lolo-poléyang*"; then, the marriage of his daughter to one of the king's sons; and, finally, the notion of government coming into the hands of strangers.

Matthes, familiar with the "traditions" of both Gowa and Boné, tells us that the ruler of the *turijéqnéq* (i.e., of the Sama) was referred to as *Lolo-poléyang*. "*Lolo*" in both Bugis and Makassar languages literally means "young." However, it takes on a different sense in conjunction with the term for ruler. Thus, in Bugis, "*Aru Lolo*" means "crown prince," or, as the Malay equivalent (*Raja Muda*) is often translated, "viceroy" or "vicereine." "*Lolo*" in "*Lolo-poléyang*," refers to this sense of the word. Rather than simply a viceroy or vicereine, that is, the governor of a country, province, or colony, who rules as the representative of a sovereign, in this case we might say *Lolo* means the governor (or governess) of hinterseas and their littorals connected through ties of genealogy and fealty to a sovereign.

"*Polé*" in both languages means "from."[82] "*Poléyang*" in Bugis means "to bring or take, chiefly homeward."[83] This suggests that the ruler of the *turijéqnéq*, the *Lolo-poléyang*, was a viceroy or vicereine who brought things homeward to Makassar, or, in the case of Boné, to Bajóé, from the hinterseas."[84]

What did Matthes mean that the government would have come into the hands of "strangers" (a curious statement, indeed, coming from a Dutchman in the colonial Indies)? This seems to mean that, since the *Lolo-poléyang*'s daughter married the son of the ruler of Boné or Gowa, then the Bajo (or Sama) no longer ruled themselves. However, a pattern of the maritime leader's daughter marrying a ruler or the ruler's son is such a common regional political strategy that it forms a trope

---

[80] "*Wie zijn die mensen met hunne witte armbanden? Dat zijn de kinderen der Badjo's, de afstammelingen der Toe-ri-djé'né's. Maar al zijt ook gij nog Badjo's, toch behoort hij niet meer u zelven toe. Al zijt ook gij nog Tidoengers (vergel. Woodenb. op* tidoeng); *toch behoort gij niet meer u zelven toe; want de koning der Tidoengers is een afstammeling van Toe-ni-sombaya.*" Ibid., 225.

[81] Ibid.

[82] "From" in Sama is *tikka*, but "return home" (Ind. *pulang*) is *molé*.

[83] Matthes, *Boegineesch-Hollandsch Woordenboek*, 141.

[84] The derivation of *lolo* as a title in Sama may well be from this overlapping context of usage with the Bugis and Makassar languages. However, it is worth noting that the term *lolo* in Tagalog, which is linguistically closer to Sama than are Bugis or Makassar, is a term of respect for elders that means "grandfather"—a reason not to draw too-hasty conclusions. It should also be mentioned that in Bugis, *Polémpang*, which may be based on the same root as *poléyang*, is a title for a head (director, leader) in Luwu, more or less the same as *gellareng*, as in: *Polémpang toAlinrang, Polémpang toRokong, Polémpang toUssu*, the three of whom, Matthes notes, were the three heads in charge of the fisheries of the ruler of Luwu. (Matthes, *Boegineesch-Hollandsch Woordenboek*, 147.) This does make one think twice about the historical possibility that the "first" *Papuq* could have come from Ussuq. As discussed below, this location is understood as important for its mythological and literary, rather than historical, connection.

in Southeast Asian literature. One could call it the *putri Laksamana* trope, marrying "the admiral's daughter."[85]

Matthes found that the people could neither tell him who this Gowa or Boné prince had been, nor were they able to show him any kind of written documents in which the event of his marriage to the *Lolo-poléyang*'s daughter appeared. Explaining that Tunisombaya is Arung Palakka, Matthes then goes on to interpret the *kelong* as meaning that the Sama "do not belong to themselves anymore" because, as the result of such a marriage, their ruler has become a descendant of Arung Palakka.[86] Therefore, the idea is, they "belong" to Arung Palakka, who, while still the ruler of Boné, also had a residence in Makassar after he and the VOC subdued it in the Makassar War.

The latter half of the verse may be translated differently, however. Matthes reads /ta/ as "not." Instead, it may be an affix. The affix /-ta/ may be a first-person plural possessive inclusive, "our."[87] Or, as it is widely used in south and southeast Sulawesi, it may signal a respectful form of the second-person plural possessive, "your." The affix /-nu/ is a familiar form of "your." Matthes's reading presumes a speaker who is non-Sama.[88] An alternate reading presumes that the speaker and the audience are all Sama, or share Sama descent. This would give the *kelong* a different interpretation. *Jari*, cognate with Indonesian *jadi*, means "become" or "became." The affix /-na/ may be his/her/its, or a nominalization of *jari*, hence, it could mean "the thing/person that became" or "its outcome/result" or "her issue."

| | |
|---|---|
| Manna Bayo-ta Bayonu, manna Tidung-ta Tidunnu. | Whoever is our/your (esteemed) Bajo, is your (familiar) Bajo, whoever is our/your (respected) Tidung, is your Tidung. |
| Tidung karaéng, jarinna Tunisombaya. | Tidung is/are *karaéng*, Her/their issue [or: the outcome], Tunisombaya [Arung Palakka]. |

---

[85] The author is currently preparing an article on the historical and literary theme of the *laksamana*'s daughter. Compare the seventeenth century boy king of Johor sitting, in all public ceremonies, on the lap of his mother, the daughter of the Laksamana (admiral). The Laksamana's family was in myriad key positions, while the Laksamana himself was in charge of the fleets of the *Orang Laut*, or Sea People. See Barbara Watson Andaya and Leonard Y. Andaya, *A History of Early Modern Southeast Asia, 1400–1830* (Cambridge: Cambridge University Press, 2015), 200. In this picture, before the regicidal usurpation of the Bendahara (prime minister), did the Laksamana's family derive importance simply from their association with the Malay royal line? Or was it perhaps the case that, as in Sulawesi, the head of the fleet himself came from a royal or noble line? Is this vision of the boy king on the lap of his mother, the Laksamana's daughter, not also a reminder of how intertwined the king's and Laksamana's lineages were, with even the Malay royal line, like Gowa's, itself descended from the highest social strata of *Orang Laut* lineages (according to the stories about Paramesvara's descendants)?

[86] Matthes, *Makassaarsche chrestomathie*, 225.

[87] In other words, "our" shared between the speaker and addressee, as opposed to the exclusive "our" that excludes the addressee.

[88] As shown in *Makassaarsche chrestomathie*, 233, where Matthes discusses these lines as part of the children's song *Kurru-kurru jangan*, named after the way it begins. His set up is as follows: "One imagines a woman who, with a child on her arm, looks from a window where she has a view of the road and, a little farther on, of the sea ..." He apparently is unaware of other contexts for understanding the *kelong*.

In this reading, Arung Palakka is the outcome of *tidung*, understood here to be the equivalent (or precursors) of Sama people who, like them, bear the status of "royalty," or *karaéng*. This is the opposite of Matthes's interpretation, in which "*Tidung* are *karaéng*, the product (*afstammeling*, descendant) of Tunisombaya." In that riddling way poetry of the region sometimes has of playing with polysemy, more than one interpretation may be possible. Given the contents of the *lontaraq* about the Sama past, with which, it seems, Matthes was not familiar, the reading I prefer is that Arung Palakka was the descendant of a union between a high-status Sama woman with the son of a Gowa ruler. The verse, then, reminds a Sama listener that Tunisombaya (Arung Palakka) descended from high-status Tidung forbears, and that you/we Sama either share in this descent, or in having Sama patrons (your Bajo) who do so.

This interpretation accords with the claims made in the manuscripts about the Sama past in Sulawesi: the daughter of the *papuq* married into the Gowa royal family and Arung Palakka was one of her descendants. "Petta Torisompaé descends from I Papuq's grandchild, and because of that there is no divorcing between the land of Boné and Bajoé."[89] The implicit contest is not about whether their lineages were intertwined. Rather, the issue is how to reckon who comes from whom. In such an exceedingly status-conscious society, genealogical precedence in the relations between elite lineages manifests as a profoundly political matter.

Matthes, imagining that the Sama persisted through time apart from such entanglements with others, and confusing biology for social and cultural practice, took the intermarriage of these lineages as something that, in itself, diminished "the Bajo." He added his voice to the chorus of colonial discourse about the threatened disappearance of sea nomads: "This much, however, is clear, that this water people [*watervolk*] is more and more starting to lose its independence and the character of its nature, so that it is becoming harder with every day to determine something regarding its origin and history."[90]

## SAMA ORAL TRADITIONS

When they were put to paper, Gowa and Talloq *patturioloang*, like the Chronicle of Boné, incorporated extant oral histories, in addition to newly composed material.[91] In a similar manner, versions of a regionally widespread oral tale about a highborn Sama woman relocated to live among another group most likely predate the composition of these *lontaraq* about the Sama past.

As a maritime people, dispersed across island Southeast Asia yet with no particular point of collective diaspora, Sama people and their different versions of this tale frustrated colonial projects to order knowledge of ethnic difference through metonymies of people and place. "The Bajo" did not fit the mold of "Javanese from the land of Java," "Balinese from Bali," "Bugis people from *tana Ugi* (the land of the

---

[89] Specifically, the claim is: "The child of Petta Rompegading, named Karaéng di Lembangparang, who became the karaéng in Gowa, took the child of I Papuq as his wife, and her child, (a) karaéng in Gowa, the female one, was the mother of Petta Torisompaé (Arung Palakka)." "History of the Bajo of South Sulawesi," OR545/263, 54.

[90] Matthes, *Makassaarsche chrestomathie*, 225.

[91] Cummings, *Making Blood White*, 82; Campbell Macknight and Mukhlis Paeni, "The Chronicle of Boné," unpublished manuscript and translation. The author wishes to thank Campbell Macknight for making this available.

Bugis), and so forth. Not only did "the Bajo" have no history of political unity, they did not even come from land. Nor did stories gathered from them over the years gratify the impulse to find their "origins," for the stories, which usually did entail migration, mentioned both different destinations as well as different points of departure.

Sourced from Sama communities in disparate parts of island Southeast Asia, in many versions the woman in the story's opening is relocated by capture. Most versions fall into one of two subgroups. In tales from the southern Philippines and eastern Malaysia, the protagonist is usually said to have come from Johor, at insular Southeast Asia's western end—the so-called "Johor princess story." By comparison, stories from southern and eastern Sulawesi and from islands both in and across the Flores Sea to its south usually place this figure's departure point in Luwu, sometimes specifying Ussuq at the head of the Gulf of Boné. Both kingdoms, Johor and Luwu, are associated in regional historical memory with prestigious centers that have royal lineages stretching back through time to an indistinct and legendary period.

Such stories have intrigued scholars and travelers, who have mostly interpreted them as clues to Sama origins or as evidence of the Sama people's desire to link themselves with the prestigious kingdoms of former times.[92] However, these stories are less about origins than explanations, on the one hand, of relocation and dispersal, and on the other hand, of intertwined relations with other groups. Would it make sense to call them "migration narratives"? Some groups in upland Southeast Asia have migration narratives that map out their histories in relation to the landscapes through which they and previous generations have moved.[93] Like the migration narratives of some people in Southeast Asia's upland areas, Sama tales of the past use a shift of locale to mark change over time. Also like migration narratives, they hint at a relationship between places and a collective past that differs from how we think of diaspora, which continually refers notions of collective belonging back to a singular place. Yet, unlike many migration narratives, these stories of the Sama past are not links in a chain of movements, nor are they set in remembered historical time.

This class of Sama stories, which is neither origin stories nor migration narratives, often purports to explain the circumstances that led to "how we Sama people got here." Sometimes they also address the wider condition of dispersal. Concluding remarks, such as "... and that's how we came to be scattered," unambiguously state this frame for understanding the story's significance. Yet, at what point such interpretive remarks were joined with the rest of a given version is unclear. These remarks also have the curious effect of turning the narrative into a just-so story.

Even without explicit framing remarks, the concern with relocation and dispersion remains evident from the thrust of the content. One finds snippets of such stories about Sama relocation and dispersion in the eighteenth-, nineteenth-,

---

[92] Frake, "The Genesis of Kinds of People in the Sulu Archipelago," 320–21; Liebner, "Four Oral Versions of a Story."

[93] Renato Rosaldo, "Perspectives on Ilongot History," in *Ilongot Headhunting, 1883–1974* (Stanford: Stanford University Press, 1980); Anna Lowenhaupt Tsing, *In the Realm of the Diamond Queen: Marginality in an Out-of-the-way Place* (Princeton: Princeton University Press, 1993); and Peter Metcalf, *They Lie, We Lie: Getting on with Anthropology* (London and New York: Routledge, 2002).

and twentieth-century literature on the region. A number of brief tales attested from the northern regions of Sama distribution trace the presence of Sama people in the Sulu archipelago of the Southern Philippines,[94] and in Borneo, or present day Eastern Malaysia[95] and Kalimantan,[96] to a departure from the prestigious former Malay kingdom of Johor. In these stories, the theft of a "princess" or high-status Bajo daughter from Johor, en route by sea to her betrothed, results in the relocation of those who were to have accompanied and protected her. A version recorded in the Philippines in 1945 goes like this:

> Centuries ago, peaceful fishermen, afraid of the shore folk, dwelt in boats off the coast of the Malay Peninsula. The beautiful daughter of their chief was stolen and taken away by the chief of the shore people, but she escaped and returned to her father's boat. Afraid of revenge, the Badjaus decided to let the next big gale take them where it would, and as a result they wound up in the Sulu Sea and made it their new home.[97]

This story, which explains how Sama people came to be in the Sulu archipelago, presents the move as unintentional. Charles O. Frake has shown how the Johor princess story has been used in the southern Philippines to bolster a fallacious rewriting of demographic history that portrays the Sama as coming to the region later than their Tausug compatriots, thus ideologically justifying the Tausug presence in Jolo.[98] The story has also had other uses. Versions like this one illustrate collective flight across the water as a response to fear of retaliation, a retaliation expected to come from those who had attempted to abduct the princess or chief's daughter, after she escaped and returned to her natal kin.

It may also be seen as a critique of stealing women, a story about the repudiation of a coerced kinship. This sort of kinship would have made the Sama chief's daughter a subordinate dependent, and would signify the subordination of her natal kin as well. Kinship in this story is no mere metaphor.[99] Rather than stand for something else, here kinship is lodged in the very constitution of intergroup

---

[94] Helen Follet, *Men of the Sulu Sea* (New York: Charles Scribner and Sons, 1945), 129–30; and H. Arlo Nimmo, *Magosaha: An Ethnography of the Tawi-tawi Sama Dilaut* (Quezon City: Ateneo de Manila University Press, 2001), 22–24.

[95] David Sopher, *The Sea Nomads: A Study Based on the Literature of the Maritime Boat People of Southeast Asia* (Singapore: Memoirs of the National Museum, 1965), 141–42 (the term "literature" in this title refers primarily to outside observers' remarks about the Bajo in the historical literature); Thomas Forrest, *A Voyage to New Guinea and the Moluccas, 1774–1776* (London, New York, Melbourne, and Kuala Lumpur: Oxford University Press, 1969 [1780]), 372; Owen Rutter, *British North Borneo—An Account of Its History, Resources, and Native Tribes* (London: Constable and Co., 1922), 73; and Yap Beng Liang, *Sistem Kepercayaan Orang Bajau Omadal, Sabah*, Jabatan Pengajian Melayu, Kertas Data no. 21, (Kuala Lumpur: Universiti Malaya, 1978), 9.

[96] Von Dewall, "Aanteekeningen omtrent de Noordoostkust van Borneo," 446–47.

[97] Follet, *Men of the Sulu Sea*, 129–30; and Sopher, *The Sea Nomads*, 145.

[98] Charles O. Frake, "Lines across the Water: The Lasting Power of Colonial Borders in Maritime Southeast Asia," *Northeast Anthropological Association Bulletin* (Fall 2011, "Borders, Margins and Passages," Anne M. Galvin, guest editor), 11–12.

[99] For counter-historical discourses that draw on kinship as a metaphor, see William Cummings, "The Dynamics of Resistance and Emulation in Makassarese History," *Journal of Southeast Asian Studies* 23, 3 (2001): 423–35.

hierarchies. The character of how it comes about matters, part of the grammar of power and prestige. Her successful escape may represent the repudiation of relations forged by the theft of a woman. Hence the story concerns not just kinship, but also the manner in which intergroup relatedness is brought about, the memory of what is acceptable and what is not, and the triumph of escape and survival.

This version therefore bears comparison with the actual historical phenomenon of Lawi's kidnapping during the post-independence conflict of the 1950s, examined in chapter five. Lawi did not escape—indeed, after she had been captured and taken away to marry a rebel military commander, her kin refused to let her return to her natal village for fear of being seen as the "enemy" by the government's forces. Yet, when rebels who participated in her capture dared to return to her village, her relatives retaliated, sending a resounding note of protest against her abduction. While in the tale above the return of the captured Sama chief's daughter led to fear of reprisals and thus to flight, the actual retaliation of Lawi's relatives gave rise to a fear of reprisals by the rebels that caused the entire village to flee.

The story related above may have resulted from some particular historical event, but it is impossible to know that for certain. Nevertheless, it had continued relevance for Sama people when Follet set it down, a relevance that reaches back into centuries of Sama social practice and precautions taken against the theft of their women—especially women of note. In the seventeenth-century southern Philippines, Francisco Combés noted that the Lutaos—those people who lived on the water—held the Subanun (*Subanos*), the river-dwellers, in a kind of vassalage. Although Combés viewed the Subanun as exceedingly "rude and barbarous, without any government; and a perpetual petty warfare is waged among them," he nevertheless remarked that their women are more chaste than those of other tribes. Whether for this reason or another, Lutao girls of rank were reared, for their own safety, among the Subanun.[100] Relatively chaste they may (or may not) have been; but being upriver certainly protected them from coastal raiding.

In another version of the Johor princess story recorded in North Borneo in 1922, the high-status Sama woman at the center of the tale was said to be the Johor Sultan's daughter. The rulers of both Sulu and Brunei fell in love with her. She was sent off to Sulu, to marry the better match, accompanied by a strong escort and war boats. The Brunei prince, in response, attacked the Johor boats and took the princess. Her Johor escorts and protectors dreaded the thought of either going on to Sulu, or going back to Johor. So they cruised the seas, picking up a living as best they could. Some, Rutter tells us, eventually formed piratical communities on the coasts of North Borneo.[101] This story explains relocation from Johor to the coasts of North Borneo. Using this story to explain the formation of piratical communities may well be attributed to Rutter, who shared the British North Borneo Company's long-standing concerns with the persistence and suppression of piracy.[102]

Other versions of the story similarly provide justification for, or an explanation of, dispersal. Pelras, in Balannipa, South Sulawesi, recorded a version told to him by

---

[100] BR, vol. 40, 11–13, http://www.gutenberg.org/files/30253/30253.txt, accessed May 5, 2013.

[101] See: Rutter, *British North Borneo*, 73, cited in Sopher, *The Sea Nomads*, 142; and Frake, "Lines across the Water."

[102] The British North Borneo Company actively settled and "pacified" the Bajau. See Warren, *The North Borneo Chartered Company's Administration of the Bajau*.

someone Bugis in which a Johor princess lost at sea is sought by the king's servants who continue their *"vie errant"* without finding her, while she winds up marrying in Boné.[103] In the mid-nineteenth century, von Dewall, writing about the north Borneo coast, recorded a version in which a Sama princess from Johor was swept away by a storm, which led him to conclude that the origin of the "Badjau" was in Johor. In this version, the people sent to look for the princess were not afraid to return to Johor, but instead got lost, and so settled on the coasts of Borneo, Celebes, and the Sulu islands.[104]

In these stories, the abduction of a woman implies that there was no marriage negotiation, no agreement about the appropriate level of bridewealth—the prestation the groom makes to a bride's family, and thus no mutual recognition of each other's status claims in social practice. Instead of this method of reproducing social class both within and across the boundaries of ethnic difference, the theft of a woman breaches the bounds of acceptability. In Sulawesi, such notions about the theft of women and unnegotiated unions are reflected in political declarations and in attitudes regarding retaliation. For instance, Cummings relates that oral and written treaties between communities contained oaths preventing the theft, seizure, or seduction of women by outsiders, and, as Chabot observed of pre-independence Makassar society, male relatives felt compelled to avenge unnegotiated unions by killing any man who ran off with their daughter, sister, niece, or cousin.[105]

Tales of relocation such as those related above conjure a view of the past set neither in a world of ethnic isolation (the colonial fantasy of sea nomads), nor one in which there is a single locus of dominant authority against which less powerful others both struggle and measure themselves. Rather, the many versions of this particular Sama oral tradition suggest a wider archipelagic social field, one in which relations among descent groups may be quite fraught and violent, and in which flight is one way out of demeaning and dangerous situations.

In contrast with the above stories, texts of two similar legends from the southern Philippines illustrate how Sama relocation was not a response to situations with other people, but instead appears to have been the result of sheer accident. In one story, the people stick their mooring stakes into the seabed to prepare for a storm or strong winds. However, instead of plunging into the seabed, their stakes

---

[103] Pelras, "Notes sur Quelques Populations Aquatiques," 157. Pelras also recorded a version in Kambuno, an island in the western Gulf of Boné, about a Bajo princess from Aceh who winds up in Luwu. Pelras (ibid., 164) also cites F. Trefers, *Het landschap Laiwoei in Z. O. Celebes en zijne bevolking*, *TAG* 31 (2nd series, 1914) on a version in which Sama arrive from the Philippines to *"Takatidung."* This could mean "Tidung atoll" or "Pirate Atoll," depending on the speaker and linguistic context. Liebner's four versions from Selayar bear a closer relation to those in the lontaraq; see Liebner, "Four Oral Versions of a Story."

[104] Von Dewall, "Aanteekeningen omtrent de Noordoostkust van Borneo," 446–47. "*De badjau zijn van djohorschen oorsprong. Eene djohorsche prinses was op zeetogt door storm verslagen geworden. De sulthan van Djohor zond eene menigte volks uit om haar optesporen. Daar de verlorene prinees [sic] evenwel niet werd wedergevonden, en de uitgezondenen reeds ver van Djohor verwijderd waren, zoodat zij den [sic] terugweg niet meer wisten, besloten zij zich neder te zetten op de kusten van Borneo en Celebes, en de groep Solokhs. De meesten wonen op het solokhsche eiland Dinawan [Palawan?]. Zij zijn over het algemeen de eilandbewoners van Borneo's noordoostkust. In mei 1849 kwamen 18 badjau-praauwen zich van Dinawan op Poelau-pandjang nederzetten en zouden de overigen, sterk 50 praawen, zich eveneens op de eilanden van Berou komen vestigen … In Boeloengan wonen geene badjaus, wel in Berou.*"

[105] See: Cummings, *Making Blood White*, 70; and H. Th. Chabot, *Kinship, Status and Gender in South Celebes* (Leiden: KITLV Press, 1996), 234–44.

instead stab and stick in a giant stingray, which takes them, while they sleep, to the Sulu archipelago. The other story is basically the same, yet in it, only the chief sets his stake, while all the other boats are tied to his.[106] In these examples, the entire story about Sama arrival in Sulu has no social impetus whatsoever. Relocation had nothing to do with intention, whether good or bad, but instead relied entirely on serendipity. These stories are included here because their explanations of relocation draw attention to chance, rather than intent, in the narrative. Whereas other versions revolved around the theft of a Sama woman, the daughter of a chief or a king, here instead one finds happenstance of mythic proportions.

In the *lontaraq* adaptation of the story about a highborn Sama woman's maritime relocation, a coincidental occurrence similarly sets the plot in motion. There is nothing particularly Bugis or "Sulawesi" about the use of coincidence as a narrative resource; nor did the *lontaraq* versions necessarily acquire their use of coincidence from the repertoire of Sama oral tales. Yet, both the above stories and the *lontaraq* versions employ fateful chance. The incident with the stingray plays a causal role in relocation, with no mention of a ruler's daughter. However, in the *lontaraq* versions, coincidence, which similarly propels the opening, directly affects the daughter of the *papuq*, the opening section's protagonist. This coincidence influences how one may interpret the way events unfold. In short, removing the intentional capture, and replacing it with chance, alters what it means for her to arrive and live among others in a new place.

This group of Sama stories is not the only one in the region to reflect ambiguities in the relations between different groups. Barbara Watson Andaya has noted how apparent contradictions in upstream–downstream (*ulu–ilir*) relations in Sumatra, not simply an outcome of European perceptions, were deeply embedded in indigenous culture and reflected in the themes of Sumatran folklore and legend. Interestingly, some of these stories involve the marriage of a woman into another group, or her abduction:

> If a typology of themes in Sumatran legend and folklore were compiled, the ambiguities in *ulu–ilir* dealings would be apparent. Numerous stories, for example, describe an ancestral hero or ruler who comes across burnt twigs or some sign of settlement further upstream, marries one of the community's daughters, and then rewards his new relatives with favors, honors, and titles in return for gifts of produce and loyal service. Other motifs invoke the deep tension inherent in this *ulu–ilir* relationship. Despite the bonds of kinship, family unity is constantly undermined by rivalries, betrayal, and dishonor. The ideal of the downstream king as a distant kinsman responsive to the obligations he owes his [upstream] relatives is implicit in *ulu* stories, but at the same time many revolve around the abduction of a beautiful upstream girl by *ilir* armies or the seizure of other precious possessions. Such tales are countered by others that tell of the brave deeds of the *ulu* ancestors who restore local honor by routing the *ilir* heroes in tests of strength and magical powers. Frequently an entire upstream community benefits by being granted freedom from tribute and labor duties.[107]

---

[106] Nimmo, *Magosaha: An Ethnography of the Tawi-tawi Sama Dilau*, 22–23.

[107] B. Andaya "Upstreams and Downstreams in Early Modern Sumatra," 547–48.

In this cluster of stories, where some contest the claims of others, the tales that counter the abduction of an upstream girl apparently restore local honor not by a direct response to an abduction, but instead by indirectly besting their downstream rivals through magic and tests of strength. Their demonstration of innate talents and prowess then allows for dispensation from the obligations of subordinates, rebalancing the scales of mutual accord.

Kinship in such tales may work as a metaphor for the relations between groups. However, since the way kinship comes about often affects the dynamics of ongoing relations and hence inheres in politics, kinship it is not merely a metaphor for political relations. Likewise, stories about the theft of women were not merely political allegory. The abduction of women and its social implications were a very real concern, beyond the confines of narrative, in actual people's lives and in politics.

## MATRILINES AND STORYLINES

It is hard to say when *LB Lemobajo* may initially have been written and incorporated this particular oral tradition about a Sama woman called I Lolo, or Putri Papuq (that is, I Lolo, the daughter of the *papuq*). Reasons internal to the manuscript itself logically suggest a date during or after Arung Palakka's rule. Primarily this comes down to the fact that the material following the story of I Lolo's relocation revolves around Arung Palakka and also presents claims about his status, his descent, and justifications of his rule. Scholarly estimations of when other chronicles were written lend support to this proposition. Scholars generally agree that the chronicles of Gowa, Talloq, Boné, and Wajoq were written in the seventeenth century, partly for reasons of style and unity of composition.[108] C. C. Macknight dates the writing of the Gowa and Talloq chronicles to shortly after 1669, their defeat in the Makassar War, and dates the Chronicle of Boné to the reign of Arung Palakka (1672–96).[109]

An intense focus on Arung Palakka was not, as one might expect, solely the concern of the Chronicle of Boné. Arung Palakka's notability in the production of historical discourse even in Makassar helps shed additional light on why he is so important in manuscripts about the Sama past. Apart from the chronicles, he appeared prominently in the *Makassar Annals*, that is, in the *lontaraq bilang* tradition sometimes called "diaries." In comparing the different texts used to prepare his critical edition, William Cummings found that the bulk of common entries concerned the 1660s and 1670s. The twenty-six common entries from the 1660s mostly deal with Gowa's conflicts with the VOC and Arung Palakka, while the sixteen from the 1670s almost exclusively address the actions of Arung Palakka. From the perspective of these common entries, Arung Palakka was "clearly the historical protagonist dominating the decade."[110] Yet, several entries about Arung Palakka, prior to the war, were also interpolated into the *Annals* after Makassar's

---

[108] J. Noorduyn, "Some Aspects of Macassar-Buginese Historiography," in D. G. E. Hal, ed., *Historians of South-East Asia* (London: Oxford University Press, 1961), 29–36; J. Noorduyn, "Origins of South Celebes Historical Writing," 143; and Druce, *The Lands West of the Lakes*, 69.

[109] Macknight, "South Sulawesi Chronicles and Their Possible Models," 325–26; and Druce, *The Lands West of the Lakes*, 70.

[110] Cummings, ed., *The Makassar Annals*, 31.

defeat. For instance, while he "subsequently become the preeminent figure in South Sulawesi for the remainder of the century,"[111] the record of his prewar exile from Makassar was later granted sufficient importance to be included after the fact.

*LB Lemobajo* and the *Badjo History* set down in Or 545/262 form part of this tradition of historical discourse in Sulawesi, sharing the aims of such *lontaraq* to "set down a statement of the status of the rulers and the ruling group more generally."[112] This was particularly important since, in the social system of south Sulawesi kingdoms, succession by primogeniture was not the rule. Rather, the pool of potential rulers was shaped by membership in a class largely determined by ascribed status, reckoned through bilateral descent. The *lontaraq* about the Sama past recognize an independent, specifically Sama source of high-status descent, and put this on a par with Makassar, specifically Gowa's, royal lineage. Hence, in addition to setting forth this status parity, I Lolo's offspring by Gowa royalty could also claim this status by virtue not only of a Gowa lineage but also through the Sama mother's line.[113] Moreover, as the *lontaraq* imply, this descent through her lineage represents an alternate source for the legitimacy conferred on Arung Palakka's rule.

During the seventeenth century, coinciding more or less with the allied Bugis and Dutch defeat of Makassar, a combination of factors enabled resolution of the power-sharing struggles between Boné's king and his council. An innovation reduced marital restrictions between families of royalty and of Boné's council. As in other parts of south Sulawesi, an ideology of "white blood" encouraged families of rulers to maintain their exclusive "purity." As such, in many kingdoms there were interdictions on marriage between the families of the rulers and those of the councils, creating a tiered, pyramidal social structure with the ruler and royalty at the top and a class of nobles beneath. However, fusing the families of king and council through intermarriage created, instead, one big nobility in which the ranking of power paralleled a blood hierarchy.[114] This would have made the elite class's social pyramid broader and given it a more flat-topped shape.

Council families that married "up" had children who inherited a higher social status, while the rulers, still preeminent, sat at the top of an expanding kin network. Facilitating the ability of low-status nobles to marry up the hierarchy may have provided a means and incentive for peripheral kin groups to marry into this expanding kin network, promoting Boné's political expansion. This innovation goes at least part way to explaining why there appears to be a shift from local integration, suggested by a preponderance of marriages between rulers and local *Arung* in the pre-Islamic sections of Bugis royal genealogies (fifteenth and sixteenth centuries), to a much greater occurrence of marriages between kingdoms in the post-Islamic

---

[111] Ibid., 90 (note 233).

[112] Macknight, "South Sulawesi Chronicles and their Possible Models," 326; and Druce, *The Lands West of the Lakes*, 69.

[113] This picture presents a curious contrast to the "Karaeng Bayo" who shares an apical position in Gowa's royal genealogy. Karaeng Bayo always seems to be taken to be male. Scholars, therefore, tend to interpret Karaeng Bayo as a representative of "stranger king" myths. Yet, like the figure in these stories, the Karaéng Bayo arose, *totompoq*, perhaps from the "underworld," or perhaps just from the sea, in contrast with the *tomanurung*, one who descended from "the heavens" or just the mountains.

[114] L. Andaya, *Arung Palakka*; Heather Sutherland, "Political Structure and Colonial Control in South Sulawesi," in *Man, Meaning and History: Essays in Honor of H. G. Schulte Nordholt*, ed. R. Schefold, J. W. Schoorl, and J. Tennekes (Dordrecht: Foris Publications, 1980), 237–38.

sections of the same genealogies, "particularly following the tumultuous events of the seventeenth century."[115] While intermarriage between realms served efforts at political consolidation, the expansion of aspiring nobility would, in turn, have dispelled minor royalty away from court centers, and augmented Bugis, and especially Boné's, political authority in peripheral regions.[116] More than just marriage politics between kingdoms, this promoted the expansion of a social and political class, while, to the extent that Boné dominated the process, it underpinned Boné's political expansion.

Bulbeck's statistical analysis of the transmission of elite Makassar titles during the sixteenth and seventeenth centuries found that, although people generally reckon descent bilaterally, the system excluded contenders by patrilineal descent toward the center. Toward the peripheries, however, it included potential title-holders by bilateral descent. What supposedly happened, then, was that men from high-status lineages could attach themselves to a wife from a lower-status lineage, and the offspring could belong to the wife's group. The privilege of "white blooded" descent allowed more powerful lineages to "dump their superfluous well-born men toward the margins," much as described for Boné above.[117] "The men thereby held exalted positions within their group ... which enjoyed greater prestige because of its attachment toward the centre. The privilege also allowed a powerful royal patriline to absorb territorial titles previously belonging to autonomous patrilines. The powerful royal retained his membership within his natal group while his wife, as the princess from the weaker line, transmitted the right of office to her husband through marriage, or to their sons through bilateral descent."[118]

In practice, people can trace their genealogies in different ways. This also holds for what appear from the center to be "in-marrying women," which not take account of the ways that those women and their descendants may have reckoned their descent through matrilines. Particularly when there is no territory to transfer, even if women take up a patrilocal residence in the center of another polity, in reckoning their descent, these women and their descendants might still emphasize matrilineality, rather than submerge it.

How women have positioned themselves and their progeny politically forms an aspect of political maneuvering worthy of further consideration. Using marriage as a way to get ahead politically was neither new, nor particularly Bugis. Across south Sulawesi, diverse groups shared beliefs both in the importance of ascriptive status, as well as in the position of women as status markers for a kin group. Moreover, strategic marriage played a role in both the development and strengthening of tributary relationships, which appear to have been part of the multicentered and

---

[115] Ian Caldwell, "Power, State and Society among the Pre-Islamic Bugis," *BKI* 151, 3 (1995): 397–98 and note 12. While the particular royal genealogies Caldwell uses to make this point are from Soppéng, this nonetheless indicates greater intermarriage among kingdoms of the peninsula generally, of which Boné was but one, yet arguably the most important one after the 1670s.

[116] Compare to Bulbeck, "The Politics of Marriage and the Marriage of Polities in Gowa," 280–315, esp. 311–12.

[117] Compare this to the many second sons of Europe's elite families who were sent off to the colonies.

[118] Ibid., 311–12.

highly decentralized political structure of south Sulawesi kingdoms certainly from 1600 on, and possibly from their early development in the fourteenth century.[119]

The status of women and their lineages were thus very important, and women made considerable effort to maneuver socially to improve the status of their descendants. For instance, the expansion of a seventeenth century political and social order in which marriage and descent were so central shaped the way noble Makassar women sought influence. They "sought influence both in the present and in the future by becoming ancestors linking later generations with influential forebears ... This was a world in which ancestors provided the social rank of their descendants. It was from their blood that one's greatness flowed."[120] Hence, it is rather curious that Karaenta ri Bontojeqneq and her famous brother, Sultan Hasanuddin, had a mother who was considered a commoner, according to information in the *Makassar Annals*.[121] It did not appear to be much of a handicap in how she conducted the politics of marriage and the marriage of polities. On the contrary, it may have impelled her to greater effort. Women such as Karaenta ri Bontojeqneq, "with their ability to marry numerous prominent men, and to bear high ranking offspring from more than one noble ... maximized their chances to become revered ancestors even as they positioned themselves as formidable individuals wielding great influence at court." Two of Karaenta ri Bontojeqneq's four marriages were to rulers of overseas kingdoms, Bima and Sumbawa, within Gowa's political ambit, and, apparently, she was so active in court politics that, in 1662, her brother temporarily exiled her.[122]

Such details that emerge fragmentarily in the dated lines of the *Annals* entries may become narrativized in the *lontaraq* chronicles and the brief historical overviews discussed earlier. These *lontaraq* writings about the past, including those about the Sama past, make up a cluster of traditions. As dialogically interrelated texts whose claims were (and sometimes still are) part of wider, overlapping fields of discourse and social interaction, a given *lontaraq* may, for instance, explicitly or implicitly, contest how the course of a war, or matters of lineage and status, are represented in another text.[123] Campbell Macknight has noted how sections of the Boné Chronicle mirror those of Gowa, especially with regard to the wars between them in the sixteenth century. He has also argued that Boné's chronicle may have been stimulated by Gowa's, or, indeed, have been a riposte to it.[124] Sometimes *lontaraq* smoothed over potentially inflammatory stories that came out in oral traditions, while at other times oral traditions might respond to written ones in order to clarify, explain, or modify accounts contained in *lontaraq* texts.

---

[119] Druce, *The Lands West of the Lakes*, 23, 26–27, 30.

[120] Cummings, ed., *The Makassar Annals*, 19.

[121] Ibid., 53 (note 108).

[122] Ibid., 19–20; see also William Cummings, "Historical Texts as Social Maps: *Lontaraq bilang* in Early Modern Makassar," *BKI* 161, 1 (2005): 40–62.

[123] On texts and language as dialogical fields of social interaction, see: M. M. Bakhtin, "Discourse in the Novel," in *The Dialogic Imagination*, ed. Michael Holquist, trans. Caryl Emerson and Michael Holquist (Austin and London: University of Texas Press, 1981), 269–422; and Bruce Mannheim and Dennis Tedlock, "Introduction," in *The Dialogic Emergence of Culture*, ed. Dennis Tedlock and Bruce Mannheim (Champaign: University of Illinois Press, 1995), 1–32.

[124] Macknight, "South Sulawesi Chronicles and their Possible Models," 325–26.

*Lontaraq* at times elided dangerous or uncomfortable memories and left unmentioned histories that might fuel anger and violence, such as the tensions that marked early relations between Gowa and Talloq. Yet, at times, oral traditions could fill in the details of what written representations had smoothed over. Such was the case with the death of Tunijalloq, known posthumously as "the one who was cut down." Nicholas Gervaise in the late-seventeenth century recorded details omitted from this unmentioned history, which, although perhaps exaggerated and containing a few errors, illustrated why, as the *Gowa Chronicle* reports, an intimate follower named "I Lolo" cut down his sovereign at sea. It was because the ruler had become infatuated with the wife of this powerful court noble and took her for his own. What written accounts leave unsaid can be as striking as what they contain.[125] Of course, in this case, what also went unsaid—perhaps because it was so obvious to contemporaries—is that a powerful court noble named *I Lolo* cut down his sovereign *at sea*. Readers here may well wonder whether this I Lolo was a Sama man of high-status descent, as his title would seem to indicate. After his regicide he reportedly "threw himself into the sea and was never heard from again."[126] Had he returned, of course, he would have been killed; it is therefore much more satisfying for storytellers to make a mystery of whether he lived.

In other cases, oral traditions offer elaborate explanations that might smooth over information that could cause offense or discomfort. For instance, the Chronicle of Gowa states that the mother of the ruler Tumapaqrisiq Kallona (r. c. 1510–46) was a slave.[127] However, an oral tradition related by Andi Ijo Karaeng Laloang, the last ruler of Gowa, told to him by his father and uncle, countered that with an elaborate story of how she was actually the daughter of the ruler of Balainipa in Mandar. When she was a young child, someone ran amok during a cockfight outside the Balainipa ruler's palace and the princess went and hid by the river. She was later found by a trader who took her to Talloq. Eventually it was known that she was the child of the ruler of Balainipa and, when she was older, she was married to the ruler of Gowa.[128]

A narrative device appears to turn her low status as a slave into an accidental transfer to ethnic others who later become cognizant of her royal descent, after which she is married to the ruler. The sequence of the narrative device is: accidental relocation, new life in the context of ethnic others, revelation of her identity, and marriage to royalty. In this story the process of effacement works in the move from written to oral. By comparison, this same narrative device makes posterity's perceptions rosier in the adaptation from oral to written in the Sama materials examined below.[129]

---

[125] Cummings, *Making Blood White*, 84–86.

[126] Ibid., 85.

[127] G. J. Wolhoff and Abdurrahim, eds., *Sedjarah Goa* (Ujung Pandang: Jajasan Kebudayaan Sulawesi Selatan dan Tenggara, n.d. [1959]), 25, cited in Druce, *The Lands West of the Lakes*, 6.

[128] Abdurrazak Dg. Patunru, *Sedjarah Gowa* (Ujung Pandang: Jajasan Kebudayaan Sulawesi Selatan dan Tenggara, 1969), 47, cited in Druce, *The Lands West of the Lakes*, 56.

[129] In an oral version of "the Story of Maturaga," collected by B. F. Matthes in the late nineteenth century, and in a manuscript version of the same story examined by William Cummings, the main character intentionally kills the ruler of the underworld by pouring boiling water into his wound. However, in the version of the story described by Wayne Bougas, the ruler of the underworld is killed unintentionally; see: Matthes, "Boegineesche en Makassarsche Legenden," in H. Van den Brink, *Dr. Benjamin Frederik Matthes*, pp. 384–85;

## SWEPT AWAY BY MYTH

In the oral versions of the tale examined above, the daughter of the Sama leader was variously: captured at sea on the way to a royal betrothal; stolen by a land chief from whom she escaped; and swept away by a storm. In the *lontaraq*, she is also swept away by accident, but the force that determines her fate is less natural than supernatural. One might say she is swept away by Bugis myth, for the plot device that causes her change of course is straight out of an episode in the Bugis epic cycle *I La Galigo*.

A number of features distinguish the *lontaraq* version of the story, along with closely related oral versions, from those found in Sama oral traditions from other parts of Southeast Asia. First, the Sama in the *lontaraq* are simply called the "Luwu Bajo." Although they get washed away from Luwu by an unexpected current and then spread out to look for I Lolo, the *papuq*'s daughter, Luwu is not taken as the collective point of origin. It is just one of the areas in which they live. Moreover, their going off to look for her is not recruited to an explanation of how Sama people came to be dispersed across the region. Instead of being preoccupied with the origins and dispersal of the Bajo, the *lontaraq* and similar oral versions focus the story on the Sama woman lost at sea. The narrative unfolds around what takes place as a consequence of her initial misadventure. Rather than concern itself with the group's relocation, as many brief oral versions from other areas do, here the audience is directed instead to her relocation among another people.

Naia ri wettu nrebbana na Wélenrénngé nalémpeq ittellona ri Ussuq,

When the *wélenréng* tree fell, there was a flood of egg-liquids at Ussuq,

nasiaccimalireng na Bajoé sibawa puwanna,

and the Bajo and their *puwang* were swept away with the current.

natabbé tona mali anaq puwanna riasenngé I Lolo.

His child, named I Lolo, was also lost.

Nataterré-terréna Bajoé llao sappai anaq puwanna.

The Bajo people scattered all over to go search for their *puwang*'s child.

Nasiaréqni wenninna siaréq toni essona assappana Bajoé ri anaq puwanna

Night and day the Bajo searched for the child of their *puwang*.

natakkoq engkana pammaséna puwang *Allahu Taala* sibawa surona

Unexpectedly, by the mercy of Allah the most High and his messenger,

naengkana naéngkalinga Bajoé karébanna anaq puwanna

the Bajo people heard news that the child of their *puwang*

naitté pabbélolanngé ri Gowa napaénréq i ri salassaqé

was picked up by a fisherman in Gowa and brought up to the palace

ri Gowa, ri bolana Sombaé.[130]

of Gowa, to the house of the *somba* [the ruler].[131]

---

Cummings, "The Dynamics of Resistance and Emulation," 426–30; and Wayne Bougas, "Bantayan: An Early Makassarese Kingdom, 1200–1600 A.D.," *Archipel* 55 (1998): 108–9.

[130] *LB Lemobajo*, 3.

[131] "The *somba*" means the Ruler of Gowa, but should not be confused with Petta Torisombaé, also known as Arung Palakka; the latter (who also became the ruler of Gowa) is the subject of the second episode in *LB Lemobajo*.

The story begins by launching straight into the best known episode of the Bugis *I La Galigo* cycle, *Ritumpanna wélenrénngé*, the felling of the *wélenréng* tree by the hero Sawerigading. Here, however, it incorporates the Sama, and does so from the beginning. Like a fable that begins "once upon a time," it first lays out the setting: the Bajo people who appeared in Ussuq or Mangkuttu in the Luwu region were called the Bajo of Luwu. In Ware there was a *raja*, the *opu* (ruler) of Ware, named Sawerigading; and a *raja* of the Bajo named I Papuq, with a child named I Lolo, who came from Mangkuttu. In this episode, Sawerigading must cut down a particular mighty tree to fashion a boat in which he will sail off to *Cina*, a location in south Sulawesi.[132] There he hopes to find I Cudai, a woman who looks just like his twin sister, with whom he had fallen in love but may not marry. With the preparatory ritual help of *bissu*, Sawerigading fells the *wélenréng* tree for his boat.[133] When the *wélenréng* tree splashes down, all the eggs that were in it create a flood of egg-liquids. The Bajo are swept away, and I Lolo, out in her boat alone, goes missing, so the people go off to look for her.[134] She is washed all the way from Luwu at the head of the Gulf of Boné, to the shores of Makassar.

This use of the well-known *wélenréng* tree episode from *La Galigo* brings the story of the Sama woman's maritime passage into the cultural universe of the Bugis and into the era of a mythical past. The Bajo connection to Luwu in this story is a literary, rather than historical, connection, which conjures an accidental reason for I Lolo's relocation to Gowa, while simultaneously placing her and her father, anachronistically, in the time and place of legendary white-blooded Bugis heroes. In starting with a *La Galigo* episode, the *lontaraq* resembles the Chronicle of Boné, which, before narratively listing a series of rulers, defeats, and alliances, gives a summary background of the mythic beginnings of the Bugis ancestors, the *tomanurung* (or those who "came down" from the heavens, as explained earlier).[135] Audiences would have no trouble distinguishing the qualitative difference between this material of myth and legend, a culturally central touchstone "storied" even in mere references to it, and the listing of historical names, titles, and occurrences that follow this first section of these two *lontaraq*.

In the long oral version related by Lo Kadér, who was familiar with a lost "sibling" manuscript, most of his telling was in Sama. Here he describes I Lolo's arrival at Gowa:

---

[132] Or 545/262. *Cina* is a legendary kingdom that appears to have been located along the Cenrana River in South Sulawesi; see Caldwell, "Power, State and Society among the pre-Islamic Bugis," 410.

[133] Although the first page or two of *LB Lemobajo* were missing, the story picked up on the first extant page with a short rendition of Sawérigading's felling of the *wélenréng* tree. The *bissu* are cross-dressing ritual specialists at former Bugis courts. In *I La Galigo*, there is at least one instance where a female character is also a *bissu*, namely, Wé Tenriabéng, Sawérigading's twin sister, referred to as I Abéng. See Sirtjo Koolhof and Roger Tol, eds., *I La Galigo; Menurut Naskah NBG 188 yang disusun oleh Arung Pancana Toa* Jilid I, transcribed and trans. Muhammad Salim and Fachruddin Ambo Enre (Jakarta: KITLV, in cooperation with Jembatan, 1995), 29.

[134] Or 545/262 leaves out the eggs and just says that when the tree fell it caused a flood and swept the Bajo away from there.

[135] Macknight and Paeni, "The Chronicle of Boné," unpublished transliteration and English translation.

Mandoré nggé' lagi kolé na ngiramang ia katintoroang na baka kangilantuangna nakarna ndaka ja anu tulumbangi – tulu ngilau tetapi para, bangina, bona tadampar mandoré. Ngge' lagi kolé na ngusi dirina, *terpaksa*, alaqna né busei Samana, bona ngongsorang ia, a bobo'na ngingkatang bulu tikolo'na, bona malutang ia ma bunda lépana, masi du lubina, batuahna iru *antara* bunda lépa baka tikolo'na, bona paléa.

*Setelah* iru nia dakau suku Goa a poré mamia pugélang lao baka jalana. Dumalang kitana lelépa. "Lépa ai ko" yuqna "oré?" "Misa timbauna bona pakai kamudi" yuqna. "Kamudina pakai batah." A, patupi ia. Tarintahna, é – nia manusiana, "O, matai kapah" yuqna. Patuku ia tarintah masi napasna. Tarintahna ingka itu – bulu tikolo. "Taha-taha" yuqna "bulu tikolo dinda itu. Ai jana nia dinda itu. Bona malasona" qna. "Dinda tika mangga janaq" yuqna "itu."

Sampé ansiniangna iru palimbaq ia ka dara. Karna kitu ia *bertindak* batingga-batingga madialang pikirangna oré. *Lapor*, batuahna, ka Karaéng Goa.

Tika ia ma *istana* ditilau ia alé *penjaga*. "Ai" yuqna. Yuqna *"Penting"* yuqna "Nia na *lapor*ku ka Karaéng."

Yuqna "Ai na ma*dilapor*nu?"

Yuqna "Nia tau – (batuk)—

Nggé'né sillongah baong Mangkasarku. Baongku Sama turus né, a di? Sasalah jana baong Mangkasarku. Lamong baong Bugis, té, *los*.[136]

There she could no longer stand the feeling of tiredness and hunger, because it was not only three nights and days, but many nights before she was cast ashore there. She was no longer able to make herself move, so was forced to take her Sama oar and stake it. Then she tied her hair to it, and coiled it around the bow of the boat. And there was still more of it, meaning between the bow and her head; then she lay down.

After that there was a Gowa person who went to look for some food with his fishing net. Walking, he saw a small boat. "What boat is this?" he asked. "It has no topsides. And it uses a rudder, as well as a tiller." He moved closer and saw—huh?! Someone's in it. "Oh, maybe dead," he said. He approached and he saw that she was still breathing. He noticed the rope of hair. "How long," he said, "the hair of this woman is! This woman is really something. And beautiful, too," he said. "I wonder where this woman is from."

At this point he came back up on shore, since, he was thinking, he didn't want to take just any old action. That is to say, he reported to the King of Gowa.

Arriving at the palace, the guard asked, "What?" "It's important," the Gowa person said, "there's something to report to the Karaéng."

"What do you have to report?" the guard asked.

"There's a person –" [he coughs; he frame shifts:]

My Makassar isn't perfect anymore. I'll just continue speaking in Sama, ok? I'd mess up in Makassar. (But contrary to what you might expect) if it were Bugis, no problem.[137]

---

[136] Words borrowed from Indonesian are in italics. "Los" is a Dutch loanword (meaning "slack," "free," "loosely") in Indonesian. The Sama particle *té* indicates something that is contrary to expectations. The Bugis *wélendréng* was known as *balindrah* in Sama.

[137] Lo Kadér, recorded July 27, 1994, Tampo, Southeast Sulawesi, transcription pp. 11–12. I

I Papuq, in the meantime, received news that his daughter had been found at Gowa and brought up to the *karaéng*'s palace. After consulting with his many "children and grandchildren," a phrase which could also be read as his "descendants," or simply "his people,"[138] he sails together with them to Gowa:

Pada (mengkali)nga i upowadaé

Upomanasa i baja ri denniarié na to pa(da) tarakka sempeq

Narékko pada maréngkalinga no obbi nassituru no pada redduq i toddoqmu muabang ngi gajomu mupatettonngi pallajarammu mupada rui i sempeqmu, tapada sempeq muttama ri Goa tapada manessai wi karébaé engakana ri Gowa ri sari bolana Sombaé anaq puwammu Loloé.

Aga napada pallebbani sempeqna ia maneng maégaé sininna anaq eppoé.

Napada mammanuq-manuqna lao sompeqna muttama ri Goa esso wenni.[139]

"Listen, everyone, to what I say:

I hope that tomorrow at early dawn we all depart together by sail.

If you all hear the call, agree, all of you, to pull out your punting poles, push your oars, stand up your boat masts, and hoist your sails, together we will sail into Gowa, together we will investigate the truth of the news that at the palace of Gowa in the house of the *somba*, is your *puwang*'s child, the *lolo*."

So all together those many descendants unfurled their sails.

Together in procession, day and night, they sailed a course to enter Gowa.

They make an impressive showing in the harbor. Just as I Papuq consults with his people, the *karaéng* consults with his ministers. An envoy goes back and forth between I Papuq and the *karaéng* with messages, decisions are weighed and agreed upon, and the leaders are shown great deference. When an auspicious day arrives and I Papuq goes up to the palace with his large entourage, they are all well-treated and served food, despite being so numerous that places must be made for them to sit outside. Finally, I Papuq is asked what brings him to Gowa, and his response is polite but a little cagey, explaining that his daughter has gone missing as a result of the flood from the *wélendréng* tree. He does not mention that he had heard that she landed and was found at Gowa. The *karaéng* wonders to himself whether I Papuq is the father of "the one (with) whom I made a shared life, who I made my wife, whose origin I do not know." And those who were gathered there, the members of his council of ministers (*adeq tomabbicara*), and the representatives of the tributary domains, in their hearts they also wondered the same thing. He suggests to his chief advisor (*tomabbicara*), and the latter agrees, that maybe it would be good if his wife whose-provenance-we-do-not-know might come and sit in the presence of the revered *karaéng*-regalia.[140]

---

have included the last line since it indicates that the teller thought listeners (his nephew and myself) might expect to hear the fisherman code switch to speak in Makassar. Neither his nephew nor I had heard the story before. His remark suggests that in the version familiar to him, such a code switch took place here.

[138] See Chabot, *Kinship, Status and Gender in South Celebes*, 149.

[139] *LB Lemobajo*, p. 4.

[140] *LB Lemobajo*, 4–10. Here the word *arajang* is used, apparently, to bestow or equate with the *karaéng* a special symbolic and spiritual source of royalty that the regalia (*arajang*) embody.

She comes out accompanied by her close attendants, and when she sees I Papuq, she requests that Karaéng Torisombaé permit her to serve *sirih* to her "karaéng," "whose name is I Papuq, and also called *Tidung Karaéng Bayoka Nisomba Tonji*" (a reference to the *kelong* verse discussed above). The *karaéng* tells her "go," and, along with all those present, he is astonished. All there in the palace say to themselves:

| | |
|---|---|
| Arung maraja ha paléq ri lau napobainé Karaénta Torisombaé, nisoko itta-ittana engka ri salassaé naéwa sipuppureng Karaénta ri laleng balékona ceppanigaé, nadeq engka rapi nawa-nawa i ri akkarungeng marajana pangulungenna Karaénta.Naengka mani puwanna napada engka paddissengetta | It appears that Karaéng Torisombaé has been married to great royalty of the east/the sea, all this time at the palace accompanying the shared fate of the *karaéng* in the embrace of the shelter of the mosquito net. No one had imagined the greatness of the one who shares the life of our *karaéng*. |
| Ri onrong akkarungenna naéwaé sisampureng Karaénta.[141] | Only after her father came did we then know the place of her realm, of our *karaéng*'s friend-of-one-*sarung*.[142] |

There followed a few days of rest, and after the *karaéng* consulted with his ministers (*adeq marilaleng pabbicara gowa*), they invited I Papuq to chose a village from among those under Gowa's protection where I Papuq and his many descendants/people could live. "'All that my many children and grandchildren want is to live in the shade/protection of the place between what is called Kalukukalukuang Point (*Tanjong*) down to Cikowang. For, living there, and occupying all the islands and deltas, all of I Papuq's many children and grandchildren [descendants] will seek their livelihood from Déwakeng all the way to Libukeng Tenngaé … so I Papuq returned and gathered his children and they made villages and set down roots [to stay]."[143]

A few years later, a ceremony was held for the child of the *karaéng* and I Lolo to be circumcised and receive his first haircut. There was no discernible difference between their clothing. "As if the grandeur of I Papuq was visibly the equivalent degree [of status] as the fineness of the *Karaéng*'s vestments." The ceremony was followed by further festivities.[144] Finally, I Papuq says to the *karaéng*: "I will keep my grandson at the palace, to be taken as a sign in Gowa of the greatness of I Papuq," and he instructs the *karaéng* that if there is another ceremony planned for I Papuq's grandson, to stand a banner of I Papuq's grandeur (or prestige) so that it may also become I Lolo's sign regarding the realm of the Bajo.[145] I Papuq also stored there at the Gowa palace a number of his regalia implements (*pakéang arajanna*) for use in certain ceremonies as a sign of the Bajo's realm (called: *cindé, ambarala* [*sic*], *tokong*

---

[141] Ibid., 10.

[142] A poetic way of saying they share a bed. A *sarung* is a piece of cloth, often with its ends sewn together to make a big tube, worn tied as clothing, but also serves as bedclothes. "*Lau*" in Bugis means "east," a word derived from the direction of the sea for most Bugis lands; "*lau*" also means "sea," cognate with Indonesian "*laut*."

[143] Ibid., 12.

[144] Ibid., 14.

[145] "I Lolo" here may refer to his daughter, but could also mean the grandson.

*duwa*, as well as some that made noises: *gendang, kettok-kettok, anak beccing, siasiaé*).[146] I Papuq also left Karaénta Torisombaé "the scale of a boat" (as in a fish scale), as a sign of I Papuq's decendants following the *karaéng* and sheltering in Gowa's shade or protection under the *karaéng*'s grandeur.[147]

| | |
|---|---|
| Nakkedana Karaénta ri (I) Papuq, | The *karaéng* said to I Papuq: |
| Tattimpaq I babanna Goa muttama, tattimpaq toi babanna Goa muwassu. | "Gowa's door is open, you come in; also [if] Gowa's door is open, you go out.[149] |
| Agi-agi rennu cenning atinna I Papuq I Lolo, ia ni napogauq napakkuwa, nakarana engkana na Lolo nangurusi Karaénta Torisombaé. | Whatever I Papu I Lolo wants in his heart then that is what will be worked on, because of Karaénta Torisombaé's shared descent.[150] |
| Naia bettuwanna riasenggé Lolo, engkana Lolo nauru sibawa Karaénta Torisombaé, I Papuq. | As for the meaning of those called Lolo, Lolo already existed, their descent is the same as Karaénta Torisombaé, [and/or] I Papuq. |
| Makkuniro nariaseng Lolo anaqna arunna Bajoé. | Hence, those called Lolo are children of the ruler of the Bajo. |
| Makkedani Karaénta Torisombaé ri (I) Papuq, "Baraq madécénggi soro rioloq I Papuq noq ri lopinna. Nasseri ni Karaénta Torisombaé enrenngé Adeq Pabbicarana Goa ri onro assiissengenna I Papuq na Karaénta Torisombaé." | Karaénta Torisombaé then said to I Papuq, "Perhaps you may wish to return to your boat. Karaénta Torisombaé and Gowa's ministers (*adeq pabbicara*) now comprehend about the situation of I Papuq's acquaintance with Karaénta Torisombaé." |
| Nasorona I Papuq I Lolo sibawa anaq eppona pada nok ri lopinna. | So I Papuq I Lolo with his descendants together went down to their boats. |
| Namarapeq na ri onrong assennangenna ri lopié enrenngé anaq eppona. Nasiaréq na ittana, siaréq tona taunna siaréq tona pariamana ittana Makkatukatuwo anak eppona I Papuq maégaé. Tamat.[148] | He was calm at his favorite place there on that boat with his people. For some time, many years, even several decades,[151] those many people of I Papuq sought their living. The end. |

---

146 Defined by Matthes in his dictionaries where he also made drawings of them. Some of these implements I saw in the possession of a very old woman on an island in the Takabonerate atoll.

147 Ibid., 14–15.

148 Ibid., 15.

149 Viz., you are free to come and go as you please.

150 Here he could be referring either to the story of the founding couple of the Gowa lineage, which through the "Karaéng Bayo" would give them a shared descent, or he could be referring to their grandson, in whom they have a common descendant.

151 *Pariamana*, a period of 8 or 12 years. Matthes 1874, p. 133. Cf. Javanese *windu*.

In Lo Kadér's telling, after I Lolo lands in Gowa, the people there are similarly ignorant about who she is. Yet in this Sama language version, her identity remains unknown to those in Gowa explicitly because she does not speak. It is not just that she is a silent character and the narrator speaks for her. Rather, the fact of her not speaking is very strongly marked. When, carried in her boat, she arrives at the stairs of the palace, she briefly regains consciousness and is asked where she is from, but she gives no answer. Her breath comes haltingly because of hunger and exhaustion, so they feed her and over time nurse her back to health. Once she has fully recovered she still does not answer when the ruler's wife (*nda datu*) asks where she is from, and so it goes, whether she is left alone or whether other young women repeatedly ask her. She does not answer—does not, in fact, speak at all.

The Gowa ruler has a dream in which he is told not to neglect this girl, because she is not just anybody. As he is getting old and his son would not be a suitable heir without a wife, he decides to marry him to this unspeaking young woman. This is agreed to by the elders and they have a simple wedding, "even though she has no *wali*" (a *wali*, in Islamic practice, is a male relative legally responsible for a bride). Hence, in this oral version, the Gowa ruler marries her to his son. After they are married, things between them are harmonious. Yet, even when she becomes pregnant, she continues not to speak. Nonetheless, despite her silence, actions symbolic of her Sama affiliation and status are described in detail, such as making a *sangkinih*, a kind of bracelet and belt amulet from pieces of fish bone tied with thread.

Lo Kadér's storytelling was interrupted at this point by my friend and sometimes-assistant, his favorite nephew, who asked: "Hang on a second, this woman who was swept away, where was she from?" Lo Kadér replied, after a pause: "Bajoé." ("Bajoé," referring not to "the Bajo" in a general sense, since he was speaking Sama and not Bugis, but rather to the place Bajoé on the coast of Boné.) "You don't know her name?" his nephew asked. To which Lo Kadér replied, "No. Shall I go on?" And his nephew eagerly said, "Yes!"

That exchange confirmed that, like the people in Gowa, we in the audience did not know her name. Nor did the audience know exactly why she did not speak, but we did know of her Sama lineage. The audience hearing this version could hardly avoid being aware that she lived in Gowa with the self-knowledge of who she was, yet was surrounded by people who knew nothing about her background.

This state was explicitly addressed in the story. The connection between her not speaking and their ignorance of her background formed the subject of an exchange between the *karaéng* and his son. The *karaéng* was curious about how things were going with the newlyweds, so he asks his son:

"Baong ai di*pakén*u na baka ndanu?"

"What language do you use with your wife?"

Yuqna, "Karaéng, misa' sikali baong." Yuqna, "tapa *silisurah*[152] néku ndaka na nia *suara*. Tapi nggé' du na tantangna, batuahna ansiniang iru nggé' daka du ia kitu. Ai-ai akataku *ikut* na du na!"

"*Karaéng*, there is no speaking at all," the son said. "I have been only decent, [yet] she's had no voice. But she also has not opposed" [meaning by this that she hasn't refused, either]. "What-

---

[152] This word was unrecognizable to both myself and Lo Kadér's nephew Kamaruddin, whose first language is Sama. I think it is an approximation (or unknown cognate) of the Indonesian word *susila*, decent or well-behaved.

"Dadi misa sikalina *bicara*?"

ever my desire, she goes along with it, too," he said.

"So there hasn't been any speaking at all?"

"Misa" yuqna. "Ruruaangné baongku, baong Bugis, baong Mangkasar na, misa" yuqna.

"None," the son replied. "Already [I have tried] all sorts of languages I know: Bugis, Makassar; there is nothing," he said.

"O, ai jana," yuq Datu itu, "suku ai ko jana na itu?"[153]

"What, I wonder," the ruler mused, "what descent group could she be from, this one?"

While in *LB Lemobajo* her lineage is revealed in the context of her father's audience with the *karaéng*, in Lo Kadér's telling, the revelation of who she is accompanies her first public act of speech, or rather, of song. In Lo Kadér's version, she continues not speaking all the way through childbirth. In contrast with her silence, the baby, once he starts to cry, cannot seem to stop. Attendants try all kinds of things: they put him to bed, they sing to him, they try Bugis songs and Makassarese songs, but nothing seems to help. In the meantime, the infant's silent mother takes a machete and goes out to find pieces of bamboo, which she then splits and bends and, bringing them back up to the house, weaves into a cradle or swing. She hangs it securely and climbs in:

A, turus tapaqna ma todah iru ningkolo, turus pugaina batitu tanangna, *seakan* malaku ia ana oré. Dijulukang ka ia. Dijulukang ka ia ampina né anana itu. Tatarintahna ana na. Soro tatarintahna, turus batuahna iru pallihna uyana. Uyana yuqna:

As soon as she sat in the swing she did this [movement] with her hands as if she were requesting the child. He was given to her. He was given to her and she rocked this child in her arms. She gazed at her child. As soon as she looked at her child, she immediately sang to him. The song went like this:

"*Manna bajo tobajoa*" qna
"*Manna cidung tociduang.*
*Cidung karaéng*
*bajo ka ni somba tongji.*"

"*Manna bajo tobajoa,*" she said
"*Manna cidung tociduang.*
*Cidung karaéng*
*bajo ka ni somba tongji.*"[155]

Turus takatonang batuahna karaéng Sama bélé. A, turus takatonnang mandoré. Bo—suku Sama bélé. Bajo batuahna, adi, Somba bélé na itu. A, ditetené, di anu, patilauang (ansiniang iru).[154]

Right away it was known that this meant she's a *karaéng* Sama. It was immediately understood over there. Wo— from Sama people! Bajo, in other words, you know? Ah, she was examined, was, what's it?—asked [about her provenance].

---

[153] Lo Kadér, transcription, 15.

[154] Ibid., 16. *Ansiniang* is a nominalization of *ansini*, which in Indonesian would be *tadi*. It indicates previousness, not origin, and has a wider semantic range than "*tadinya,*" the closest Indonesian equivalent. So in using this word to talk about who this mysterious woman was or where she was from, it did not imply some place (or descent) as an ultimate origin, but rather

A number of times I asked people familiar with this story why they thought she did not speak. Generally the response was shoulder shrugs, except for one man who pointed out that, after all, she had arrived in Gowa, so maybe she just did not speak the Makassar language. However, there seems to be more to it than that.

In both oral and written versions, she arrives at Gowa accidentally by dint of a flood caused by the mythical *wélenréng* tree. She is unconscious and cannot be identified. Her unplanned voyage and fortuitous arrival set important constraints on how one may understand the story. Accident forecloses the interpretive possibility of seeing her presence in Gowa as the result of any intentional human action. Perhaps if one had no familiarity with other versions of the story from around the archipelago, this would seem little more than quirky. However, since so many versions of the story in this class of narratives entail her capture by others, it is hard not to draw the conclusion that here, accidental relocation stands in place of capture. The affront and insult of capture, which demeans status not just of individuals but of kin groups, is out of place and irreconcilable in a form of writing that emphasizes and aims to bolster, not to diminish, genealogical worthiness and status. Euphemizing capture this way effaces it from the story, thereby removing it as an explanation for the protagonist's relocation and her nonnegotiated marital union.

The woman's identification gets further deferred, in the *lontaraq* version, by her silence regarding her parentage and provenance, and, in Lo Kadér's oral version, by her muteness. This renders her socially illegible to those in her new setting. The unveiling of her identity is the climax of the story, by revealing at once that she is both Sama as well as from an elite lineage.

The use of coincidence or accident as a literary device to alter the interpretation of a narrative by obscuring something potentially offensive or inflammatory (e.g., capturing a woman and marrying her without a negotiation between kin groups), appears not only in stories from Sulawesi, but also in stories from the wider archipelago. Ruzy Hashim finds another sort of "accident" in the *Sejarah Melayu* (the Malay Annals). There, the accidental closing of a door causes a key character to commit suicide because he reads this as an action taken by the sultan, whom he presumes he has angered and thus whose favor he has lost. Hashim argues that this scribal ploy of focusing attention on the accident as a reason for the character's suicide basically obviates the reader's or audience's ability to interpret his suicide as an act of protest.[156]

---

only what had been just prior—where she had come from (before here), who she was descended from (before herself).

[155] In this rendition of the *kelong*, Tidung has been changed to "cidung." As an approximation of what the *kelong* says, this verse is unmistakable, but also untranslatable, even as its intent is clear: to convey that the Sama also have an elite lineage due the same sort of respect that other royalty receive. An older Sama man on Pulau Kambuno recalled there being more than just this one couplet. Moreover, in the version he recalled, this particular couplet came out in response to a perceived insult and not simply in an effort to stop her baby's crying and thus ending her own silence. The point is that this phrase in the couplet and what it signified maintained a prominent place in a somewhat different version of the story. In fact, it was much less common for me to hear "tellings" of the story than it was to encounter references to the narrative through allusions to or approximations of this *kelong*.

[156] Ruzy Hashim, "Bringing Tun Kudu out of the Shadows: Interdisciplinary Approaches to Understanding the Female Presence in the Sejarah Melayu," in *Other Pasts: Women, Gender and History in Early Modern Southeast Asia*, ed. Barbara Watson Andaya (Honolulu: Center for

What is the significance of the Sama story's adaptation to this Bugis manuscript medium? Why was the story taken up? Under what conditions did it makes sense to entextualize the story, extracting it from one context of circulation and re-embedding it in another, with new discursive parameters and circuits of oral and written production?[157] Entextualization always serves political goals.[158] To make sense of the strong memory of descent through this Sama matriline, it is worth recalling that the entextualization moved the story into a specifically Bugis linguistic and cultural context. Given the claims made in subsequent sections of the *lontaraq* about Sama genealogical precedence in relation to Arung Palakka, and a past of ties between Bugis rulers and Sama lineages from which "viceroys" and "vicereines" to Boné were chosen, the story's entextualization must have occurred when demonstrating these ties greatly mattered. Doing so may have mattered to people "on both sides," that is, to both Bugis and Sama kin, as well as to those descended from both, particularly through this Bugis–Sama lineage. The text provides a way to understand those interconnections. Moreover, in addressing its audience, the text contributes both to the creation, and to the reproduction, of a "public" with stakes in the politics of smoothing over potential offense and according status recognition.

This bears a remarkable similarity to the political savvy with which Arung Palakka incorporated men from Tiworo into his elite guard. When Arung Palakka offered sixty men from Tiworo a prestigious way to serve him and Boné, conferring upon them positions in his guard of prime commanders, he provided a kind of recognition that softened the blow of Tiworo's demolition. This bestowal of rank (and arms) on former foes allowed Arung Palakka to include them politically and militarily within the orbit of Boné's authority. Bugis-language *lontaraq* manuscripts similarly offered a medium to recognize the standing of particular Sama lineages, and to embody and attest to their longstanding relationship with Boné. Manuscripts were passed on intergenerationally, helping to reconstitute those connections. No more enduring "proof" of lineage existed than such texts, whose dissemination, recopying, and resuscitation in new oral versions helped to reproduce the memory of the precedence and recognition they proclaimed. No more public recognition of status claims existed than their confirmation in negotiated marriages, a contrast to their abrogation in capture, which is why, in the *lontaraq* versions of the story, a very public wedding resolves the plot in the story's dénouement.

---

Southeast Asian Studies, University of Hawai'i at Mânoa, 2000).

[157] On entextualization, see R. Bauman and C. L. Briggs, "Poetics and Performance as Critical Perspectives on Language and Social Life," *Annual Review of Anthropology* 19 (1990): 59–88; C. L. Briggs and R. Bauman, "Genre, Intertextuality, and Social Power," *Journal of Linguistic Anthropology* 2, 2 (1992): 131–72; S. Gal and K. A. Woolard, "Constructing Languages and Publics: Authority and Representation," in *Languages and Publics: The Making of Authority*, ed. S. Gal and K. A. Woolard (Manchester: St. Jerome, 2001), 1–12; M. Silverstein and G. Urban, eds., *Natural Histories of Discourse* (Chicago: University of Chicago Press, 1996); and Joseph Sung-Yul Park and Mary Bucholtz, "Introduction. Public Transcripts: Entextualization and Linguistic Representation in Institutional Contexts," *Text and Talk* 29, 5 (2009), 483–500.

[158] Briggs and Bauman, "Genre, Intertextuality, and Social Power"; C. L. Briggs, "Metadiscursive Practices and Scholarly Authority in Folkloristics," *Journal of American Folklore* 106 (1993): 387–434.

### BEYOND LOCALIZATION: MOBILITY, BORROWING, AND TRANSFORMATION

If these stories were treated as products of a purely local character, the difference between capture and accident would probably not attract notice. Bringing together both attestations and manuscripts from different parts of the insular world to one analytical space reveals that they form a class of narratives joined by the logic of their plot structure and the placement of a Sama woman at their center. Rather than a search for the ur-story among them, as if there were an original version, or its putative origins, examining how the narrative transformed invites instead an effort to historicize the change.

Understanding the narrative's reinvention in the Bugis context, and its portability through the social networks that cross the maritime world, takes a "local" product of writing and de-provincializes it. People often view cultural products in a given language as representative of a single ethnic group and place. Yet the materials examined here, whether told by someone Sama or passed on through Sama hands, traversed both maritime space as well as languages and narrative contexts. Translation from one language to another, and, furthermore, into writing, involved much more than just a transposition. It entailed reformulations in terms of genre and structure, as well as new repertoires of reference and resolution.[159]

Why do manuscripts move about? As discussed above, many manuscripts are relocated during times of military upheaval. Yet people also traveled to obtain manuscripts, to copy them, and, especially, to "borrow" them. When tracing the other three manuscripts that were so-called siblings to *LB Lemobajo*, I learned that a genealogy had apparently been separated from the manuscript that Kalabeq ("Puah Habeq") had held at Pulo Balu in the Tiworo Straits. While most of the manuscript had been burned during the 1950s along with about two hundred houses across the water from Pulo Balu at Boné Boné, the genealogy was twice "borrowed" by relatives. First, a cousin, Mappé, borrowed it and brought it from Pulo Balu back across the Gulf of Boné to Kanalo in the Pulau Sembilan Islands off Sinjai. The reason why he borrowed this part of the manuscript was to prove his lineage to his third wife, the non-Sama Karaeng Ngai Daeng Puji. It then moved with him to Ara, but was there only five years before his brother, Makka, borrowed it and brought it across the Flores Sea to Labuanbajo to prove his descent to someone who reportedly was not Sama.[160] These people borrowed manuscripts to substantiate their claims of high-status descent to a potential spouse and to non-Sama others who had no knowledge of kin connections and status divisions among and between Sama communities.

Similarly, in Kambuno, two women, Atibulaéng and Hatimung, mentioned that their grandmother, Lolo Inja, had had a *lontaraq*. Lolo Inja was considered Sama by her father, Andi Malaniung Petta Rani, and by his first wife, her Sama mother, Opu Janniméng—names accompanied by the Bugis titles "Andi" and "Opu." Andi

---

[159] See also Ronit Ricci, *Islam Translated: Literature, Conversion, and the Arabic Cosmopolis of South and Southeast Asia* (Chicago: University of Chicago Press, 2011).

[160] Fieldnotes, Lolo Moto, Pulo Balu, April 6, 2000. Moto's father, Lolo Raitung, was the brother of Kalabaq's mother, Lolo Ambiq; Fieldnotes, Lo Kadér, Tampo, April 16, 2000; Fieldnotes, Haji Buraéra, Rantéangin, North Kolaka, March 6, 2000; Fieldnotes, Johari, Ara, South Sulawesi, October 26–27, 1999; and Fieldnotes, Madeq Ali, Kanalo Satu, South Sulawesi, October 2, 1999. Madeq Ali confirmed other statements that the genealogy had been brought to Labuanbajo during the DI-TII period. Compare this to Liebner, "Four Oral Versions of a Story," 119.

Malaniung himself was widely acknowledged to be Sama, his Sama father having lived in the Salabangka Islands, and his Sama mother, Lolo Sarine, being from Tinobu in Lasolo Bay. Andi Malaniung reportedly took the *lontaraq* from his daughter, Lolo Inja, to give to his fourth wife, a Bugis woman named Asyok. The granddaughters, in fact, did *not* dress this up as "borrowing," and seemed to disapprove; but neither did they call it "stealing." He apparently took the *lontaraq* to demonstrate his *lolo* descent to his fourth wife. Simply demonstrating access to and possession of a *lontaraq* would have been sufficient proof of such descent. Yet it likely recorded his own antecedents. Gifting it to his fourth wife provided a way for her and their offspring to substantiate their own claims to high-status descent.[161]

Processes of textual transmission and transformation from areas outside Southeast Asia to areas within it have been the focus of considerable scholarly work (e.g., studies of the *Mahabarata*, the *Ramayana*, and the *Book of One Thousand Questions*). In this work, the mobility of actual manuscripts often remains implicit. Yet some scholarship on literary interchanges from South Asia and the Middle East to the archipelago underscores this dimension of Southeast Asian literary history.[162] South Sulawesi, like the region itself, also has textual traditions that are not derived from elsewhere. With good reason, these tend to be the focus of specialists. However, what one scholar, Denys Lombard, called an "excessively ethno-linguistic vision" has the potential to obstruct research on the connections and exchanges among writing produced and exchanged between people of the region's many shores.[163] In contrast with his characterization, or perhaps caricature, of a patchwork of specialist knowledge, scholarship on interregional textual adaptation and recent work on South Asian literary cultures have discredited arguments that collapsed notions of identity into primordial linguistic or literary formations.[164] More attention to textual interchange within the region might reveal a great deal about the interactions among people of different groups and how they interpreted and reinterpreted their social worlds, in a way that attends to the complexity of littoral society.[165]

---

[161] Atibulaéng, Pulau Kambuno, South Sulawesi, November 8, 1999; and Fieldnotes, November 8, 1999.

[162] Vladimir Braginsky, *The Heritage of Traditional Malay Literature: A Historical Survey of Genres, Writings and Literary Views* (Leiden: KITLV, 2004); Laurie Sears treats knowledge of these Indian epics in the Javanese context as inseparable from the history of their colonial study in the nineteenth century, yet also examines them as a kind of "living tradition" with ongoing reformulations in contemporary genres; see Laurie Sears, *Shadows of Empire: Colonial Discourse and Javanese Tales* (Durham and London: Duke University Press, 1996). The *Book of One Thousand Questions* was adapted to Javanese, Malay, and Tamil, as well as to Bugis, although the latter is not examined in Ricci's *Islam Translated*.

[163] Denys Lombard, "Réflexions sur le Concept de 'pasisir' et sur son Utilité pour l'Étude des Littératures," in *Cultural Contact and Textual Interpretation*, ed. C. D. Grijns and S. O. Robson (Dordrecht: Foris Publications, 1986), 19–20.

[164] For more on such non-primordial approaches to analysis see, for instance, Ricci's discussion of "tellings" in *Islam Translated*; and Indrani Chatterjee, "Captives of Enchantment? Gender, Genre, and Transmemoration," in *History in the Vernacular*, ed. Raziuddin Aquil and Partha Chatterjee (New Delhi: Permanent Black, 2008), 250–87. Also see Mark Gamsa, "Cultural Translation and the Transnational Circulation of Books" *Journal of World History* 22, 3 (2011): 553–75.

[165] Lombard, "Réflexions sur le Concept de 'pasisir,'" 19–20.

This remains a challenge, however, since texts in the region have a knack for being hard to find. In the nineteenth century, James Brooke tried in vain to procure texts from the Bajo at Bajoé, who he said claimed to have books in the Bugis syllabary. His efforts to find *lontaraq* fared little better inland among the Bugis near Lake Tempe. There he heard only of some compendia with sayings of their wise men, and "several volumes of the voyages and adventures of Sawira Gading," or Sawerigading, the main figure in the *La Galigo*, and a name that local *rajas* bestowed on Brooke as a bit of flattery.[166] Disappointed at the dearth of texts, he complained in his journal that the list of Bugis works drawn up by John Leyden, mentioned for the first time only in 1811, may have been influenced by native exaggeration.[167]

It was not just a problem with Bugis texts. In the nineteenth century, Europeans and Southeast Asians alike complained about the difficulty of locating Malay texts, and were willing to travel far to obtain copies. One example of this is particularly intriguing. A manuscript of the Muslim heroic legend *Hikayat Raja Handak* reveals that a person called Kari Telolo in Makassar arranged for a scribe to travel to Semarang, in Java, to make a copy of the manuscript there as early as 1797.[168] "Kari," or *kare*, is a form of the Makassar language title *karaéng*. "Telolo" is probably the name "Tulolo," which appears in the *Makassar Annals*. However, to an ear schooled in reading Sama titles across the cross-cultural contexts of Sulawesi, "Kari Telolo" could well be Karaéng To Lolo. Whichever the case, she or he was willing to go to great lengths to obtain a copy of a particular manuscript in the late-eighteenth century, a manuscript in Malay, and have the scribe make a copy, presumably to be brought back to Makassar. This was no small excursion. To get from Makassar to Semarang at that time meant sailing 633 miles (1,018 km), comparable to sailing from Rome to Tripoli, just to have someone copy a manuscript. While this shows how people literally went to great lengths to obtain manuscripts, it also illustrates their mobility, interregional communication about the products of writing, and practices that crossed cultural and linguistic borders.

Another example illustrates the movement of a manuscript from Makassar to Johor in the sixteenth century, marking "the enthusiasm with which the Johore court greeted the 'history brought from Goa', that is, the 1536 version of the *Malay Annals*."[169] Equally intriguing, the *Gowa Chronicle* reports that during the reign of Tumaparisiq Kallonna (c. 1510–46), the *sabannaraq*, I Daeng Pamatteq, who was also a *tumailalang* (one of a trio of ministers who acted as intermediaries within Gowa), first "made Makasar lontaraq," meaning that he made documents.[170] One can but wonder whether this *sabannaraq*, like some others, was Sama, and how his reported

166 Brooke and Mundy, *Narrative of Events in Borneo and Celebes*, 116.

167 Ibid.; John Leyden, "On the Languages and Literature of the Indo-Chinese Nations," *Asiatic Researches* 10 (1811): 158–289; and Sirtjo Koolhof, "*Sureq, Lontaraq, Toloq*: Manuskrip dan Ragam Sastra Bugis" (*Sureq, Lontaraq, Toloq*: Manuscripts and Kinds of Bugis Literature), *International Journal of Malay World Studies* 25 (2007): 171.

168 Ian Proudfoot and Virginia Hooker, "Mediating Time and Space: The Malay Writing Tradition," in *Illuminations*, ed. Ann Kumar and John H. McGlynn (Jakarta: The Lontar Foundation and New York and Tokyo: Weatherhill, Inc., 1996), 77.

169 P. E. de Josselin de Jong, "The Character of the Malay Annals," in *Malaysian and Indonesian Studies: Essays Presented to Sir Richard Winstedt on His Eighty-Fifth Birthday*, ed. John Bastin and R. Roolvink (Oxford: Clarendon Press, 1964), 241.

170 G. J. Wolhoff and Abdurrahim, *Sedjarah Goa*, 18, cited in Cummings, *Making Blood White*, 42 (note 17), 216, 238 ("*tumailalang*"); and Cummings, *A Chain of Kings*, 32, 107.

authorial achievement related to his maritime travels. Was it he who brought the 1536 version of the *Malay Annals* to Johor from Gowa?

Up until the nineteenth century, manuscripts were not objects of commerce. Instead, they were inherited or lent out. During the nineteenth century, European collection efforts led to a considerable traffic in manuscripts, and there is little doubt that European demand stimulated manuscript production, for many were copied specifically for the purpose.[171] In 1842, John Crawford was able to sell his collection of 136 Malay, Bugis, and Javanese manuscripts and books to the British Museum for £250—down from the £516 he had been asking.[172]

Different circuits of exchange arose, with different logics behind them. Thus, on the one hand, as part of constructing colonial knowledge, a commercialized effort to collect manuscripts built steam in the nineteenth century; and on the other hand, manuscripts with content that had particular social relevance to those who kept, lent, inherited, and otherwise obtained them circulated through more restricted access, inheritance, and borrowing practices. Most Malay manuscripts were embedded in particular social relations and access to them was governed by those relationships. Texts of dynastic histories or potent religious knowledge could be handled only by experts or social insiders whose knowledge matched the contents. Owners of manuscripts of "recreational literature" did lend them, though not for pecuniary reward, and these owners were anxious about their care and eventual return. For instance, on a blank page of a nineteenth century copy of the *Hikayat Hang Tuah*, a note in a hand different from that in the text indicated that the manuscript belonged to the Sultan of Pahang—who ruled in the 1890s—and asks whoever might borrow it to return it quickly. Yet social proprieties made it difficult to press for the return of property.[173]

A similar remark about borrowing that reflects this difficulty appears on the last page of a manuscript recounting the history of Baku, a Makassar locality:

> It is greatly to be regretted that the *lontaraq* telling about this was borrowed by Sombaya [the ruler of Makassar] at the time of the installation of Arung Pao [the ruler of Baku]. He asked to just borrow it but has not yet returned it until this time. It was borrowed by an old woman named I Maniya. She asked to borrow it in order to copy it. There were (other *lontaraq*) taken by the Dutch; there were others that were lost; there were others that were burned by Sombaya of Gowa.[174]

---

[171] Roger Tol, "A Separate Empire: Writings of South Sulawesi," 219, and Proudfoot and Hooker "Mediating Time and Space," 77–78, both in *Illuminations*, ed. Kumar and McGlynn.

[172] P. R. Harris, *A History of the British Museum Library 1753–1973* (London: British Library, 1998), 134, cited in Annabel Teh Gallop, http://britishlibrary.typepad.co.uk/asian-and-african/2013/12/reading-malay-manuscripts-with-children.html, accessed August 3, 2014.

[173] Proudfoot and Hooker, "Mediating Time and Space," in *Illuminations*, ed. Kumar and McGlynn, 77; and Cummings, *Making Blood White*, 560, 562, 564.

[174] Manuscript N 16, p. 15, in William Cummings's private collection, most of which are copies of privately owned manuscripts borrowed (probably from relatives) by his Makassarese language tutor during fieldwork: "His family connections and social ties were critical in gaining access to these texts." The remark above is hard to date precisely, but is probably from the late-nineteenth or early twentieth century. Cummings, "Rethinking the Imbrication of Orality and Literacy," 537 (note 5); also see Cummings, *Making Blood White*, 52-53.

"Serious" texts like dynastic histories (chronicles) or potent religious knowledge were governed by restricted access, according to the relationships in which they were embedded, while "recreational" texts could be lent out, but were difficult to get back. As with Malay manuscripts, manuscripts in Sulawesi were embedded in social relationships that restricted access to varying degrees.[175]

Manuscripts moved on maritime conveyances. Their mobility was not primarily the result of the spread of religion and conversion. For instance, although there were Muslims in Champa (on the coast of central Vietnam) in the fifteenth century and earlier, Islam was a consequence rather than a cause of the close relations between Malays and Chams. When the Chams adapted the Malay *hikayat*, the Malay texts were borrowed in pre-Islamic form, without any of the later Muslim alterations.[176] As with materials coming from outside the region, textual mobility within it also relied on a world of maritime activities.

Even manuscripts that did not cross great distances by sea nevertheless received a broad enough reading or hearing to contribute to clusters of contested traditions. Scholars of Southeast Asia have focused with increasing subtlety and sophistication on such clusters of contested traditions, indeed, not collapsing "identity" with primordial views on literary production, but, on the contrary, critically examining the relationship between social belonging and regional literary formations. To some degree this reflects much wider shifts in scholarship that put contestations over meaning at the center of culture, analyzes them as part of social practices among interpretive communities, and seeks to historicize their dynamics. Such interdisciplinary work at the intersections of social, cultural, and literary histories considers how the "transformation of these stories is part of the transformations involved in the movement from pre-colonial to colonial and post-colonial politics."[177]

## COLONIAL CODA: THE FAIRYTALE IN BURGHOORN'S TYPESCRIPT

Pieter Burghoorn, a Dutchman in the Indies, heard another version of the story about a highborn Sama woman at sea who weds a man from another ethnic group. At some point between his hearing it when he lived in the Indies during the 1920s and its appearance in a typescript he sent to Jacobus Noorduyn in 1968, he wrote it down and it became a colonial fairytale.

---

[175] Cummings, "Rethinking the Imbrication of Orality and Literacy," 535, 537. Jane Drakard found that in Barus, Sumatra, Malay manuscripts were part of contested traditions and royal genealogies were sequestered with other heirloom objects, wrapped in a cloth, and treated as part of state regalia. *LB Lemobajo* had been wrapped in a red velvet cloth. Jane Drakard, "Ideological Adaptation on a Malay Frontier," *Journal of Southeast Asian Studies* 17, 1 (1986): 39–57.

[176] Reid, *Charting the Shape*, 46; Henri Chambert-Loir, "Notes sure les relations historiques et littéraires entre Campa et Monde Malais," in *Actes du Séminaire sur le Campa* at the University of Copenhagen, May 23, 1987 (Paris: Centre for History of Civilizations of the Indochinese Peninsula, 1988), 98–101.

[177] Adrian Vickers, "'Malay Identity': Modernity, Invented Tradition and Forms of Knowledge," in *Contesting Malayness: Malay Identity across Boundaries*, ed. Timothy Barnard (Singapore: NUS Press, 2004), 48; see also Susan Rodgers, *Print, Poetics and Politics: A Sumatran Epic in the Colonial Indies and New Order Indonesia* (Leiden: KITLV Press, 2005; and Jane Drakard, *A Kingdom of Words: Language and Power in Sumatra* (New York: Oxford University Press, 1999).

Jacobus ("Koos") Noorduyn was a scholar with expertise on Celebes, who, for much of his career, served as director of KITLV, where he began working in 1962.[178] Burghoorn sent Noorduyn a typescript some eighty pages in length about "the Badjau" sea people. The typescript drew on what he had learned during his time living and working in Celebes between 1923 and 1930.

Burghoorn initially posed a bit of a mystery, as records of him and his work in any official capacity appeared neither in the *Landbouw* registers nor in the *Regeringsalmanak* for the 1920s and the 1930s.[179] Born in Delft in 1904, it turns out that he served from 1921 to 1927 in the colonial navy as an assistant mechanic and then a mechanic. Different from the Royal Netherlands Navy, the colonial navy played a civil administrative and coast guard role in the Indies under the colonial administration and the governor general.[180] What happened after 1927 is not visible in the colonial archives. However, this civil administrative role of the colonial navy, and his skills as a naval mechanic, explain how he came to hold the positions he mentions in his typescript. By Burghoorn's own reckoning, he was in various parts of Celebes for most of the 1920s. From 1923 to 1926, he stayed in the Balangbalangan islands, a sparsely distributed group of islands that stretches across much of the Makassar Straits between southeastern Borneo and the west coast of Celebes. When he served as a superintendent of work in administrative units under indirect rule (*opzichter Landschapswerken*), he made dozens of trips in the Tolitoli area at the northwest end of Celebes, for which he often made use of Sama boats. Finally, he traveled around the east coast of Celebes and often come in contact with the Sama when he worked from 1927 to 1930 as head of the technical service with the fisheries office on Celebes' northeast coast.[181]

The typescript contains a collection of elaborately descriptive technical passages about native industry. These are hung on a narrative frame that re-presents the

---

[178] On Noorduyn's career, see Poeze and Schoorl, eds., *Excursies in Celebes*.

[179] I am grateful to Sirtjo Koolhof for help with checking these. Personal communication, Sirtjo Koolhof, July 12, 2004.

[180] NA, Ministry of Colonies: Stamboeken Burgelijke Ambtenaren, Serie A, 1836–1927, access number 2.10.36.22, inventory number 950, folio 542, register GM2. I also could find no record of him during the pre-World War Two decades in either inventories 2 or 19 of the other Ministry of Colonies Registration cards for East Indies civil servants (*stamkaarten Oost-Indische Ambtenaren*). On the colonial navy, see J. A. A. Wijn, ed., *Tot in de verste uithoeken: de cruciale rol van de Gouvernements Marine bij het vestigen van de Pax Neerlandica in de Indische Archipel 1815–1962* (Amsterdam: De Bataafsche Leeuw, 1998).

[181] P. Burghoorn, "De Badjaus," unpublished typescript and letter, c. 196, KITLV DH 1240. The quirky page numbering follows Burghoorn's original: "… *bij mijn verblijf in midden Celebes en wel in de vorstendom Tolitoli en Boeool …*" (p. 1a/4); "*Toen ik van 1927 tot 1930 op de Oostkust van Celebes rondtrok kwam ik veel in aanraking met een goedmoedig zeevolkje …*" (p. 1/II); "*De Balangbalangan-eilanden werden door mij voor het eerst bezocht in de jaren 1923 tot 1926 …*" (p. 4/X); "*Ik zelf ben tientallen malen in die omgeving geweest* [Poelias, westcoast, Tolitoli region] *daar ik als opzichter Landschapswerken in die omgeving veel gebruik maakte van hun prauwen*" (p. 5/X); and "*… toen ik als Hoofd Techn. Dienst bij de Zeevisserij op het Station Air-Tembaga zat, noord-oostkust van de Minahasa …*" (p. 6/X). My thanks to Henk Schulte Nordholt (personal communication, April 30, 2012) for help with sorting out the term *opzichter Landschapswerken*. According to Burghoorn's daughter from his second marriage, Burghoorn's first family died during World War Two. After the war he remarried and became an Indonesian citizen, but returned with the family to the Netherlands in 1957, and about five years later they became Dutch citizens. I am grateful to his daughter, Wil Burghoorn, for sharing her knowledge about him (personal communication, October 12, 2015).

version of the story he heard about a Sama princess lost at sea. Burghoorn also provides a brief pseudo-historical introduction, scattered remarks that illuminate his nostalgia for innocent natives and his critical disdain for "white civilization," as well as analytical digressions that aim to help the reader distinguish "the Badjau" from others with whom they might be confused.

Although Burghoorn had a great deal of firsthand knowledge about life on the coasts of Celebes, he explicitly apologized in his letter to Noorduyn for the unscholarly way his manuscript was written, wishing he had not been so ignorant of cultural anthropology at the time he undertook his travels some forty years earlier. Lamenting the unscientific result of his efforts, he ends the letter with: "It has thus become an ordinary story. I have sometimes thought that it could be made into a fine 'documentary' film. A good script-writer can take it in all kinds of directions … and still remain a documentary."

His lack of training notwithstanding, Burghoorn depicted richly detailed scenes and offered frank observations that reveal the considerable amount of time he spent among "Badjau" communities on Sulawesi's coasts and offshore islands. He describes a remarkable range of activities: from the play of boys and girls in the water and the proficiency they develop—equally, he insists—in swimming, diving, and sailing, to the production of salt and sago and the manufacture of lines and sails. With similar attention to detail, he describes the methods of righting capsized boats and the exquisite skill and cooperation required in the risky hunt for rays. Burghoorn was a patient observer and a careful reporter of technical skills and material processes of production, a sort of connoisseur of practical techniques. Although he regretted his lack of scholarly training, he nevertheless comes across as a dedicated purveyor of knowledge about native industry, as one might expect of someone in his position.

He was not, however, as skilled an observer of social forms or processes of communication. In fact, apart from the narrative frame in which he embeds these descriptions of skill, technique, and material production, his typescript bears strikingly little description of what could be called "the social." Nonetheless, although he does not describe much about local perspectives and the dynamics of interactions, the technical and practical flavor of his descriptive passages sets them apart from the narrative frame. This frame is a version of the story in which, as he would say, a "Badjau princess" gets lost at sea and ends up marrying the son of a sultan.

Burghoorn's own attitudes toward "the Badjau," as well as toward the Dutch, do, at points, come through in the text. As he wrote neither for a Sama audience, nor for others in and around Celebes, but rather for a Dutch one, he expended some effort to describe who the Badjau were and who they were not. The tenor of his efforts reveals a rather romantic view of the Badjau as a simple folk. He paints them with a kind of coastal pastoralism, emphasizing what he took to be their nonaggressive nature. Dutch colonials, by contrast, were the target of his criticism and cynical asides. Burghoorn reflected, for instance, on how "white civilization" had an immoral view of nakedness, and his sarcastic comments suggest that this "civilization" was accompanied by profuse amounts of gin. He also expressed profound disapproval of how little Malay (the lingua franca) the Dutch in the Indies were able to speak, which they nevertheless managed to use in a most impertinent manner. Burghoorn's view of simple sea nomads went hand in hand with a sense that civilization corrupts. In part it reflected a more widespread view in which some natives, and especially those in the past, appeared to be unsullied by a modernity presumably borne by colonial Europeans.

The typescript's nostalgia was probably deepened by the retrospective lens through which Burghoorn viewed the past: a time before the war, and before the loss of the colony; back in the old days, *tempo doeloe*, literally, the "time before." Although he mentions in his cover letter that three-quarters of the work had already been done when he received Noorduyn's encouragement, we cannot be completely sure which parts were composed when. Romantic views of sea people as simple folk were common among Europeans in the late-colonial period and Burghoorn's typescript is an interesting illustration of such views, in particular, for how he employed such perspectives in trying to differentiate "the Badjau" from others.

He disentangles similar sounding terms, distinguishing between *badjau, batjo,* and *badjo*.[182] "Badjau" (*bajau*), the name he used to refer to these sea people, was different from "*batjo*" (*baco*), "the Makassar language term for 'youth,' used in the same spirit as the word '*djongos*' on Java."[183] These youth, he explained, were used as stevedores along the inter-island trade routes at stops that did not have proper ports.[184] Although, he admits, both were sea people of a sort, he thought that outsiders often confused them with each other. He, personally, "never saw a combination of these two wholly different people." As for "*badjo*" (*bajo*), a word he had seen on maps, he offers contradictory explantions. In one he describes it as an amalgamation of the terms *badjau* and *batjo*. In the other, he echoes the common folk etymology, a corruption of the Malay word "*badjak*" (*laut*) for "pirate." He blames the corruption of the word for "bandit" on the careless mispronunciation of Malay by the Dutch.[185]

Curiously, Burghoorn seems to have no awareness of the widespread and longterm use of *bajo* as an exonym for the Sama among other groups in the region.[186] Nor does he appear to have any cognizance of the autonym "Sama," which suggests that he neither spoke Sama, nor grasped how they drew some very basic social distinctions between themselves and other descent groups. The absence of "Sama" or related terms is particularly striking when he moves beyond mere folk etymology to distinguish "the Badjau" from the historical "pirates" of the region. One would expect, but does not encounter, mention of the notorious Balangingi Sama of the southern Philippines in this discussion.[187] In making his case for the difference between the Badjau and pirates from the Southern Philippines, Burghoorn asserts that the Badjau are peaceable (*vreedzame*). "Not that they are not eminent

---

[182] In contemporary spelling, respectively: *bajau, baco,* and *bajo*.

[183] Burghoorn, 1a/8.

[184] Burghoorn also mentions that this small-scale trade was carried by natives on cargo ships, or *laadboten*. Burghoorn, p. 4/X. This is the plural of the Dutch term *laadboot*, undoubtedly the source for the name of the Indonesian cargo boat common in Sulawesi, called *perahu lamboq,* or *la^mboq*.

[185] Ibid.; "corruption," "verbastering," Burghoorn, 1a/8.

[186] In addition to its common use in the Sulawesi region, "Bajo" (ᨅᨍᨚ) also appears in Bugis-language manuscripts of the eighteenth and nineteenth centuries. As previously mentioned, in the Makassar language it appears as "*Bayo*," equivalent to *Turijéqnéq*, "people of the water."

[187] James Warren has written copiously on the Balangingi Samal; see, for example, James Warren, *Iranun and Balangingi: Globalization, Maritime Raiding and the Birth of Ethnicity* (Honolulu: University of Hawai'i Press, 2002); Warren, *The Sulu Zone, 1768–1898.*

fighters, on the contrary. But they are not aggressive."[188] He was very invested in this view of the peaceable Badjau. In a passage where he treats a story of Sama dispersal from Johor as fact, this supposedly peaceable character of the Badjau again supports an effort to distinguish them from others:

> That the notorious pirates were named 'Magindanoas' [*sic*] as well as 'Badjogubang,' can have given rise to the notion that they would also be descendants of the Badjaus of Johor. But they are anthropologically [*sic*] wholly different and have a very divergent form. Also they speak a language, probably "Tagala" [viz., Tagalog], that in no part resembles the Badjau language. The language spoken by the "real" Badjaus reminds one of a dialect in the Komerin district of South Sumatra. Further, their whole way of acting [that of the pirates], their manner of sea travel, their boat construction and aggressiveness, differ so strongly from the real Badjau that I cannot accept that they ever would have belonged to this group.[189]

Basically what he argues here is that, on the basis of boat construction, aggressiveness, a racial view of physical form, and the sound of a language he clearly does not speak, the "real Badjau" are not the same as Southern Philippines "pirates." He cannot accept that the so-called Badjogubang pirates share an ethnic affiliation or descent with those he considered the real Badjau. The claim of phonological resemblance to a south Sumatra dialect implicitly supports the notion of a Johor origin in the version of the tale he relates about a Bajo princess.

As is obvious from his descriptive passages, Burghoorn spent enough time among the Badjau to bear witness to certain practices or skills, processes of manufacture, a stunning location, or particular delicacies. Nevertheless, the typescript offers only two instances of him interacting with anyone "Badjau." One, which places him on their boats, comes in relation to his role as superintendent of work in administrative units under indirect rule. His description of a misguided attempt to get them to perform statute labor in agriculture provides some context that helps to clarify the character of his place on their boats:

> Once an Indonesian official in the Dutch [colonial] service tried to turn them into farmers. This man, himself coming from the "agrarian Bugis," considered anyone who was not a farmer a vagrant—this in contrast to the seafaring Bugis from the coastal regions. It led to a huge fiasco. Luckily a Dutch civil servant intervened in a timely manner and it was decided that the Badjaus not only could not be forced to do agriculture but that they should be allowed to perform their statute labor [*herendiensten*] at sea. And ultimately the Badjaus were a very small percentage of the whole population. Thus it was decided that the Badjaus would only perform statute labor if a civil servant needed to be moved along the coast and there was no other way to go, such as for small crossings from one

---

[188] *"In sommige boeken wordt gesproken van een Badjaugroep die naar de Philipijnen zou zijn getrokken. Van hier uit zouden zij aanvallen gedaan hebben op de kusten en eilanden van de Minahasa en de westkust van Celebes tot aan Tolitoli toe. Maar zulke verhalen passen in het geheel niet in het karakter van de vreedzame Badjau's. Niet dat zij geen uitstekende vechters zijn, integendeel. Maar zij zijn niet agressief."* Burghoorn, 1a/1.

[189] Burghoorn, 1a/2-3. By "anthropologically," he seems to mean here physical appearance—elsewhere he explains that the Badjau are pigeon-toed.

island to another. I stayed several times in these regions which had the size of a few Dutch Provinces but where at the most there were only two civil servants. For longer distances these [two civil servants] preferred to wait for a better, motorized connection.[190]

Hence, Sama labor was occasionally used for short-distance coastal transportation. Such labor, he explained, was paid, but people had little desire to work for a wage since food was plentiful. Partly as a result, and partly because, one suspects, most Sama people were able to avoid such labor "obligations," it became possible to arrange for one person to substitute for another's required service. Some people consequently made a kind of calling of such work.[191] This description clarifies the relationships involved when he mentions that he often made use of Bajo boats in his role as superintendent.[192]

The other instance in which he interacts with Sama people places him at the heart of the typescript's narrative structure. Its organization shuttles the reader back and forth between sections of realist reportage, and passages of pure romanticism. For instance, he juxtaposes the dramatic story of the Badjau princess with a passage in a realist historical register about an eighteenth century attempt, purportedly by Boné's ruler, to put a Boné prince on the Johor throne. The claimant was supposedly a grandson of the lost Badjau princess, who, in the version of the story familiar to Burghoorn, had originally come from Johor. So, Burghoorn's logic went, the basis for the legitimacy of the Boné prince's claim to a royal position in Johor was the notion that he descended, through her, from a lesser but still quite prominent line of Johor. Although unconvincing historically, the point here is that he addresses his audience on the field of "fact," even if his facts are wrong.

Contrast with that approach his idyllic description of the Salabangka Islands:

In these gorgeous surroundings the Badjau chose to make their home. The crystal clear water is a deep blue color and runs to emerald green toward the shallows and the coasts. This splendor of colors, seen in the harsh light of the tropical sun and with the grey-white background of the islands' bluffs, totally devoid of vegetation, give to this group [of islands] a more than fairy-like beautiful image, an image that in its reality far surpasses fantasy. The outcrops [*uitlopers*] of these rock formations, which sometimes ended up in thin shoals on the beaches, were also gloriously beautiful. And striking against these outcrops with a piece of iron, one gets a sound like that of a church clock, and each outcrop gives a different pitch. One fancies oneself really in a fairyland there.[193]

Amidst this enchanting portrayal of the Salabangka Islands he sets the scene in which he hears the story that frames the rest of his material. It is the only place in the entire typescript, except when he gets ferried about by someone doing statute labor, that he appears within the narrative, a witness to, and participant in, the goings-on.

---

[190] Burghoorn, 1/II–3/II. Burghoorn uses "Indonesian" anachronistically here.

[191] Ibid.

[192] Burghoorn, 5/X.

[193] Burghoorn, 1/XIV.

Looking back on those days when he traveled around the east coast of Celebes, he explains that he slowly became better acquainted with these sea people:

> And after a few months of associating with them they became rather more obliging, especially with their narratives. I noted that if, at sea, they were ever unexpectedly overtaken by a storm, they would shout at their loudest: O, Princess Papu, please help your children! And so I wondered who indeed this Princess Papu should be, who helps them out in time of need. Was she a Dewi, a Goddess? And one day, on a dazzling moonlit evening when the full moon hung like a fireball in the heavens, I sat with them on the shore of one of the islands in the fantastically beautiful Salabangka Archipelago on the southeast coast of Celebes. An impressive evening in a striking place on the beach. An evening that cannot be described, but which one could only "live to see," which could only be "experienced." And on this solemn evening, in this nearly sacred place, I heard as the first, and probably also the only white person, the story of Princess Papu.[194]

Without grasping who, or what, a *papuq* was, Burghoorn took "Papu" to be her name, while the word *putri*, which can mean either a daughter of someone respected or a princess, shed the former sense completely.

Burghoorn does not say much more about the setting than this. He offers no description of the teller, no mention of song, and no depiction of the rest of the audience, if there was one. He delivers only this setting of would-be colonial ethnography, and with it, primes the reader to follow a series of scenes dispersed throughout the typescript in which he tells his rendition of the tale he heard. He describes a dispersion story in which the Badjau princess gets swept away in a storm, and her father, the sultan, sends the people to look for her. The sultan makes a "judgment" against the Badjaus: because of their "carelessness" in looking out for his daughter, they must search for her and may not return without finding her. Yet, more than this, he also condemns them to a life of not settling permanently on land and of making their living entirely from what they find at sea and on the strand. Hence, in Burghoorn's version, their way of life in the littoral is explained as a punishment. He tells us that in the process of fanning out from Johor to look for her, groups dropped off along the way due to age, weariness, and ill-health, with young Badjau stepping in to take care of them. They eventually become a range of maritime-oriented ethnic groups from Riau to Borneo to eastern Celebes, including the Salabangka islands, where he heard the story.

In Burghoorn's version, within the frame of the story, Putri Papu, after she regains consciousness, tells about her voyage: about her decision to weigh the anchor of a fine new boat, the dead calm before the storm, and her worrying about whether she would come out of it alive. Yet currents and winds eventually abate, the boat turns out to be well-provisioned (as Burghoorn seemed to think all Bajo boats are), and, with some citrus and even a Bajo-style tinder box, her courage and lust for life return.[195] She is, as it happens, perfectly able to stay alive away from land, at least for the time being. It was important, Burghoorn tells us, that she had reached the current below the Borneo coast:

---

[194] Burghoorn, 3–4/II.

[195] Burghoorn, 1/XII–3/XII.

Was zij in de stroom onder de Java-wal terechtgekomen dan was zij vermoedelijk door de Floris Zee en de Banda Zee op de Tanimbar-eilanden of de Nieuw Guinea-kust afgegaan. Wat er dan met haar gebeurd was laat zich gemakkelijk raden. Maar zeker was de geschiedenis van Poetri Papoe dan nooit geschreven geworden. Op de Tanimbar eilanden en op Nieuw Guinea heerste een slavernij en kanibalisme van de ergste vorm. Beter zou zij dan tussen de eilanden door de Indische Oceaan ingedreven zijn en daar omgekomen in de golven. Dit zou nog een betrekkelijk zachte dood geweest zijn in vergelijking met de verwachtingen op genoemde kusten. Maar gelukkig kreeg de oostelijke stroom haar te pakken en met stroom en wind ging het op Celebes aan.

Had she wound up in the current below the Java coast, then she would probably have gone off through the Flores and Banda Seas to the Tanimbar Islands or the New Guinea coast. What then would have happened to her is easily guessed. But for certain the history of Poetri Papoe would then never have been written. In the Tanimbar Islands and in New Guinea reigned a slavery and cannibalism of the worst form. It would be better for her to float between the islands into the Indian Ocean and there perish in the waves. This would have been a relatively mild death in comparison with the expectations on the aforementioned coasts. But luckily the easterly current took hold of her and off she went with wind and current to Celebes.[196]

Rather than washing up on Gowa's beach, her fateful voyage ends when she is found at sea by another boat, that of a Boné prince:

Eindelijk, na zeer zorgvuldig manoeuvreren, kwamen zij langszij van de prauw. Maar wie schets hun verbazing toen zij in die prauw een beeldschoon meisje zagen liggen slapen. Uit haar gehele wezen, hoe haveloos zij er op dat moment ook uit zag, uit haar gehele wezen straalde haar hogeafkomst, haar adeldom. Misschien was het wel een dewi, een fee.

Finally, after maneuvering very carefully, they came alongside the boat. But who could describe their surprise when they saw, lying asleep in this boat, a very beautiful maiden. However ragged she appeared at that moment, her nobility, her high birth, radiated from her entire being. Maybe she was even a goddess, a fairy.

Snel en voorzichtig bracht men het prauwtje langszij van het admiraalschip zonder haar wakker te maken, zonder haar to storen. Daartoe had men de moed niet. En de jonge kroonprins keek vol bewondering op de schone slaapster neer. Dit moest een princes zijn, dat was zo te zien.

Quickly and carefully they brought the little boat alongside the flagship without waking her, without disturbing her. For that they had not the courage. And the young crown prince looked down upon the sleeping beauty full of admiration. This must be a princess, that much was clear to see.

Toen Putri Papu uit de slaap ontwaakte was zij reeds aan boord van

When Putri Papu woke from sleep she was already aboard the flagship and

---

[196] Burghoorn, 3/XII–4/XII. Burghoorn nowhere mentions knowledge of written accounts of this story other than his own, so, presumably, when he says, "would never have been written," he means by himself.

het admiraalschip en stond de Kroonprins van Boné naast haar. En daar de Boeginezen zich bij hun vaart op Malakka ook de Maleise spraak hadden meester gemaakt kon de Kroonprins met haar spreken en vol verwondering hoorde hij naar haar avontuurlijke verhaal, het verhaal van "de reis van Putri Papu."

the Crown Prince of Boné stood beside her. And as the Bugis, from their voyaging to Malacca, had also mastered the Malay language, the Crown Prince could speak with her, and he listened to her adventurous story full of wonder, the story of "the voyage of Putri Papu."[197]

Having regained consciousness aboard the flagship and narrated her voyage, the story turns back to the narrator's perspective.

Met grote interesse had de Kroonprins het verhaal van Poetri Papoe aangehoord. En als Sultansdochter en Kroonprinses werd zij door de Sultanszoon met alle eerbied en onderscheiding, haar hoge rang waardig, behandeld.

De jonge vorst was niet alleen geroerd door haar jeugd en uitzonderlijke schoonheid maar evenzeer door haar moed en "zeemanschap". –En vooral dit laatste was voor hém, een zoon der zee, wel iets heel bijzonders.

En Poetri Papoe, kon zij ongevoelig blijven voor haar jonge, mooie redder ?? Een Sultanszoon en een goed zeeman ?? Hij kende haar taal en haar volk, dat had hij op zijn reizen geleerd. En de zoon der zee had de dochter der zee gevonden.

The Crown Prince had listened to Putri Papoe's story with great interest. And as a Sultan's daughter and a crown princess she was treated by the Sultan's son with every respect and distinction dignifying her high rank.

The young prince was not only moved by her youth and exceptional beauty but as much by her courage and "seamanship." And this last especially was for him, a son of the sea, really something quite special.

And Poetri Papoe, could she remain unfeeling to her young, handsome rescuer? A Sultan's son and a good seaman? He knew her folk and her language, which he had learned on his voyages. So the son of the sea found the daughter of the sea.[198]

Scholars of the region, familiar with examining its literary products, caution against projecting or imposing European categories in the analysis of Malay and Indonesian literary genres.[199] Here, instead, we seem to have a reading, or more properly, a hearing, of the story about a highborn Sama woman's maritime voyage filtered through certain European genre expectations. In contrast with the other oral and written versions of the story, in Burghoorn's version, she does not land on a strange coast but rather is rescued by the crown prince of Boné. Her own provenance and ethnic affiliation do not remain a mystery until her lineage is

---

[197] Burghoorn, 3/XI.

[198] Burghoorn, 4/XII–5/XII.

[199] Sears, *Shadows of Empire*, esp. 75–120; Sweeney, *A Full Hearing*; and Shelly Errington, "Some Comments on Style in the Meanings of the Past," *Journal of Asian Studies* 388, 2 (1979): 231–44.

revealed; rather, there is no hiding the fact that she is a princess, because nobility radiates from her entire being even while she sleeps, in a disheveled state.[200] Nor does she keep silent, but instead relates her story directly as soon as she wakes. Burghoorn suggests the view that perhaps she is, after all, a goddess or a fairy, fittingly, since in the end, the son of the sea finds the daughter of the sea, a boy-meets-girl fairytale. Despite all these differences, Burghoorn's reformulation—intentional or not, we have no way of knowing—rests on narrative devices used in previous reframings. Her maritime voyage is the result of an accident, here, a storm. Although she does not arrive on the shores of another kingdom, she is nevertheless encountered in an unconscious state. These devices, familiar in the story's adaptation to the Bugis-language context, became available to Burghoorn, who took the figure of an unconscious Sama woman at sea, and turned her, literally, into "sleeping beauty" (*de schone slaapster*).[201]

This fairytale would not have been possible without Burghoorn's view of the Badjau as *goedmoedig zeevolkje*: good-natured or innocent little sea folk, nary a piratical bone in their bodies.[202] A romantic view mired in stereotypes of peaceable (*vreedzame*) sea nomads, it set them apart, constitutionally, from an earlier era's pirates, who had been reined in by the power of steam and late-colonial technologies of rule well before the decades when Burghoorn served in Celebes.[203]

Burghoorn's depiction of the story about a highborn Sama woman's relocation built on the adaptations in Bugis-language manuscript versions and related Sama retellings, while these differed again from the array of Sama capture narratives sourced from various archipelagic locations. These differences are of interest not as a matter of folkloric butterfly collecting, but, rather, because comparing them reveals features of cultural history. Understanding the cultural history of how Sama capture narratives got taken up and adapted to new media and different narrative forms tells us about the relation between their entextualization and the social contexts in which it took place. Whereas Burghoorn's recounting illustrates how ideologies of modernity and fallen natives combined with the late colonial lull in piracy to permit portrayal of "the Badjau" as quaint and innocuous, the Bugis-language manuscripts and related oral versions present a social environment filled with preoccupations about the significance of lineage and how kin and political ties get formed and remembered.

To depict a woman's unnegotiated union and relocation to a virilocal residence—whether a would-be "husband's" or that of a captor—would undermine the *raison d'être* of such genealogical narratives, which (unless one is depicting a foe) aim to shore up the reputation and prominence of particular lineages. Such narratives instead foreground claims of genealogical worthiness, such as the

---

[200] Radiating light or an aura is a feature common to Javanese *wahyu* tales; see: Sears, *Shadows of Empire*, 49, 205; Nancy K. Florida, *Writing the Past, Inscribing the Future: History as Prophecy in Colonial Java* (Durham and London: Duke University Press, 1995), 39 (note 75), 205 (note 238), 287–88, 287 (note 5). However, here, although she radiates high birth and nobility, no light or aura is specified, and no other version mentions any similar phenomenon.

[201] Burghoorn, 3/XI.

[202] Burghoorn, 1/II.

[203] Burghoorn, 1a/1, 2/XIV. Eric Tagliacozzo, "Kettle on a Slow Boil: Batavia's Threat Perceptions in the Indies' Outer Islands, 1870–1910," *Journal of Southeast Asian Studies* 31, 1 (2000): 70–100; Ger Teitler, "Piracy in Southeast Asia: A Historical Comparison," *MAST* 1, 1 (2002): 67–83; Jennifer L. Gaynor, "Piracy in the Offing."

precedence of one lineage over another in the genealogy of a particularly prominent figure like Arung Palakka, or the existence of ties of political office and kinship that rest on claims to lineage status parity. Even if their details may be hard to verify, these features illustrate not only the importance of ascribed status and genealogical precedence, but also the social, textual, and narrative practices that have supported them, among the people of south Sulawesi's peninsula and in the littoral society of the hinterseas historically connected to it.

Examining this cultural history also tells us about the relationship between social belonging and regional literary formations, in particular, how analytically misguided it is to collapse notions of identity and belonging into separate silos of primordial linguistic and literary production. The narrative of a Sama woman's relocation sits in both a Sama and a Bugis cluster of traditions. Analyzed within the context of the latter, it emerges as laden with stakes in a broader field of contestations. How the story was adapted to Bugis-language manuscripts and transmitted by Sama people over generations illustrates not only the movement of a narrative from one linguistic context to another, but also illuminates a literary formation that straddled both Bugis and Sama social worlds. This works against reductive views about ethnic groups and literary production, on the one hand, while also working against reductive views about ethnic groups and social formations on the other. While capture was effaced from the story, it remained a narrative about a Sama woman's maritime relocation and, replete with demonstrations of belonging to the upper rungs of an interethnic littoral society, focused on the matriline that descended from her, in a status-competitive world of interethnic kinship and politics. Through the media of oral and manuscript transmission, it reproduced both descendants' belonging to this elite Sama matriline, and secured the inclusion of this lineage among a transgenerational interethnic social class.

# CHAPTER FIVE

## STAKES AND SILENCES: LAWI'S CAPTURE DURING THE DARUL ISLAM REBELLION

Hajjah Lawi knew the story about I Lolo, and how she wound up at the Gowa palace with a child by Gowa royalty. She remembered hearing it from her great aunt, *nenek* Naria, when Lawi was still small and lived in Pulo Balu. Although the story provided its Sama audience with a narrative resource for lineage pride, it so thoroughly euphemized and effaced any possibility of reading "captured" or "kidnapped" in the narrative, that it could not, or at least did not, serve Lawi as an allegory for her own experience.[1]

This chapter returns to Lawi's story, introduced at the beginning of the book. An oral history, with all the caveats this entails about memory's fallibility, this story offers more than just the means to critique the limitations of the nationalist perspective evident in the archival traces of events during the 1950s.[2] Recollections by participants and witnesses present an opportunity to delve deeply into the qualitative dimensions of social and political dynamics. Such oral histories illustrate how a land-based power made efforts to gain access to maritime people by forging kin connections, bestowing titles, and maintaining the threat of violence. The fact that this example of intergroup politics in the maritime world comes from so recent a period underscores the durability of capture as a tool of intergroup politics. It also shows that marrying a woman with a high-status Sama lineage remained a method for attempting to gain followers from among those with skills, knowledge, and networks in the maritime world.

Lawi's daughter Morgana, as she aged, came to understand that she had been raised by her father's sister and deceived about her mother's identity. Her belated discovery of her Sama mother and her maternal kin underscores why stories about Sama interethnic unions remain relevant, particularly in how they exhort progeny to recall not just descent from high-status forebears, but also descent through a Sama matriline. Although in some contexts genealogies may be reckoned in ways that leave the Sama matrilines in interethnic unions deemphasized or submerged, for descendants to recall this matriline is to engage in a practice of social reproduction.

---

[1] Author's interviews with Hajjah Erna and Hajjah Lawi, Wawo, North Kolaka, June 22, 2011. That the placename "Wawo" is identical to the name of the last *datu* or "*raja* Bajo" at Boné may just be coincidence.

[2] See also Shahid Amin, *Event, Metaphor, Memory: Chauri Chaura, 1922–1992* (Delhi: Oxford University Press, 1995).

## DARUL ISLAM COMES TO TIWORO

When Lawi was taken from her village in 1954, Indonesia was barely a nation and Lawi was barely a woman.[3] She had been promised to Umar, a young man she had had her eye on, and although no formal gift exchange—no deal-sealing—had yet taken place between the families, her relatives had already begun to gather the quantities of rice that would be needed for a wedding. Then the rebels came to take her.[4] These were the fighters of the DI-TII, the Darul Islam movement in Sulawesi, one of three main branches of the rebellion. They took Lawi to their commander, Jufri Tambora, so he could marry her.

While the different branches of Darul Islam shared certain goals for Islamic governance articulated against a new center-weighted national administration, each also grew out of a particular history rooted in separate regional concerns. This same point about the conflicting interests of the center and the regions applies as well to the other armed movements that the new nation contended with in its tumultuous early years, although none is adequately explained by this alone.[5]

Following the Japanese occupation, Indonesian national independence was hard won in combat and over negotiating tables, and, in terms of territory, achieved in a piecemeal fashion. Yet even after the nation assumed more or less its current shape, political and military reorganization as well as local processes of social revolution—and, in some places, counter-revolution—remained the focus of a complex series of different, if structurally related, struggles. At first, the new republic in revolution consisted only of Java and Sumatra, and comprised but one part of an overarching federal structure together with a group of states initiated by the Dutch. Some of these states were quite substantial, but none loomed as large as the State of Eastern Indonesia (*Negara Indonesia Timoer/Groote Oost*).

When this state was dissolved into the Indonesian Republic in 1950, and revolutionary fighters returned from Java to Sulawesi, they found themselves disqualified from service in a reorganizing national military. This denial of their active participation in the new military was particularly galling, given that the right to serve had been granted to the former soldiers of the Royal Netherlands Indies Army (KNIL, Koninklijk Nederlands Indisch Leger), the enemy against whom these fighters had struggled during the revolution.[6] Kahar Muzakkar, a fairly prominent

---

[3] The year is reckoned based on correlation with an administrative report about related events, discussed below. Lawi is often referred to as "Haji Lawi" for having fulfilled a pilgrimage to Mecca. Although most Indonesians refer to women who have done so as "Hajjah," local practice is to not use the gender marking. Since she was still quite young in the 1950s, I have decided not to use her title when discussing events of that time. Similarly, for her brothers Haji Syamsuddin and Haji Buraéra, I drop the title when discussing events before they made the pilgrimage. When he was young, Haji Buraéra was known as Mbulé.

[4] Author's interview with Habiba. Habiba is Lawi's sister-in-law, by one of her brothers. She mentioned the rice gathering and that the gift exchange had not yet taken place. While Habiba clarified their marital status, Haji Lawi herself had mentioned the prospective groom, Umar, sometimes in Sama called Ummareng (the /e/ is an unstressed schwa), was Haji Subaéda's son. Lawi said in 2011 that they (the rebels) had shot him. Author's interviews with Haji Lawi.

[5] A good place to begin to learn about the variety of regional dynamics during and after the revolution is Audrey R. Kahin, ed., *Regional Dynamics of the Indonesian Revolution* (Honolulu: University of Hawai'i Press, 1985).

[6] Barbara S. Harvey, "Tradition, Islam, and Rebellion: South Sulawesi 1950–1965" (Ph.D. dissertation, Cornell University, 1974), 192–219.

figure in the revolution who led many of the men from Sulawesi, was denied the post he felt was his due. Along with the disfranchisement of those who had fought under him on Java, as well as those who had fought against the reimposition of Dutch rule in Sulawesi, this refusal formed the initial impetus for a rebellion that soon allied itself to the Darul Islam movements in West Java and in Aceh.[7]

The Darul Islam conflict in Sulawesi lasted through the 1950s, and in some areas until 1965, when Kahar was reportedly killed. During the conflict, ordinary people had to negotiate the efforts of two would-be powers that wished to hold sway. "Govern" is too dainty a word to describe the methods used by each side in this conflict in their attempts to prevail as the predominant ruling force. On one side was DI-TII; on the other was the Jakarta-based national military, namely, the Indonesian National Army—or TNI—and the Mobile Brigade, still at that point called *Mobrig*, which played a prominent role in southeast Sulawesi.[8] Research on DI-TII for the most part neglects southeast Sulawesi. Nevertheless, the peninsula and its surrounding waters and islands were thoroughly swept up in the conflict from its early years.[9]

By 1952, conditions in the Straits of Tiworo were already unsafe, as fighters from each side alternately arrived on the shores around its edges and came to the villages on its islands.[10] The straits remained a disputed area throughout the years of the conflict, a "border zone" (*daerah perbatasan*) rather than a rebel-held region (*daerah defakto*), in part as a result of its geography. Although DI-TII managed to exert some influence there, neither side had the wherewithal to territorialize and hold the straits, and instead could only terrorize its people and try various tactics to turn them into followers. This led people in the straits to employ stratagems of appeasement and evasion, and when these did not work, flight.

One way noncombatants negotiated the conflict was to have village heads that each side would view as an ally. This was called "having two heads" (*berkepala dua*). Yet, having two heads also referred to a broader set of practices for dealing with armed visitors, and a concomitant political philosophy regarding conditions in the straits. Hence, as Buraéra once mentioned, "the people in those islands, they were

---

[7] Ibid., 217–39.

[8] Mobrig's role was evident in the comments of many subjects whom I interviewed. Although Barbara Harvey's dissertation concentrates on South Sulawesi, it also shows the prominence of Mobrig's presence in Sulawesi's southeastern regions, for instance, in the major battle at Kasipute after DI-TII attacked the Mobrig post there in October 1957. See Harvey, "Tradition, Islam, and Rebellion," 406. Mobrig (which later changed its acronym to "Brimob"), had its roots in the Tokubetsu Keisatsutai, the Japanese-occupation era's special police force, a highly trained, heavily armed mobile police force formed in 1944 in each residency on Java and Madura. See M. Oudang, *Perkembangan kepolisian di Indonesia* (Djakarta: Mahabarata 1952), 46–47, cited in *Java in a Time of Revolution: Occupation and Resistance, 1944–1946*, Benedict Anderson (Ithaca: Cornell University Press, 1972), 131, note 30. In this same note, Anderson mentions that John Smail remarked that the Tokubetsu Keisatsutai had particular importance as the one heavily armed force remaining after the dissolution of the other people's forces, the Heihō and the Peta, under the Japanese. See John R. W. Smail, *Bandung in the Early Revolution, 1945–1946* (Ithaca: Cornell Modern Indonesia Project, 1964), 60, note 12.

[9] DI-TII in Sulawesi had two divisions: "Division 40,000" and the Hasanuddin Division, each with four regiments. Jufri Tambora was commander of a regiment in the Hasanuddin Division. Barbara Harvey lists him in this position in 1957–59, but it is certain that he was already a commander at least by 1954, based on documents and interviews discussed below. Harvey, appendix IX, 466–67.

[10] Author's interview with Haji Buraéra, March 5, 2000.

all *kepala dua*," all two-headed. Throughout Tiworo, during my field research, the straits' predominantly Sama people widely used the term "having two heads" to describe how they managed the conflict in "the time of the gangs" (*waktu gerombolan*). It was a strategy common in other areas as well. Pragmatically, having two heads entailed demonstrating a certain even-handedness when men from either side of the conflict showed up. They were received well (*jemput baik-baik*) and served (*dilayani*) kindly, and eventually went on their way. Under the circumstance, serving only one side could be fatal (*bisa-bisa melayang jiwa*, literally, your soul could take flight). Having two heads was the only way to remain in place and still be relatively safe when either side came through. Although giving both sides a positive reception was risky and did not eliminate their suspicions, such suspicions were apparently also quelled by the influence of money. In other words, both sides in turn had to be paid off. As one man put it, "The one from the left comes, you give. The one from the right comes, you give."[11]

To have two heads, moreover, entailed keeping each side in the conflict in the dark about one's dealings with the other side. In other words, Sama people in the straits intentionally and actively created spaces of ignorance to keep what went on with one side from becoming known to the other. Such spaces thus took shape differently from the sort of unknown spaces that institutions create in the process of producing and organizing records. They were different again from the shadows cast by the politics of colonial disregard.[12] Here, in contrast, regular people knowingly fostered these obscured spaces, creating zones of ignorance in which disregard might, to their benefit, flourish.

Take, for instance, reports of Darul Islam's numbers in the straits. The village head of Bontu-Bontu, which straddled the tips of two small islands at the straits's eastern end, made a report at three in the morning on March 18, 1954, to the district head's intermediary in the town of Raha. He reported that twenty Darul Islam men, eight with firearms, had appeared in Bontu-Bontu.[13] During field research, an elderly man I happened to travel with on my way from Bontu-Bontu to Raha met my query about the DI numbers in this report with a laugh. DI men showed up, he explained, but people from the straits commonly over-reported Darul Islam's presence. They did this to discourage the government's forces, which were short-staffed but no less demanding, from venturing out to the islands as well.

This explanation alerted me to the problem that even the hard-to-come-by numbers on DI-TII in the archives were unreliable. It also served as a reminder to take even mundane archival reports with a grain of salt. Interviews and oral histories are frequently beset by the question of how their production and perspective affects the material that they put forward. Yet all source materials face these questions about production and perspective. In this case, an oral source acts as a check on a set of archival materials, raising questions about how their bureaucratic character and seemingly neutral nature too often foster a naive reliance on the apparent reliability of such documents. Hence, a participant's recollection throws this report's

---

[11] Ibid.

[12] Mary Douglas, *How Institutions Think* (Syracuse: Syracuse University Press, 1986), 69; Ann Laura Stoler, *Along the Archival Grain: Epistemic Anxieties and Colonial Common Sense* (Princeton: Princeton University Press, 2010), 25–26, 278.

[13] "Warta Politik bulan Maret 1954 Daerah Sulawesi Tenggara," ANRI Makassar, Propinsi Sulawesi 1950–1960, reg. 359.

claims in a critical light, illuminating knowledge and practices hidden in the shadows. Such comments have great analytical value for critiquing contemporaneous archival materials. However, as important as this methodological point is, the shadows themselves present a compelling matter that deserves analytical attention.

People in the straits cultivated such spaces in order to evade and to negotiate the conflict. The nonpartisan position of village leaders, the explicit politics of having two heads, and the generalized practices informed by these politics—including the judicious use of misinformation, and not divesting others of their misapprehensions about Sama people—all made it possible for noncombatants to keep the warring forces at bay. They employed these means to eke out spaces to survive—not geographic spaces, but spaces that were no less material for their formation in shared knowledge and practices. Such knowledge and practices were not shared simply through membership in a particular ethnic group, but rather among people who communicated with each other from similar structural positions vis à vis the combatants. These groups formed interlinked interpretive communities, or "publics," throughout the affected littorals. In these social and epistemological spaces they gained some critical elbow room to persevere under intermittent but intensive scrutiny and duress.

Such methods had their limits. People in the Tiworo Straits also commonly fled when combatants showed up on their beaches. Residents "stepped aside" or "evacuated" (*menyingkir*), a term that included temporary relocation, long-term withdrawal, and sometimes permanent resettlement. In some cases, quick returns were not possible, as both sides apparently burned villages as a tactical measure. Darul Islam burned villages in the hope that flight would drive people into Darul Islam-dominated areas and preclude their return. The TNI burned villages to deprive Darul Islam of potential recruits from regions beyond TNI control—in effect, this meant anywhere outside of the few towns and the cities they held, such as Raha, Kendari, and Makassar.[14] Many people from Tiworo and the surrounding coasts fled to the safety of these more populous enclaves, and to spots across the Gulf of Boné, as well as across the Flores Sea. Sometimes they established new settlements, but usually they went to places where other Sama people already lived.[15]

Beyond propelling migration and exacting donations in Tiworo, Darul Islam also demonstrated its power in other ways and attempted to forge social networks that might sustain the movement. Demonstrating its power involved more than a show of guns and gore. For instance, Jufri Tambora, the DI-TII regiment commander for much of Southeast Sulawesi, boasted that, while officers under him might gather two or four boats to conduct their business in the straits, when *he* toured the waters of Southeast Sulawesi he commandeered "forty boats."[16] This image, intended to impress the populace with both his power and Darul Islam's, was reminiscent of the

---

[14] Author's interviews with Buraéra and Tuhpa, March 5, 2000. Dozens of people mentioned that both sides burned villages, which left people unable to return home and drove them to other locations. On the discourse of forest and city during the rebellion, see Esther Velthoen, "*Hutan* and *Kota*: Contested Visions of the Nation-State in Southern Sulawesi in the 1950s," in *Indonesia in Transition: Rethinking "Civil Society," "Region," and "Crisis,"* ed. Hanneman Samuel and Henk Schulte Nordholt (Yogyakatya: Pustaka Pelajar, 2004), 147–74.

[15] Natasha Stacey, *Boats to Burn: Bajo Fishing Activity in the Australian Fishing Zone* (Canberra: ANU E-Press, 2007).

[16] Author's interview with Jufri Tambora, March 6, 2000.

archipelago's long history of the symbolism of fleets of state. Jufri toured the straits and other nearby coasts to impress, to compel, and to be served. Such demonstrations of power arguably focused less on territorial acquisition than on efforts to expand and consolidate the movement's social supports. But perhaps Lawi's abduction illustrates this point better.

To say that Darul Islam used social means of expansion and support is not to imply that coercion was absent. Yet it is not quite clear to what degree the movement coercively forged and exploited social networks as a matter of conscious strategy. I should stress that I am not suggesting that the kidnapping of women was a programmatic and widespread part of Darul Islam's tactics. Nonetheless, Lawi's capture was not impromptu, but planned. I piece together her story partly from archival documents, but mostly from her own recollections and those of her close relatives.

## LAWI'S KIDNAPPING

Unceremoniously grabbed and hauled away—such is the image we commonly have of kidnapping and capture. However, that is not how things went for Lawi. She was chosen beforehand, sought, taken, transported by boat, marched, and then given a wedding ceremony more or less at gunpoint. Her looks had something to do with it—she was known as a beauty; so did the skills of her people, as well as her own lineage. Lawi's grandmother, Manihing, was the first wife of Anakoda Manting, a renowned boat builder and mariner, said to come from Talia Kendari, a Sama settlement on the southern point at the entrance to Kendari Bay.[17] Their only child, Lawi's father, Haji Usman, was born at Pulo Balu in the Straits of Tiworo. A trader, Haji Usman had also been Pulo Balu's *imam* before the "time of the gangs."[18] Lawi's mother, Mbakala, was born to Lo Ngasi and Lo Mantu. The title "Lo," an abbreviation of "Lolo," marks their high-status Sama descent. Lo Ngasi, Lawi's maternal grandmother, was said to descend as well from a royal Buton lineage. Lo Mantu originally came from Palima in north Boné, South Sulawesi. A former village head of Pulo Balu, he was said to have "opened" or founded it, although archival evidence suggests that Pulo Balu was occupied by maritime people since at least the seventeenth century. Perched at the tip of its eponymous island, the village of Pulo Balu sits opposite Muna Island's northwest point, its houses jutting out into the waters of the straits, and its boats lying at anchor offshore. Like other villages in the straits, it could only be reached by boat, but, by the same token, the strait's protected waters gave access to passages in all directions.

---

[17] Anakoda Manting, a.k.a. Nakoda Manting and Mboq Manting. Mboq Manting's boat was named *Bintang Sedang*. He was said by some to be descended from Mandar, although one person said from Kolaka. Haji Buraéra was unsure of where his forebears came from, but said that he himself came from Talia Kendari. He had reportedly been given a letter of identification (or introduction) from the Dutch, apparently in recognition of his boat-building skills. These skills were said to be passed on through his descendants in villages throughout this region, both through learning and apprenticeship, as well as by mere fact of descent.

[18] Author's interview with Haji Buraéra, March 5, 2000. Haji Lawi was among those who thought he descended from people from Mandar. Author's interview with Haji Lawi, June 22, 2011.

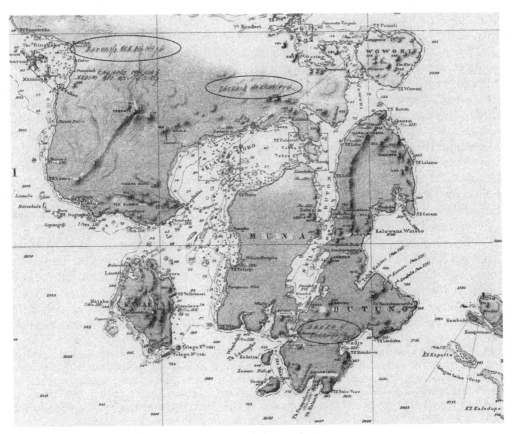

Detail of the chart of the east coast of Sulawesi, from late in the Darul Islam period, ca. 1962.
Note the areas, circled, marked *daerah berbahaya* ("dangerous area").
Hydrography Office of the Indonesian Navy 1959, reprinted 1962. Source: Cornell University Map Library

Lawi's "in-laws" were impressive, too. Jufri Tambora had grown up playing with Kahar Muzakkar, the leader of Darul Islam in Sulawesi.[19] Jufri's brother, M. Ali Kamri, and his sister, Sitti Hami, each also exercised tremendous influence during the Darul Islam period over regions along the northeast coast of the Gulf of Boné. Sitti Hami became Kahar Muzakkar's fourth wife and ran a trading operation, or a smuggling ring, depending on your perspective, which helped to support Darul Islam materially.[20] Upon Lawi's being wed to Jufri, one could say that she had been married into a relatively important Bugis family. Numerically dominant in Sulawesi's southwestern peninsula, the Bugis are also known for their history of seafaring and migration, as well as for their commercial acumen and their occasionally prominent role in national and regional politics. Yet while these siblings might lay some claim to the "white blood" of an elite Bugis lineage (even as they contested continuation of the colonial-era aristocracy's privileges), their

---

[19] Author's interview with Jufri Tambora, March 6, 2000.

[20] In fact, the three siblings—Sitti Hami, M. Ali Kamri, and Jufri—each apparently had say over particular portions of Southeast Sulawesi in the north Kolaka region. Sitti Hami and Jufri were full siblings, and M. Ali Kamri, their younger half-brother, shared the same father. Author's interviews with Haji Buraéra, March 5, 2000; and with Di Alie Kamrie, his mother Sitti Hasisa, and other family members of M. Ali Kamri, June 22, 2011.

authority sprang more from their ties to Kahar Muzakkar, and their own involvement in the leadership of the Darul Islam movement in Sulawesi.

When the DI men came looking for Lawi, her grandmother grabbed Lawi's younger sister, Najamin, and hid in the mangroves at a neighboring island.[21] Although Lawi was taken (Sama: *dialaq*), or "kidnapped" (Indonesian: *diculik*), as she and others often called it, she was accompanied by a number of close relatives, seven in all. These included her mother, Mbakala, with her baby Bicce (Marhabia), still nursing; her sister-in-law Habiba; her brother Syamsuddin; and an uncle named Marhalim. They traveled by boat for a day and a night, stopping at islands along the way: Pulo Maloang, Pulo Gala, Pulo Maginti, Pulo Masudu, and then onto the peninsula southeast of Boépinang. During this journey they were showered with bullets by the central government's forces. A further trudge inland and uphill brought them finally to Jufri's local base at Puulémo, near Marampuka. The next day Lawi was wed to Jufri.[22]

The presence of all these companions might make one wonder whether "captured" or "kidnapped" adequately describe the situation.[23] However, numerous interviews made it clear that the circumstances were far from consensual.[24] Lawi said that her uncle, Marhalim, counseled her to comply with whatever they told her to do: "Whatever is asked, you just do it." "So that," she said, "is how I responded." Given the presence of guns at the ceremony, this was probably good advice.

---

[21] Author's interview with Najamin, June 27, 2011. My interview with Habiba suggests that the *gerombolan*, or rebels, often came to the islands to find pretty, young women. She also stated that many women were *disuruh kawin*, ordered to marry, but she did not know specifics about any others. Haji Lawi's given name, Aluwia or Alwia, was also commonly shortened to Awi and to Hawi. She was additionally known as Haji Sitti Alwia, and as Ibu Erna, Mamanya Erna, or Maqnya Erna—i.e., "Erna's mother."

[22] Author's interviews with Haji Lawi, May 4, 2000; Habiba, June 27, 2011; and Haji Mansyur, March 25, 2000. Haji Muda and Made Ali were also brought along.

[23] The men who took her were said to have carried a photograph of her, which proved to be untraceable. This came up in interviews in 2000, and again with her daughter in 2011. The latter, although of course not a witness at the time, also mentioned that one of Jufri's men was named Herman (Ermang). She said Herman was a sort of *"bencong"* (man who cross-dresses)—the kind who often assists with bridal couples. (This is a practice I have also seen in a Sama village; probably related historically to the functions of *bissu*, Bugis transvestite ritual priests, who persist despite the Bugis having been Muslims since the seventeenth century.) Initially, Herman came alone with the photograph, and Lawi's family hid her. Then he went away and came back with a number of Jufri's men, who surrounded the house (Haji Erna, June 21, 2011). Numerous relatives in different parts of Tiworo and beyond referred to the events surrounding Lawi's capture and her union with Jufri Tambora. Although seventy-five analog audio cassettes of interviews (variously sixty and ninety minutes long) were originally recorded in 2000, only some of those interviewed went into substantial detail about this situation and its repercussions. The most important interviews in this regard were those with Haji Lawi herself, on May 4 2000; Haji Buraéra, March 5, 2000; Haji Mansyur and Mustakim (two of Lawi's brothers), March 24 and 25, 2000; Jufri Tambora, March 6, 2000; and Habiba, June 27, 2011.

[24] Cynthia Werner discusses consensual and nonconsensual forms of bride kidnapping, and the rise of the latter in post-Soviet Kazakhstan; see Cynthia Werner, "Bride Abduction in Post-Soviet Central Asia: Marking a Shift towards Patriarchy through Local Discourses of Shame and Tradition," *Journal of the Royal Anthropological Institute* 15, 2 (2009): 314–31. The research discussed here offers a detailed examination of a particular nonconsensual bride kidnapping during the DI-TII period, and, as such, must be sharply differentiated from fairly common forms of "elopement" (*kawin lari*) in the region that generally have the bride's consent and are not carried out under threat of violence.

Although she recalled neither the month nor the date, the wedding was legitimate (*sah*), performed, she said, on a Friday, a Muslim holy day. Legitimizing the ceremony also seems to have been the main purpose of bringing along the relatives, to bear witness and to replace the absent father with other male representatives, in accord with Muslim practice. Apparently the rebels had no interest in holding the relatives there for any longer than necessary, as they were sent on their way the following day. All, that is, except for Lawi and her young sister-in-law, Habiba.[25]

A few days later, Lawi and Habiba were escorted back to Pulo Balu. Everyone in the village came to the beach to greet them. However, only Habiba disembarked. The families gathered by the water's edge did not permit Lawi to come ashore. Instead they insisted that she return, "go home" to Marampuka, where Jufri was based. She was, in a word, banished (*diusir*). Had she been allowed to return, the TNI and Mobrig, the central government's forces, might assume that the villagers were in league with Darul Islam. None of them, the villagers that is, would be able to show their faces in Raha, the only nearby town.[26] It would have impeded the efforts of those who relied on Raha to conduct trade and to obtain provisions like rice. It also would have ruled out the town as a refuge from the conflict. Worse still, if the central government's forces believed her family and neighbors were in cahoots with DI-TII, they would become its targets or "bullet bait" (*umpan peluru*).

REVENGE

Lawi's father, Haji Usman, was not in the village when she was taken. He had sailed, along with his youngest son, Buraéra, on a trading trip to Lombok.[27] When they got back and found out that Jufri's men had taken Lawi, it hit her father very hard. Lawi later heard someone describe his reaction this way: the sound he made, it was like a goat wailing.[28] (For the uninitiated, this is truly a gut-wrenching sound.) Habiba recalled, "He was beside himself. The house and yard were filled with people watching over him. He screamed, he cried, he called out for his child, Lawi."[29]

The homecoming of Haji Usman and Buraéra happened to coincide with the return to Pulo Balu of two DI men delegated to look for additional family members

---

[25] In 2011, Haji Lawi reiterated that at the ceremony there were guns by her side, and that her uncle Marhalim had told her "you just answer (his/their) call" (*menyahut ki saja*). Petta Solo performed the ceremony. Author's interview with Haji Lawi, June 22, 2011. In 2000, Lawi had called Petta Solo "Daeng Massuro." Buraéra, while not a witness to the "wedding," also mentioned the ceremony's legitimacy. Habiba, along with her husband, Haji Salam (in Sama, "Salang"), commented on its legitimacy as well. Author's interviews with Haji Lawi, May 4, 2000; Haji Buraéra, March 5, 2000; and Habiba, June 27, 2011. In addition, the extended family of Jufri and Sitti Hami's half brother, M. Ali Kamri, also classified or considered Lawi's marriage to Jufri as legitimate. Unlike Jufri, this brother had only had one wife and had many children. Many of these grown children were present, some unmarried, some married and with their spouses and children. Much of my conversation was with M. Ali Kamri's eldest child, named after the rebellion: Di Alie Kamri (pronounced "Dey," as the "Di" was from "D.I.," for "Darul Islam." Author's interviews with Di Alie Kamri and family, June 22, 2011.

[26] Author's interview with Habiba, June 27, 2011. Habiba called the TNI the *tentara kota*, the city army, a neat opposition to the common association of DI-TII with the *hutan*, or forest.

[27] Author's interview with Haji Buraéra, March 5, 2000.

[28] Author's interview with Haji Lawi, May 4, 2000.

[29] Author's interview with Habiba. "*Uu—dia mengamuk. Penuh itu rumah di bawah kolong itu penuh ora(ng) jaga dia. Dia be(r)teriak, mi, menanggis, dia panggil mi anaknya, Lawi.*"

who might join Lawi, and to take them back to their base.[30] These DI men were recognized by Lawi's relatives who had been brought to Puulémo and Marampuka for the wedding ceremony. The DI men now not only sought others to join Lawi, but apparently also asked Haji Usman for money. Haji Usman already harbored resentment over his daughter's abduction. He did not take this fleecing lightly. Habiba recalled his reaction: "'What do these people want with us—doing this? We've already been offended and on top of it they ask for money!' In the end," she said, "these people, these gang members, they wanted a lift back to another island. All the tough guys were sought for this: Marhalim, Wa Sunia, Sumeng (my cousin), and Wa Itang. It was all tough guys who saw them back. [Though] one of them bowed out."[31] Haji Usman summoned these four strong, trustworthy men, and although one backed down, the others took the two rebels and their own steady nerve out in a boat.[32]

Once out on the water, they told the two DI men, "We'll grill you up some squid. We'll make you some squid later. You just have a rest." After they fell asleep, they bludgeoned them, stabbed them with a spear, and tossed their bodies into the sea. Habiba had heard Marhalim's first-hand account of events at the time, and her recollection of what he described was chilling.[33] "'After getting speared,' he said, 'he'd appear again [on the surface of the water], rising like this. *Jabbed* him again.' It was only two of them that, y'know—. And they clubbed their heads. Those guys, of course they had wooden things to hit with because it was a boat. Yeah—they hammered, hammered his head. Hmph. After that he'd sink, and then float up again. He got jabbed again by Marhalim, that toughie. Wa Itang, though, he ran off."[34]

After they killed the two DI men and dumped their bodies in the sea, they sent the blood-soaked boat upriver to the government post at Kambara on Muna's northwest end. "Those officials, Mobrig, whatever, they came down to have a look. Maybe [they thought] it's true that he [Haji Usman] was resentful [*sakit hati*], because they took his child. So he killed those thugs [*gerombolan*]. The upshot of it

---

[30] Author's interview with Haji Buraéra, March 5, 2000.

[31] Author's interview with Habiba, June 27, 2011. "'*Apa mau dibikin kami ini orang—ini begini? Sakitnya kita punya hati, dia mau minta lagi uang.' Akhirnya dia orang anu, e—ini gerombolan, mau diantarpulang. Cari mi semua orang jago: Abanya—Pak Marhalim, itu ada namanya Wa Sunia, Sumeng saya punya sepupu, Wa Itang. Semua orang jago, yang antar dia pulang. Satunya dikasi turun.*" Later in the interview she substitutes "Kaputi" for "Sumeng," probably a nickname for her cousin.

[32] Author's interviews with Habiba, June 27, 2011, and Haji Buraéra, March 5, 2000. Haji Buraéra talked about what happened without naming names. Haji Lawi described how she came to learn about the involvement of Marhaling (Marhalim) and Summeng (author's interview, May 4, 2000), discussed below.

[33] "*E, masih anu katanya, itu, masih mau dibakarkan cumi-cumi. Itu. Dia orang. Hm, dibakarkan cumi-cumi, itu, katanya dia orang ini Marahlim. Nanti kita bakarkan, tidur, mi. Sarena{?} [Setelah] dia tidur, bawa dipalu mi, ada mi dipalu, ditombak. Ya. Mati, mi. Dibuang di laut.*" Author's interview with Habiba, June 27, 2011.

[34] "*Kalau ditombak, katanya, begini dia muncul lagi, naik begini. Ditombak lagi. Hanya dua orang saja yang anu. Ada mi pukul kepalanya. 'Tu orang bikin memang anu—'tu orang bikin memang pemukul itu kayunya—ya kapal. Ya palu, palu kepalanya. Anh. Habis itu dia jatuh dia muncul lagi, ditumbuk lagi sama Marahlim itu yang jago.* [Habiba's husband laughed in the background during this story.] *Itu Wa Itang dia lari.*" Ibid. Lawi's daughter Haji Erna and her husband, Mappésamma, were also familiar with the story of how the two men had been taken out in a boat and killed (author's interview, June 21, 2011).

was, that's why we weren't harassed by the city-army. It was because of that, sending their blood up [the river in a boat]."[35] One of the DI corpses washed ashore on a nearby island, while the bloody boat served as proof that local people had taken action against the rebels. Habiba expressly credited their killing and this delivery of proof with protecting the villagers from, as she called them, the "city-army," the central government's forces.

## DISCOURSE IN THE ARCHIVES

It is likely that Habiba was right, that killing the DI men is what protected the villagers from harassment by the TNI and the Mobile Brigade. Government officials clearly had some sense of what had happened and knew that local people had taken things into their own hands. But how much did they know about these deaths and what did they comprehend were the reasons for them?

The government tried to track Darul Islam in Southeast Sulawesi by the reports it received about them. After ousting them from Boépinang proper and from Kasipute at the strait's western end, a report noted in March 1954: "During the time of the monthly report, the movements of the bands [*gerombolan*] appear to return to the vicinity of the islands of Tiworo—Tembako, Bembe, Tobea, Massaloka, Muna, Kabaena, and the waters of the Tiworo Straits." That is, they returned not only to the islands and waters of the straits, but also to the areas surrounding it: Tembako and Bembe islands sit southwest of Massaloka Island at the straits's western entrance, the Tobea islands ("Large" and "Small Tobea") lie at the straits's eastern end, Muna borders it to the southeast, and Kabaena tames the winds and currents coming from the southwest. The report's author was not surprised to find Darul Islam again venturing into this area, since the number of army and Mobile Brigade personnel stationed on the peninsular mainland were not, in his estimation, equal to the breadth of the region they had to protect. Moreover, as the previous month's report stated, not only was the region broad, it was also "made up of thousands of islands."[36]

Despite the central government's success at taking Kasipute in 1954, this relative dearth of personnel resulted in a situation where "the remnants of the bands roaming about Laiwui on the peninsula can still appear from time to time to carry out their terror."[37] At the same time, Tiworo's geography presented at least as much of a challenge for the central government as it did to Darul Islam: "A portion [of the TII] also runs outside the region in control of the Army by using boats to go to the above mentioned islands—islands that have always been the destination of troublemakers [*pengacau*] because there are still no armed instruments of the state there owing to their location and the difficulties of communication."[38] In short, the

---

[35] "*Turun itu petugas, Mobrig apa itu dia lihat—o, betul paleq* [= *barangkali*] *ini, dia sakit hati, diambil anaknya. Dia bunuh itu gerombolan. Sampai kita tidak diganggu sama tentara kota. Lantaran itu mi. Dikasi naik darahnya.*"

[36] "Warta Politik bulan Maret 1954 Daerah Sulawesi Tenggara," ANRI Makassar, Propinsi Sulawesi 1950–1960, reg. 359; and "Warta Politik bulan Februari 1954 Daerah Sulawesi Tenggara," No. 286: Rahasia [secret report], Bau-Bau, 5 April 1954, ANRI Makassar, Propinsi Sulawesi 1950–1960, reg. 359. The Mobrig post at Kasipute, attacked by DI-TII in 1957, was presumably established in 1954.

[37] "Warta Politik bulan Maret 1954 Daerah Sulawesi Tenggara."

[38] Ibid.

report suggested that the central government lacked boots on the ground as well as boats in the water.

Among the six incidents listed in this report, three of which pertained to Tiworo, one toward the end of the month gave the report's author particular cause for optimism. It was the only incident not perpetrated by the rebels: during March 26–27, 1954, "a marauder [*gerombolan*] landed at Kambara, Tiworo island, but the people there together took action and killed him."[39] Although the report's author is confused about the location of Kambara, and strictly speaking there is no single island that bears the name "Tiworo," this unusual report certainly seems to refer to the retaliatory killing discussed above.

The geographic confusion about Tiworo and Kambara is understandable for someone unfamiliar with the region, which was likely the case for whomever authored the report. Kambara is situated a bit inland from Muna's northwest coast. Yet this stretch of Muna's coast is considered part of the Tiworo area. Looking at it as many local people do, not from the land toward the straits, but rather from the waters and shores of the straits toward the land, Kambara is located in a kind of inland fringe, on the landward periphery of the straits. Even contemporary administrative divisions reflect this, including a swath of northern Muna in *Tiworo kepulauan*, "archipelagic Tiworo" or "Tiworo and the islands (associated with it)."[40] The inclusion of northern Muna, and with it Kambara, as part of this area, rests on the fact that most of the area's villages are located among the islands, shores, and inland margins of the straits, with settlement of Muna's northern interior sparse until relatively recent government agricultural and demographic interventions. Moreover, the maritime-oriented people of the islands and littoral were inseparable from the historical kingdom of Tiworo, whose seventeenth century fortifications on the coastal fringe of Muna's northwest shore lay only a short hop across the water from Pulo Balu.[41]

In addition to the report's inadequate grasp of the area's geography, it demonstrates confusion about where the killing took place. The government itself seems to have maintained an armed post at Kambara during "the time of the gangs," and the report indicates that the killing took place there, rather than, as Habiba reports, in a boat that was left to drift into Kambara. The report also states that there was only one murder, but it was widely acknowledged among witnesses from Pulo Balu that when the boat departed from its waters, this Stygian crossing carried not one victim but two.

Compounding the confusion, the report gets the motive for the killings wrong, proclaiming that "the actions of the marauders ... only constitute the act of taking revenge, directed at none other than the people [*rakyat*], because the people are fed up with forced donations from them, and are aware that the gangs that roam about Southeast Sulawesi in general and especially on the Laiwui mainland and the aforementioned islands are not the true army of Islam as they propagandize."[42]

---

[39] Ibid.

[40] While the islands in the straits are collectively referred to as the Tiworo islands (*pulau-pulau Tiworo*), and *kepulauan Tiworo* would mean the Tiworo archipelago, the compound *Tiworo kepulauan* ("Tikep" for short) is closer to "archipelagic Tiworo" or "Tiworo and the islands (associated with it)." The same holds for the South Sulawesi area known as "Pangkep," *Pangkajene Kepulauan*.

[41] About the historical kingdom of Tiworo, see chapter three.

[42] "Warta Politik bulan Maret 1954 Daerah Sulawesi Tenggara."

Although this statement seems to get it right that people were fed up with extortion, here the author, worked-up to quite an impressive froth, apparently got the dynamics of revenge backward. He words his report as though the rebels were retaliating against the people, when, indeed, it was the other way around.

"The people" in the passage above, the *rakyat*, has a distinctly nationalist ring, especially when juxtaposed with other terms in the report, such as "marauding bands" and "troublemaking thugs" (*pengacau gerombolan*), used to refer to the central government's foes. In the marginalia, one of the report's readers criticizes certain terms for being out of line with official discourse. Thus, he struck the term "fleeing people" (*orang-orang pelarian*) and in the margin substituted "refugees" (*pengungsi-pengungsi*). Refugees are people who seek refuge in a safe place from something that befell or attacked them, whereas "fleeing people" are simply intent on getting away. In other words, a certain moral cachet attaches to "refugees," as charges, which implicitly positions the government on the side of giving assistance to those whom it might paternalistically regard—at least ideologically—as its people. The central government's forces were nevertheless also said to engage in tactics that drove people from their homes.

Finally, the report contains a curious reference to the rebels as "the CTN" (*Corps Tjadangan Nasional*, the National Reserve Corps), which prompted a vigorous response in the margin. Where the report states that on March 17, "the CTN entered Tobea and totally looted it," one reader retorted: "There is no longer any CTN!"[43] It seems such a small detail, but the reaction underscores its significance. The CTN was meant to be a transitional organization for former revolutionary fighters and guerillas who had struggled against the reimposition of Dutch authority after the Japanese Occupation. Perhaps ten thousand of these former guerrillas were to become the responsibility of the BRN (*Biro Rekonstruksi Nasional*, National Reconstruction Bureau), for demobilization and retraining in civilian life, while another five to six thousand were to be commissioned into the CTN. On March 24, 1951, at a ceremony in Makassar, Lieutenant Colonel Kosasih, the acting *panglima* (commander) of TT-VII, the Seventh Army and Territory (*Tentara dan Teritorium*), which covered all of eastern Indonesia at the time, commissioned the CTN/Preparatory Brigade Hasanuddin with Lieutenant Colonel Kahar Muzakkar as its commander. Two-hundred fifty men from each of its five battalions participated, were given arms, and then returned to their designated areas (*rayon*) to await a final settlement between the former guerrillas and the TNI. However, the two sides did not manage to reach a mutually agreeable settlement. When the time came on August 17 (Indonesia's Independence Day) for the installation ceremony that would transition the former guerrillas from reservists to active duty members of the military, the dignitaries at the parade ground in Makassar waited in vain, for by then the CTN members, now rebels, had withdrawn to the forest and within days fighting started in earnest.[44] To call Sulawesi's DI-TII the "CTN" in a report written in 1954 was, to say the least, highly unusual. On the one hand, it seems to refuse DI-TII recognition as a genuine Islamist rebellion and to imply its ongoing subordination to the TNI. On the other hand, the marginalia, "There is no longer any CTN!" underscores how the designation "CTN" worked against the

---

[43] Ibid.

[44] Harvey, "Tradition, Islam, and Rebellion," 231–39.

delegitimizing grain of official terminology, which labeled them as "marauders" or "gangs," a species lower even than rebels.

Beyond the question of the rebels' credentials and the legitimacy of their struggle, the report made clear that in these documents, at least—produced by the central government's agents for higher government officials—the ideological battle took place over decidedly nationalist territory. This is clearly revealed both in the assertion that DI-TII was no longer CTN (!), cast out, as it were, from the nationalist fold, as well as in the portrayal of the revenge killing as an act carried out by "the people" against the central government's foes. The documents give no indication that, in fact, the killing had other, decidedly more "local" causes.

This contrast between the nationalist discourse in the reports and the recollections of those directly involved in Lawi's capture and the fallout from it brings to mind, among other works, Shahid Amin's book, *Event, Metaphor, Memory*. There, too, the discourse of official history, while intertwined with local events, also betrays a disregard, even an ignorance, of how local dynamics and their meanings both played a causal role in events, and in how people remembered them. Here, the political report from 1954 gave no indication that the Darul Islam men were murdered largely in retaliation for Lawi's kidnapping.[45]

It is also possible that some in the government or the military (often one and the same) knew more than what was revealed in the report. One is especially tempted to think so in light of the fact that Lawi's uncle, Marhalim, became village head when the village of Pulo Balu was formally reestablished in 1965. Yet such an expression of confidence in him need not have relied on knowledge of his role in the DI men's killings. He did, after all, come from a lineage that counted respected boat builders, an *imam*, and *punggawa* (local leaders) among its members. Even if his role were known, though, Lawi's almost certainly remained obscured. For while the interpretive frames of official reports may have disregarded the social dynamics actually at play, it is also fair to say that it was in the people's best interests to keep officials ignorant about those dynamics by creating spaces of silence.

## SILENCES

Sama people had many reasons not to talk. Three reasons worthy of mention are the silence of fear, the silence of protection, and the silence of righteous mourning or indignant loss. As many people implied in interviews, and Habiba stated outright, when Lawi was taken, "people could not speak." It was not that no one said anything. Rather, "people could not speak—they were forced (*terpaksa*) [not to]. If one spoke, one's mouth would be filled with bullets."[46]

Lawi herself kept another silence, one that prevented retaliation against those who killed the two DI men who showed up again in Pulo Balu after her father returned from Lombok. Yet, how did Lawi know who had done the deed? When Lawi returned to Pulo Balu with Habiba, she had intended to fetch some clothes, but was instead turned away by her family and neighbors.[47] Apparently, she made a

---

[45] In pulling apart these threads, I wish to indicate not just the divergence of the interpretive frames of reference, but also the causal role played by local meanings and dynamics in the first place. As I see it, while not abjuring nationalism's relevance, this point places the present work amidst a post-orientalist historiography.

[46] Author's interview with Habiba, June 27, 2011.

[47] Ibid.

second attempt to retrieve some clothing not long after the two men were killed. However, when she and her escort arrived at Pulo Balu this time, they found that the village had completely disbanded. Everyone had fled out of fear that the rebels might, in turn, retaliate.[48] Or almost everyone fled. In the dark of night, Lawi encountered her younger brother, Syamsuddin, who had hidden himself. In whispers he related how the DI men had returned and been killed. When she returned to the DI-TII base, she kept that knowledge of who committed the murders very close to her chest. Word of the DI men's demise soon reached Puulemo via other mouths, and Lawi recalled how the people there had talked about it. Yet, only she knew who had carried it out, and she never revealed that secret. "They wanted to go and respond [in kind]. But they could not. He who is guilty is the one who gets killed. It wasn't really known—only I knew—that it was Marhalim and Summeng who, it was said, did it."[49] This particular social logic, in which targets of revenge had to be limited specifically to the actual perpetrators, is a logic that would not have held up when I first met Haji Lawi. At that time, during the early post-Suharto era's violent conflicts of the late 1990s and early 2000s, talk of revenge commonly drew on communalist presumptions, that is, revenge was often aimed at members of a group, rather than at particular individuals. Looking back from such a vantage point, Lawi's ability to forestall a reprisal by keeping such knowledge to herself seems a distant, almost quaint notion, hard to believe. Yet during the 1950s, her silence saved her relatives' lives.

Finally, her mother, Mbakala, who had fled to the town of Raha when the village disbanded, endured repeated questioning by the central government's soldiers: the TNI and Mobrig. Habiba said that Mbakala died of a broken heart from the loss of her favorite child, and recalled her streams of tears and her silence in the face of the military's scrutiny.[50] Mbakala kept the military ignorant about her daughter, whose taking she could not prevent. For the sake of her family and co-villagers she had to keep silent around the soldiers and police, who could do nothing to bring her daughter back. A tearful silence, then, of righteous mourning and indignant loss.

## COMMANDEERING SAMA BOATS

Men were also taken by Darul Islam. Yet they were not taken with the intent to wed them, literally, into the movement.[51] Back when Pulo Balu disbanded, Buraéra initially fled to the town of Raha, but soon returned to Tiworo to join people from Pulo Balu and three other straits villages who had decamped to Muna's northwest end. There the local military post lent them at least a semblance of security. Yet the location posed certain challenges for these Sama people, who found it difficult to get by at this remove from the coast. Hence, with the government's permission, they relocated downriver, closer to the shores that stood opposite Pulo Balu across the channel, to pursue their livelihoods. TII forces took them by surprise there, for

---

[48] Author's interviews with Haji Lawi, May 4, 2000; and Haji Buraera and Haji Tuhpa, March 5, 2000.

[49] Author's interview with Haji Lawi, May 4, 2000.

[50] Author's interview with Habiba, June 27, 2011.

[51] Ironically, in the latter years of the rebellion, and largely by coincidence, Lawi's brother, Buraéra, wound up marrying a Bugis woman, Tuhpa, related to one of the DI men killed in retaliation for Lawi's kidnapping.

rather than approach up the mouth of the river or through the mangrove channels, they instead landed around the point and cut inland on foot across an uninhabited area to take out the military post. Then they advanced down the river to the Sama village near the coast.[52]

When people there realized what was happening, everyone who could do so jumped into boats to get away. The rebels moved quickly, ordering some people to take them on board, while others were directed to lead the way out to sea, to ensure that everyone came along. At some point, once out in the straits, the rebels changed their minds about bringing up the rear of this impromptu flotilla. Perhaps they felt it was unbecoming to be followers in such a situation. Whatever the reason, all of a sudden they decided that they had to be out in front, leading. This was a precious opportunity for the Sama people, now behind them, to turn tail, which they did, fleeing hither and yon across the water. Buraéra laughed so hard recollecting this scene that he had to wipe the tears from his eyes. It had been foolish of the rebels to decide to lead the way instead of bringing up the rear—whether the decision was strategic or borne of hubris. But Buraéra's story was poignant, as well, for ironically, he had been in one of the boats with the rebels. In his heart he must have cheered on his Sama friends and relatives, yet also felt his own fate become more uncertain as he watched them slip away.[53]

After his capture, Buraéra was pressed into fighting for the TII. Initially, he was placed in a battalion where his superior was Suparman, Jufri's nephew.[54] Jufri himself, as mentioned earlier, was commander of one of the four regiments that constituted the TII's Hasanuddin Division, the division that operated in southeast Sulawesi. The other TII division in Sulawesi, which operated in its southwestern peninsula, was called Division 40,000. Its name memorialized the 40,000 Sulawesians supposedly killed as a result of the brutal tactics used by "Turk" Westerling and his commandos during a Dutch "pacification campaign" in late 1946 and early 1947.[55]

Jufri's regiment in the southeastern peninsula and nearby islands had five battalions. One, led by Hasan Hasra, was located in Lasolo, up the peninsula's east coast, north of Kendari. The second, under the leadership of Asmada, was located in Wawotobi, in the central part of the peninsula's interior. The third battalion, under Suparman, operated in the region of Boépinang and included parts of the peninsula's western and southern coasts, as well as sections inland. The fourth battalion, under Andi Bachtiar, worked in the region around Punggaluku, at the peninsula's southeastern end. This area also included Loraya and Lainea on the straits's northeastern shore and Pulo Tobea at its eastern entrance. Finally, the fifth, under Haeru Sahada, operated in and around the Tukang Besi islands.[56] As with the divide

---

[52] Author's interview with Haji Buraéra, 5 March 5, 2000.

[53] Ibid.

[54] Ibid.

[55] George Kahin wrote that, during this campaign in Sulawesi (Celebes), probably between five hundred and a thousand people were killed in arbitrary summary executions conducted in villages, and that at least ten thousand likely were killed during the course of the whole campaign. He does not indicate where these figures came from or on what they were based. He also noted that Republican authorities maintained that about 29,500 civilians were killed in this campaign. George McTurnin Kahin, *Nationalism and Revolution in Indonesia* (Ithaca: Cornell Southeast Asia Program Publications, 1952 [2003]), 356.

[56] Author's interviews with Jufri Tambora, March 6, 2000; and Andi Bachtiar, April 17, 2000.

between the forest and the city in south Sulawesi, most of the southeastern peninsula was more-or-less controlled by DI-TII, with the exception of Kendari; the towns of Kolaka, Raha, and Bau-Bau; and, at times, Boépinang.[57] Although Jufri and his men gained some influence in Tiworo, the straits remained a contested area throughout the years of the conflict.

Operations in and around Tiworo often started from the vicinity of Boépinang. For part of the 1950s, Jufri based his regiment headquarters in Kasabolo, along the coast just west of Boépinang, while Suparman's battalion headquarters were located inland in Rakadua, just north of Boépinang. Even though at some point during the rebellion the Mobile Brigade maintained a post in the town of Boépinang itself, it seems DI-TII managed to work around it, for they organized boat departures from Barangga along the coast to Boépinang's west, or from Pulau Pasudu (Masudu) offshore from Marampuka to Boépinang's east.[58]

Jufri and his men used Sama people and boats to transport them to locations across the water. At first, they commandeered transportation from Sama who came from the area of Boépinang, primarily at Barangga. However, after they removed numerous people from Sama villages on Kabaena, principally from Sikeli and Malandahi, and relocated them to Rakadua on the peninsula, Jufri thereafter used these people instead to conduct operations in Tiworo and nearby areas. This is as close as DI-TII came to maintaining any kind of regular naval capacity in the region.[59] DI-TII did not fight at sea, but, to get across the water, they relied heavily on commandeering Sama boats as needed. Mostly they used *jarangka*, single-outrigger boats that could hold about twelve people. However, after Jufri made further inroads in Tiworo, he made greater use of the *pajala* commonly found there,

---

Mohammad Nasir took over Suparman's battalion (number 22) when Suparman died, during or before 1957, the year DI-TII attacked Mobrig at Kasipute (Kasepute) in the western end of the straits. The battle at Kasipute in October of that year, an effort to take it back after it had been lost to the central government's forces in 1954, was the largest battle to that point in the conflict in Sulawesi. Barbara Harvey places Kasipute "near Kolaka." However, Kasipute, which is not located on the Gulf of Bone, but, rather, is on Tiworo's shores, lies about fifty miles from Kolaka as the crow flies, over mountainous terrain, and about three times that far around the coast. Kahar himself led four- to five-thousand troops in the attack on the Mobile Brigade in Kasipute. DI-TII was only defeated in this battle with the aid of navy and air force shelling and bombing, plus the mobilization of additional Mobrig and army units from the regional territorial command, KDM-SST. Harvey, "Tradition, Islam, and Rebellion," 376. Suparman was said to have died when a boat he was on sank in the Gulf of Bone. Author's interview with Di Alie Kamri, June 21, 2011 (at Erna's house).

[57] Harvey, "Tradition, Islam and Rebellion"; and Velthoen, "Hutan and Kota," discuss the divide for south Sulawesi. DI-TII people periodically slipped into the population centers from time to time.

[58] Author's interview with Buraéra, March 5, 2000; on Pulau Pasudu, author's interview with Jufri Tambora, March 6, 2000.

[59] See Ali Hadara's master's thesis, which takes simple smuggling reports as proof of "maritime guerillas" (*gerilya laut*) in "the Tiworo Sea" without showing any naval combat or effort to differentiate it from clandestine trade. Hadara also cites as evidence DI-TII plans that never came to fruition, and relied on interviews with urban sources who do not appear to have spent time in Tiworo during the conflict. Ali Hadara, "DI-TII di Sulawesi Tenggara: Studi Kawasan Laut Tiworo (1950–1965)" (master's thesis, University of Indonesia, 1998). Harvey lists in an appendix on DI-TII's structure from 1957–59 that M. Lantana Fachri served as Representative of the RII (Indonesian Islamic Republic) Navy (Harvey, "Tradition, Islam, and Rebellion," 466). However, the name never came up in the course of my research on DI-TII in Southeast Sulawesi.

large boats that could each hold about twenty men. The choice of vessel depended in part on availability and in part on need. A trip from Barangga to Sikeli on Kabaena could reasonably be done in a *jarangka*, but *pajala* were useful for somewhat longer trips and those that required more men.[60]

While his battalion commanders might make do with a few boats, Jufri, as mentioned earlier, professed to step out in no less than forty boats. According to him, he made his first tour of Tiworo, around the entire area, in 1957, stopping at Sikeli from where he also claimed to have toured the island of Kabaena on a horse. From Kabaena he crossed east to the large neighboring island of Muna. He continued through the Tiworo Straits all the way to the Tobea islands at the straits's eastern mouth, and beyond this to Wowoni off the peninsula's eastern coast. At other times he and his men island-hopped from Pulo Masudu directly through the straits, to Pulo Maginti, Pulo Gala, Pulo Rangko, Pulo Balu, Pulo Mandike, and Pulo Tiga, among others. In 1958, however, a trader procured a *jonson* for him, an outboard motor, which was practical at least for traveling to Kabaena, and his sailing days were numbered.[61]

Not so Buraéra. At first, Buraéra wound up with Suparman's battalion simply because they were the regiment most active in Tiworo. Before long he functioned as Suparman's guard or escort and received special training as part of a detachment. Eventually this led to him meeting Jufri, his powerful brother-in-law, and to finding a way out of the center of combat. Jufri delegated him, in his capacity as a trader, to ply the waters for Darul Islam, which is how, in a modest cargo boat (*lamboq*), Buraéra became a smuggler for the rebellion, traveling regularly to Dili in Portuguese Timor, to Singapore, and back again to Sulawesi.[62]

## TRADE, FEAR, AND KINSHIP

Many traders for DI-TII in this region of Indonesia shipped their cargo to Rantéangin, located far up the east coast of the Gulf of Boné, in what is now the district of north Kolaka. At Rantéangin, the spine of a mountain range, like a long, gnarled finger, reaches down nearly perpendicular to the shore with a fast-flowing river beside it. A dramatic view, it also serves as a prominent landmark on which sailors out in the Gulf of Boné can take sightings. Near Rantéangin, Sitti Hami, who was Jufri's sister and Kahar Muzakkar's fourth wife, ran a major trading—or smuggling—operation, from her house in Wawo. The cavernous, empty warehouse where we spoke, oddly out of place in this semi-rural setting, once stored bullets, arms, fatigues, and much more.

During the Darul Islam rebellion, Sitti Hami exercised considerable influence over southeast Sulawesi's commerce. Buraéra said she controlled the economy, monopolizing trade in the area, which was heavily dependent on shipping. Regular people, people without special standing in the movement, were not permitted to conduct trade without her permission. Her influence appears to have extended along the eastern Gulf of Boné, across the waters around Kabaena, and through Tiworo, but dissipated toward Buton and the Tukang Besi islands. Part of how she exercised control was by assuming the authority to issue documents for the movement's

---

[60] Author's interviews with Jufri Tambora, March 6, 2000; and Haji Buraéra, March 5, 2000.

[61] Ibid.

[62] Author's interview with Haji Buraéra, March 5, 2000.

traders to carry with them. She probably learned the details of how to do this from Jufri, who had experience with the forms and uses of such documents from when he functioned as harbormaster at Kolaka during the Japanese occupation. An informant for the Japanese who looked for Dutch spies, Jufri had been responsible for dealing with the comings and goings of boats. He was the one who arranged their papers.[63]

Among the papers Sitti Hami issued were "false letters" (*surat palsu*), in other words, forged documents, complete with official stamps. DI-TII stole stamps for this purpose. For instance, if a stamp from Langara on the island of Wowoni were used, they would forge the signature of the village head there at the time, whose name was Undaq. For the stamp from Taliabo, relatively close to Sulawesi but in north Maluku, they signed Yunus, for the village head there. The same goes for the stamp from Wanci or Wangi-wangi in the Tukang Besi islands. The papers would also indicate the amount and type of cargo, and the destination—say, Surabaya. But in fact they all issued from the same place: Sitti Hami.[64] DI-TII operated as far south into the Flores Sea as Jampea in the Bonerate Atoll.[65] However, beyond such areas connected with coastal society to the north, outsiders knew little of circumstances in Sulawesi, and papers that looked legitimate allayed the suspicions any outsiders might have had about the mariners carrying them.[66]

Many people from Sulawesi had opened shipping businesses throughout the region, so it was usually possible to find trade connections once one crossed the Flores or Java Seas. However, sometimes the actual goods did not quite match the "official" cargo, and some things had to be loaded with particular care. For example, as Buraéra recalled, Gresik, East Java, is where he picked up "army uniforms—if we wanted to load them, we would pretend to be taking fresh water in a large water jar [*tempayan*]. We carried it right in front of the police post."[67] It was risky business. If caught, goods would get confiscated and the next stop would be jail. At the same time, Buraéra said that the profit he got from this work often doubled the value of the goods and he could count on at least seventy percent. He admitted that once he did get caught, in Tanjung Balei, near Singapore, when carrying coffee and other goods from Sumatra, but he got away. His methods apparently involved more than simply exchanging goods directly between Sulawesi and other areas, instead trading up for profit along his journey in the time-honored tradition of the region's sailors. Many items were salable in Singapore and other major ports of the region. He was, moreover, far from the only smuggler moving goods between Singapore and southeast Sulawesi, so certain channels of clandestine exchange had already been established.[68]

---

[63] This came up in my discussion with Jufri about his biography. During my interviews with Jufri, he did not connect his experience handling documents with Sitti Hami's role in Darul Islam. He had previously, albeit briefly, been a teacher in the Kolaka area, but had a disagreement with the Javanese head of the school. After he quit, he found this work as an informant for the Japanese. He said he worked as harbormaster for *Bensa Ongkōkai*, "Bensa Transportation." Author's interview with Jufri Tambora, March 6, 2000. See also the related discussion in the beginning of the Introduction.

[64] Author's interview with Haji Buraéra, March 5, 2000.

[65] Something I had earlier been surprised to learn during field research in November 1999 on Latondu and Rajuni, islands in this group.

[66] Author's interview with Haji Buraéra, March 5, 2000.

[67] Ibid.

[68] See the series of secret reports that begin on January 20, 1954, with information regarding

Some items required particularly special connections. For instance, Buraéra mentioned how difficult it was to trade anything at the harbor in Dili. If one needed an article of clothing to wear personally, that was one thing. But doing deals in quantity was quite another. The harbor was tightly controlled, trade worked on a system of orders, and local stores were largely owned by Arab merchants. For the most part, Buraéra was not hooked into the right networks in Dili. However, there was one important contact in Dili whom Jufri also mentioned separately, a trader named Orlando. Orlando was interested in buying copra, widely smuggled at the time. He dealt in, among other things, ordnance left behind after the Japanese occupation. "That Orlando," said Jufri, "that guy was my friend. He sent me bombs, whatever, all kinds of things."[69] In the archives, while looking for first-hand

smuggling conducted two months earlier between Singapore and southeast Sulawesi. Thirty-nine boats, twenty of which were witnessed came from Wowoni, northern and southern Buton, and a couple of the Tukang Besi islands. At least some of these were almost certainly Sama, as the particular places mentioned have Sama villages (and no others) on their coasts. In Wowoni, there is only a Sama village, so there is no mistaking it for "Butonese." The informant described a system whereby the smugglers were escorted into and out of Singapore's waters by the motorboats of a particular Chinese merchant. The smugglers carried coffee, copra, and other goods. The report's author also described how, for the past few years, as far as the Customs and Duties office in Buton's port at Bau Bau knew, there were no boats from Riau delivering *gambir*. Yet there was no shortage of *gambir* in the Bau Bau region. *Gambir* is used in betel chewing as well as in tanning and dyeing. The report surmised it was being offloaded at other places in the region. See Letter of Polisi Negara Kantor Wilayah Buton Dinas Sekuriti, and related letters between Customs and Duties officials, the police, and the governor's office, ANRI Makassar, Propinsi Sulawesi, Reg. 359. Buraéra had been caught at Tanjung Balei on Karimun island, not to be confused with the Tanjung Balei in North Sumatra, across the Malacca Straits from Kuala Lumpur. Author's interview with Haji Buraéra, March 5, 2000.

[69] Author's interviews with Haji Buraéra, March 5, 2000; and Jufri Tambora, March 6, 2000. Arms for DI-TII in Sulawesi came from a number of sources, including from sympathizers in the TNI itself. For one thing, TNI defectors would bring their weapons over to the TII, and then hope to be reintegrated to the TNI at a higher rank. See Harvey, "Tradition, Islam, and Rebellion," 238, on these "jungle promotions." Buraéra said that some fighters, such as Andi Selle, began as DI men "on the inside" (of the government's military), but wound up profiting from trade with both sides. Harvey describes Andi Selle as one of the TNI's "early successes," and she notes how Kahar, later in the rebellion, was able to make both territorial and commercial deals with Andi Selle and Andi Sose, another ex-CTN commander. Both men effectively became "TNI warlords … so that local operations were not carried out against [Kahar] in the extensive areas under their control. Selle, in particular … was an excellent source of arms and supplies … always willing to sell to the highest bidder, and to work out arrangements as long as he got his cut." Harvey goes on to say that Pare-Pare, where Selle was based, near supplies of copra, was an old smuggling harbor (indeed, at least since the fifteenth century), with easy connections to Borneo and even Singapore. See Harvey, "Tradition, Islam, and Rebellion," 236, 264. On the importance of copra in the political economy of Sulawesi in this period, see Barbara S. Harvey, *Permesta: Half a Rebellion* (Ithaca: Cornell Modern Indonesia Project, 1977). Probably for lack of oral and written sources, Harvey characterized southeast Sulawesi's role at the time this way: "Southeast Sulawesi, with the exception of the island of Buton, was an area of largely uninhabited jungle. Its political significance was negligible" (Harvey, *Permesta*, 44). She relied, as most historians do, on documented figures and interviews with prominent personages. Her resulting statement adopts the metropolitan view. See Velthoen, "*Hutan and Kota.*" Hence, the historiography on DI-TII has largely disregarded Southeast Sulawesi, despite the movement's substantial presence there and the fact that significant battles were fought in Southeast Sulawesi. It was certainly not uninhabited, and conflict over this area lasted for more than a decade, which says something about its political significance. With the establishment of martial law in 1957,

accounts by sailors, I came across reports about smuggling from Portuguese Dili. Yet they never seemed to catch any smugglers. When I mentioned this to Buraéra, he said, very quietly at first, "Yeah, we just might have come out on top. Y'know sailors, they're pretty gutsy when it comes to breaking government regulations."[70]

"Smuggling" can be a sensitive term, since it implies the recognition of certain political structures, which, in this case, were certainly being contested. As Jufri said, "if it's our enemies talking, they'd call it 'the black market.' But we just called it regular trade." He went on to draw the parallel with terms that delegitimized the movement (*gerakan*), or rebellion (*pemberontakan*), as a whole: "Because the thing is, those city people, [and] our PKI [communist] enemies, they'd say that I'm in a 'gang' [*gerombolan*]. But I don't get that—'gang member.' 'Gangs'—that's evil people. There is no organization."[71]

DI-TII, indeed, had a military organization, some degree of administrative structure, as well as a system for conducting trade. Sitti Hami's efforts to control this trade were hardly unusual in light of colonial and early post-colonial attempts to monopolize, in particular, the lucrative copra trade.[72] However much it was organized, though, the smoke and mirrors of forged letters were a concession to the need to work around the central government that Darul Islam fought. Having an organization, of course, justified neither side's tactics or methods. Despite his protest of the label "gang," Jufri was perfectly up front about his methods: "I'd say: good luck or bad, I've come here to improve you. But if you want to refuse my orders, want to put up resistance to me, I'm the one with the weapons. See these? Arms. Lots of them. They'd choose. You want to live or die? If you want to live, you come with me. If you want to die, you can defy me. Hmph—you there, I kill you."[73]

---

officials tried to reinstitute a government copra monopoly, which required all copra from South and Southeast Sulawesi to go through Makassar (see Harvey, *Permesta*, 115–16). However, mariners from Southeast Sulawesi by this time had decades of practice skirting such attempts to control its copra trade (not to mention earlier histories of smuggling). Neither the colonial government nor the republic had the ability to police the waters effectively. Moreover, archival documents show that, even where there was a customs office, such as at Buton, its monitoring of trade was unreliable, to say the least. See: "Letter of 11 September 1954 Bau-Bau, secret. Subject: smuggling at Singapore. Sent to the Governor of the Province of Sulawesi (copy of letter No. 36 of 27 February)" and the related letter "20 January 1954, Vice Commander, National Police, Buton District Office, Security Division," ANRI Makassar, Propinsi Sulawesi 1950–1960, reg. 359.

[70] "*Iya. Boleh jadi kita menang. Orang perahu itu, berani-berani melanggar peraturan pemerintah.*" Buraéra 5 March 2000. My thanks to John Wolff for suggesting "we might just have" and "gutsy" here, and for weighing in with humor and erudition on the shortcomings of literal translations of colloquial speech (personal communication, July 24, 2013).

[71] To some degree this remark echoed discourses of the recently ended late-Suharto period, when the government warned people to be vigilant about "OTB," Organizations without Shape (*Organisasi Tanpa Bentuk*), implying the possibility of a communist resurgence and enlisting the population against it. The government thereby tried, but largely failed, to foment paranoia and distract the public from criticisms of the government. Some fifteen years later, it was particularly amusing to see the incisive economist Kwik Kian Gie apply the same term, OTB, to the network of like-minded capitalists that included the so-called "Berkeley mafia." See HMINews.com, "Sri Mulyani Indrawati (SMI), Berkeley Mafia, Organisasi Tanpa Bentuk (OTB), IMF dan World Bank (WB)" May 30, 2010, http://hminews.com/news/1618/, accessed August 10, 2013.

[72] Harvey, *Permesta*.

[73] *Saya bilang: Saya datang di sini untuk perbaiki ko, untung-untung jahat. Tapi kalau mau menolak saya punya perintah, mau perlawanan dengan saya, saya yang punya senjata. Lihat di sini (se)njata, banyak.*

DI-TII used arms and fear to control not just territory, but bodies. People were forced to relocate to rebel-held areas and the threat of violence was used to extort their compliance. However, fear for one's immediate survival did not control smugglers. One might think they could potentially just sail away, but it was not that simple. If people from other branches of the movement, or other smugglers, reported back that one had tried to exit the movement, this could have serious consequences. A smuggler might stray or lie low for a spell, as Buraera did. But if smugglers strayed, Darul Islam gave them reasons to return. Lawi was apparently just such a reason.

It was while discussing the arms trade and his "friend" Orlando that Jufri himself brought up his union with Lawi, a subject that he connected directly with the topic of fear. I asked whether many Sama people used to convey information to him—that is, about arms and their potential acquisition—or whether such knowledge only came through particular people. Since archival research on such networks is difficult, and beset by the perspective of the state, I wondered if Jufri might provide some details about how his information networks worked.

What he offered in reply was a grand, if vague, "Oh, *all* of them." All Sama people brought him information? Not likely. Was he, in saying this, just avoiding specifics? Or was this of a piece with his forty-boats-come-with-me-or-I'll-kill-you self-image? From what I understood, Sama people had not exactly been tripping over each other to tell him useful things. Even so, it would not be impossible for him to believe something like this, given—aside from his overweening confidence— the sorts of strategies many Sama people employed during the rebellion that resulted in telling power holders what they wanted to hear. Skeptical and curious to learn more, I mirrored his comment as a follow-up question: "All of them?"

His response, offered as an explanation, was: "I wed a *raja* of the Bajo. She was [or: they were] afraid." "How's that?" I asked. "I married a high-status descendant of the Bajo." I countered, "Did you? So what's the story with that?" "Just that. I married someone whose ethnic group was the Bajo people."[74] His last comment may

---

*Dia pilih: mau hidup atau mati. Kalau mau hidup, ikut sama saya. A, kalau mau mati, bisa menentang. Mmh, saya bunuh ko itu.*" Author's interview with Jufri Tambora, March 6, 2000. A great deal of back story could be given about Jufri: his capture along with other *palopo pejuang* (strugglers, fighters) and imprisonment during the revolution; how he was sentenced to death along with five other leaders, then had the sentence commuted to life and actually served nine months in Cipinang prison before being released after the Round Table Conference for RIS sovereignty; his grasp of how Kahar's position shifted with the army's change from Sudirman to Nasution; his training in Java—X07 started there, but then was disbanded because of Nasution's rise; and his participation in KGS (*Komando Grup Seberang*, the Outer Islands Commando Group), command of which was given to Kahar (rather than leadership of the South Sulawesi unit of the new Territorial Command for Eastern Indonesia). The rest of the story can be filled in by Barbara Harvey's work. But perhaps most important for the present work, Kahar Muzakkar and Jufri were childhood pals, schoolmates, and scouts. This was an undeniably important factor in Kahar's reliance on his childhood friend, which he cemented through an alliance: Kahar's marriage to Jufri's sister Sitti Hami.

[74] The literal translation renders this as "she was afraid," which Lawi undoubtedly was, but the context and construction suggest that *dia* here may also refer to *Bajo*, meaning that not only she, but *they* were afraid. When he described his methods of intimidation, Jufri used *ko* and *dia* in a similar manner to refer to any person in a collective abstract (they). The "*to*" appears to be interference from Bugis, meaning "people/person." "*Saya kawin to rajanya orang Bajo. Dia takut.*" "*Bagaimana?*" "*Saya kawin dengan bangsawannya orang Bajo.*" "*Ya? Terus, bagaimana cerita itu?*" "*Itu, bangsanya* [sic] *orang Bajo saya kawin.*"

have contained a malapropism, substituting *bangsa*, "nation, people, race," for *bangsawan*, "nobility or aristocracy." Either way, though, his remarks show him thinking in the aggregate. In other words, his comments underscore that he was not just marrying a pretty young Bajo woman (because he could), but a *raja*, one from a "kingly" or high-status lineage.

Jufri thus explicitly linked clandestine maritime trade, on the one hand, and Lawi's ethnic affiliation and ascribed status on the other. She was picked because she was Bajo and came from a prominent lineage. The first of Jufri's many wives, she was the only Sama one, and the only one known to have been kidnapped for the purpose.[75] Even assuming it is true that none of the others had been kidnapped, one could hardly conclude that there had been a lack of coercion, since, as more than one woman remarked, in those days, if Jufri asked for something, who would have had the audacity to refuse?[76] Indeed, the link Jufri made explicit between clandestine maritime trade and his marriage to a woman from the class of *raja* Bajo was forged and reinforced through both kinship and fear.

## AMPHIBIOUS SURVIVAL

Buraéra stressed that Darul Islam used marriage as a tactic. In his view, his sister Lawi's marriage to Jufri was not a one-time aberration, but rather an intentional strategy. He reckoned that he, himself, had only been able to gain access to Jufri and work out a better situation for himself because of the kin connection. "When I reached there this occurred to me, because the *gerombolan* have a *taktik* that always makes—always has someone who joins [*masuk*] and marries, so that there's whatsit—so that there's a kind of protection." "They had a method," I asked, "it was planned that way?" "Yes!" he said, laughing, "it's clear to see." When we discussed Jufri's sister Sitti Hami, he pointed out that her marriage to Kahar Muzakkar followed the same strategy (*siasat*).[77]

The marriage tactic was also used with an important figure who came over to DI-TII with his men late in the decade from another rebellion, Permesta:

That Permesta guy, Gerungan, the one who came and joined with DI-TII, he was made a battalion commander straight off. He had been a major. Kahar right away had him marry his sister. That was their tactic. But his underlings couldn't handle it, all the restrictions of Islam, so they reversed course and ran off. The poor babies at the time, they were still small and were left behind with their mothers ... When they merged with DI-TII, [Gerungan's men] had all been given positions [viz., rank]. Things were divided up. They were given houses, training, but who could know—over time they couldn't handle it.[78]

---

[75] Jufri had eleven wives, but two or three may have come after the end of the conflict. Author's interview with Haji Erna, June 22, 2011.

[76] The phrase that came up repeatedly was: *siapa berani menolak?* (Who would be brave [enough] to turn him down?) This sentiment was reminiscent of the comments made by an anonymous Sama man whose boat and services had been commandeered by DI-TII, for which he later served jail time at the end of the rebellion: better three years in jail than dead (for refusing to help DI-TII).

[77] Author's interview with Haji Buraéra, March 5, 2000.

[78] "*Itu Permesta, itu yang datang mengabungi sendiri di anu, di DI-TII. Langsung itu di— dia punya Komandan batalyon. Gerungan, Mayor pangkatnya. Langsung dikasi kawin dengan saudara perempuan*

Gerungan had been a graduate of the Dutch military academy at Breda and considered one of the most intelligent and capable officers in Eastern Indonesia. Although little is known about his arrival in the south in the late 1950s or his initial contacts with Kahar Muzakkar, he brought with him some two hundred men, three quarters of whom were armed—an infusion of arms and expertise that delighted Kahar. Two companies of these troops shared in the success of an attack and three-day occupation of Malili in January 1959. However, due in part to disputes over reorganization and weapons, Gerungan and most of his men were said to have tried to flee, which led to two weeks of fighting. Defeated, Gerungan and his men were given the choice to convert or be executed, and chose the former. Thirty or forty of this Permesta group who had not tried to flee were allowed to remain Christians. Subsequently, Gerungan caused no further trouble, studied Arabic, taught at the DI military academy in Latimojong, and is said to have become one of Kahar's most trusted followers.[79]

If Buraéra is correct about these kinship tactics and this instance of putting them into play, then Gerungan had become Kahar's brother-in-law. Buraéra was certainly in a position to know, since his own sister-in-law, Sitti Hami (Jufri's sister), was married to Kahar. It appears that Gerungan may thus have had multiple reasons—a military position, support for the movement's aims, a new family, preserving his skin—to stay with DI, not to mention to convert.

Political and military history on the rebellion remains largely silent on the importance of such connections. Barbara Harvey's foundational research did, however, acknowledge that family ties between the rebels and civil and military officials in the towns both assured DI of assistance and also impeded implementation of harsh policies of suppression. Many people in the towns had relatives in the *hutan* (jungle, woods), and these relatives were "virtual hostages, in the sense that should the members of the family in the government or TNI support firm action, the members of the family in the *hutan* might be killed in revenge."[80] Yet

---

*Pak Kahar. A, itu taktiknya itu. Tapi yang bikin anu, dia punya anak buah, karena tidak tahan anu, larangan-larangan hukum Islam. A itu mi, sehingga balik haluan, melarikan diri. Bayi kasihan pada waktu itu, masih anak-anak, masih kecil ditinggalkan, sama ibunya. Kalau waktunya menggabung diberikan jabatan semua. Dibagi-bagi, disini ada juga. Ada rumah, ada pelatihan. Dibagi-bagi. Tahu-tahu lama-kelamaan tidak bisa, mi, menahan lama. A, melarikan diri, mi." Ibid.*

[79] According to Terance Bigalke, Gerungan had begun to collaborate with Frans Karangan on organizing a Greater Toraja movement in Central Sulawesi that would be associated with Permesta. However, before the plans amounted to anything concrete, they quarreled and went their separate ways. Karangan's TNI company aided Javanese troops (Brawijaya) against Permesta, and Gerungan first joined with Permesta and then with Kahar's DI-TII. See Terance W. Bigalke, *Tana Toraja: A Ssocial History of an Indonesian People* (Singapore: Singapore University Press, 2005), 260. Barbara Harvey noted that D. J. Somba, another of the Permesta leaders, who had been a lieutenant colonel in the TNI, promoted Gerungan to commander when, on February 19, 1958, the KDM-SUT (the North Sulawesi District Military Command) broke relations with the Sukarno central government. This information comes solely from interviews with Somba in the early 1970s. Gerungan led Permesta's RTP (*Resimen Tim Pertempuran*, Combat Team Regiment) "Anoa" in Central Sulawesi, headquartered in Poso. It may be that Gerungan neither agreed with nor saw much of a future for himself in the TNI under martial law established in 1957, and, as Harvey points out, Gerungan was aware of earlier discussions between Permesta officers in the south on the possibility of reaching some agreement with Kahar. Harvey, "Tradition, Islam, and Rebellion," 404–11. Poso, where RTP Anoa was headquartered in the 1950s, lies deep in the Tomini Gulf.

[80] Harvey, "Tradition, Islam, and Rebellion," 263.

the tactics Buraéra described go beyond what Harvey explains essentially as using family members with kin on the other side to negotiate and manage threats. Besides this, one gets a picture of how forging kin ties through marriage constituted part of vital alliance-making processes that expanded the rebellion and socially supported it.

If forging kin connections was part of the calculus that went into DI-TII's military and political decision-making, not just incidental to it as in any civil war, then it may be worth considering why our methodologies apparently make these phenomena of war and kinship so hard to think about together, particularly for recent history. By drawing on memories that would never make it into an archive, one can bend these frameworks—history of the family on the one hand, political and military history on the other—back toward each other, to retrace the connections between rebellion and kinship, loyalty and fear. Analyzing them in the same space reveals the dynamics of how they worked together.

Lawi's presence among the rebels would not have forestalled any government reprisals, for she had no kin in positions of note in the towns. Rather, her capture provoked a reprisal from her family beyond the government's knowledge. While the men killed by her relatives had been looking for others to join her, and hence made her an instrument to expand the movement socially, the reasons for her kidnapping went beyond a desire to increase DI's numbers. Because her father was a Sama trader, her people knew boats and the sea. Moreover, she came from a high status lineage that counted among its members both local political and religious leaders (recall her father had also been an *imam*), a lineage with some pull among dispersed yet interconnected Sama communities. Her capture, therefore, could potentially provide DI-TII a route to access better material support; in particular, the specialized skills and knowledge pertinent to the region's maritime infrastructural networks.

This is evident from the association Jufri himself made between the clandestine arms trade and his marriage to Lawi. It is also revealed more concretely in the trusted relationship Jufri and his sister developed with Lawi's brother Buraéra. Buraéra claimed to have become Jufri's personal adjutant and described how, like a shill who convinces onlookers in a swindle, he played Jufri's stooge, helping him come off as looking tougher at times than he really was.[81] This accommodation was part of how Buraéra got through the conflict: he was, he said, amphibious. Initially, "*amfibi*" had been a title (*gelar*) bestowed on him by his friends among the TII's battalion and company commanders, a play on his ability to get by on land as well as at sea, one of the "sea people," but nonetheless quite at home on land.

Yet *amfibi* turned out to have another more specific meaning as well, a term this old salt used to explain his own position in his recollections. As a smuggler, he had to be "amphibious," working for one side while playing the other. He had to be able to survive in both worlds. In contrast with Jufri's bravado, this slight but spry man conveyed, with admixtures of satisfaction, mirth, and self-effacing gestures, how he had, in those days, through wits and pluck, scraped by with his life. In addition to smuggling, he had apparently also been captured by the Mobile Brigade, and for a time, before he escaped from them, was brought on operations around Boépinang and Kabaena.

Buraéra explained that when the movement first began, Sama people were the only ones who had not been implicated in it. They had not gotten mixed up with the rebels. The reason why they were not involved, he said, was because they were

---

[81] Author's interview with Haji Buraéra, March 5, 2000.

ignorant, they did not know anything about politics.[82] This may have been more or less true, depending on what one means by "politics." Yet it also reflects a common stereotype with roots in the colonial period of the Bajo as innocent sea nomads (or ex-sea nomads). Buraéra related, for instance, that if he happened to come across an army guy on operations, he would just tell him that he was Bajo. This itself was often defense enough to be left alone. It was so useful a perception that, apparently, others claimed to be Bajo just to avoid the conflict. "All those people who fled from south Sulawesi and then got their identity cards in Muna, the ethnic group that they declared there was Bajo. If a soldier looked at it, they'd say: 'Oh, a Bajo person, this is someone who doesn't know anything … The people living over there are Bajo [they would say].' But, in fact, they were Bugis."[83] Although over the years I had many times encountered people who hid—or, as Erving Goffman would say, "covered"—their Sama affiliations when among non-Sama Indonesians, this was the first time I had heard of Bugis people pretending to be Bajo.[84]

Hiding behind the presumption of harmlessness (as a Bajo person) only worked as a strategy for Buraéra so long as no one "outed" him as part of DI-TII. Buraéra, "just a Bajo guy," was picked up by the Mobile Brigade, brought on operations, and presumed not to have connections with Darul Islam. At Kabaena, on one of these operations with the Mobile Brigade, he was recognized by a certain Mohammad Nurung, one of the *gerombolan*, and someone he had known well. Buraéra, or one of his companions, shot Nurung in the leg. He lived, but, Buraéra realized, this person would just cause trouble, and indicated to the commander of the operation that it would be better to just finish him off. "I really regretted it, too. But I thought, well, it's for my safety. Because if he's safe, I'm screwed."[85]

After the conflict had ended and almost all the rebels had "returned" to the republic, a euphemism that puts a nice face on surrender, the central government's intelligence people apparently gave Buraéra considerable leeway, since they understood that if anyone knew where Jufri was still holding out, it would be Buraéra. Buraéra, for his part, did not want Jufri to be killed, because, he said, he was an in-law (*ipar*), and also because "he was very smart and, moreover, a guerilla.

---

[82] "*Waktu operasi, waktu pertama ada gerakan, cuma suku Bajo yang tidak terlibat, tidak ada anu, campur dengan gerombolan…Pertama, alasannya, orang bodoh, orang Bajo itu bodoh, tidak tahu politik. Tidak tahu apa-apa.*" Ibid.

[83] "*Asalnya ditangkap, lalu—. Jadi semua itu pelarian-pelarian dari Selatan, ambil KTP di sana di Pulau Muna. Dinyatakan sukunya disitu, suku Bajo. Dilihat tentara, orang Bajo, orang tidak tahu apa-apa ini…penduduk di sana, suku Bajo. Padahal Bugis.*" Ibid. At Pulo Tiga, on March 29, 2000, Mboq Amang, born during World War Two, talked about how they were always scared during the "time of the gangs" and fled from place to place, like many people. Amang's father (Masak) was of Muna and Buton descent, and his mother (Pondeq) was from Muna. When asked "and you?" Mboq Amang replied: "My father's from Muna so I don't know what his kids are. I guess live at the Bajos and become Bajo is what it's called." *Tidak tahu, mi. Bapakna orang Muna tidak tahu mi anaknya orang apa. Tinggal di Bajo jadi orang Bajo barangkali namanya.* They spoke Bajo at Amang's house, but if someone who spoke Muna (or the Tiworo dialect of it, "*bahasa Tiworo*") or Bugis came by, then they would code switch into one of those languages. This picture of multilingualism occurred on a few of the islands in central Tiworo, and in Tanjung Pinang on Muna's north shore. By contrast, Sama was the lingua franca in Pulo Balu and at locations in most of the eastern and western ends of the straits.

[84] Erving Goffman, *Stigma* (New York: Simon and Schuster, 1963), 102–4.

[85] "*Merepotkan saja ini orang … sama komandan operasi, lebih baik diselesaikan saja. Saya menyesal juga, tapi saya pikir, a, keselamatan saya. Kalau dia yang selamat, saya yang celaka.*" Haji Buraéra, 5 March 2000.

If someone in the family leaked [information about where he was to the government], it could be learned from the official. A little mistake like that could get you killed."[86] Despite the kidnapping of Lawi, and Buraéra's own capture and impressment with DI-TII, it came to matter that Jufri was his brother-in-law, but by the same token it also mattered that he was one seriously fearsome relation.

## MORGANA'S FATE

After nine years of enduring hardship in the woods of the Southeast Sulawesi peninsula, moving around from one place to another whenever it seemed their location was discovered, Lawi said she learned that the people with whom she shared adversity and daily life were "just plain good people." When the conflict was over, she made her way to Raha, where she was reunited with her father, and they returned to Tiworo.[87]

When she returned, she must have been pregnant, because her son Daulat, her fourth child by Jufri, was born there. The first, born among people who may still have seemed strangers to Lawi, sadly did not make it past the first few days.[88] Lawi's other two children were daughters. Erna, who was very young when she returned to Pulo Balu with her mother, grew up without ever meeting her older sister, Morgana. Morgana grew up thinking that Sitti Hami was her mother.

When Morgana was about six months old, her aunt Sitti Hami took her.[89] Sitti Hami's marriage with Kahar did not produce any progeny, and she was said to have had a fondness for Morgana. Adoption is fairly common in Indonesia, and occasionally young Sama children decide, apparently on their own, to go live with an aunt. However, this was different. For one thing, Sitti Hami was not Sama, but Bugis. She was the sister of the man who had had Lawi kidnapped. We do not know what Lawi may have felt at the time Morgana was taken: powerless, despondent, and resentful? Perhaps relieved? After all, her marriage to Jufri was coerced, and although she said she was never forced, sometimes willingness is the handmaid of survival. What is certain is that, if Lawi had not been taken from Pulo Balu, she would not have borne Morgana, and thus Morgana could not have been taken from her.

---

[86] "*Itu Pak Jufri orang pintar baru gerilya. Tidak mungkin. Kan, dia tahu kalau famili. Familinya bocor, tercium dari petugas* [literally, "if the family leaks, it's sniffed out (or "smellable") from the official"]. *Salah sedikit, dibunuh.*" Author's interview with Haji Buraéra, March 5, 2000.

[87] Author's interview with Haji Lawi, May 4, 2000.

[88] Author's interview with Mayana, June 21, 2011; and Haji Erna, June 22, 2011. The supposition that Lawi had been pregnant when she returned after the rebellion occurred to me while talking with Habiba about Lawi's children. Lawi would have had frequent contact with Habiba when she first returned to Raha. Author's interview with Habiba, June 27, 2011. Sometimes her son was called "Daula." His full name was Syahrur Daulat. It bears the sense of "sovereign prince" or "fortunate royal," a fine and very Islamic name for the son of a Darul Islam commander and a Sama woman of high-status descent. Indeed, even though slavery has been outlawed in Indonesia for decades, among Sama people in much of Sulawesi, a custom persists in which it is not deemed fitting for children descended from slaves to have such Islamic-sounding names. Instead they may, for instance, have lyrical names from Indonesian words, like "key" (Kunci) and "forest" (Rimba). Other Sama people, but not necessarily other Indonesians, accordingly "read" information about descent from such naming practices.

[89] Author's interview with Haji Lawi, May 4, 2000.

"Fata Morgana" was named by Jufri. This choice of names was fitting, for its allusion to "fate" and "illusion." Morgan le Fay (Fata Morgana [Ital.], Morgain la fée [Fr.]) was a figure of Arthurian legend. *Fata* in the name appears to come from the Italian for "enchantress," as well as from the Latin for "fates" (sing. *fatum*). The latter invoked the Fates, mythological personifications of destiny who spun, measured, and cut the thread of life. Among other things, the Fata Morgana of legend wove illusions, presumably the source for the contemporary sense of "fata morgana," meaning "mirage," referring specifically to a form of floating illusion associated with the Straits of Messina. Lawi's child, Fata Morgana, was to have a life structured, at least at first, by an illusion. Yet, as fate would have it, she was eventually demystified.[90]

Morgana ("Mor," as she was called) was never led to believe that anyone other than Jufri was her father. Yet, when she was in middle school, she began to wonder whether Sitti Hami was really her mother, since Jufri and Sitti Hami were siblings. After she finished elementary school in Wawo, she had to walk over to Rantéangin, two or three kilometers away, to attend middle school. This is where Buraéra lived. A promise he made forbade Morgana from frequenting his house because, it was feared, he might reveal to her the secret that her real mother was Lawi. However, a young Sama relative who came from Tiworo to live for a time at Buraéra's house was visited there by his father, and the latter wanted to see this daughter of Lawi's, who was, for him, on the order of a grandchild. Somehow or other, with the help of one of Buraéra's children (perhaps on the way to or from school), he managed to meet Morgana on the sly. He told her: "Your mother is in Raha. That's not your mother here." Morgana reportedly kept this encounter to herself for a long time. Her schooling later continued in Makassar, where she lived with Jufri's wife Haji Ruga and attended college. There in Makassar she apparently had some confirmation of the truth.[91]

In 1979, Lawi had a broken tooth and Jufri came to Kendari, the provincial capital of Southeast Sulawesi, with money for her to have someone replace it. He flew from Makassar to Kendari with Haji Ruga, their small child, and Morgana. Lawi had moved with her daughter Erna and son-in-law, Mappésamma, from Tiworo to a

---

[90] Jufri was said to have named the children. To be clear, I do not mean fate as opposed to causality, but rather the sense of events beyond individual control that turn out in a particular way. See: Richard Price, "Preface to the Edition of 1824," in *The History of English Poetry from the Close of the Eleventh Century to the Commencement of the Eighteenth Century*, vol. I, ed. Thomas Warton (London: printed for Thomas Tegg, 1840), 34; and Carolyne Larrington, "The Enchantress, the Knight and the Cleric: Authorial Surrogates in Arthurian Romances," *Arthurian Literature* 25 (2008): 43–65. Curiously even more apt, yet very likely unknown to Jufri, in the earliest written version in which she appears (the Latin *Vita Merlini*, written by the Norman-Welsh Geoffrey of Monmouth in the mid-twelfth century), the name was "Morgen," cognate with Irish "Muirgen," and identified with Welsh derivates meaning "born of the sea." See: J. Rhys, *Celtic Folklore* (Oxford: Clarendon Press, 1901), 373; and J. Rhys, *Studies in the Arthurian Legend* (Oxford: Clarendon Press, 1891), 22; cited in Lucy Allen Paton, "Studies in the Fairy Mythology of Arthurian Romance," published PhD dissertation (1894), *Radcliffe College Monographs* No. 13 (Cambridge: Radcliffe College, 1903), 9, notes 6–8. See also: James Douglas Bruce, *The Evolution of Arthurian Romance* (Geneva: Slatkine Reprints, 1974), 79, note 85; and Emily Rebekah Huber, "Geoffrey of Monmouth: Introduction," http://d.lib.rochester.edu/camelot/text/geoffrey, accessed October 13, 2015.

[91] Author's interview with Haji Erna, June 22, 2011. Wawo's middle school at the time was still called "Sanawiya," not "SMP." The Sama relative who came to stay with Buraéra was Rajulan.

relative's house on the outskirts of Kendari, because Erna's husband had recently taken up a teaching position in a high school in Kendari.[92] When Morgana traveled to Kendari with Jufri and Haji Ruga, they stayed at a modest inn run by someone in the family, a man said to be Sitti Hami's son—although whether biologically by someone other than Kahar or "adopted," like Morgana, was unclear. In any case, this man and his wife informed Morgana that her mother, Lawi, was presently there in Kendari. Morgana and Jufri took a pedicab out to meet her. It was late afternoon when they arrived at the house. There on the steps sat a woman who Morgana went up to and hugged straight away. Only, the story goes, she thought to herself that people had always mentioned that her mother was pale, and this woman was not pale. Mappésamma, who happened to witness this, told her, "That's not your mother. That's your aunt. Your mother's inside." She had mistakenly hugged Lawi's younger sister, Banong. Then Morgana went inside and met her mother for the first time in some twenty-two years.[93]

Ironically, in 1982, Mappésamma got another promotion and became the head of a middle school in Wawo. As a result, Lawi was faced with the dilemma of whether to return to the area where Jufri still kept a house, a place in which Sitti Hami still wielded some influence, and where Morgana had been taken and raised apart from her. Not to go with Erna and Mappésamma to Wawo would have meant deciding whether to live in Kendari, in Raha, or in Pulo Balu, apart from her daughter Erna for the first time. Initially she refused to go back to Wawo. Erna recalled what her mother said: "I do not want to go along." But after considerable cajoling and reassurances that, after all, she would be in the house with Erna and her family, and Jufri would not be there with them, Lawi decided to go with them to Wawo. They stayed for about the first six months in Sitti Hami's house, before their own place was ready. Then, Erna said, "At that time my father came, and summoned us, me and the children [to see him at his house with one of his wives]. Mama did not want to go. So I went. She held out. We were there for three nights."[94]

Morgana, a grown woman at this point, did not settle in the Wawo area. Born when her mother was on the move with Darul Islam, taken by Sitti Hami, and raised under a lie, after she left she never looked back.[95] As discussed further below, Morgana's history reveals the precariousness of social reproduction when a woman is captured and her descendants are denied the memory of their matriline. It also underscores the power relations that undergird such forgotten pasts. Together with Lawi's history, Morgana's story moreover brings to mind the Putri Papuq narrative, with its maritime relocation of a Sama woman of high status descent to live among powerful others, the attempt to confer legitimacy on her unnegotiated union, and the question of whether that union's offspring will be able to know their matriline. Yet, also like the Putri Papuq story, Morgana's experience underscores submerged genealogy's resilience, when descent through the matriline is emphasized and perpetuated in practices of recalling the past.

---

[92] They stayed in Kendari-ceddi—a very Bugis name for a very Sama settlement.

[93] Ibid. Mappesamma had separately told the latter parts of the story of this reunion in much the same way. This was before Haji Erna sat down and related both what she herself remembered and what she was told by Morgana about her own growing skepticism and knowledge about her true parentage when she was young.

[94] Ibid.

[95] Ibid. After the reunion in Kendari, she returned to Makassar, went on with her life, and became a college teacher.

Hajjah Sitti Alwia (Si Lawi), 2011; author's photo

## CAPTURE MARRIAGE AND THE MEMORY OF MATRILINY

The Oxford scholar R. H. Barnes once remarked that marriage by capture has a long genealogy in anthropology, yet it always seems to take place in another time or among the neighbors of whomever the ethnographer happens to be interviewing. Despite attempts to divide up different sorts of capture marriage into neat taxonomies, and a tendency to see the practice overall as a unitary institution, he neither thought it likely that "the problem of capture marriage" had a single explanation, nor, given the number of people affected and the mixture of motives, that a single explanation would ever be sufficient.[96] All the more reason, then, to historicize the practice. Yet, for historians of Southeast Asia, marriage by capture also remains analytically elusive for how it straddles two divergent tacks of inquiry in the literature: on the one hand, maritime raiding and the taking of slaves, and, on the other hand, the expansion of polities through elite marriage strategies. This sort of capture, moreover, remains elusive for the most mundane—and hence the most

---

[96] R. H. Barnes, "Marriage by Capture," *Journal of the Royal Anthropological Institute* 5, 1 (1999): 57, 59, 69.

powerful—reason, namely, how the practice is inextricably ensconced in the idiom of kinship.[97]

Historically, in Southeast Asian societies, chiefs and kings created broad networks of affinal ties that ran horizontally and vertically through the socio-political hierarchy, enabling these rulers to build political coalitions. Subordinates presented daughters and sisters to rulers as acts of fealty, and women given in marriage cemented alliances between elites. Elite polygamy was "an indication of status and a diplomatic weapon."[98] It was therefore incumbent on Southeast Asian sultans, *rajas*, and chiefs to accrue large surpluses of prestige good wealth that would allow them to acquire high-status and politically strategic wives, since bridewealth payments traditionally passed from prospective grooms to the families of selected brides.[99] Yet, in-marrying women, initially the fulcrum of an alliance, could also lead to the breakdown of relations and a polity's fragmentation. "Foreign wives," that is, women of rank who started off as strangers in an unfamiliar virilocal residence, could become the focus of factional competition to seize primacy for their progeny at the death of a ruler. Poor treatment of such high-ranking women could lead to interpolity warfare. The exchange of women thus constituted a crucial part of how political relations were formed and maintained. Hence, while overlord–vassal relations that involved continued reciprocity were often modeled after the kinship bonds of families, however much familial terms provided metaphors for political relationships in the region, it was also the actual exchange of women that "made these bonds tangible, for the children that resulted from subsequent unions became the living symbol of irrevocable kinship."[100]

The children of marriage by capture are no less the sign of irrevocable kinship. Yet while people in cognatic societies trace descent from both maternal and paternal lineages, recalling these lineages over subsequent generations may not entail the recollection or reinscription of how particular unions came about. In other words, unless capture gets taken up in narrative and reproduced, over time the memory of capture is likely to fade, even as genealogical memory—including descent from different ethnic groups—gets reproduced. Hence, kinship forms a vehicle of material social practice through which political relations may be expressed, perpetuating the memory of connections between ethnic groups. Yet genealogical reckoning may also be the vehicle through which the history of those political relations—how coercive alliances came about—may be forgotten. In other words, people may perpetuate through genealogical reckoning the memory of connections between ethnic groups, even as the underside of those connections—their character, how they were forged—might fall into obscurity.

---

[97] Although Janet Hoskins does not address capture, per se, she has written about the fragile boundary between women transferred as slaves, and women given as brides in Kodi, Sumba. See Janet Hoskins, "Slaves, Brides, and Other 'Gifts': Resistance, Marriage and Rank in Eastern Indonesia," in *Slavery and Resistance in Africa and Asia: Bonds of Resistance*, ed. Edward A. Alpers, Gwyn Campbell, and Michael Salman (Routledge, 2005), 109–26.

[98] See: Anthony Reid, *Southeast Asia in the Age of Commerce, 1450–1680*, vol. 1: *The Land Below the Winds* (New Haven: Yale University Press, 1988), 151; and Junker, *Raiding, Trading, and Feasting*, 294.

[99] See: Reid, *Land Below the Winds*, 146; and Junker, *Raiding, Trading, and Feasting*, 293.

[100] Barbara Andaya, "Political Development between the Sixteenth and Eighteenth Centuries," in *The Cambridge History of Southeast Asia*, vol. I, ed. N. Tarling (Cambridge: Cambridge University Press, 1992), 408, 419, 420; and Junker, *Raiding, Trading, and Feasting*, 294.

In Lawi's case, Jufri and his people patently made an effort to create a wedding that could in some sense be called legitimate. This involved a formalistic sort of adherence to religious strictures under threatening circumstances. Viewed in retrospect by her relatives, this legitimacy did not seem to be obviated by the fact that the arrangement was brought about by the use of force and threats to gain compliance. Yet their actions at the time indicated clearly that her "kidnapping" was perceived as wrong or unjust. Not only was Lawi taken and the wedding coerced, but her capture also further breached propriety by intervening in preparations already underway with a suitor who looked certain to work out agreeably.

Lawi's relatives' disapproval of Jufri's actions was not simply because he neglected to seek and obtain her parents' approval. Rather, her abduction completely violated widely accepted procedures of proposal and negotiation between kin groups, as well as the exchange of bridewealth or *mas kawin*, the marriage payment (in Arabic, *mahar*). In Sulawesi, and in many other parts of the archipelago, negotiation and prestation (or the gift of bridewealth) commonly recognizes, and in some cases realigns, the relative status of those being wed, and by extension that of their natal kin. Writing of southern Sulawesi before the 1950s, Hendrik Theodorus Chabot remarked that "social status ... signifies in the first place the possibility to marry." Then as now, a marriage expresses a status relationship obtaining in that moment, with upward social striving crowned in the marriage of one's children, since this establishes and demonstrates the standing one has personally gained, within the bounds set by one's descent.[101] Since, as Chabot discussed, a certain equality of marriage partners was assumed, one who rose in standing through personal qualities and achievements, and on this basis was able to marry off one of his children to a member of a group considered a bit higher,

> ... has attained the highest goal. The standing that he has built up is, as it were, fixed by this circumstance. In a later social evaluation of his children, his achievement is used as a basis of judgment. His kin honor in him the man who has raised the standing of their group, for as kin they in principle are and remain his equals and thus rise with him. [Hence] ... wedding feasts ... are the gauge of social standing.[102]

What, then, are the social implications of marriage by capture? This breach of procedures that accord mutually acceptable social recognition of a bride's lineage and its public demonstration, not only has consequences for her own kin at marriage, but also for her progeny afterward. For instance, it left Lawi's children vulnerable to a kind of internal expropriation—as Lawi and Morgana experienced with the latter's "adoption" by Sitti Hami.

Lawi and her kin accepted, or perhaps accepted the wisdom of regarding, her union with Jufri as legitimate. Even so, when the opportunity presented itself, Lawi did not facilitate the appearance of mutuality, for when Jufri supposedly voiced his intention to make a formal proposal to her parents as a kind of post-hoc gesture, Lawi discouraged him from doing so. Her message was, What is the point? He had

---

[101] Chabot, *Kinship, Status, and Gender*, 134–35.

[102] Chabot, 135. See also Susan Bolyard Millar, *Bugis Weddings: Rituals of Social Location in Modern Indonesia* (Berkeley: Center for South and Southeast Asian Studies, University of California Berkeley, 1989).

already taken and married her.[103] Lawi's refusal to allow this public sanction, this maneuver to gain the semblance of approval, was a rejection that forestalled Jufri from further intimidating (or effectively bribing) her family into giving their consent after the fact. Her "why bother" attitude, if true, also denied him an appearance of propriety that he did not deserve.

Here, then, capture short-circuited the usual steps leading to marriage, literally by-passing procedures already underway. At the same time it abrogated the need for that which, through negotiations, exchanges, and celebration, in the usual course of things, would produce social recognition of such unions and mutual recognition of kin groups' status. Technically, Lawi may in the end have been married to someone of equal or higher status. But it matters how this marriage came about. Lawi's subjection and that of her kin contributed to making her a particular sort of dependent. Her procreative power was appropriated, and the social capital of her lineage status extorted to expand the movement and to improve its maritime capacities. In short, her marriage to Jufri enabled him to extend his and the movement's reach socially and to leverage specialized infrastructural resources and skills particular to the maritime world and its clandestine traffic. However, his ability to do these things met with definite limits.

Did her relatives really regard the marriage as legitimate, in retrospect? And if they did not, what consequences would that imply? Posing this counterfactual question underscores the importance of those living symbols of irrevocable kinship, since the way that people regard the marriage would directly redound to how they regard its progeny. Dependency exacted through capture without some form of legitimacy produces something like the status of a slave. Yet rather than the "social death" debated in the scholarship on slavery, perhaps one could view the result of Lawi's capture, with a "legitimate" ceremony, as a status realignment downward that would affect her kin and descendants.[104] Surely, to regard Lawi's marriage as other than legitimate would have been to cast disgrace upon what was already a shame. Curiously, by the late 1990s, among her younger relatives, the fact that she was so closely related by marriage to Kahar Muzakkar himself took on a kind of romantic late-Suharto-era anti-government aura.

And then there is Morgana, who, as a youth, wondered how it was that her supposed mother and father were also sister and brother. If Lawi had not had other children, and Morgana had never learned the truth, then, indeed, Lawi's capture and marriage would have resulted in a kind of social death—her inability to reproduce socially, and her progeny's Sama matriline sinking into obscurity. Fortunately, the fiction of Morgana's parentage could not be maintained, and the revelation of the truth gave her back more than just her matrilineal descent. It also introduced her to an array of maternal kin, who, while unable to return to her what had been misappropriated, at least readily and warmly welcomed the effort to bridge the long years of unknowing.

---

[103] Author's interview with Haji Erna, June 22, 2011.

[104] "Social death" as opposed to a relation of property was put forward by Orlando Patterson as the key phenomenon in a continuum of slavery systems. See Orlando Patterson, *Slavery and Social Death* (Cambridge: Harvard University Press, 1985).

# CHAPTER SIX

# CONCLUSION: MARITIME HISTORY IN AN ARCHIPELAGIC WORLD

Maritime history is not simply terrestrial history with water added. The challenge, as the Indian Ocean scholar Sanjay Subrahmanyam put it, is to write a history that is "conceptually oriented towards the sea rather than the land."[1] However, transposing a territorially conceived model—the ocean basins approach—to the investigation of what takes place offshore, does not always work, particularly for Southeast Asia.[2]

Focusing on the littoral has become an important concept for maritime history, thanks in large measure to another Indian Ocean scholar, Michael Pearson, apparently independent of Denys Lombard's work on Asian maritime history and his interest in the *pesisir*, the coastal area. Pearson suggested that people along the coasts of a given sea or ocean have more in common with those across the water than with those nearer at hand in their own hinterlands.[3] This is a provocative and promising notion with much evidence to back it up. Yet, it raises questions as well. To what extent did littoral societies share commonalities? If, as Pearson proposed, a mixture of maritime and terrestrial influences makes the study of littoral society a paradigm for maritime history in general,[4] then one important task for maritime history is to understand littoral societies, including the connections and unities formed by specific ties among littoral networks.

Another task, however, is to analyze the divisions within and among littoral societies: whether linguistic, in economic relationships, through kinship and religious practices, the engagement of aesthetic repertoires, the play of gender ideologies, or the efficacy of political idioms. This means determining who participated in such networks historically, what they did, and how they mattered in contests over trade, followers, and clout—all questions that, for comprehending the central and eastern archipelago, call for the use of Southeast Asian sources alongside whatever other sources can be found.

Not to do so, for Southeast Asia, risks wading unawares into powerful discursive currents that draw on the imagery of sea nomads and sea gypsies as stateless wanderers. Against this strong pull, one can historicize how generations of

---

[1] Sanjay Subrahmanyam, "Afterthoughts: Histories in Bottles," in *The Sea: Thalassography and Historiography*, ed. Peter N. Miller (Ann Arbor: University of Michigan Press, 2013), 277–83.

[2] See Gaynor, "Ages of Sail, Ocean Basins, and Southeast Asia."

[3] See: Michael Pearson, "Littoral Society: The Concept and the Problems," *Journal of World History* 17, 4 (2006): 354; and Eric Tagliacozzo, "Trade, Production, and Incorporation: The Indian Ocean in Flux, 1600–1900," *Itinerario* 26, 1 (2002): 75–106.

[4] Pearson, "Littoral Society," 354.

interested observers—from Combés to Brooke and beyond—looked from a distance at stilt-house settlements in the shallows, yet talked about their inhabitants as though they lived only on boats. Such a projection of romantic fantasy may have some basis in reality, yet it only holds water by turning a blind eye to evidence of the long history of lives lived in interlinked littorals. To analyze and present counter-evidence to a history of such representations is but one approach that complements the project of revealing the participants and dynamics of littoral networks.

Littoral networks, permeated by both unities and divisions, linked urban areas to myriad nonurban coastal locations in archipelagic Southeast Asia. People lived in a variety of littoral locales, and many also moved between them. Hence, a priority in this book has been to attend to networks of littoral society that reached far beyond urban centers, in order, literally, not to miss the boats. Instead, to "follow the boats" through real waters and trace them by their textual wakes has served as a guiding principle for investigating the maritime past. In general terms, this means more than pointing out the existence of networks and connections. Even counting the frequency of certain connections, where one is able, may explain little about how those links were made, what exactly they connected, how they mattered, what sustained them, and how their significance may have changed or been forgotten over time.

Yet to investigate significance also means, figuratively, to get in the boats. It entails engaging with how things looked from the littoral and from movement between intertidal zones, and taking on board for consideration how people represented the connections that linked them over the waters. To be sure, indigenous manuscripts present no less ideologically laden content than the colonial archives. Yet where, in juxtaposition, they shed light on each other, they clarify certain topics, themes, and areas of practice.

Although it is well known that Southeast Asia's extensive nonurban coasts provided important commodities, such as trepang, fish, salt, and pearl shell, not a great deal other than this appears in the literature about the varieties of material and social practices in which littoral people historically engaged. While different centers at various times sought influence over particular littorals and the people in them, some maritime-oriented people were based in cities, while others in littoral locales maintained a measured distance from centers of politics and trade. What, besides trade, politics, and war linked regional littoral networks? Kinship, for one,[5] and networks of cultural production, for another. The creation and reformulation of genealogical narratives, an important part of how people gauged their relative positions, intimately linked the region's more densely settled areas with people dispersed in villages of both hinterlands and hinterseas. To look beyond trade at these other sorts of connections requires using sources that truck in different "units of analysis" less responsive to quantification, and calls for picking up potentially unfamiliar methodological instruments.

Tiworo, deemed a nasty pirates' nest in the seventeenth century, and briefly mentioned by Valentijn in the eighteenth century for its infamous reputation, then slipped into obscurity. Under the *pax Neerlandica*, by the early twentieth century outsiders commonly categorized the region's maritime people on a continuum that

---

[5] Peter Boomgaard, Dick Kooiman, and Henk Schulte Nordholt, eds., *Linking Destinies: Trade, Towns and Kin in Asian History*, VKI 256 (Leiden: KITLV Press, 2008).

ranged from animist "sea gypsy" to "piratical Moor." These classifications were sometimes ethnicized. Yet such externally drawn distinctions glossed over how many of the people so labeled would, in their shared language, have recognized each other by the same autonym, "Sama."[6] Hence, as with names applied to upland Southeast Asians, they provide a cautionary tale about the limits of reading colonial sources against the grain. Sama people's own narratives should also not be taken at face value. This book has shown how they were part of the maritime past, helping to produce, yet also caught in, networks of interethnic relations cross-cut by practices and ideologies of gender, kinship, and social class.

In the latter half of the seventeenth century, mariners from Tiworo's littoral communities supplied far-flung allies in trade and war, between Makassar and the Moluccas. The VOC and its allies targeted Tiworo as a result of the interests it shared with Makassar and the actions it undertook with Makassar and on its behalf. Tiworo's defeat in 1655, accompanied by the taking of three hundred women and children as spoils, was rationalized as payoff by the VOC to keep the fighters of their local allies well-disposed to further exploits. Although sources say the captured people went to Ternatans and Mardijkers, rather than being shipped to Batavia to be sold as slaves, what became of them is unknown. Some likely wound up as slaves, and may have gone to Batavia with Mardijkers returning there, while others were absorbed into non-Sama communities elsewhere that, for them, were new. In either case, they were in a position of subordinated dependency and separated from their families. One cannot discuss their new social positions or their strategies of survival in the abstract, except to say that their unnegotiated standing as strangers would likely have been public knowledge in places where most people knew each other by face if not by name. Many would know that the stranger women and children had been taken in war and arrived through expropriation. Their status, "achieved" by capture and relocation, created hierarchies of social class that paralleled the boundaries of ethnic difference. Descendants might "lose" such status by absorption and forgetting amidst the new community.

In contrast, marriages contracted between members of different ethnic groups, particularly between elite lineages among political allies, ramified in forms of social stratification that cut horizontally across ethnic groups. Since ascribed status followed from lineage, forms of writing such as genealogies and genealogical narratives proved fecund for processes of social reproduction that hinged on the recognition of status. For instance, "proving" descent with an inherited or borrowed family manuscript could demonstrate to the family of a potential spouse the suitability of a prospective marriage partner, and this mattered particularly when kin groups forged ties across the boundaries of ethnic groups with unfamiliar people. Manuscripts had portability and intergenerational staying power that for some Sama demonstrated claims to precedence vis à vis other lineages, including those of other descent groups. When others recognized such claims, it afforded the possibility to reproduce socially. Hence, while genealogical narratives, like marriage, made such claims manifest, they buttressed how elite marriages ramified in forms of social stratification that cut horizontal layers across ethnic groups.

---

[6] Specialists of things Bugis might be reminded that this is also the autonym most commonly used in the southern Philippines, hence, not likely to be "explained" by the Bugis term *tau sama*.

The capture of a highborn Sama woman and her maritime relocation structured the basic lineaments of a story whose versions were widely shared among Sama people in different parts of the region. When adapted to Bugis modes of representing the past, narrative devices euphemized capture in these stories, obscuring its socially subordinating implications. By creating accident in the place of intention, these devices shielded audiences from the perception of a diminished standing and from social discomfort. In the pre-lontaraq Sama oral traditions, memorializing capture may initially have been part of why such narratives had been created in the first place. So it seems ironic that such stories should lose, through capture's effacement, what may have been their initial *raison d'être*. However, the reasons for remembering things change with their historical context.

Although the details remain somewhat hazy on precisely how it came about that this Sama story was adapted to Bugis-language lontaraq, nevertheless, the adaptation effectively wiped from the narrative all but the traces of capture's relevance to intergroup hierarchies. Instead the story's adaptation was harnessed to claims of genealogical precedence and status parity. It also framed the significance of subsequent parts of the manuscript, which enumerated ties between a particular Sama lineage and the Bugis realm of Boné. Knowledge of this story, but especially inheritance or ownership of its embodiment in manuscript, formed socially valid evidence in support of claims beyond the bounds of the text, in other realms of social practice, such as kinship and politics.

Prominent Sama people also appear in lontaraq texts from Makassar, which show them deeply involved in Makassar's seventeenth-century trade, politics, and kinship networks. After the second defeat of Makassar's ally Tiworo, rather than see its men taken down in slaughter and its women and children reduced by capture, Arung Palakka instead handpicked sixty men, armed them, and gave them rank, making them half of his guard of prime commanders. Gaining prestige through such a position with Boné probably had greater appeal to them than did other options, such as remaining allied with Makassar or fleeing to other locations. On Arung Palakka's part, this was a clever and pragmatic political maneuver to forward his aims in trade and war, since these mariners were exceedingly valuable assets to any such endeavors in the archipelagic world. By conferring high rank on these men from Tiworo, Arung Palakka ensured that they gained a stake in his, and Boné's, successes. Given that marriage was a key component in seventeenth-century alliance-making, it would not be surprising if Arung Palakka also sought to cement their new political orientation with marriages to his relatives. Certainly, if the Sama *papuqs* who became Makassar's harbormasters were an example and precedent, Boné may well have been gratified to gain Tiworo's skilled and probably well-connected mariners.

*Intertidal History* presents a very different picture of maritime people, and in particular of the Sama, from what one usually finds in the literature. We have primarily come to know them as collectors of marine produce for the China trade, and, in the late eighteenth and nineteenth centuries, as slave-raiding clients of the southern Philippines' Sulu sultanate. Stereotypes of regional sea people alternately depict them as meek nomadic animist sea gypsies, or, in a contrasting stereotype, as fierce Muslims prone to piratical raiding. Yet what this book shows fits with neither of those images. Sama families fled eastward from Boné with their lontaraq to Tiworo and beyond, to escape early nineteenth- and early twentieth-century conflicts that had come to Bajoé's shores. Yet, long before this, Sama leadership, nautical skills, and knowledge, as well as an alliance with Tiworo, had been vital to seventeenth-century Makassar. While a sizable number of Tiworo's seventeenth-century mariners disbanded from the straits and traveled west under a new alliance with Boné, their relocation was not stateless nomadic wandering, nor simply to raid or gather goods. Rather, they moved as a result of changes in the power dynamics of political relationships, a politics in which they took part.

As this book makes clear, maritime people, including the Sama, were not peripheral to regional states—at least not during the seventeenth century. On the contrary, polities such as Makassar and the Bugis realm of Boné sought them out and forged connections with them, to access their skills, knowledge, and networks, which were crucial to success in the commercial, military, and political world of the archipelago. To delve into the past of maritime-oriented people, such as the Sama, necessitates that one consider their relations with others, be they Makassar, Bugis, Ternatan, or Dutch. To study these social and political interactions is to take a fairly broad view of the complex society of the littoral. Amidst the archipelago's littoral networks sat the nonurban maritime hub of Tiworo, whose geography helped shape its place in the history of archipelagic dynamics. A vital ally with boats, mariners, and interests of its own, Tiworo played a key role with Makassar against VOC domination of the spice trade, providing a strategic distant harbor for Makassar's fleet and a nautical staging area for the conflicts further east. Tiworo continued to participate in interlinked scales of political economy, as it shifted from intense collaboration in maritime activities to the dissolution of this density of ties, pivoting from hinterseas to backwater. Its subsequent bonds with the Bugis realm of Boné ran through a Sama lineage dispersed on scattered shores of the central archipelago. The long political relationship between Boné and the Sama, memorialized in manuscript, formed a portable past. It started with the story of a woman who traveled across the sea.

# BIBLIOGRAPHY

**Archival Sources**

ANRI Makassar, Propinsi Sulawesi 1950–1960, reg. 359

British Library

Cense Collection (OR), KITLV

The John Rylands Library, University of Manchester

Kantor Yayasan Kebudayaan Benteng Ujung Pandang

Leupe Collection, Nationaal Archief (NA; National Archives of the Netherlands)

Library of the French National Assembly

Museo Galileo, Florence

Noorduyn Collection (DH), KITLV

Nederlands Bijbelgenootschap Collection, University Library, University of Leiden
(NB), UBL

*Straits Times*

VOC 1602–1799, Vereenigde Oost-Indische Compagnie Archive, access number
1.04.02, NA


**Unpublished Manuscripts**

Burghoorn, P. "De Badjaus." Typescript and letter, c. 196, KITLV DH 1240.

The Chronicle of Boné.

Lontaraq Bajo Lemobajo.

*Makassaarsche en Boeginesche handschriften van het Nederlandsch Bijbelgenootschap*,
Makassar and Bugis language manuscripts of the Netherlands Bible Society.

*Sja'ir Sipelman* (viz., Speelman). MS no. XVI in the Leiden Juynboll catalogue.

*Tolok Rumpakna Bone*. University Library, University of Leiden: ms cod.or. 6773.


**Books and Articles**

Abendanon, E. C. *Midden-Celebes Expeditie. Geologische en Geographische Doorkruisingen
van Midden-Celebes (1909–1910)*. 4 vols. Leiden: Brill, 1915–18.

Abidin, Andi Zainal. "Notes on the Lontara' as Historical Sources." Trans. The
Editors. *Indonesia* 12 (October 1971): 159–72.

Amin, Shahid. *Event, Metaphor, Memory: Chauri Chaura, 1922–1992*. Delhi: Oxford
University Press, 1995.

Ammarell, Gene. *Bugis Navigation*, Monograph No. 48, Yale Southeast Asia Series.
New Haven: Yale University Southeast Asia Studies, 1999.

*Ambtelijke Adviezen van C. Snouck Hurgronje, 1889–1936*. 3 vols. Rijksgeschiedkundige
Publicatiën, Kleinen Serie 35. The Hague: Martinus Nijhoff, 1965.

Andaya, Barbara Watson. *The Flaming Womb: Repositioning Women in Early Modern Southeast Asia*. Honolulu: University of Hawai'i Press, 2006.

———. *To Live as Brothers: Southeast Sumatra in the Seventeenth and Eighteenth Centuries*. Honolulu: University of Hawai'i Press, 1993.

———. "Political Development between the Sixteenth and Eighteenth Centuries." In *The Cambridge History of Southeast Asia, from Early Times to c. 1800*, Vol. I, ed. Nicholas Tarling. Cambridge: Cambridge University Press, 1993, 402–59.

———. "Upstreams and Downstreams in Early Modern Sumatra." *The Historian* 57, 3 (1995): 537–52.

Andaya, Barbara Watson, ed. *Other Pasts: Women, Gender and History in Early Modern Southeast Asia*. Honolulu: Center for Southeast Asian Studies, University of Hawai'i at Mânoa, 2000.

Andaya, Barbara Watson, and Leonard Y. Andaya. *A History of Early Modern Southeast Asia, 1400–1830*. Cambridge: Cambridge University Press, 2015.

Andaya, Leonard Y. "Cultural State Formation in Eastern Indonesia." In *Southeast Asia in the Early Modern Era: Trade, Power and Belief*, ed. Anthony Reid. Ithaca: Cornell University Press, 1993, 23–41.

———. *The Heritage of Arung Palakka: A History of South Sulawesi (Celebes) in the Seventeenth Century*. The Hague: Martinus Nijhoff, 1981.

———. "Historical Links between Aquatic Populations and the Coastal Peoples of the Malay World and Celebes." In *Historia: Essays in Commemoration of the 25th Anniversary of the Department of History, University of Malaya*, ed. Muhammad Abu Bakar, Amarjit Kaur, and Abdullah Zakaria Ghazali. Kuala Lumpur: Tha Malaysian Historical Society, 1984, 34–51.

———. *The World of Maluku: Eastern Indonesia in the Early Modern Period*. Honolulu: University of Hawai'i Press, 1993.

Anderson, Benedict. *Java in a Time of Revolution: Occupation and Resistance*. Ithaca: Cornell University Press, 1972.

Baker, Brett. "South Sulawesi in 1544: A Portuguese Letter." *Review of Indonesian and Malaysian Affairs* 39, 1 (2005): 61–85.

Bakhtin, M. M. "Discourse in the Novel." In *The Dialogic Imagination*, ed. Michael Holquist, trans. Caryl Emerson and Michael Holquist. Austin and London: University of Texas Press, 1981, 269–422.

Barnes, R. H. "Marriage by Capture." *Journal of the Royal Anthropological Institute* 5, 1 (1999): 57–73.

Bauman, R., and C. L. Briggs. "Genre, Intertextuality, and Social Power." *Journal of Linguistic Anthropology* 2, 2 (1992): 131–72.

Bauman, R., and C. L. Briggs. "Poetics and Performance as Critical Perspectives on Language and Social Life." *Annual Review of Anthropology* 19 (1990): 59–88.

Bigalke, Terance W. *Tana Toraja: A Social History of an Indonesian People*. Singapore: Singapore University Press, 2005.

Bijaksana, Satria, et al. "Status of Tree-ring Research from Teak (*Tectona grandis*) for Climate Studies." *Jurnal Geofisika* 2 (2007): 2–7.

Blair, Emma Helen, and James Alexander Robertson, eds. *The Philippine Islands*. 44 vols. Cleveland, OH: A. H. Clark Co., 1903–09.

Blaeu, Willem Janszoon. *India quae Orientalis dicitur et Insula Adiacentes*. Amsterdam, 1664.

Blust, Robert. "The Greater Central Philippines Hypothesis." *Oceanic Linguistics* 30 (1991): 73–129.

———. "The Linguistic Macrohistory of the Philippines: Some Speculations." In *Current Issues in Philippine Linguistics and Anthropology: Parangal Kay Lawrence A. Reid*, ed. Hsiu-Chuan Liao and Carl R. Galvez Rubino. Manila: Linguistic Society of the Philippines and SIL Philippines, 2005, 31–68.

Boomgaard, Peter, Dick Kooiman, and Henk Schulte Nordholt, eds. *Linking Destinies: Trade, Towns and Kin in Asian History*, VKI 256. Leiden: KITLV Press, 2008.

Bor, Livinus. *Amboinse Oorlogen, door Arnold de Vlaming van Oudshoorn als superintendent, over d'Oosterse gewesten oorlogaftig ten eind gebracht*. Delft: Arnold Bon, 1663.

Borschberg, Peter. "The Seizure of the Santa Catarina Revisited: The Portuguese Empire in Asia, VOC Politics and the Origins of the Dutch-Johor Alliance, 1602–c.1616." *Journal of Southeast Asian Studies* 31, 1 (2002): 31–62.

Bottoms, J. C. "Some Malay Historical Sources: A Bibliographical Note." In *An Introduction to Indonesian Historiography*, ed. Soedjatmoko. Ithaca: Cornell University Press, 1965, 2007; and Jakarta: Equinox, 2007, 156–93.

Bougas, Wayne. "Bantayan: An Early Makassarese Kingdom, 1200–1600 A.D." *Archipel* 55 (1998): 83–123.

Braginsky, Vladimir. *The Heritage of Traditional Malay Literature: A Historical Survey of Genres, Writings and Literary Views*. Leiden: KITLV, 2004.

Brascamp, E. H. B. "De ontdekking van djatibosschen op Pangesana in 1727." *Tectona* 11 (1918): 723–43.

Briggs, C. L. "Metadiscursive Practices and Scholarly Authority in Folkloristics." *Journal of American Folklore* 106 (1993): 387–434.

Brink, van den. H. *Dr. Benjamin Frederik Matthes, zijn leven en arbeid in dienst van het Nederlandsch Bijbelgenootschap*. Amsterdam: Nederlandsch Bijbelgenootscap, 1943.

Bronson, Bennet. "Exchange at the Upstream and Downstream Ends." In *Economic Exchange and Social Interaction in Southeast Asia*, ed. K. L. Hutterer. Ann Arbor: Center for Southeast Asian Studies, University of Michigan, 1977, 39–52.

Brooke, Sir James, and Captain Rodney Mundy. *Narrative of Events in Borneo and Celebes, down to the Occupation of Labuan: From the Journals of James Brooke, Esq., Rajah of Sarawak, and Governor of Labuan*. Vol. 1. London: John Murray, 1848.

Brooke, Sir James, and Henry Keppel. *The Expedition to Borneo of Her Majesty's Ship Dido for the Suppression of Piracy with Extracts from the Journal of James Brooke*. 3rd ed. London: Chapman and Hall, 1847.

Brown, D. E. "Brunei and the Bajau." *Borneo Research Bulletin* 3, 2 (December 1971): 55–58.

Bruce, James Douglas. *The Evolution of Arthurian Romance*. Geneva: Slatkine Reprints, 1974.

Bulbeck, F. David. "The Landscape of the Makassar War." *Canberra Anthropology* 13, 1 (1990): 78–99.

———. "New Perspectives on Early South Sulawesi History." *Baruga* 9 (September 1993): 10–18.

———. "The Politics of Marriage and the Marriage of Politics in Gowa, South Sulawesi, during the 16th and 17th Centuries." In *Origins, Ancestry and Alliance: Explorations in Austronesian Ethnography*, ed. James J. Fox and Clifford Sather. Canberra: Department of Anthropology, Research School of Pacific and Asian Studies, The Australian National University, 1996, 280–315.

———. "A Tale of Two Kingdoms: The Historical Archaeology of Gowa and Tallok, South Sulawesi, Indonesia." PhD diss., Australian National University, 1992.

Caldwell, Ian. "Form Criticism and Its Application to Bugis Historical Texts." In *Language and Text in the Austronesian World: Essays in Honor of Ulo Sirk*, ed. Y. A. Lander and A. K. Ogloblin. München: Limcom Europa, 2008, 301–12.

———. "Power, State and Society among the Pre-Islamic Bugis." *BKI* 151, 3 (1995): 394–421.

———. "South Sulawesi AD 1300–1600; Ten Bugis Texts." PhD diss., Australian National University, 1988.

Canfield, D. Lincoln. "Spanish American Data for the Chronology of Sibilant Changes." *Hispania* 35, 1 (February 1952): 25–30.

Cense, A. A. "Eenige aantekeningen over Makassaars-Boeginese geschiedscrijving." BKI 107, 1 (1951): 42–60.

Cense, A. A. "Old Buginese and Makassarese Diaries." *BKI* 122, 4 (1966): 416–28.

Chabot, H. Th. *Kinship, Status and Gender in South Celebes*. Leiden: KITLV Press, 1996.

Chambert-Loir, Henri. "Notes sur les relations historiques et littéraires entre Campa et Monde Malais." In *Actes du Séminaire sur le Campa* at the University of Copenhagen, May 23, 1987. Paris: Centre for History of Civilizations of the Indochinese Peninsula, 1988, 95–106.

Chatterjee, Indrani. "Captives of Enchantment? Gender, Genre, and Transmemoration." In *History in the Vernacular*, ed. Raziuddin Aquil and Partha Chatterjee. New Delhi: Permanent Black, 2008, 250–87.

Combés, Francisco, S. J. *Historia de las islas de Mindanao, Iolo, y sus adyacentes*. 1667. Reprint, Madrid, 1897.

Cortesão, Armando, and Avelino Teixeira da Mota, eds. *Portugaliae Monumenta Cartographica*. Archivio Stato. Lisbon: Coimbra University Press, 1960.

Cummings, William P. "Historical Texts as Social Maps: *Lontaraq bilang* in Early Modern Makassar." *BKI* 161, 1 (2005): 40–62.

———. *Making Blood White: Historical Transformations in Early Modern Makassar*. Honolulu: University of Hawai'i Press, 2002.

———. "Rethinking the Imbrication of Orality and Literacy: Historical Discourse in Early Modern Makassar." *Journal of Asian Studies* 62, 2 (2003): 531–51.

Cummings, William P., ed. and trans. *A Chain of Kings: The Makassarese Chronicles of Gowa and Tallok*. Leiden: KITLV Press, 2007.

———. *The Makassar Annals*. Leiden: KITLV Press, 2010.

*Dagh-register gehouden int Casteel Batavia vant passerende daer ter plaetse als over geheel Nederlandts-India*. 31 vols. The Hague: Martinus Nijhoff and Batavia: Landsdrukkerij, 1887-1931.

Dalgado, Sebastião Rodolfo. *Glossario Luso-Asiatico*. Hamburg: Helmut Buske Verlag, 1982 Reimpression, Coimbra 1919.

Day, Tony. *Fluid Iron: State formation in Southeast Asia*. Honolulu: University of Hawai'i Press: 2002.

———. "Ties that (Un)Bind: Families and States in Premodern Southeast Asia." *Journal of Asian Studies* 55, 2 (1996): 384–409.

"De expeditie naar Zuid-Celebes in 1905–1906." *Indisch militair tijdschrift*, Extra bijlage [supplementary issues] 35, 37. Batavia [Jakarta]: Kolff, 1915–16.

*Documenta Indica II*. Rome: Monumenta Historica Soc. Iesu, 1950.

Douglas, Mary. *How Institutions Think*. Syracuse: Syracuse University Press, 1986.

Dourado, Fernão Vaz. *Atlas of 1580*. http://www.wdl.org/en/item/8918/view/1/40/. Accessed March 29, 2014.

Drakard, Jane. "Ideological Adaptation on a Malay Frontier." *Journal of Southeast Asian Studies* 17, 1 (1986): 39–57.

———. *A Kingdom of Words: Language and Power in Sumatra*. New York: Oxford University Press, 1999.

———. *A Malay Frontier: Unity and Duality in a Sumatran Kingdom*. Ithaca: Cornell Southeast Asia Program, 1990.

Druce, Stephen C. *The Lands West of the Lakes: A History of the Ajattapareng Kingdoms of South Sulawesi 1200–1600 CE*. Leiden: KITLV Press, 2009.

Dunmore, John, ed. and trans. *The Pacific Journal of Louis-Antoine de Bougainville, 1767–1768*. London: The Hakluyt Society, 2002.

Errington, Shelly. "Some Comments on Style in the Meanings of the Past." *Journal of Asian Studies* 388, 2 (1979): 231–44.

Ferrand, Gabriel. "Malaka, le Mālayu et le Malāyur." *Journal Asiatique* XI (1918): 431–38.

Findlay, Alexander G. *A Directory for the Navigation of the Indian Archipelago, China, and Japan*. 2nd ed. London: Richard Holmes Laurie, 1878.

Florida, Nancy K. *Writing the Past, Inscribing the Future: History as Prophecy in Colonial Java*. Durham and London: Duke University Press, 1995.

Floris, Peter [Pieter Willemsz]. *Peter Floris: His Voyage to the East Indies in the* Globe, *1611–1615, the Contemporary translation of his Journal*, ed. W. H. Moreland. London: Hakluyt Society, 1934.

Follet, Helen. *Men of the Sulu Sea*. New York: Charles Scribner and Sons, 1945.

Forrest, Thomas. *A Voyage to New Guinea and the Moluccas, 1774–1776*. London, New York, Melbourne, and Kuala Lumpur: Oxford University Press, 1969 [1780].

Fox, James J. "The Transformation of Progenitor Lines of Origin: Patterns of Precedence in Eastern Indonesia," In *Origins, Ancestry and Alliance: Explorations in Austronesian Ethnography*, ed. James J. Fox and Clifford Sather. Canberra: Department of Anthropology, Research School of Pacific and Asian Studies, The Australian National University, 1996, 13–53.

———. "Notes on the Southern Voyages and Settlements of the Sama-Bajau." *BKI* 133, 4 (1977): 459–65.

Frake, Charles O. "Conference Report: The Muslim Peoples of the Southern Philippines," *Current Anthropology* 14, 3 (1973): 326–29.

———. "The Cultural Construction of Rank, Identity and Ethnic Origins in the Sulu Archipelago." In *Origins, Ancestry and Alliance: Explorations in Austronesian Ethnography*, ed. James J. Fox and Clifford Sather. Canberra: Department of Anthropology, Research School of Pacific and Asian Studies, The Australian National University, 1996, 319–32.

———. "The Genesis of Kinds of People in the Sulu Archipelago." In *Language and Cultural Description: Essays by Charles O. Frake*, selected and introduced by Anwar S. Dil. Stanford: Stanford University Press, 1980, 311–32.

———. "Lines across the Water: The Lasting Power of Colonial Borders in Maritime Southeast Asia." *Northeast Anthropological Association Bulletin.* Fall 2011, 7–20.

Gal, S., and K. A. Woolard, eds. *Languages and Publics: The Making of Authority.* Manchester: St. Jerome, 2001.

Gallop, Annabel Teh, and Bernard Arps. *Golden Letters: Writing Traditions of Indonesia.* London: The British Library; and Jakarta: Yayasan Lontar, 1991.

Gamsa, Mark. "Cultural Translation and the Transnational Circulation of Books." *Journal of World History* 22, 3 (2011): 553–75.

Gaynor, Jennifer L. "Ages of Sail, Ocean Basins, and Southeast Asia." *Journal of World History* 24, 2 (2013): 309–33.

———. "Flexible Fishing: Gender and the New Spatial Division of Labor in Eastern Indonesia's Rural Littoral." *Radical History Review* 107 (Spring 2010): 74–100.

———. "Piracy in the Offing: The Law of Lands and the Limits of Sovereignty at Sea." *Anthropological Quarterly* 85, 3 (2012): 817–57.

———. "Maritime Ideologies and Ethnic Anomalies: Sea Space and the Structure of Subalternity in the Southeast Asian Littoral." In *Seascapes: Maritime Histories, Littoral Cultures, and Transoceanic Exchanges*, ed. Jerry H. Bentley, Renate Bridenthal, and Kären Wigen. Honolulu: University of Hawai'i Press, 2001, 53–68.

George, Kenneth M. "Felling a Song with a New Ax: Writing and the Reshaping of Ritual Song Performance in Upland Sulawesi." *Journal of American Folklore* 103, 407 (1990): 3–23.

———. *Showing Signs of Violence: The Cultural Politics of a Twentieth Century Headhunting Ritual.* Berkeley, Los Angeles, and London: University of California Press, 1996.

Gillis, John R. *Islands of the Mind: How the Human Imagination Created the Atlantic World.* New York and Hampshire: Palgrave Macmillan, 2004.

Gin, Ooi Keat. *The Japanese Occupation of Borneo, 1941–1945.* London and New York: Routledge, 2011.

Goffman, Erving. *Stigma.* New York: Simon and Schuster, 1963.

Hadara, Ali. "DI-TII di Sulawesi Tenggara: Studi Kawasan Laut Tiworo (1950–1965)." MA thesis, University of Indonesia, 1998.

Hall, Kenneth R. "Coastal Cities in the Age of Transition: Upstream–Downstream Networking and Societal Development in Fifteenth and Sixteenth Century Maritime Southeast Asia." In *Secondary Cities and Urban Networking in the Indian*

*Ocean, c. 1400–1800,* ed. Kenneth R. Hall. Lanham: Rowman and Littlefield, 2008, 176–204.

———. "Economic History of Early Southeast Asia." In *The Cambridge History of Southeast Asia, From Early Times to c. 1800,* Vol. I, ed. Nicholas Tarling. Cambridge: Cambridge University Press, 1993, 183–275.

———. "Local and International Trade and Traders in the Straits of Melaka Region: 600–1500." *Journal of the Economic and Social History of the Orient* 47, 2 (2004): 213–60.

———. *A History of Early Southeast Asia: Maritime Trade and Societal Development, 100–1500.* Lanham: Rowman and Littlefield: 2011.

———. "Sojourning Communities, Ports-of-Trade, and Commerical Networking in Southeast Asia's Eastern Regions, c. 1000–1400." In *New Perspectives on the History and Historiography of South and Southeast Asia, Continuing Explorations,* ed. Michael Arthur Aung-Thwin and Kenneth R. Hall. Abingdon and New York: Routledge, 2011, 56–73.

Harris, P. R. *A History of the British Museum Library 1753–1973.* London: British Library, 1998.

Harvey, Barbara S. *Permesta: Half a Rebellion.* Ithaca: Cornell Modern Indonesia Project, 1977.

———. "Tradition, Islam, and Rebellion: South Sulawesi 1950–1965." PhD diss., Cornell University, 1974.

Hashim, Ruzy. "Bringing Tun Kudu out of the Shadows: Interdisciplinary Approaches to Understanding the Female Presence in the Sejarah Melayu." In *Other Pasts: Women, Gender and History in Early Modern Southeast Asia,* ed. Barbara Watson Andaya. Honolulu: Center for Southeast Asian Studies, University of Hawai'i at Mânoa, 2000, 105–204.

Henley, David. "Review of James Warren, *The Sulu Zone*: The World Capitalist Economy and the Historical Imagination." *Bijdragen tot de Taal- Land- en Volkenkunde* 156, 4 (2000): 834–38.

Heeres, J. E., ed. *Corpus Diplomaticum Neerlando-Indicum.* The Hague: Martinus Nijhoff, 1931.

Heersink, Christiaan. *The Green Gold of Selayar: A Socio-Economic History of an Indonesian Coconut Island c. 1600–1950s, Perspectives from a Periphery.* Amsterdam: Vrije Universiteit, 1995.

Hoskins, Janet. "Slaves, Brides, and Other 'Gifts': Resistance, Marriage and Rank in Eastern Indonesia." In *Slavery and Resistance in Africa and Asia: Bonds of Resistance,* ed. Edward A. Alpers, Gwyn Campbell, and Michael Salman. London and New York: Routledge, 2005, 109–26.

Huber, Emily Rebekah. "Geoffrey of Monmouth: Introduction." The Camelot Project, 2007. http://d.lib.rochester.edu/camelot/text/geoffrey, accessed October 13, 2015.

Ittersum, Martine Julia van. "Hugo Grotius in Context: Van Heemskerck's Capture of the Santa Catarina and Its Justification in De Jure Praedae (1604–1606)." *Asian Journal of Social Science* 31, 3 (2003): 511–48.

————. *Profit and Principle: Hugo Grotius, Natural Rights Theories, and the Rise of Dutch Power in the East Indies, 1595–1615.* Leiden: Brill, 2006.

Jacobs, Hubert. *Conversions in the Country of Macassar in a Paris Imprint of 1546.* Rome: Pontificia Università Urbaniana, 1968.

————. "The First Locally Demonstrable Christianity in Celebes, 1544." *Revista Quadrimestrial Studia* (1966): 282–302.

Josselin de Jong, P. E. de. "The Character of the Malay Annals." In *Malaysian and Indonesian Studies: Essays Presented to Sir Richard Winstedt on His Eighty-Fifth Birthday,* ed. John Bastin and R. Roolvink. Oxford: Clarendon Press, 1964, 235–41.

Junker, Laura Lee. *Raiding, Trading and Feasting: The Political Economy of Philippine Chiefdoms.* Honolulu: University of Hawai'i Press, 1999.

Kahin, Audrey R., ed. *Regional Dynamics of the Indonesian Revolution.* Honolulu: University of Hawai'i Press, 1985.

Kahin, George McTurnin. *Nationalism and Revolution in Indonesia.* Ithaca: Cornell Southeast Asia Program Publications, 1952 [2003].

Keifer, Thomas. "The Sulu Sultanate: Problems in the Analysis of a Segmentary State." *Borneo Research Bulletin* 3, 2 (December 1971): 46–51.

Knaap, Gerrit. "Headhunting, Carnage, and Armed Peace in Amboina, 1500–1700." *Journal of the Economic and Social History of the Orient* 46, 2 (2003): 165–92.

————. *Kruidnagelen en Christenen: De Verenigde Oost-Indische Compagnie en de bevolking van Ambon 1656–1696.* Dordrecht and Providence: Foris, 1987.

Koolhof, Sirtjo. "The 'La Galigo': A Bugis Encyclopedia and its Growth." *BKI* 155, 3 (1999), 362–87.

————. "The *La Galigo* as Bugis History." In *The Indonesia Reader,* ed. Tineke Hellwig and Eric Tagliacozzo. Durham: Duke University Press, 2009, 115–20.

————. "The Sleeping Giant: Dynamics of a Bugis Epic (South Sulawesi, Indonesia)." In *Epic Adventures: Heroic Narrative in the Oral Performance Traditions of Four Continents,* ed. Jan Jansen and Henk J. Maier. Munster: LIT, 2004, 98–111.

————. "*Sureq, Lontaraq, Toloq:* Manuskrip dan Ragam Sastra Bugis." [*Sureq, Lontaraq, Toloq:* Manuscripts and Kinds of Bugis Literature], *International Journal of Malay World Studies* 25 (2007): 171–86.

————. "*Sureq* versus *Lontaraq*. The Great Divide?" In *Language and Text in the Austronesian World: Essays in Honor of Ulo Sirk,* ed. Y. A. Lander and A. K. Ogloblin. München: Limcom Europa, 2008, 327–33.

Koolhof, Sirtjo, and Roger Tol. "The Delight of the Dutch *Compagnie*: On the *Toloqna Musuq Boné* by Daéng ri Aja." *Jambatan* 11, 3 (1993): 99–108.

Koolhof, Sirtjo, and Roger Tol, eds. *I La Galigo; Menurut Naskah NBG 188 yang disusun oleh Arung Pancana Toa* Jilid I, transcribed and trans. Muhammad Salim and Fachruddin Ambo Enre. Jakarta: KITLV, in cooperation with Jembatan, 1995.

Larrington, Carolyne. "The Enchantress, the Knight and the Cleric: Authorial Surrogates in Arthurian Romances." *Arthurian Literature* 25 (2008): 43–65.

Leyden, John. "On the Languages and Literature of the Indo-Chinese Nations." *Asiatic Researches* 10 (1811): 158–289.

Liang, Yap Beng. *Sistem Kepercayaan Orang Bajau Omadal, Sabah*. Jabatan Pengajian Melayu, Kertas Data no. 21. Kuala Lumpur: Universiti Malaya, 1978.

Liebner, Horst H. "Four Oral Versions of a Story about the Origin of the Bajo People of Southern Selayar." In *Living through Histories: Culture, History and Social Life in South Sulawesi*, ed. Kathryn Robinson and Mukhlis Paeni. Canberra: ANU Dept. of Anthropology, Research School of Pacific and Asian Studies; and National Archives of Indonesia, 1998, 107–33.

———. "Indigenous Concepts of Orientation of South Sulawesian Sailors." *BKI* 161, 2 (2005): 269–317.

Ligtvoet, A. "Beschrijving en Geschiedenis van Boeton." *BKI* II (1878): 1–112.

Locher-Scholten, Elsbeth. "'Een gebiedende noodzakelijkheid': Besluitvorming rond de Boni-expeditie 1903–1905." In *Excursies in Celebes*, ed. Harry Poeze and Pim Schoorl. Leiden: KITLV, 1991, 143–64.

Lombard, Denys. "Réflexions sur le Concept de 'pasisir' et sur son Utilité pour l'Étude des Littératures." In *Cultural Contact and Textual Interpretation*, ed. C. D. Grijns and S. O. Robson. Dordrecht: Foris Publications, 1986, 19–24.

Ma Huan. *Ying Yai Sheng Lan: The Overall Survey of the Ocean's Shores*, trans. and ed. J.V.G. Mills. New York and London: Cambridge University Press, 1970.

Macknight, C. C., and Mukhlis. "A Bugis Manuscript about Praus." *Archipel* 18, 1 (1979): 271–82.

———. "The Concept of a 'Work' In Bugis Manuscripts." *Review of Indonesian and Malaysian Affairs* 18 (1984), 103–14.

———. "The I La Galigo Epic Cycle of South Celebes and Its Diffusion." *Indonesia* 17 (October 1974): 160–69.

———. "Notes on the Chronicle of Boné." In *Living through Histories: Culture, History and Social Life in South Sulawesi*, ed. Kathryn Robinson and Mukhlis Paeni. Canberra: ANU Dept. of Anthropology, Research School of Pacific and Asian Studies; and National Archives of Indonesia, 1998, 45–55.

———. "South Sulawesi Chronicles and their Possible Models." In *Vasco da Gama and the Linking of Europe and Asia*, ed. A. R. Disney and E. Booth. New York: Oxford University Press, 2000, 322–32.

MacLeod, H. "De onderwerping van Makassar door Speelman, 1666–1669." *De Indische Gids* (1900), 1269–97.

Manguin, Pierre-Yves. "The Amorphous Nature of Coastal Polities in Insular Southeast Asia: Restricted Centres, Extended Peripheries." *Moussons* 5 (2002): 73–99.

———. "The Vanishing *Jong*: Insular Southeast Asian Fleets in Trade and War (Fifteenth to Seventeenth Centuries)." In *Southeast Asia in the Early Modern Era: Trade, Power and Belief*, ed. Anthony Reid. Ithaca: Cornell University Press, 1993, 197–213.

Mannheim, Bruce. *The Language of the Inka since the European Invasion*. Austin: University of Texas Press, 1991.

Matthes, B. F. "Boegineesche en Makassarsche Legenden." In *Dr. Benjamin Frederik Matthes Dr. Benjamin Frederik Matthes, zijn leven en arbeid in dienst van het Nederlandsch Bijbelgenootschap*, ed. H. Van den Brink. Amsterdam: Nederlandsch Bijbelgenootscap, 1943, 384–85.

———. *Boegineesch-Hollandsch Woordenboek*. The Hague: Nijhoff, 1874.

———. *Makassaarsche chrestomathie: Oorspronkelijke Makassaarsche geschriften, in proza en poëzyI*. The Hague: Nijhoff, 1883.

———. *Makassaarsch-Hollandsch Woordenboek*. Amsterdam: Frederik Muller, 1859.

Metcalf, Peter. *They Lie, We Lie: Getting on with Anthropology*. London and New York: Routledge, 2002.

Miksic, John. *Singapore and the Silk Road of the Sea, 1300–1800*. Singapore: NUS Press, 2013.

Millar, Susan Bolyard. *Bugis Weddings: Rituals of Social Location in Modern Indonesia*. Berkeley: Center for South and Southeast Asian Studies, University of California Berkeley, 1989.

Mills, J. V. G. *Eredia's Description of Malacca, Meridional India and Cathay*. Kuala Lumpur: Malaysian Branch of the Royal Asiatic Society, 1997.

Nimmo, H. Arlo *Magosaha: An Ethnography of the Tawi-tawi Sama Dilaut*. Quezon City: Ateneo de Manila University Press, 2001.

Noorduyn, J. "The Wajorese Merchants' Community in Makassar." *BKI* 156, 3 (2000): 473–98.

———. "Origins of South Celebes Historical Writing," In *An Introduction to Indonesian Historiography*, ed. Soedjatmoko. Ithaca: Cornell University Press, 1965, 2007; and Jakarta: Equinox, 2007, 137–55.

———. "Some Aspects of Macassar-Buginese Historiography." In *Historians of South-East Asia*, ed. D. G. E. Hall. London: Oxford University Press, 1961, 29–36.

Noorduyn, J., ed. "De Handelsrelaties van het Makassaarse Rijk Volgens de 'Notitie' van Cornelis Speelman uit 1670." In *Nederlandse Historische Bronnen* vol. 3. The Hague: Martinus Nijhoff, 1983, 96–123.

Nordholt, Henk Schulte. "The Invented Ancestor: Origin and Descent in Bali." In *Texts from the Islands: Oral and Written Traditions of Indonesia and the Malay World*, ed. Wolfgang Marschall. Bern: Institute for Ethnology, 1994, 245–64.

Omar, Rahila. "The History of Boné A.D. 1775–1795: The Diary of Sultan Ahmad as-Salleh Syamsuddin." PhD diss., University of Hull, Centre for South-East Asian Studies, 2003.

Oudang, M. *Perkembangan kepolisian di Indonesia*. Djakarta: Mahabarata 1952.

Ovalle, Padre Alonso de. *Historia del Réino De Chile*. Rome: Francisco Caballo, 1646.

Pallesen, Kemp. *Culture Contact and Language Convergence*. Manilla: Linguistic Society of the Philippines, 1985.

Park, Joseph Sung-Yul, and Mary Bucholtz. "Introduction. Public Transcripts: Entextualization and Linguistic Representation in Institutional Contexts." *Text and Talk* 29, 5 (2009), 483–500.

Paton, Lucy Allen. *Studies in the Fairy Mythology of Arthurian Romance, Radcliffe College Monographs* No. 13. Cambridge: Radcliffe College, 1903.

Patterson, Orlando. *Slavery and Social Death*. Cambridge: Harvard University Press, 1985.

Patunru, Abdurrazak Dg. *Sedjarah Gowa*. Ujung Pandang: Jajasan Kebudayaan Sulawesi Selatan dan Tenggara, 1969.

Pearson, Michael. "Littoral Society: The Concept and the Problems." *Journal of World History* 17, 4 (2006): 353–73.

Pérez-Mallaína, Pablo E. *Spain's Men of the Sea: Daily Life on the Indies Fleets in the Sixteenth Century*, trans. Carla Rahn Phillips. Baltimore and London: Johns Hopkins University Press, 1998.

Pelras, Christian. "Célèbes-sud avant l'Islam, selon les premiers témoignages étrangers." *Archipel* 21,1 (1981): 153–84.

———. "Les premières données occidentales concernant Célèbes-sud." *BKI* 133, 2 (1977): 227–60.

———. "L'oral et l'écrit dans la tradition Bugis." *Asie du Sud-Est et le Monde Insulindien* 10 (1979): 271–97.

———. "Notes sur Quelques Populations Aquatiques de L'Archipel Nusantarien." *Archipel* 3 (1972): 133–68.

Pires, Tomé. *The Suma Oriental of Tomé Pires, an Account of the East, from the Red Sea to Japan, Written in Malacca and India in 1512–1515; and The Book of Francisco Rodrigues, Rutter of a Voyage in the Red Sea, Nautical Rules, Almanack, and Maps, Written and Drawn in the East before 1515*, trans. Armando Cortesão. London: The Hakluyt Society, 1944.

Price, Richard. "Preface to the Edition of 1824." In *The History of English Poetry from the Close of the Eleventh Century to the Commencement of the Eighteenth Century*, vol. I, ed. Thomas Warton. London: printed for Thomas Tegg, 1840, 9–95.

Proudfoot, Ian, and Virginia Hooker. "Mediating Time and Space: The Malay Writing Tradition." In *Illuminations: The Writing Traditions of Indonesia*, ed. Ann Kumar and John H. McGlynn. Jakarta: The Lontar Foundation and New York and Tokyo: Weatherhill, Inc., 1996, 49–78.

Ptak, Roderich. "China and the Trade in Cloves, Circa 960–1435." *Journal of the American Oriental Society* 113 (1993): 1–13.

———. "China and the Trade in Tortoise Shells (Sung to Ming Periods)." In *Emporium, Commodities and Entrepreneurism in Asian Maritime Trade, c. 1400–1750*, ed. Roderich Ptak and Dietmar Rothermund. Stuttgart: Franz Steiner Verlag, 1991, 195–222.

———. "The Northern Trade Route to the Spice Islands: South China Sea-Sulu Zone-North Moluccas (14th to Early 16th Century)." *Archipel* 43 (1992): 27–56.

———. "From Quanzhou to the Sulu Zone and Beyond: Questions Related to the Early Fourteenth Century." *JSEAS* 29 (1998): 269–94.

———. "Some References to Timor in Old Chinese Records." *Ming Studies* 17 (1983): 37–48.

Real Academia Española. *Diccionario de la lengua castellana, en que se explica el verdadero sentido de las voces, su naturaleza y calidad, con las phrases o modos de hablar, los proverbios o refranes, y otras cosas convenientes al uso de la lengua […] Compuesto por la Real Academia Española*. Madrid: Imprenta de Francisco del Hierro, 1726.

————. *Diccionario de la Lengua Castellana por la Real Academia Española*. Madrid: Imprenta Real, 1817.

Reid, Anthony. *Charting the Shape of Early Modern Southeast Asia*. Singapore: ISEAS, 2000.

Reid, Anthony. "A Great Seventeenth Century Indonesian Family: Matoaya and Pattingalloang of Makassar." In *Charting the Shape of Early Modern Southeast Asia*, ed. Anthony Reid. Singapore: ISEAS, 2000, 126–54.

————. "The Rise of Makassar." *RIMA* 17 (1983): 117–60.

————. "The Rise of Makassar." In *Charting the Shape of Early Modern Southeast Asia*, ed. Anthony Reid. Singapore: ISEAS, 2000, 100–102.

————. *Southeast Asia in the Age of Commerce, 1450–1680*, vol. 1: *The Land Below the Winds*. New Haven: Yale University Press, 1988.

————. "The Structure of Cities in Southeast Asia, Fifteenth to Seventeenth Centuries." *Journal of Southeast Asian Studies* 11, 2 (1980): 235–50.

Rhys, J. *Celtic Folklore*. Oxford: Clarendon Press, 1901.

————. *Studies in the Arthurian Legend*. Oxford: Clarendon Press, 1891.

Ricklefs, Merle Calvin. *A History of Modern Indonesia Since c. 1200*. Stanford: Stanford University Press, 2001.

Ricci, Ronit. *Islam Translated: Literature, Conversion, and the Arabic Cosmopolis of South and Southeast Asia*. Chicago: University of Chicago Press, 2011.

Rodgers, Susan. *Print, Poetics and Politics: A Sumatran Epic in the Colonial Indies and New Order Indonesia*. Leiden: KITLV Press, 2005.

Rosaldo, Renato. *Ilongot Headhunting, 1883–1974: A Study in Society and History*. Stanford: Stanford University Press, 1980, 31–60.

Rutter, Owen. *British North Borneo—An Account of Its History, Resources, and Native Tribes*. London: Constable and Co., 1922.

Salim, Muhammad, trans. *Transliterasi dan Terjemah Lontarak Tolok Rumpakna Bone*. Ujung Pandang: Departemen Pendidikan dan Kebudayaan Propinsi Sulawesi Selatan, 1991.

Sather, Clifford. *The Bajau Laut: Adaptation, History, and Fate in a Maritime Fishing Society of South-eastern Sabah*. Kuala Lumpur and New York: Oxford University Press, 1997.

Schendel, Willem van. "Geographies of Knowing, Geographies of Ignorance: Jumping Scale in Southeast Asia." *Environment and Planning D: Society and Space* 20, 6 (2002): 647–68.

Scott, James. *The Art of Not Being Governed: An Anarchist History of Upland Southeast Asia*. New Haven: Yale University Press, 2009.

Sears, Laurie J. *Shadows of Empire: Colonial Discourse and Javanese Tales*. Durham and London: Duke University Press, 1996.

Sears, Laurie J., and Joyce Burkhalter Flueckiger. "Introduction." In *Boundaries of the Text: Epic Performances in South and Southeast Asia*, ed. Laurie J. Sears and Joyce Burkhalter Flueckiger. Ann Arbor: Center for South and Southeast Asian Studies, University of Michigan, 1991, 1–16.

Silverstein, M., and G. Urban, eds. *Natural Histories of Discourse*. Chicago: University of Chicago Press, 1996.

Smail, John R. W. *Bandung in the Early Revolution, 1945–1946*. Ithaca: Cornell Modern Indonesia Project, 1964.

Solís, Don Antonio de. *Historia de Nueva España*. Madrid: Bernardo de Villa-Diego, 1684.

Sopher, David. *The Sea Nomads: A Study Based on the Literature of the Maritime Boat People of Southeast Asia*. Singapore: Memoirs of the National Museum, 1965.

Speilbergen, Joris van. *The East and West Indian Mirror, Being an Account of Joris van Speilbergen's Voyage Round the World (1614–1617), and the Australian Navigations of Jacob Le Maire*. Trans., with notes, and intro. J. A. J. Villiers. London: Hakluyt Society, 1906.

Stacey, Natasha. *Boats to Burn: Bajo Fishing Activity in the Australian Fishing Zone*. Canberra: ANU E-Press, 2007.

Stapel, F. W. *Cornelis Janszoon Speelman*. The Hague: Martinus Nijhoff, 1936.

———. *Het Bongaais Verdrag*. Groningen; The Hague: J. B. Wolters, 1922.

Sterkenburg, G. J. van. *Een Glossarium van Zeventiende-Eeuws Nederlands*. Groningen: Wolters-Noordhoff, 1981.

Stoler, Ann Laura. *Along the Archival Grain: Epistemic Anxieties and Colonial Common Sense*. Princeton: Princeton University Press, 2010.

Subrahmanyam, Sanjay. "Afterthoughts: Histories in Bottles." In *The Sea: Thalassography and Historiography*, ed. Peter N. Miller. Ann Arbor: University of Michigan Press, 2013, 277–84.

Sutherland, Heather. "Political Structure and Colonial Control in South Sulawesi." In *Man, Meaning and History: Essays in Honor of H. G. Schulte Nordholt*, ed. R. Schefold, J. W. Schoorl, and J. Tennekes. Dordrecht: Foris Publications, 1980, 230–45.

———. "A Sino-Indonesian Commodity Chain: The Trade in Tortoiseshell in the Late Seventeenth and Eighteenth Centuries." In *Chinese Circulations: Capital, Commodities, and Networks in Southeast Asia*, ed. Eric Tagliacozzo and Wen-Chin Chang. Durham and London: Duke University Press, 2011, 172–99.

———. "*The Sulu Zone* Revisited." *Journal of Asian Studies* 35, 1 (2004): 133–57.

———. "Trepang and Wangkang: The China Trade of Eighteenth-Century Makassar c. 1720s–1840s." *BKI* 156, 3 (2000): 451–72.

Sweeney, Amin. *A Full Hearing: Orality and Literacy in the Malay World*. Berkeley: University of California Press, 1987.

Tagliacozzo, Eric. "Kettle on a Slow Boil: Batavia's Threat Perceptions in the Indies' Outer Islands, 1870–1910." *Journal of Southeast Asian Studies* 31, 1 (2000): 70–100.

———. "Trade, Production, and Incorporation: The Indian Ocean in Flux, 1600–1900." *Itinerario* 26, 1 (2002): 75–106.

Taylor, Paul Michael. "Introduction." In *F.S.A. de Clerq's Ternate: The Residency and Its Sultanate*, trans. Paul Michael Taylor and Marie N. Richards. Washington: Smithsonian Institution Libraries Digital Edition, 1999 [1890], i–xviii.

Teitler, Ger. "Piracy in Southeast Asia: A Historical Comparison." *MAST* 1, 1 (2002): 67–83.

Temminck, Coenraad Jacob. *Coup-d'oeil général sur les possessions néerlandaises dans l'Inde archipélagique.* 3 vols. Leiden: A. Arnz, 1846–1849.

Teeuw, A. "Indonesia as a 'Field of Literary Study': A Case Study—Genealogical Narrative Texts as an Indonesian Literary Genre." In *Unity in Diversity: Indonesia as a Field of Anthropological Study,* ed. P. E. de Josselin de Jong. Dordrecht: Foris Publications, 1984, 38–62.

Tedlock, Dennis, and Bruce Mannheim, eds. *The Dialogic Emergence of Culture.* Champaign: University of Illinois Press, 1995.

Tiele, P. A. *De Europeërs in den maleischen archipel.* Vol. III. The Hague: Nijhoff, 1880.

Tol, Roger. *Een Haan in Oorlog: Toloqna Arung Labuaja, een Buginees Heldendicht.* Leiden: KITLV, 1990.

———. "A Royal Collection of Bugis Manuscripts." *BKI* 149, 3 (1993): 612–29.

Tsing, Anna Lowenhaupt. *In the Realm of the Diamond Queen: Marginality in an Out-of-the-way Place.* Princeton: Princeton University Press, 1993.

Valentijn, François. *Oud en nieuw Oost-Indiën,* v. I. Dordrecht: J. Van Bram, 1724.

Velthoen, Esther. "*Hutan* and *Kota*: Contested Visions of the Nation-State in Southern Sulawesi in the 1950s." In *Indonesia in Transition: Rethinking "Civil Society," "Region," and "Crisis,"* ed. Hanneman Samuel and Henk Schulte Nordholt. Yogyakatya: Pustaka Pelajar, 2004, 147–74.

———. "Pirates in the Periphery: Eastern Sulawesi 1820–1905." In *Pirates, Ports, and Coasts in Asia: Historical and Contemporary Perspectives,* ed. John Kleinen and Manon Osseweijer. Singapore: Institute of Southeast Asian Studies, 2012, 200–21.

Verheijen, Jilis A. J. *The Sama/Bajau Language in the Lesser Sunda Islands.* Pacific Linguistics, Series D, No. 70, Materials in Languages of Indonesia, No. 32. Canberra: Dept. of Linguistics, Research School of Pacific Studies, The Australian National University, 1986.

Vickers, Adrian. "'Malay Identity': Modernity, Invented Tradition and Forms of Knowledge." In *Contesting Malayness: Malay Identity across Boundaries,* ed. Timothy Barnard. Singapore: NUS Press, 2004, 25–55.

Vingboons, Johannes. "Map of the Southern Part of Celebes, Ceram and Timor." In *Atlas Blaeu–van der Hem.* Vienna: Austrian National Library, 1665–68.

Vink, Markus. "Mare Liberum and Dominium Maris: Legal Arguments and Implications of the Luso-Dutch Struggle for the Control over Asian Waters, ca. 1600–1663." In *Studies in Maritime History,* ed. K. S. Mathew. Pondicherry: Pondicherry University, 1990, 38–68.

———. "'The World's Oldest Trade': Dutch Slavery and Slave Trade in the Indian Ocean in the Seventeenth Century." *Journal of World History* 14, 2 (2003): 131–77.

Von Dewall, H. "Aanteekeningen omtrent de Noordoostkust van Borneo" (Medegedeeld door J. Hageman). *Tijdschrift voor Indische Taal-, Land- en Volkenkunde* 4 (1855): 423–58.

Vosmaer, J. N. "Korte Beschrijving van het Zuid-oostelijk Schiereiland van Celebes, in het bijzonder van de Vosmaers-Baai of van Kendari; verrijkt met eenige Berigten omtrent den stam der Orang Badjos, en meer andere aanteekeningen." *Verhandelingen van het Bataviaasch Genootschap van Kunsten en Wetenschappen* 17 (1839): 61–184.

Wade, Geoff. "An Early Age of Commerce in Southeast Asia, 900–1300 CE." *Journal of Southeast Asian Studies* 40, 2 (2009): 221–65.

Warren, James F. *Iranun and Balangingi: Globalization, Maritime Raiding and the Birth of Ethnicity*. Honolulu: University of Hawai'i Press, 2002.

———. "The North Borneo Chartered Company's Administration of the Bajau, 1878–1909: The Pacification of a Maritime, Nomadic People." MA thesis, Ohio University Center for International Studies, 1971.

———. *The Sulu Zone, 1768–1898: The Dynamics of External Trade, Slavery, and Ethnicity in the Transformation of a Southeast Asian Maritime State*. Honolulu: University of Hawai'i Press, 2007.

———. "Who Were the Balangingi Samal? Slave Raiding and Ethnogenesis in Nineteenth-century Sulu." *Journal of Asian Studies* 37, 3 (1978): 477–90.

Weiland, Petrus. *Kunstwoordenboek*. Rotterdam: D. Bolle, 1858.

Werner, Cynthia. "Bride Abduction in Post-Soviet Central Asia: Marking a Shift towards Patriarchy through Local Discourses of Shame and Tradition." *Journal of the Royal Anthropological Institute* 15, 2 (2009): 314–31.

Wijn, J. A. A., ed. *Tot in de verste uithoeken: de cruciale rol van de Gouvernements Marine bij het vestigen van de Pax Neerlandica in de Indische Archipel 1815–1962*. Amsterdam: De Bataafsche Leeuw, 1998.

Wisseman-Christie, Jan. "State Formation in Early Maritime Southeast Asia: A Consideration of the Theories and the Data." *BKI* 151, 2 (1995): 235–88.

———. "States without Cities: Demographic Trends in Early Java." *Indonesia* 52 (October 1991): 23–40.

———. "Trade and Early State Formation in Maritime Southeast Asia: Kedah and Srivijaya." *Jebat* 13 (1984/85): 43–56.

Wolhoff, G. J., and Abdurrahim, eds. *Sedjarah Goa*. Ujung Pandang: Jajasan Kebudayaan Sulawesi Selatan dan Tenggara, n.d. [1959].

Wolters, O. W. *History, Culture, and Region in Southeast Asian Perspectives*. Rev. ed. Ithaca: Southeast Asia Program Publications, 1999.

# Index

## A

Abendanon, Éduard Cornelius 56.
Abu Lais (Sultan) 66.
Alie, Sarib. *See* Tuwanna I Dondang.
Ambon 36, 69–70, 79, 85, 86, 97.
    *See also* Great Ambon War.
Andaya, Leonard 97.
Angkor 62.
Arcat 38, 41.
Aroe Bakoe. *See* Arung Bakung.
Arumponé 83, 120, 124.
Arung Bakung, 18–21.
Arung Palakka, 9, 11, 30, 99–104, 107.
Asahudi 70–71, 75, 79.
Ayuddhya 67.

## B

Baabullah (Sultan) 66, 74.
*baixos* 47–48.
Bajo 10, 22, 66, 127, 128–30, 145; boats
    160–61; dispersion myth 141–42;
    European depictions of 23–24, 192;
    origin of term 44–53, 158; raja 188–89.
    *See also* Bajoé.
Bajoé 17, 19, 21–22, 108, 120–21; flight
    from 117–18; growth of 28; lords of
    122. *See also* Bajo.
*baJuũs* 24, 40–44.
Banda 29, 36, 38, 40, 50, 67, 72, 83,
    85, 97.
Barasaq 94.
Baringeng (Puwang). *See* Palettéi (To).
Basilan 23, 44–45.
Batavia 9, 70, 77, 79, 85, 86, 97, 122, 203.
Batoij 14.
Bengkalis 41.
*Berkepala dua, see* having two heads.
Bima 27, 36, 38, 139
Binsen Ongkōkai 3–4.

Blaeu-Van der Hem Atlas 15.
Boano 71.
Boné, Dutch war with 19.
Bontosunggu (Karaeng) 92–95.
Bor, Livinus 75.
Borneo 17, 34–35, 36–38.
Bougainville, Louis-Antoine de 50–51, 72.
Braudel, Fernand 9.
Bronson, Bennet 61.
Brook, James 17–18, 22–24, 153, 202.
Brunei 26, 27, 45, 133.
Bugis 20, 22–23, 82–84, 101–3; kingdoms
    90; language manuscripts 8, 11, 20, 30,
    92, 107–8, 204; lineage 109, 113, 130,
    173–74, 192. *See also* Boné.
Boné, realm of 5, 8, 22, 28, 66, 204–205.
    *See also* Bugis.
Buraéra 3–5, 172–94.
Burghoorn, Pieter 155–64.
Burma 37.
Buton 15, 19, 27; alliance with VOC
    105–6; claims over Tiworo 21, 103–4;
    conflict with Tiworo 98–101.

## C

Camucones 44. *See also* Sama.
Cappalaya 66.
capture, practice of 8–9, 41, 70, 79–82.
    *See also* piracy, slavery.
cartography 14, 60. *See also* maps.
*Celates* 24, 40–44.
Celebes; European knowledge of 14–15;
    maps of 57.
Cense, A. A. 92–95.
Ceram 70–71.
Ceylon 84.
Champa 27, 62, 155.
Chinese trade 28, 29, 34, 69.
chronicles 110.

cloves. *See* spice trade.
clove (spice) islands. *See* Moluccas.
Combés, Francisco 23–24, 45.
Coromandel 37, 97.
Corps Tjadangan Nasional 179–80.
Council of the Indies 97.
CTN. *see* Corps Tjadangan Nasional.

**D**

Darul Islam (DI) 3, 9, 168–72;
    rebellion 3–5.
*datu* 26, 122.
descent. *See* kinship politics.
DI-TII. *See* Darul Islam.
Dourado, Fernão vaz 15, 56.
*Dromedaris* 14.

**E**

English; conflict with Dutch 84–85;
    trade 69, 85.
ethnogenesis 26.
Eurocentrism 1.

**F**

Fatimah Banri 89.
fleeing people 179.
Flores 88.
Floris, Pieter 24, 43, 49.
Fox, James J. 88–89.
Frake, Charles O. 26, 44, 132
Funan 62.

**G**

genealogies 20, 65, 81, 108, 164–65,
    197, 203. *See also* kinship politics.
Gervaise, Nicholas 140.
Gillis, John 60.
Gilolo. *See* Halmahera.
Glarang (*gellarang*) 123.
Gowa 81–87, 94; alliance with Talloq
    60–61, 66, 81; court (Makassar) 5;
    Chronicle of 140, 153; and the
    spread of Islam 83.

Great Ambon War 11, 29–30, 66–79.
    *See also* Ambon.
Gresik 36, 185.
Guard of Prime Commanders 11, 30,
    106, 107, 150, 204.

**H**

Haerlem, Jan van 104.
Hairun (Sultan) 66.
Hall, Kenneth 10.
Halmahera 35, 39.
Hami (Sitti) *See* Sitti Hami.
Hasanuddin (Sultan) 11, 14, 84.
having two heads, practice of 169–70.
Heemskeerk, Jacob van 15.
hinterseas, definition of 29, 33, 61–62,
    91, 121.
Hitu 70.
Hoamoal 70–71, 77, 79, 80, 81.
Hustaert, Jacob 14, 75, 77, 80.

**I**

Indian; model 12; trade 29, 69.
Indonesian Islamic Army (TII) 3–4, 31.
Indonesian National Army. *See* Tentera
    Nasional Indonesia (TNI).
intertidal history 1, 9, 29, 204;
    definition of 6–7.
Iranun 26, 45.

**J**

Jacobs, Hubert 59.
Jailolo 27.
Jakarta. *See* Batavia.
Japanese Tramp Shipping Transport
    Company 4.
*jarangka* 183.
Java 12, 29, 36–38, 40; the Java route 36.
Johor 27, 68, 131–34, 153, 159–60.
Jolo 23, 44–45, 51, 132.
*jong*. *See* junks.
Jufri Tambora 168, 169, 171, 173, 184,
    188–89; early career 3–4, regiment
    182–83.
junks 37. *See also* paraos (*perahu*).

# K

Kabaena 15, 98, 177, 183–84, 191, 192.
Kahar Muzakkar 168, 173–74, 179, 184, 189, 199.
Kaledupa 15.
Kalisusu 105.
Kampar 36, 41.
Kampong Tiworo 20.
Kampungsiang 59.
Kanjilo (Kareng) 82, 93.
karaéng 87, 90, 130, 145.
Karaeng Bayo 65, 87, 109, 137, 146.
Kelang 71, 77.
kelong 126–27.
Kendari Bay 17–20, 172.
kinship politics 4–7, 31, 88, 91–92, 184–89, 197, 204.
Kolaka 4, 172–73, 183–85.
Kumbewaha 74.


# L

Laala 70, 80, 81.
La Galigo 109, 112.
Labakkang 19,
Laiwui 19, 177, 178.
Lamakera 88.
Lawi 3–5, 31, 133; kidnapping of 172–99; marriage to Jufri 4, 189. *See also* Buraéra.
Lepo Lepo 19.
Lingga 41–42.
linguistic borrowing 52–53, 57.
littoral society 1, 5, 6, 10, 28, 39, 165, 201–202. *See also* intertidal history.
Lohia 86, 99, 104–5.
Loki 70.
*lolo* 20–21.
Lombok 3, 175, 180.
Lontaraq Bajo Lemobajo (LB Lemobajo manuscript) 89, 113, 116, 118–26, 136–37.
Lutau 23, 44–45, 47, 133.
Luwu (Luwuq) 83, 89, 90, 120, 131, 141–42.


# M

Ma'daremmeng (La) 83.
Maetsukyer, Willem 75, 77.
Magellan 35, 51.
Majapahit 27, 62.
Makassar 114–15, 204–205; alliance with Sama 96–97; Annals 91; description of 38, 53–55, 58; literature 109, 125–27, 139, 153; relations with the Dutch 68–69, 83–84, 107, 137; relations with Tiworo 5, 66–79; rise of 67; war with Boné 66. *See also* Makassar War.
Makassar War 11, 27, 30, 68, 82–87, 107–8.
Makkulle Ahmad (I Daeng) 92, 95, 96.
Makkulle (I Daeng) 85, 92, 95–96.
Malacca 36–43; seizure of 67.
Malay Chronicles 71.
Manassaq (Daeng) 95.
Mandar 28, 83, 90, 110, 140
Mandarsyah 74, 80, 84, 105.
Manggappa (Daeng) 96.
Mangkuttu 89, 142.
Manguin, Pierre-Yves 62.
Manila 26.
Mappaq (I). *See* Makkulle (I Daeng).
maps, Descelier's 54, 56, 57; Vaz Dourado's 56; Lopo Homem's 56, 57; Francisco Rodrigues' 46, 48.
maritime networks 1, 7.
maritime people. *See* sea people.
marriage, negotiated 30, 81–82, 95, 167, 191. *See also* kinship politics.
Matoaya (Karaeng) 68, 93.
May, Jan Corneliszoon 15.
Mboq (I) 93–95.
Melaka 27, 39, 67.
Mindanao 23, 44–45, 51.
Moluccas 34, 42, 50, 66, 69, 74, 203; and its islands 35; and Java 72; description of 36–38. *See also* spice trade.
Morgana, 193–95.
Muna Island, description of 11, 14–16, 86, 100.

**N**

negative space 13.
northern littoral route 29, 33–63, 72, esp. 36.
Noorduyn, Jacobus 156–58.
Numalo (Daeng) 92–93, 95, 96.


**O**

oceanic turn 13.
*Orang Laut. See* sea people.


**P**

Pahang 38, 42, 67.
Paiva, Antonio de 54–56, 59–61, 67.
Pajala 183.
Palakka (Arung). *See* Arung Palakka.
Palembang 42, 71.
Palettéi (To) 20–21, 121. *See also* Arung Bakung.
Pancana. *See* Muna Island.
Pangesane. *See* Muna Island.
Pankajene 57, 59, 61, 63.
Pantsiano. *See* Muna Island.
*papuq* (Sama leaders) 29, 88–89, 92, 107–8.
Paqnakkukang 83, 84, 96.
Paramesvara 42, 71.
*paraos* 38–39, 41.
Patani 27, 38, 67–69.
Pattingalloang (Karaéng, Tumamenang ri Bontobiraeng) 58, 93.
*pax Neerlandica* 15, 22, 108, 202.
Pegu. *See* Burma.
Pelras, Christian 56–57, 89.
pesisir 201.
Pigafetta, Antonio 51.
Pinto, Manuel 56.
piracy 18, 38–39, 87, 164.
Pires, Tomé 24, 34, 36, 38, 47, 60, 71; description of *baJuũs* 40, 67; description of *Celates* 40–42, 67; description of Makassar 29, 39; *Suma Oriental* 33, 36.
Pliny the Elder 33.
Poengawa 123.
Poolman (Captain) 105.

Puah Basar 123.
*Purim. See* Bengkalis.
puwang 20.


**Q**

Quanzhou 34.


**R**

raiding. *See* capture. *See also* piracy.
Ramayana 33.
raja 142.
Reid, Anthony 10.
Riau islands 109.
Rodrigues, Francisco 47.
Rogers, Woods 51.
Roos, Gerrit 74, 78, 79.
Rupat 38, 41.


**S**

*sabannaraq* 8, 85, 88, 94–97, 153.
Saenaq (I) 95.
Sama 22, 97; Balangingi 26, 44, 158; importance in Makassar trade 28; leaders 65; lineages 20–21; origin of term 44–47; sources regarding 8; Sama narrative 107. *See also* sea people, Bajo, Lutau.
Sandao 95.
Sapeh 38.
Sawitto 94.
sea cucumber. *See trepang.*
sea gypsies. *See* sea people.
sea people 1, 3, 7, 22–28, 42, 129, 156; naming in non-Sama languages (exonyms) 44–45, 158–60; as pilots 49–52; political allegiance of 25–27, 40; stereotypes of 25–26, 204. *See also* Sama, Bajo.
Segeri (Karaeng) 117.
Semporna Islands 25,
Siam 38, 42.
Sidenreng 119.
Singapore 36, 42, 71, 184, 185.
Sitti Hami 4, 184–85.

slavery 9, 38–39, 79–80, 199; Dutch 80–81. *See also* piracy.
smuggling 4.
southern littoral route 29, 36–37, 70.
Speelman, Cornelis 30, 42, 97–99, 101, 102, 105; remarks on Tiworo 12, 105–6; on the treaty with Buton 105.
Speelman's War. *See* Makassar War.
Speilbergen, Joris van 15, 68, 72.
spice trade 33–34, 65, 67–70.
Sombaopu 98.
Soppeng 83, 119.
Srivijaya 27, 71.
Steijger, David 98, 101–5.
Subanun (Subanos) 133.
Sula Islands 77, 85, 87, 96, 97.
Sulu 26–27, 34–35, 45–46, 81, 90, 132–35.
Sulu Sultanate 26, 204.
Sumbawa 36, 38, 139.
Suppa (Suppaq) 54, 56, 94.


**T**

Talloq 28, 53, 93, 96, 130, 140; alliance with Gowa 60–61, 66, 81; Chronicle of 39, 58, 88, 90, 94, 136.
Tambora, Jufri. *See* Jufri Tambora.
Tanakeke 51.
Tausug 26, 46, 132.
temporal scale 9.
*teluk rantau* 61–62.
Tentera Islam Indonesia (TII). *See* Indonesian Islamic Army.
Tentera Nasional Indonesia (TNI) 3, 169, 171, 175, 177, 179, 181, 186, 190.
Ternate 27, 35; relations with Portuguese 66.
Tidong 44. *See also* Sama, piracy.
Tidore 27, 35, 66, 98.
Tiele, Pieter Anton 56.
Tiworo; atlases depicting 16–18; centrality of 87; European portrayals of 15; geographic description of 177–78; historical background 11–21; Kingdom of 178; organization of 12–13; relations with Buton 102–4; relations with Makassar 5, 30, 63, 65; relations with Ternate 66; war with VOC 29–31, 65, 73–78, 86–87, 97–105. *See also* Bajo, Great Ambon War, Makassar War, piracy, Sama.
Tobunku 66, 77, 80, 85, 96, 105.
Tunijalloq 94.
tributary relations 91.
transnationalism 7.
Treaty of Bungaya 98, 118–19.
*trepang* 18, 26, 28, 202.
Tumamenang ri Agamana (Karaeng). *See* Matoaya (Karaeng).
Tumenanga ri Makkoayang 90, 94.
Tumenanga ri Taenga. *See* Bontosunggu (Karaeng).
Tumamenang ri Papambatuna 93.
Tuwanna I Dondang 19, 20.


**U**

Ujung Tanah 67.


**V**

Valentijn, François 11–12, 16, 202.
Vlaming, Arnold de 14, 16, 73–80, 86.
Vondel (Dutch poet) 93.
Voorst (Commander) van 101, 103.
Vosmaer, J. N. 17–21, 120, 123–24.
Vosmaer's Bay. *See* Kendari Bay.


**W**

wali 147.
Warren, James 26.
Wesenhagen (Commissioner) van 85–86.
Wolters, O. W. 61.
Wajo 83, 119.
white blood 109, 137–38, 142, 173.
Wowoni 16, 77, 99, 184, 185.


**Z**

Zomia 7.